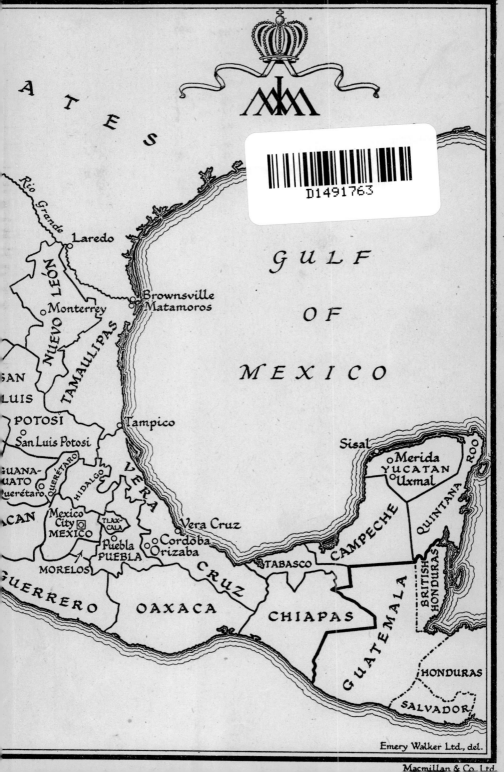

ATES

Río Grande

Laredo

NUEVO LEÓN

Monterrey

TAMAULIPAS

Brownsville
Matamoros

GULF

OF

MEXICO

SAN
LUIS

POTOSI

San Luis Potosi

GUANA-
JUATO
Querétaro

QUERÉTARO

HIDALGO

VERA

Tampico

Sisal

Merida
YUCATAN
Uxmal

QUINTANA ROO

ACAN

Mexico
City
MEXICO

TLAX-
CALA

Puebla
PUEBLA

MORELOS

Cordoba
Orizaba

Vera Cruz

CAMPECHE

CRUZ

TABASCO

GUERRERO

OAXACA

CHIAPAS

GUATEMALA

BRITISH HONDURAS

HONDURAS

SALVADOR

Emery Walker Ltd., del.

Macmillan & Co. Ltd.

D1491763

56688

18)=

UNIVERSITY COLLEGE LIBRARY
CARDIFF

This book must be returned on or before
the last date stamped below. Borrowers
breaking this rule will incur a fine of 3d. per
volume per week or part of a week.

c17894   1d per volume per day,

1 MAY 1962		
6 DEC. 1964		
18 JAN 1965		
24. JUN. 1965		

BOOKS BY H. MONTGOMERY HYDE

✲

THE RISE OF CASTLEREAGH

THE EMPRESS CATHERINE AND PRINCESS DASHKOV

LONDONDERRY HOUSE AND ITS PICTURES

PRINCESS LIEVEN

JUDGE JEFFREYS

With the Marchioness of Londonderry

THE RUSSIAN JOURNALS OF MARTHA AND CATHERINE WILMOT

MORE LETTERS FROM MARTHA WILMOT : IMPRESSIONS OF VIENNA

With G. R. Falkiner Nuttall

AIR DEFENCE AND THE CIVIL POPULATION

THE EMPEROR MAXIMILIAN I OF MEXICO

From the portrait by Jean Adolphe Beaucé in the National Museum of Mexico
in Chapultepec Castle, Mexico, D.F.

By courtesy of the Government of Mexico

MEXICAN EMPIRE

THE HISTORY
OF MAXIMILIAN AND CARLOTA
OF MEXICO

BY

H. MONTGOMERY HYDE

LONDON
MACMILLAN & CO. LTD
1946

Á MI ESTIMADO CONOCIDO
GEORGE R. G. CONWAY
SINCERO AMIGO DE MÉJICO
EN CUYO BUEN RETIRO Á CUERNAVACA
SE CONCIBIÓ ESTE LIBRO

7.4.48

PREFACE

IN 1936, while working in the Austrian State Archives in Vienna where many of the private and secret papers of the imperial family are preserved, I became aware for the first time of the existence of a considerable amount of material, both documentary and printed, relating to the last Mexican Emperor and his consort. Some of this material had previously been seen and used by Count E. C. Corti, who was the first student permitted to examine the imperial collections on the collapse of the Austro-Hungarian monarchy in 1918. Shortly after my visit a full account of the so-called *Maximilianarchiv* from the pen of the collection's official keeper appeared in the *Inventare des Wiener Haus- Hof- und Staatsarchiv*, vol. 5, edited by the late Dr. Ludwig Bittner and published in Vienna in 1937.

But this was not the only repository of source material for the lives of Maximilian and Carlota. There was the western hemisphere. I realized that it would be unwise for me to attempt to write a biography until I had been, among other places, to Washington and Mexico City. For this facility I had to wait several years. Eventually in 1942 a visit to Mexico was arranged, and I was able to return there in the following year. These visits enabled me to collect the necessary additional material. They were fortunately supplemented by opportunities for research in a number of libraries and public archives in the United States of America. Some idea of the extent and variety of the sources which it was necessary to examine in order to complete this work may be obtained from the bibliographical chapter in it.

In 1945 it was my lot to spend the last months of my war service in Austria and Italy, where I was able to revisit Vienna and also to see the neighbourhood of Trieste and Milan which all bear many memories and unmistakeable traces of Maximilian and Carlota.

To the numerous individuals and institutions on both sides of the Atlantic who have helped me I wish to express my thanks for their inexhaustible kindness and patience. I am particularly indebted to the following :

In Mexico : the Government of the Republic for access to the National Archives and to the Archives of the Ministry of Foreign Affairs ; Mr. George R. G. Conway for his generous advice and hospitality and for unrestricted use of his unique collection of manuscripts and printed books on Mexico preserved at Cuernavaca ; Mr. Ian Walker, late H.M. Vice-Consul in Mexico City, for accompanying me to Querétaro and enabling me to cover the ground of Maximilian's last campaign in the literal sense ; Lic. Edmundo O'Gorman, Mr. Vladimir Dillon and Col. J. D. W. Holmes of Mexico City, and Sr. Eduardo B. Rendón of Cuernavaca, for allowing me to draw on their knowledge of Mexican character and history.

In the United States : Alfred A. Knopf, Inc., for permission to quote from Mrs. Alison Phillips's excellent translation of Count Corti's *Maximilian und Charlotte von Mexiko* ; the staffs of the Library of Congress, Washington, D.C., the United States National Archives, Washington, D.C., the Library of the University Club, New York, N.Y., the New York City Public Library, and the Library of the University of Texas, Austin, Texas.

In Austria : the late Dr. Ludwig Bittner and the late Dr. Lothar Gross for special facilities for research in the helpful State Archives in Vienna ; Count E. C. Corti for a number of corrections and for his kindness in allowing me to use his fine library in Vienna which has happily survived the hazards of war and military occupation.

In England : the Trustees of the British Museum and of the London Library and the Librarian of the Admiralty for the use of printed books in their charge ; Count Carl Lónyay for reading this book in typescript, Professor and Mrs. W. Alison Phillips for reading it in proof, and all three for making a number of suggestions for its improvement which I have been glad to incorporate in the text.

To those in the four countries who have authorized the reproduction of pictures or documents in their possession I am also grateful. Particulars will be found beneath each illustration.

H. MONTGOMERY HYDE

32 Wilton Place
London, S.W.1
December, 1945

CONTENTS

ILLUSTRATIONS

GENEALOGICAL TABLE

Francis I
(1768–1835)
Emperor of Austria and last Holy Roman Emperor,
m. (1) Elizabeth of Württemberg; (2) Marie Therese of Naples; (3) Ludovica d'Este; (4) Caroline of Bavaria

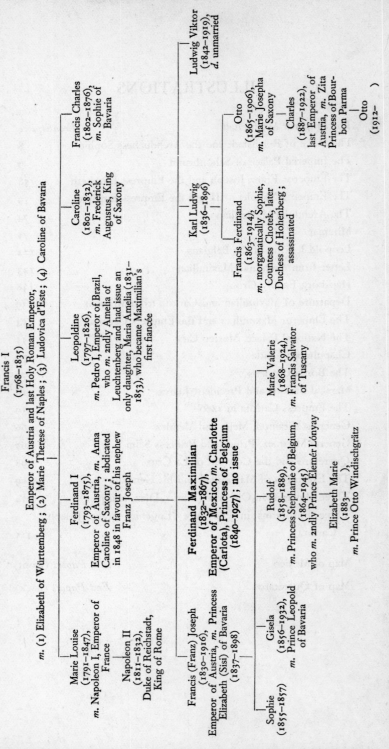

- **Marie Louise** (1791–1847), *m.* Napoleon I, Emperor of France
  - **Napoleon II** (1811–1832), Duke of Reichstadt, King of Rome

- **Ferdinand I** (1793–1875), Emperor of Austria, *m.* Anna Caroline of Saxony; abdicated in 1848 in favour of his nephew Franz Joseph

- **Leopoldine** (1797–1826), *m.* Pedro I, Emperor of Brazil, who *m.* 2ndly Amelia of Leuchtenberg and had issue an only daughter, Maria Amelia (1811–1853), who became Maximilian's first fiancée

- **Caroline** (1801–1832), *m.* Frederick Augustus, King of Saxony

- **Francis Charles** (1802–1876), *m.* Sophie of Bavaria
  - **Francis (Franz) Joseph** (1830–1916), Emperor of Austria, *m.* Princess Elizabeth (Sisi) of Bavaria (1837–1898)
    - Sophie (1855–1857)
    - Gisela (1856–1932), *m.* Prince Leopold of Bavaria
    - Rudolf (1858–1889), *m.* Princess Stephanie of Belgium, who *m.* 2ndly Prince Elemér Lónyay
      - Elizabeth Marie (1883–), *m.* Prince Otto Windischgrätz
    - Marie Valerie (1868–1924), *m.* Francis Salvator of Tuscany
  - **Ferdinand Maximilian** (1832–1867), Emperor of Mexico, *m.* Charlotte (Carlota), Princess of Belgium (1840–1927); no issue
  - **Karl Ludwig** (1836–1896)
    - Francis Ferdinand (1863–1914), *m.* morganatically Sophie, Countess Chotek, later Duchess of Hohenberg; assassinated
    - Otto (1865–1906), *m.* Marie Josepha of Saxony
      - Charles (1887–1922), last Emperor of Austria, *m.* Zita Princess of Bourbon Parma
        - Otto (1912–)
  - **Ludwig Viktor** (1842–1919), *d.* unmarried

I. *Boyhood*

MAXIMILIAN I, King of Bavaria, had numerous offspring by two wives. Several of his daughters married German sovereigns, Caroline, the eldest, becoming the fourth wife of the Austrian Emperor Francis. When it was proposed that Caroline's younger half-sister Sophie should marry the Hapsburg Archduke Francis Charles, one of the Emperor's sons by a former marriage, the bride elect threw herself at her parents' feet and protested vigorously at the fate in store for her. " That imbecile ! " she sobbed. " Never ! " However, she was told that the alliance had been decided upon some years before at the Congress of Vienna, and that settled the matter. Sophie was accordingly wedded to her Archduke in the year 1824, and the fact that her own half-sister became her mother-in-law was not regarded as being in any way unusual for those times : it merely added another strand to the tangled skein of German Imperial Family relationships.

The Archduchess Sophie was probably the handsomest of " the Bavarian sisters of misfortune ", as the King's daughters were known ; she was certainly the cleverest and most determined. As she took leave of her parents after the wedding ceremony she said with a defiant toss of her head : " I have resolved to be happy, and I am going to be ". Henceforward the whole course of her life was to exemplify this resolution, supported as it was by a dominating personality, marked willpower and an undying devotion to the cause of the Roman Catholic Church.

Sophie was not in love with Francis Charles, whose intellectual attainments, it must be admitted, were not of a particularly high order. Furthermore, for the first six years of their married life her husband gave her no children. It was not altogether surprising that her natural desire for intelligent companionship should find expression in the most romantic and at the same time pathetic figure in the Imperial Court. This was the young Napoleon Francis, Duke of Reichstadt, son of the

1

first Napoleon by the Austrian Emperor Francis's daughter Marie Louise. The good-looking Duke, who had been born into the purple as King of Rome, was virtually held a prisoner in the Austrian capital, although he was regarded by his father's supporters as the rightful heir and titular ruler of the French people under the style of Napoleon II. Politically he was no more than a pawn on the European chess-board which it suited the Austrian Chancellor Prince Metternich to move about at will. As an individual Napoleon Francis was a brilliant dreamer who hoped to stage a successful come-back with the help of his Bonapartist partisans. For encouragement and sympathy in his schemes he looked in vain to his mother, who was not interested and in any case was much too busy with her morganatic husband and lover in the Italian Duchy of Parma, which he ruled, to devote any time to her son's upbringing. In his life the place of mother and sister was taken by Sophie. To his empty boyhood she gave the only warmth of friendship and understanding he had known.

At this time Napoleon Francis was mastering the rudiments of military training and chafing under the restraints of barrack-room discipline. The young couple would spend hours together in Sophie's cheerful apartment in the Hofburg, Vienna's imperial palace, where they would talk about the first Napoleon, for Sophie's Bavarian father had been one of the French Emperor's staunchest allies. At other times she would play graceful Italian airs on the pianoforte while the young Duke would listen enraptured and dream of a restoration of his dynasty. " I will go, if France calls me," he said, " but it must be Imperial France, not anarchy." For a short time during the hot July days in 1830 Napoleon's heir thought that his hour had come, for there was revolution in Paris and the tricolour flew again. But the Fates decreed otherwise. Louis Philippe the " citizen King ", about whom the first Napoleon had warned his son, ascended the French throne complete with bourgeois impedimenta of umbrella and galoshes, while the unfortunate Napoleon the Second languished in his Viennese hot-house.

In 1831 the Duke was twenty years old. " He radiated youth and beauty ", wrote a friend who saw him at the British Ambassador's New Year ball in the white, silver and green uniform of an Hungarian Grenadier Regiment. " The dull pallor of his face, the melancholy curve of his mouth, his penetrating glance so full of fire, the harmony and poise of his movements endowed him with a charm that was irresistible." With the twenty-six-year-old Archduchess Sophie, the only woman who counted in his life, his friendship now developed into strong affection. During the summer of 1831 they saw a great deal of each other. At the imperial summer palace at Schönbrunn his apartments were situated directly above hers, which he could reach unknown to the Court servants by a small connecting staircase. To exactly what degree of intimacy this means of communication developed there is no means of discovering. One can only conjecture, for the lovers left no correspondence to show it.

It is known that Napoleon Francis was extremely fond of children. Sophie's first child, Franz Joseph, had been born in the previous year, and the young Duke's joy at its birth was scarcely less than its mother's. He would fondle the infant for hours on his knee and amuse him with his watch-chain and other trinkets. By the time the Court returned to Vienna for the winter Sophie was again with child. It will never be known for certain who was responsible for its conception — Sophie's husband the Archduke Francis Charles, or Napoleon's *l'aiglon*, the Duke of Reichstadt. It may well be in this unborn child, which he was barely to live to see, that Napoleon II fulfilled the destiny which he strove so arduously and so vainly to achieve in his lifetime.

The young man's health was bad, giving his friends serious cause for alarm. He began to lose weight and developed an unpleasant cough. He found difficulty in shouting orders on the parade-ground. Then one day as he was about to go on parade he was seized with a violent fit of coughing and began to spit blood. He could not disguise the dread truth from himself. He had consumption. Nevertheless, he continued to go on parade in all weathers, spent hours in the saddle, and seemed to take a fiendish delight in taxing his weak frame to the point of exhaustion. With the coming of summer in 1832 his condition grew worse. Sophie gave up some of her rooms in the Schönbrunn palace so that he might be more comfortable. It was a stroke of tragic irony that they were the very rooms which the lad's illustrious father had occupied after he had vanquished the Austrian armies in the great campaigns of Austerlitz and Wagram.

Early in June Sophie returned to the palace after a short absence in Vienna. She was now in her eighth month, and from then on until the moment of her confinement she saw the ailing Napoleon Francis every day. They would still go for walks together in the lovely palace grounds, and when the young man was too weak to walk he would be carried into Sophie's private garden where, in a beautiful setting of terraces and fountains, there was a little pavilion or summer-house. Here the Duke would stretch out on a long armchair every afternoon wearing " a dressing-gown of red-and-white stripes with white trousers and a Greek cap that showed his blonde curls ". Sophie would read to him, while he would play languidly with the infant Franz Joseph and stroke his hair.

A week later the rupture of an abscess in one of his lungs precipitated the final crisis. The physicians abandoned all hope and advised that he should receive the comforts of religion. To guard him from the painful impression that he was already a dying man, Sophie told him that he must join with her in receiving the Sacrament and " unite their prayers for obtaining he, his health, and she, a happy delivery ". This ceremony duly took place in the private chapel at Schönbrunn, Sophie kneeling by his side and supporting him with her arms. That evening he declared he felt better, much refreshed and relieved. Some days later, after his mother, Marie Louise, had arrived from Italy, the invalid collapsed and was put to bed, and Sophie saw that the end was near. Nevertheless, Sophie kept up her long vigil by his bedside, although she herself was ill and in constant distress.

One day early in July Sophie did not come to Napoleon Francis's room and in anxious tones the dying Duke asked where she was. He was told that her pains had begun. Thereafter from hour to hour he sent for news of her. Next day, it was July 6, 1832, they told him that the Archduchess Sophie had been safely delivered of a second son and that the newly-

4

born would be called Ferdinand Maximilian — Ferdinand after the Emperor Francis's eldest son and heir to the Austrian crown, and Maximilian after her Bavarian father. A day later the infant Archduke was baptized with the assistance of several high dignitaries of the Church. Napoleon Francis felt at peace.

The dying man lingered on for two more weeks. The end came during a violent thunder-storm which broke over the palace in the early morning of July 22. Sophie was still confined to her room, and when the sad news was broken to her later in the day she was stunned with grief. For several hours she lost consciousness, her milk dried up, and a high fever set in. For the next few days her own life was despaired of. Gradually she recovered, but it was not the same Sophie.

When she emerged from her sick-room into the light of public view her friends no longer found the gay and understanding Archduchess that they knew. All gentleness seemed to have left her. It was a bad omen for the infant Ferdinand Maximilian.[1]

2

The imperial summer palace of Schönbrunn was a magnificent place containing over fourteen hundred rooms and one hundred and thirty-nine kitchens, in addition to a riding school, menagerie and rare botanical gardens. But the main building was always chilly and lacked adequate internal heating. The infant babes of the Archduchess Sophie were almost always suffering in consequence from " colds in the head ". According to modern ideas, the rooms assigned to the Archducal family were practically unfit for human habitation. Disorder, dust and dirt appeared on every side. The elder baby's room was actually situated above the guards' lavatory, an arrangement which produced the most unpleasant effects, especially in summer-time. That the little Archdukes survived such an infancy at all is due partly to the good constitutions with which they were born and partly to the tender care lavished upon them by their nurse.

[1] Amongst the papers left by Metternich at his death in 1859 there is supposed to have been a secret letter from the Emperor Francis which established that Maximilian had Napoleonic blood in his veins. The Archduchess Sophie is also alleged to have confessed as much to a priest. See Bibliography below, p. 337.

The nurse, as befitted her distinguished charges, came of a noble German family. Baroness Louise Sturmfeder was no ordinary nurse. She had a profound distrust for the physicians of the time, and in an age when it was commonly believed that consumption was caused by cold atmosphere she strongly advocated a regime of fresh air and exercise. The Aja or "Amie", as she was known, loved her charges dearly, but the elder child was unquestionably her favourite. For a time she regarded the new baby "Maxi" as an interloper — "the step-child" — while "Franzi" was her "own boy". Maxi was barely three years old when he saw this. Looking at her with his big blue eyes he said : "Amie, you know I love you just as much as you love Franzi". The Baroness melted and gradually her jealousy disappeared.

It was inevitable that Maximilian should play second string to his brother, and the effect in the formation of his character was unfortunate. He perpetually strove to be better than his brother in everything. Yet they were essentially different. Maxi was dreamy and temperamental, liking books and music ; Franzi was industrious and methodical and despised the arts as "those things", diplaying a strong preference for soldiering instead. But in spite of their fundamental differences which made themselves apparent in their characters at an early stage, no shadow darkened their relations as children and later as boys. That they were happy together, and that Franz in particular loved his younger brother, is borne out by a few letters written by Franz in the schoolroom which have survived.

When he was five, Maxi developed some infectious complaint, probably measles, and was isolated in his rooms in the palace. The elder brother wrote to him every day until he was released from quarantine. Franz had developed a remarkable aptitude for drawing and he devoted this talent to the invalid's diversion. "I have a very bad cold in my head", wrote Franz in one of his boyish notes, "and have a tallow plaster round my neck every night when I go to bed, but this shall not prevent me from writing to you and sending you drawings in anticipation of the delight of our being together again." A little later Franz wrote : "We are amusing ourselves very well here with our cannon and with reading, although it is not half as jolly as when we are all together upstairs and can have all sorts of games and occupations ". Then again : " Grandmama has given me a fortress. After it has been set up it can be bombarded with a little cannon which makes it collapse. It is so nicely made and garrisoned with cardboard soldiers. Farewell, I shall continue to contribute as much as I can to your entertainment."

As each boy passed his sixth birthday he was removed from the tender care of the Aja and handed over to a tutor for schooling in earnest. Each boy had his own tutor who was in turn subordinate to the Chief of the Household or Ajo Primo. This latter individual was a Frenchman, Count Heinrich Bombelles, who had been recommended by the ex-Empress Marie Louise. For each boy he drew up a formidable scholastic curriculum which grew steadily more exacting as the pupils increased in age and included an amazing variety of subjects. When they were seven they put in thirty-two hours' study a week divided between religious instruction, German, writing, geography, history, French, Hungarian, Bohemian and drawing. Each year the hours of study grew longer, until at seventeen each lad spent fifty-five hours a week on a wide range of subjects which included, in addition to the foregoing, book-keeping, law, technology, Italian, Polish, military studies and " diplomatic ". In addition, the students were thoroughly trained in the sciences of dancing, fencing, riding, swimming and gymnastics.

This curriculum, although varied and intensive, was not unenlightened. " No superstition," said Maximilian's tutor to him, " for it is the limit of fear and weakness." Hence Count Bombelles strictly forbade the boys to carry rosaries, because, as the younger brother had occasion to remember in later life, " such practices easily led to superstitious fetishism and mechanical prayer without soul or understanding ". Similar emphasis was laid upon physical training, and in the summer months lessons frequently took place outside in the open air. " We are having a jolly time here ", wrote Franz from Schönbrunn in 1841 : " from nine in the morning to half-past five in the afternoon we are in the garden, where we also dine : and we swim, too, every day. At five we either go for a walk or have gymnastics, but on Wednesdays—like today—I go for a ride." But while Franz did not really feel at home on horseback, Max early showed signs of becoming a dashing and even reckless horseman. " I cannot ride slowly ", Max confessed. He loved to gallop madly across country, which gave him some idea of " the delight of flying " as well as the sensation of " no longer belonging to this weak earth ". Indeed from his earliest days he was a firm believer in the possibility of aerial travel. " I still augur something wonderful from attempts at flying ", he wrote as a young man ; " and if ever the balloon theory should become a reality I shall devote myself to travelling in the air and am certain that I shall find in it the perfect concentration of enjoyment."

Physically the Archduke Ferdinand Max grew up quickly and his height was set off by his frank blue eyes and fair hair. A slightly receding chin hinted at a certain weakness of character which was undoubtedly promoted by the light-hearted and easy-going ways of so many of his Viennese friends and contemporaries. Nevertheless, the sense of moral values which his teachers inculcated was of the highest. Twenty-seven precepts which he assumed as the guiding rules of life he wrote down on a card. This card, which he invariably carried on his person, included such admirable self-admonitions as " Never joke with one's inferiors, never converse with the servants ", " Listen to all ; trust few ", " Never let oneself be carried away by the first impression ", and " When taking any step, think of the consequences ". If these precepts were not always observed, the fact that the young man should have reminded himself so frequently of them at least shows a commendable striving after perfection in those moral virtues of which he felt that he fell short.

Unlike his elder brother, Max developed a taste for the distant and exotic. On his ninth birthday he was given a small thatched cottage which was erected for him under the shade of the large trees which stood near the celebrated *Boulingrin*, that same bowling-green on which poor Napoleon Francis had spent most of his time during the last painful weeks of his life and where Franz Joseph used to fire off his toy cannon. Whilst looking through the books of pictures in the Court library Max had come upon some savage tribesmen of Africa in their native

THE ARCHDUCHESS SOPHIE OF BAVARIA
MOTHER OF FRANZ JOSEPH AND MAXIMILIAN

From the portrait by Josef Kriehuber in the
National Library in Vienna

THE DUKE OF REICHSTADT (NAPOLEON II)
HOLDING THE INFANT ARCHDUKE FRANZ JOSEPH

From the water-colour by Johann Ender in the Albertina Collection
in Vienna

The little girl is the Bourbon Princess Caroline of Salerno
She later married the Duke of Aumale, son of the French King Louis Philippe and uncle of Carlota

THE IMPERIAL PALACE OF SCHÖNBRUNN

From a contemporary engraving

dress, and he therefore adorned the cottage with replicas of their weapons and built a kind of kraal or compound with stakes. In the evenings a fire gleamed merrily while a huge stone idol and a boa-constrictor's skin which hung from one of the trees completed the native scene. On one side of the cottage beside a picturesque waterfall Max slung a hammock between two of the trees, " near to which ", as he put it when reminded of the scene many years later, " sat a handsome and intelligent green parrot presented to me in those merry days by Napoleon's widow ".

In this happy world of make-believe Max used to ponder about far-off climes and he formed the resolution to travel. The first opportunity of seeing something of the real world outside the confines of Austrian Court life came a few years later when in the late summer of 1845 he was taken on a trip to Venice and Trieste. The two tutors made up the party along with Franz Joseph and a younger brother, Karl Ludwig, who was a year younger than Max.

The journey from Venice to Trieste was made by sea, and Max was enchanted by it. He had made up his mind now. He wanted to be a sailor.

3

In 1835 the Emperor Francis died, but his grandson Max, who was three years old at the time, did not really remember him. The young Archduke did, however, have a lively recollection of the late monarch's political testament, which had been drafted by the astute old Chancellor Prince Metternich as a guide to the new Emperor, who was Francis's eldest son Ferdinand. " Do not shift the foundations of the edifice of State ", so ran this remarkable document. " Reign and change nothing ; plant yourself firmly and unswervingly in the soil of the principles by whose constant observance I not only guided the Monarchy through storm and stress but also secured for it the high place which it occupies in the world." In addition to Austria proper, the Empire included Hungary, Bohemia, Croatia, Slovenia, Galicia, Bukovina and the Italian provinces of Lombardy and Venice. Ferdinand now meekly acquiesced in the continuance of a political system which had been perfected over a period of twenty years by Metternich. In fact, the new monarch was so weak and incapable that he readily allowed all the business of government to be executed on his behalf by a commission known as the Conference of State. " Poor Ferdy is an idiot," said the Viennese to each other, shaking their heads.

The Conference of State consisted of four ill-assorted individuals — the Archduke Francis Charles, heir to the throne and father of Franz and Max, whose mental capabilities were very little above those of the reigning Emperor; the Archduke Ludwig, a Conservative of the narrowest type; the Imperial Chancellor Prince Metternich, himself the apotheosis of reaction, and the Finance Minister Count Kolowrat, a Conservative who posed as a Liberal less out of any sense of conviction than from a desire to thwart the Chancellor, with whom he was scarcely on speaking terms. The Archduchess Sophie, though no more a Liberal than the Finance Minister, was not impervious to the signs of discontent which were increasing not merely in Hungary and Italy but in the heart of the Austrian Empire. She was acutely aware, too, that, since the Emperor Ferdinand was incapable of having any children, the succession must devolve upon her husband and ultimately upon their eldest son. Her great ambition was to see this son firmly seated on the throne and ruling a loyal and satisfied people. Hence she entered warmly into the Finance Minister's intrigues against the old Chancellor and his puppet Emperor.

The scheming Sophie hoped that her political ambitions would be achieved gradually and constitutionally. But events moved more swiftly and more radically than she anticipated. The year was 1848, that political *annus mirabilis*. The trouble started in Paris. There the mob rose in February and dethroned its bourgeois ruler Louis Philippe, umbrella, galoshes and all. The revolutionary hysteria quickly spread to Austria. Soon the mob was thundering outside the Chancellery in Vienna while Metternich sat glumly at his desk, and a delegation of burghers endeavoured to induce him to resign. " We have nothing against your person, Prince," pointed out an alderman in the delegation, " but everything against your system." In a few minutes the leader of the mob was in the building and forcing his way to the Chancellor's study. Metternich opened the door. The intruder gasped : " Another five minutes and I shall vouch for nothing." Metternich saw the point. He turned calmly to the delegation and informed its members that, as they evidently believed his continuance in office would imperil the welfare of the monarchy, he would resign.

To the Archduchess's consternation the revolutionary ferment spread rapidly and did not stop short even of the Imperial Majesty. On May 15, 1848, just a fortnight after Metternich's dramatic resignation, a crowd of students forced their way into the Hofburg where the whole imperial family was then living, and literally at the point of the musket obliged the unfortunate Emperor Ferdinand to grant a popular constitution. By this time the Court was thoroughly alarmed. Ferdinand was induced to migrate to Innsbruck under the pretext of a pleasure excursion, taking with him Sophie and her sons. The Archduchess was indignant but had no alternative. As she put it, " I could have borne the loss of one of my children more easily than I can the ignominy of submitting to a mass of students. In the future the shame of the past will seem simply incredible."

While news of risings in other parts of the Austrian dominions were received by the uneasy imperial family, the work of restoring law and order was entrusted to the Governor of Prague, Prince Windischgrätz, a severe military disciplinarian, who allowed himself a free hand for the purpose and in whom incidentally the Archduchess Sophie found a valuable ally for her dynastic plans. In August the Court was able to return to Vienna, where a revulsion of popular feeling set in momentarily in favour of the feeble Emperor, but a second rising, which took place in October and resulted in the murder of the Minister of War, drove the Court away again. This time the Emperor sought the security of the old fortress town of Olmütz in Moravia. Meanwhile Windischgrätz and his troops quickly reduced Vienna and drowned the insurrection in blood.

During the next six weeks a curious tragi-comedy was played out at Olmütz. Putting their heads together, Sophie and Windischgrätz decided upon a joint plan of action. They must persuade the weakened Emperor to abdicate, while her husband, Francis Charles, would renounce his claims to the throne, thus leaving the way open to her son Franz. The first step in this carefully prepared campaign was the appointment of a strong constitutional government headed by Windischgrätz's brother-in-law, Prince Felix Schwarzenberg, an energetic mixture of soldier, diplomat and roué with even less mercy in his make-up than Windischgrätz. The next move was securing the Emperor's agreement to surrender his imperial heritage. There was no difficulty over this as Ferdinand had long been tired of his care of state, which he proved only too willing to hand over. With his brother and heir Francis Charles the planners encountered harder going. Like most weak characters, Francis Charles proved obstinate. He pointed out that his father would never have approved the shirking of his divinely ordained responsibilities. It now happened most fortunately that a vision of the late Emperor appeared before the eyes of the puzzled Francis Charles as in a dream and announced that it was his will that the Archduke should stand aside in his son's favour. The part of the imperial ghost, it may be added, was successfully undertaken by a courtier who was in Sophie's pay and was later suitably rewarded for his pains. The trick worked, Francis Charles retired this time for good into political obscurity, and the eighteen-year-old Franz Joseph agreed to shoulder the imperial burden.

Of the young Archdukes only Franz himself was in the secret from the beginning. Max was not informed until the last moment, and even then, to keep up appearances, the boys did lessons with their tutors as usual. On December 1, 1848, while the boys were struggling with the elements of canon law, the Emperor issued an invitation to all members of the Court, Government and imperial family to attend the Archbishop's palace early the following morning to hear an important announcement.

Punctually at the time appointed Archduke Max arrived with his younger brother Karl to find the throne-room packed with people and buzzing with excitement and curiosity. Immediately afterwards the Emperor and Empress came in with their household, followed by the Archduchess Sophie and the youthful Franz Joseph. Ferdinand took a seat before the throne, and amid tense silence rose and read a brief declaration in which he stated that important reasons had induced him to resign in favour of his nephew the Archduke Franz Joseph, while his beloved brother the Archduke Francis Charles had renounced his right to the succession. With this Ferdinand embraced the new Emperor, who had approached and knelt down before him. " God bless you," he said in a voice breaking with tears. " Be good. God will protect you. I was glad to do it."

Thus Franzi became Emperor of Austria. As he left the throne-room accompanied by his aide-de-camp Count Grünne, everyone present is said to have wept. Someone outside in the palace came up to the new Emperor and addressed him as " Your Majesty ". Franz Joseph started back suddenly, realizing the full import of the change which had just taken place. He turned and said simply : " Farewell, my youth ! "

The new Emperor's first task was the pacification of his disturbed dominions. The rebellious Italian provinces were easily subdued by the veteran Marshal Radetzky, but the kingdom of Hungary could only be recalled to the imperial fold with the aid of Russian troops which the Tsar Nicholas supplied. Max accompanied his brother the Emperor during the Hungarian campaign. With the Austrian first army corps under General Schlik they entered the town of Raab, which had been evacuated by the Hungarians on June 27, 1849, and they actively participated in the fighting which took place between Raab and Komorn. The fall of Buda a fortnight later foreshadowed the end of the campaign and enabled the Emperor and his brother to return to Vienna. A short time afterwards the rebel army capitulated.

To the terrible aftermath Maximilian at least was not insensible. The Hungarian Minister President and thirteen Hungarian generals were executed, over a hundred other Hungarian notables were hanged or shot, and nearly two thousand individuals imprisoned. This horrible vengeance was approved by the Emperor and carried out with the utmost rigour by the Austrian Commander-in-Chief, Baron Haynau, who became notorious for the public floggings of women which he ordered.

Thus were the Austrian provinces made safe for autocracy, but Maximilian felt disgusted. " We call our age that of enlightenment ", he wrote in his diary when reminded of these unhappy events some time later, " but its shadowy side will also be commented on. In very many cities of Europe posterity will regard with amazement and horror the chambers in which without any question of law mere force has, under the influence of hateful revenge, condemned people to death at the notice of a few short hours, perhaps because they wanted something different from that desired by the power that stands above law."

4

In 1850, greatly to Maximilian's delight, came the first real opportunity of satisfying his taste for the sea. For his benefit a party was got up for a trip to Greece and Asia Minor in the imperial corvette *Vulcan*. The vessel sailed from Trieste at the beginning of September under the command of Admiral Julius Wissiak of the Austrian navy, and the other members of the party included, in addition to Maximilian, his younger brother Karl Ludwig; Prince Jablonowsky, a young man of their own age; an elderly scholar called Kaltenbeck ; the boys' drawing master, Professor Geiger, and the Court Physician, Dr. Fritsch. Maximilian kept a diary of the voyage, which showed that at the age of eighteen he was already a shrewd observer and, unlike his elder brother the Emperor, possessed quite a pleasing sense of humour.

For the past seventeen years — virtually since the time Greece had achieved her independence — the country had been ruled by Maximilian's Bavarian cousin Otto, and during his absence, as, for example, occurred on the occasion of this visit, by his beautiful young wife Amalie, daughter of the Grand Duke Augustus of Oldenburg. This couple dearly loved their adopted land, but in spite of the fact that since 1843 the monarchy had at least in theory become constitutional, it could not be said at any time to have been either enlightened or particularly successful. The country was still a constant prey to attempted revolts and outbreaks of brigandage. Unfortunately, to quote an acute contemporary English observer,[1] Otto " took no measures to root out the social evils that caused the one, or the political evils that produced the other. The King could form no firm resolutions himself, and he reposed no confidence in his ministers. They were indeed not worthy of much, for both Bavarians and Greeks displayed far more eagerness to obtain ministerial portfolios than zeal in performing the duties of the offices with which they were entrusted. King Otto observed the meanness of their intrigues and the selfishness of their conduct. . . . To ensure complete subserviency no minister was allowed to remain very long in office, and men were usually selected without influence or ability and frequently without education."

Although Maximilian's views on Greece were naturally to some extent coloured by family considerations, the grateful traveller was by no means blind to the true state of affairs in the country. " As all men who fought in the War of Independence have the right to bear arms," he wrote in his diary, " robbery becomes especially easy to them. Often in the middle of a town a house is attacked. . . . Banditti in Greece are an understood thing. It appears that the morality of the Greeks is not raised by the ideas of King, fatherland, and brotherly love. Their own advantage is their guiding star. Even the marriages are not from affection, but in most cases bargains of convenience ; and the reflection that you are committing a wrong upon another vanishes with them before the pleasure of filling their own pockets."

A few days after leaving Trieste the *Vulcan* steamed into Patras, where the party disembarked and arranged with the Austrian Consul to ride across country to Nauplia where the corvette would pick them up. " The horses ", noted Maximilian in his diary, " awaited us before the Consul's house, who received us on the steps in front in his morning *négligé*. Only a few of the beasts and their bridles would bear inspection. The poor nags were in a frightful state of emaciation, and their harness was a conglomeration of chains, ropes, and bits of leather.

[1] George Finlay, the historian of Greece.

The contractor, whom we will call Demetry, was busily employed in dividing the beasts among the riders, and at the same time praised their qualities inordinately, in which the Consul, whose equestrian comprehension appeared to be very weak, supported him zealously." As a protection against the sun, Maximilian sported a Chinese parasol " made of extraordinarily light stuff ", which, in spite of the ridicule of his companions, served him in good stead. This incongruous excursion was attended by two gendarmes who were a mixture of Bavarian and Greek — " their heads belonged to their fatherland and their clothes or uniforms were Greek ".

The hundred and twenty miles between Patras and Nauplia by way of Corinth were covered without mishap, although in the last stage of their journey the travellers narrowly escaped being attacked by a band of robbers who successfully plundered another party in the same neighbourhood. At Nauplia they found the *Vulcan* riding at anchor, and the journey was immediately resumed on board in the direction of the Piraeus.

At the port they were met by the Austrian *chargé d'affaires* and the King's Chamberlain, General Griva, who invited them on behalf of Their Majesties to lodge in the royal palace. " He is one of the few in whom the King has entire confidence ", noted Maximilian of this official, " and in the fatal Revolution he showed his strength of character. The history of his past is somewhat obscure, and there are malicious stories afloat which describe him as having some taste for robber life. His exterior corresponds with this last supposition. He has a gloomy, somewhat lowering countenance. His complexion and hair are extraordinarily dark, so that he gains much from the becoming Grecian attire."

On their arrival in Athens Maximilian and his brother were conducted to the palace, where they were immediately received by the Queen, who appeared to greet them " in an elegant morning toilet ". Queen Amalie was now thirty-two years old, and in Maximilian's opinion united " dignity and amiability in a rare degree ". Later in the day they joined her for her daily ride. " The Queen descended the broad marble steps, and sprang with great agility on a Turkish horse which awaited her." The rest of the party followed Her Majesty's example and galloped past the guards in the palace square. "The Queen on horseback is a truly pleasant, agreeable sight", noted Maximilian. "She rides splendidly, has a firm seat, and guides her horse at full gallop over places which many of our famous riders would scarcely pass at a foot's pace."

The usual sightseeing excursions were made in this agreeable manner, and Maximilian did not seem to think that Amalie exposed herself to any risk in her rides. In fact, remarked the young man, "it is easily to be seen that it is the Queen who supports the newly established throne of Greece by her personal influence over the affections of her people". However, Maximilian could not deny that it was this same people which seven years earlier had threatened the royal pair with deposition if the King refused to grant a constitution. It so happened that the anniversary of the Revolution of 1843 fell during Maximilian's visit, and the young Archduke accompanied Her Majesty to the Metropolitan Church where, in the words of her guest, she was expected "to pray for the preservation of institutions which had plunged her beloved Hellas in confusion". On this occasion Maximilian noticed that "she was pressing her lips firmly together instead of opening them in prayer". What the visitor failed to observe, and what indeed ought to have been a great object lesson for him in later years, was that the Greek throne, in spite of the personal virtues of its occupants, did not really rest upon the solid support and goodwill of the Greek people.[1]

From Athens the *Vulcan* sailed eastward across the Aegean Sea to Smyrna. "The first morning in Asia Minor," noted Maximilian, "the first in the Ottoman empire, smiled on us joyfully. Before us lay the East with its wealth, its vegetation, its thousand dazzling appeals to the senses. The blossoms of Asia opened before us ; our long-cherished dreams were realized." Into this tourist's paradise the party plunged eagerly. They all bought Persian carpets in the celebrated Bazaar at prices which Maximilian considered "extraordinarily low ", and

[1] In 1861 an unsuccessful attempt was made to assassinate Queen Amalie by a youth who fired a pistol at her as she was returning through the streets of Athens from her evening ride. A few months later another revolution broke out which drove the royal couple from the country for ever.

they cheerfully submitted to the rigours of the Turkish bath alleviated by the accompanying pleasures of narghile pipes and lemonade sherbet. They were entertained by the Turkish Governor Ali Pashi to a magnificent dinner at which " out of particular politeness and courtesy the Governor tore off a soft bone " from the roast and presented it to his distinguished guest " with an amiable smile, exactly as if it had been a flower ".

Maximilian was particularly interested in discovering the Slave Market in Smyrna, which, it must be admitted, he did with considerable difficulty since, as he put it, " the Turks pretend to the Christians that it no longer exists, feeling a kind of shame at this barbarous sale of human beings ". There was no doubt that it did exist, and at the Archduke's suggestion the drawing master, Johann Geiger, went to some pains to record the scene. Maximilian remembered clearly what he saw there. " The sight of a naked woman frightens me," he confessed afterwards. " I am made to believe that sin is unbearably attractive."

The truth was that the Archduke Ferdinand Max was growing up.

5

Very soon after his return from this short voyage Maximilian entered the Austrian navy with the rank of Lieutenant.[1] His country's naval power at this time could hardly be said to be imposing. Every florin spent on this service was grudged, and in the interior of the Empire it was scarcely known there was a navy at all. The revolt of the Italian provinces had proved that the Austrian fleet, such as it was, was unready, while the admirals were slow to put to sea. Although after the risings in 1848 the service was reinforced by a number of North Germans and Danes and the supreme command was given to the Danish Admiral Dahlerup, both officers and ratings were still largely composed of natives of the Italian provinces, and orders to the crews were invariably given in the Italian rather than the German tongue — factors which were to prove of considerable assistance to Lombardy and Venetia in their final struggle for independence.

[1] His appointment was gazetted October 26, 1850.

Furthermore, morale was poor throughout the service.

From the moment he entered the service Maximilian became aware of this lamentable inefficiency and he talked to his fellow officers of how it could best be remedied. At first he could get no one to listen to him with the solitary exception of a young ensign named Wilhelm Tegetthoff, who was his senior by a few years. The two became firm friends, and Tegetthoff prayed that if the latest recruit could only interest his imperial brother in the subject, there might be some hope for the future of the Austrian navy. Meanwhile Maximilian threw himself into his new duties with a zest which earned him the Emperor's warm commendation. "From all I hear, Max is flourishing," wrote Franz Joseph at this time, "strong as a bear, merry as ever, always to be found on board ship, and on top of all that he works hard." The young naval officer spent much of his time at the fleet base in Trieste where he took a villa and set up an appropriate bachelor establishment. The plain-spoken Danish sailor, to whom he reported for duty on his first arrival in the port, admitted that he was genuinely impressed by the Archduke's keenness and intelligence.[1]

Early in 1851 arrangements were made by Admiral Dahlerup for Maximilian to take a cruise to the West Indies, and a frigate of the imperial navy was specially fitted out for the purpose. However, on the very day on which he was due to embark, he developed typhoid fever. He became so ill that his mother was sent for to his bedside, and for several days his life was in grave danger. Various theories were advanced as to the cause of the malady. In some quarters it was attributed to a surfeit of oysters of which he partook during a visit to Venice, while others suggested that a deliberate attempt had been made by an ill-wisher of the Austrian imperial house to poison him. At this time typhoid was endemic in the military establishments in Trieste, and it is more likely that the Archduke became infected through drinking contaminated water in one of them. His

---

[1] Hans Birch Freiherr von Dahlerup (1790–1872) commanded the Austrian fleet from 1848 to 1852. His memoirs, *In österreichischen Diensten* (2 vols. Berlin, 1911), which give an interesting picture of Austrian naval affairs at this time, show that he was constantly the victim of Court intrigues which hampered his work and eventually led to his being retired.

recovery was slow, and it was not until after midsummer that he was able to return to his post, when a tour of the principal Italian and Spanish ports was planned to take the place of the voyage to the West Indies which he had missed.

The trip took three months and was made on board the *Novara*, a 1,500-ton two-decked sailing frigate of 50 guns which was then the pride of the Austrian navy. This vessel, whose name, in Maximilian's words, " was a good omen to every Austrian ",[1] sailed from Trieste on July 30, 1851. The Archduke took his turn with the other officers in keeping watch, and a bout of bad weather which they encountered soon after setting sail showed that he was fast developing a real sense of seamanship. A week after leaving Trieste the *Novara* dropped anchor in the Bay of Naples, and the usual shore excursions were planned for the ship's company. These included the inevitable ascent of Vesuvius, in whose crater Maximilian watched eggs boil and deposited the empty wine bottle from which he had joyfully toasted his companions.

For the past twenty years the kingdom of Naples and Sicily, known as the Two Sicilies, had been ruled by the Bourbon monarch Ferdinand II, who, whatever golden opinions he had formerly earned as an enlightened ruler, had been notorious for his tyrannical government since the collapse of the revolution which had infected his kingdom in common with the rest of Europe in 1848. He had begun by annulling the constitution which he had sworn faithfully to observe, while about the same time the wanton bombardment and sacking of Messina by his savage troops had acquired for himself the unenviable nickname of " Bomba ". At the very moment the Archduke Maximilian set foot for the first time in Naples Liberal circles throughout Europe were discussing in terms of indignant horror the state of the Neapolitan monarch's prisons, which contained nearly 40,000 political prisoners suffering from the vilest conditions. The rising English statesman William Gladstone had visited these infernos during the previous winter, and had just published

---

[1] The town of Novara, thirty miles west of Milan, was the scene of the battle between the Austrians and the Piedmontese on March 23, 1849, which resulted in the complete defeat of the latter and caused the abdication of the Piedmontese-Sardinian King Charles Albert in favour of his son Victor Emmanuel, later first King of United Italy.

his celebrated letters to the British Foreign Minister, Lord Aberdeen, on what he termed " the negation of God erected into a system of government ".[1]

Since the revolution Ferdinand had withdrawn from Naples, and was living quietly in the near-by fortress of Gaeta with his German second wife Maria Theresa and their numerous family. The tall strong man " with cropped hair and beard, and with a laced three-cornered hat ", who received Maximilian on his arrival in Gaeta, turned out to be " Bomba " himself. The visitor was graciously invited to stay a few days, and then was immediately introduced to the Queen and her nine children, who were paraded for his benefit. " A peculiar taste of the King," noted Maximilian, " with which the Queen is not at all pleased, is to have all the hair of the children shaved off." He had to admit that he found the general atmosphere dull and depressing. " The King is very busy, and, as is frequently the case with people who work all day, is fond of a commonplace insignificant company." As for his host's lodgings, added Maximilian in his diary, " the rooms in which the royal couple live are small and plain — I might say too plain, particularly as regards the furniture ; one might be inclined to take the dwelling for one of a not very high officer. Plain furniture stands in the rooms, a few antiquated knicknacks fill the table, and on the papered walls hang large English prints representing tiger and bear hunts, such as are perhaps to be found in the apartments of our bachelors." At dinner Maximilian found that " macaroni alone gave brightness to the table ", and he wondered whether " in this fine kingdom macaroni is substituted for bread in the prayers ". As a crowning example of royal habits, Ferdinand, to Maximilian's utter astonishment, ordered cigars after dinner and " compelled us, notwithstanding our remonstrances, to smoke in the presence of the Queen ".

Of the system of organized tyranny by which Ferdinand's Neapolitan kingdom was governed Maximilian saw, or rather was allowed to see, little evidence. While being driven round the fortress, however, he noticed a large number of men in scarlet dress and heavy chains who were working on repairs to one

[1] Gladstone's Letters to Lord Aberdeen were first published in July 1851.

of the walls. Maximilian was told that these were "military" prisoners, "expiating important crimes". A little later the wife of a "condemned criminal" carrying a little boy rushed towards the King's carriage and, notwithstanding the danger of being crushed by the wheels, refused to let go until one of the attendant guards forcibly dragged her away screaming, on which the poor woman dropped her naked child on the ground and flung herself on him in wild grief. "The scene was a sad one", noted Maximilian with a touch of Teutonic smugness, "and illustrated the strong, perhaps exaggerated, feelings of the people of the South."

The *Novara*'s next port of call was Leghorn, where an expedition was made into the interior of what was then known as the Grand Duchy of Tuscany and was to all intents a vassal state of the Austrian crown. Tuscany's ruler, another cousin of Maximilian, the Grand Duke Leopold, was in fact maintained on his tottering throne by the Austrian army. The absence of any Court life in Lucca, where Leopold was then living, depressed the Archduke. "Most of the Italian cities have a medieval stamp and so it is with Lucca", he wrote. "However, as the numerous divisions of this Peninsula have been done away with and the smaller states have been swallowed up in the larger, these towns appear deserted and dead, an impression which is increased by the scarcity of shops." But with Florence, the Grand Duchy's capital, and all its artistic joys Maximilian was enchanted, and he hated to leave this fair city. "My parting with Florence filled me with sadness", he wrote in an interesting passage of metaphor in his journal. "I was parting from a high-souled, beautiful, intellectual woman. Whilst Naples appeared to me only as a sensual beauty, a voluptuously charming woman offering herself for momentary enjoyment and had only to be wooed to enjoy on her bosom joyous hours, Florence has to be understood in order to worship her, and it is at her feet that one comprehends the present by the past."

6

By no means the least pleasant welcome awaited the voyagers in the British fortress town of Gibraltar. On arrival they immediately went to present their respects at the old Franciscan convent in the main street which was then the residence of His Majesty's viceroy. Here they were greeted in person by the Governor, Sir Robert Gardiner, a "thin man in a black dress coat and white gouty slippers", who had fought the Peninsular War under the Duke of Wellington and was now in his seventieth year. On the following evening His Excellency gave a large dinner in honour of the distinguished visitors. "All the best society of Gibraltar filled the salons of the Governor", noted Maximilian afterwards. "The strains of our national anthem greeted us with the most friendly welcome and impressed us with a feeling of festivities at home. The aged Governor, in the full uniform of a general of artillery covered with the finest military decorations, received us as a friend. After the usual presentations, in which Old England always behaves a little awkwardly, everyone gave his arm to his lady, and to the strains of music we entered the brilliantly lit large hall which was appropriately adorned with the colours covered with victories of the regiments stationed at Gibraltar."

From his place "between the amiable Governor and his friendly lady" which he had been allotted on this occasion, the young Archduke observed with interest the characteristic dining habits of the English which he admitted pleased him greatly. Before each guest stood a decanter of sherry which facilitated the "strange . . . but very friendly custom of the English of drinking to each other" as well as the more formal toasts. The latter included the health of the Austrian Emperor, which, to Maximilian's agreeable astonishment, was proposed by Sir Robert Gardiner in German. "If the grammar was not always correct", remarked Maximilian, "it went to our hearts, for it was our mother tongue." Perhaps the pleasantest habit of all concluded the banquet. "After the toasts", noted Max, "the ladies left the table to await the arrival of the gentlemen in the salon, who still comfortably gave themselves up to wine and conversation. It seems strange when the ladies at the desire of the gentlemen humbly march away from the table. Many blame this habit as barbarous ; I like it. The ladies ought to learn that they have to obey the men. To what an exaggerated and senseless gallantry shown towards the ladies leads is shown to us by the immorality of France."

In some ways this visit to " the Rock " stood out in Maximilian's mind as the most agreeable recollection of the voyage, and in addition it brought him for the first time into close touch with a British colony and provided him with a useful insight into the English character. He was taken on a complete tour of the fortifications, including the famed rock-hewn " galleries ", and the Governor even organized a riding party for his benefit to see the cork woods across the Spanish frontier. " During this party ", wrote Maximilian, " we had the pleasure of learning how perfectly hospitable and amiable the English are when they wish to be so. The sons of Albion are endowed with the gift of making their guests comfortable if they really like them, of being cordial when it comes from their heart, but they are stiff and cold — nay, even wanting in politeness — when they cannot see sufficient ground for a pleasant manner, and this unconscious frankness becomes them very well."

The remaining Spanish itinerary included the sights of Cadiz, Seville, Malaga and Granada, in all of which churches and bull-fights seemed to prove the principal attractions. In Seville the national dancers came in for some attention, and the party ordered some " slim girls with sparkling eyes " to stage a special performance for their benefit. " Like a voluptuous sultan ", wrote Maximilian, " I took my seat on a sofa to smoke cigarettes while enjoying the seductive spectacle, a pleasure which at the commencement was also enjoyed by my permission by the Russian Consul and his two stiff virginal sisters, but who escaped later frightened by the somewhat uncertain movements of a pretty dancer of seventeen."

But there were more solemn moments than these when, for instance, before leaving Seville, Ferdinand Max heard in the Cathedral an early Mass before the tomb of his ancestor and namesake, Ferdinand, who had ruled Castile six centuries earlier and had later become a saint of the Church.[1] " A sacred stillness reigned in the chapel, half illuminated by candlelight and the

[1] Besides being Maximilian's lineal ancestor, Ferdinand III of Castile (1199–1252) was the father of Eleanor, wife of the English King Edward I. He was canonized in 1671.

dawn ", so the scene appeared to the Archduke. "Amongst the solemn coffins the shrine of Ferdinand was radiant in silvery magnificence ; at its foot the officiating priest raised the most holy offering to Heaven, and I knelt as a traveller in a foreign country, a descendant of the great saint. I felt edified, and I invoked for those at home the intercession of the great saint, who knew how to unite the powerful sword with holiness of life."

This feeling of ancestral pride received a further stimulus when Maximilian visited the celebrated tombs of " the Catholic Kings " in Granada and experienced a tremendous thrill of awe and excitement.[1] "I looked right into the dead still faces of the stone likenesses of my ancestors ", he wrote afterwards ; " they were great men who enacted a portion of history, who have done something on this earth, have begotten a mighty far-ruling race, and now rest alone in a solitary chapel. *Vanitas vanitatum !* Instead of the glittering court surrounding them as formerly, a poorly clad sacristan now takes a torch, opens a small iron door, and leads me down narrow steps into a low musty vault without any embellishment, any ornament—where the naked truth grins. On this the eye of the forgetful heir never looks, and what the world does not see, it does not adorn. Here rest these proudly royal couples in narrow, small, dreadful bare coffins."

Maximilian was acutely conscious that at that moment in Spain he was the closest legitimate descendant of the departed sovereigns, closer than the reigning Queen Isabella II and her offspring. "Here I felt that the family feeling lives even after centuries," reflected Maximilian, " and a melancholy regret moved my soul to see the great dead thus forsaken and not thought of by the new dynasty. I, in simple dress, stand by the coffins of those on whose sunny throne our family would still rule if there had not been a Charles II." [2]

[1] In 1496 Joanna, daughter of the " Catholic " monarchs Ferdinand of Aragon and Isabella of Castile, married Philip of Hapsburg, Duke of Burgundy and son of the Holy Roman Emperor Maximilian I. Their son Emperor Charles V succeeded to all the Hapsburg dominions and also to the throne of Spain. Ferdinand, Isabella, Joanna and Philip are all buried in the Capilla Real in Granada Cathedral.

[2] Charles II, King of Spain and direct descendant of Ferdinand and Isabella, died in 1700 and was the last of the Spanish Hapsburg monarchs. He made a will in favour of the French King Louis XIV's grandson Philip of Anjou, who succeeded him as Philip V, thereby establishing the Bourbon succession in Spain which lasted, with a few brief interruptions, until 1931.

Darkness began to envelop this dismal vault as the sacristan unlocked a small room adjoining and left Maximilian. In a few minutes the sacristan returned with the regalia of the Catholic King Ferdinand of Aragon. Proudly and yet with a touch of sadness Maximilian took in his hand the circlet of gold which had once crowned that monarch's brow, and he grasped the once powerful sword which Ferdinand had drawn in defence of Christendom. A truly grandiose and fantastic picture swam before his eyes and captured his vivid imagination. Could he not, he thought, draw such a sword in order to win such a crown for himself?

It was indeed a dazzling dream of empire which the Archduke Ferdinand Maximilian conjured up as he stood before the shrine of his ancestors in the Cathedral of Granada. That it should one day be realized in himself was his peculiar destiny.

II. *Travels*

THE winter season in Vienna which followed Maximilian's first Mediterranean voyage was particularly gay and brilliant. The Archduchess Sophie gave no less than seven Court balls, and there were innumerable less formal dances at which Maximilian and the Emperor as well as the younger brother Karl Ludwig all appeared. Dancing was then the great passion of the aristocratic Viennese society. The baton of the imperial orchestra was in the able hands of the younger Johann Strauss, that great master of the waltz, composer of the " Blue Danube " and other familiar melodies of old Vienna. Although many of these gatherings were informal, they were nevertheless strictly exclusive. Only the diplomatic corps and members of those Austrian families having the requisite number of quarterings in their arms attended. Flirtations between the younger unmarried couples were frequent but innocent. Competition on the part of the ladies to dance with the imperial brothers was keen, and those favoured in this manner were known as *Kaisercontesserln*. The mothers and chaperones were condemned to watch the proceedings from narrow hard benches without backs, the Archduchess Sophie among them conspicuous with her gold lorgnette. Herr Strauss never dropped his baton on the last waltz until the figures on the benches were dozing or asleep, the candles spluttering in their sockets and the first rays of the morning sun struck the ballroom floor.

Among the *Kaisercontesserln* was the pretty pink-cheeked nineteen-year-old Countess Paula (or Pauline) von Linden, whose father was Minister of Württemberg, one of the petty German kingdoms which enjoyed diplomatic representation at the Court of Vienna. Maximilian had met her during the previous season and had become immediately attracted. During his voyage on the *Novara* he had thought about her a great deal. It was a typical boy-and-girl romance, but on the part of the Archduke it now developed into something approaching a passion — into much more than the pretty young Pauline realized at the time. Regardless of the comments of the Court, and in particular of the disapproving glances which she received through his mother's lorgnette, Maximilian eagerly seized the opportunity provided by every waltz and cotillon to hold her in his arms to the intoxicating strains of Herr Strauss's music.

Came Shrove Tuesday 1852, the last day of the season's "Carnival", when the dancing ended punctually at midnight, for in the Catholic Court there was naturally no dancing during Lent. Two dances were arranged for this gala day — one, a *déjeuner dansant* at the house of Prince Auersperg which lasted from noon until six o'clock in the evening, and the other a short ball beginning at eight and, as befitted the season's end, given by Archduchess Sophie herself in the Hofburg.

As Pauline von Linden was putting on the new white frock which her mother had chosen for this occasion, a bouquet of flowers arrived at the house addressed to her. The flowers bore no card, and Count von Linden, who saw them, told his daughter that she could not accept a bouquet from an unknown admirer. Pauline, who thought that the flowers might have been sent by the love-lorn Archduke Max, told her parents that they had come from an elderly Countess of her acquaintance, since she felt that if her guess was correct the Archduke would be disappointed if she appeared at the ball without them. In these circumstances Pauline was allowed to carry the bouquet in her hand, as the custom then was. At the Auerspergs' she found that Maximilian was deputizing officially for his brother the Emperor, and she therefore imagined that he would lead off the first cotillon with the lady of the house. To Pauline's intense astonishment Ferdinand Max approached her and requested the honour, saying as he did so, "I am glad you are carrying my flowers." The young girl looked shyly at her partner and felt a certain thrill which continued throughout the evening.

Pauline returned home to change for the imperial ball. As she was leaving the house to get into her carriage the same messenger who had brought her the flowers earlier in the day appeared with a fresh and more beautiful bouquet. Pauline was delighted ; she accepted the gift joyfully and drove off to the

Hofburg. As she entered the palace she encountered the younger Archduke Karl Ludwig, leaning against one of the doors. His gaze caught the flowers, and he winked knowingly as she passed. So he's in the secret too, she thought. As events turned out, Karl Ludwig was not the only member of the imperial family who knew.

Max was in the great ballroom waiting for her in a dream of excitement and infatuation. As usual he danced the first cotillon with her, and also most of the other dances on this short evening's programme. Shortly before midnight the orchestra struck up the last tune, a waltz. The gentlemen selected their partners, and the couples soon whirled round feverishly — Max and Pauline among them — anxious to drain the intoxicating cup of rhythm to the last drop. Suddenly the first stroke of midnight was heard on the clock, the tempo of the music slackened, the dancers moved more and more slowly — until at the final stroke conductor Strauss dropped his baton and the music stopped altogether. The dancers dispersed. The Carnival was over.

As Max and Pauline bade each other a fond good-night, neither knew that it was the end of their brief romance and that they had danced together not only the last waltz of the season but the last in their lives. Next day Maximilian was ordered back to his naval duties in Trieste, and shortly afterwards, as the result of a hint dropped to the King of Württemberg, the Minister von Linden was transferred with his wife and daughter to another post in Berlin. It was not difficult for the Archduchess Sophie to arrange these matters.

2

At this time the greater part of the Austrian fleet, consisting of five two-decker sailing frigates of the old type, was lying in Venice, and the Emperor determined to accompany his brother there and sail with the squadron to Trieste. As the squadron was about to put off in the face of threatening weather, the Admiral in command declined responsibility for the monarch's safety. Franz Joseph immediately summoned the commanders of the five vessels before him and enquired whether they would get under way were he not on board. On receiving the reply that they would obey orders, the Emperor commanded them to disregard his presence and announced that he would sail with his fleet. The squadron thereupon put to sea with the Emperor and Maximilian on board the Admiral's flagship and encountered a terrific storm. One of the frigates foundered and went down with all hands, but the flagship and the other vessels managed to limp into port all considerably damaged.

Maximilian's strong passion for Paula von Linden was originally revealed to the Empress-Mother through some poems which she discovered by chance in her younger son's rooms. To Franz Joseph, it is true, these verses, like all Max's poetical compositions, were " practically unintelligible ", but to the alert and watchful eye of Sophie they told a clear tale. The affair must not be allowed to develop. Accordingly Maximilian was peremptorily informed that he must have no further communication with the young lady, and to secure his compliance the more easily he was ordered to sea again almost as soon as he had returned to Trieste. A four-month voyage was planned to cover Sicily, the Balearic Isles, Spain, Portugal, Madeira and North Africa. If the trip partook more of a pleasure cruise than a routine naval operation, it was because Archduchess Sophie let it be known that she wished to combine two kinds of business. Should her Ferdinand Max be able to find a suitable bride in any of the royal Courts he might visit in addition to improving his professional talents as a sailor, so much the better.

A considerable amount of fresh ground was broken on this expedition, and in many ways it proved more instructive than the voyage of the previous year. In Messina harbour Maximilian found the French battleship *Charlemagne*, " a beautiful ship of the line of eighty guns, distinguished by its excellent arrangements and great cleanliness, which are not always to be found among the French ". As the first large steam-driven naval vessel to be built by the French Government, this battleship was naturally of great interest to the officers and men of the *Novara*, and Maximilian welcomed the opportunity of being able to inspect her thoroughly. " We wandered through all parts of the ship ", he noted afterwards, " and were especially pleased with an excellent powder magazine, which looked like a library, and where there was a machine worked by steam-power intended to make sea water drinkable : unfortunately this has not met with success, but it is worth notice."

A week or two later the *Novara* sailed into Port Mahon, the capital town of Minorca, and there a further useful experience awaited Maximilian. The English Mediterranean fleet, consisting of six battleships, a frigate and another steam vessel, lay at anchor under the flag of Rear-Admiral Sir James Dundas, " a tall, portly, fine man with an extremely pleasant face that makes one like him ". The Commander-in-Chief immediately invited him on board his flagship H.M.S. *Britannia*, a three-decker of 120 guns, and conducted him to his spacious comfortable cabin, " the principal charm of which is a long balcony ", where he presented the admiring Archduke to his wife, whom the custom of the service in those days permitted to accompany her husband at sea. Maximilian was then shown over the battleship, while her complement of " 1,000 cheerful men " were reviewed on deck for his benefit. He was most impressed by the air of comfort, cleanliness and quiet efficiency which prevailed everywhere on board. He noted particularly the solid mahogany tables in the cabins, the fine silver plate and china in the wardroom, and the two horses which the Admiral kept for his personal use in order to be able to make shore excursions. In short, the visitor found the *Britannia* " a picture of the strength and greatness of the British navy ". Above all he liked the pleasing mixture of the practical and the comfortable. " The English are clever ", was his considered conclusion, " and very well know that the more agreeable things are made to the officers and midshipmen on board, the more they love their ship and the easier they find to bear their absence from land. The Englishman is at home in his ship and asks nothing better, for indeed it would be difficult to find anything better anywhere."

So the voyage continued, and at every port to which their frigate put in, Maximilian and his brother officers had some new and interesting experiences. Maximilian recorded what he saw in his diary, and although much of what he wrote down was dull and commonplace, from time to time he would notice something which would make him pause and think, and in so doing would throw light on the development of his character and mind. In Valencia, for example, he was taken to see a silk factory, and on this subject he expressed himself characteristically :

In the whole world there is nothing more tedious to me than a factory. Everything goes on with such a mathematical regularity calculated to the very second ; and human genius shows the working people by its wonderful inventions how useless is their little bit of common sense. They are in fact mere machines.

We are living in the unhappy time of change. . . . I can never accommodate myself — or at least I cannot at present — to see the rich owner of a factory producing in quantities articles which satisfy the extravagant luxury of the rich, whilst his workmen are serfs by reason of the mere power of his money, pale shadows of men who in a state of stupor and for the needs of their stomachs sacrifice their bodies to his money bag. I cannot forget my fellow men even for the most beautiful new machines ; my valuation of the so-called genius of our century does not reach to that height. In a factory I always feel uncomfortable. . . . Everything appears to me as if only made for the moment. We live in the century of haste, and with this the factories seem to harmonize.

It was unfortunately just such well-intentioned but half-baked sentiments as these that were to land Maximilian in constant difficulties when he achieved a position of political authority some years later.

In Algiers, where the *Novara* dropped anchor in the heat of summer, Maximilian and his companions found fresh fields to explore. The acquisition of Algeria by the rapidly growing French Empire of Napoleon III had only recently been completed, and all parties in France were exploiting it for their particular ends. " Algiers has become a watchword for France," remarked Maximilian with a fine touch of accuracy, " so that in these days it is placed at the head of every proclamation whether by the Napoleon, the Orleans or the Bourbon party, and alike whether the intention be to perplex or to benefit those who are addressed." But it was the aggressive and ambitious Louis Napoleon who was making the most of the conquest which Maximilian was able in a manner to survey from the late Arab ruler's palace in the Kasbah. " There in a fit of despotic rage ", noted Maximilian, " the Dey struck the French Consul with a fan, to which blow France owes her possession of Algiers, but owes also the loss of many thousands of human lives and many millions of francs. Algiers is a sort of safety-valve for France ; it carries off her bad blood, but also takes some of the good with it. Up to the present time it has been an uncertain possession, yet a field of action for French bravery and for untried theories."

Perhaps the most memorable part of this visit was an excursion which the party made into the Atlas Mountains, where they were received by General Yusuf, a former Tunisian Bey, who had become a high officer in the French army, taken a Parisian wife and embraced the Catholic faith. Maximilian found him " the one really chivalrous being in Algeria. . . . He is brave as a lion and wise as a serpent, both of which qualities the French adore. He never appears like a parvenu, for he himself talks of his past life ; he rather gives the impression that the French are receiving a favour in his services, and that he stands free and independent on his own self-created foundation." The gallant Yusuf, it may be added, regaled his guests with truly Oriental hospitality, dispensing iced champagne and Arab dancing girls with an equally lavish hand. Maximilian, who participated in these pleasures, salved his conscience with the reflection that " one may for once as a traveller sacrifice propriety, as this is a necessary portion of the complete picture ".

July 6, 1852, found Maximilian in the lovely island of Madeira. It was his twentieth birthday, which according to the laws of Austria signified his coming of age. The day began with the playing of the imperial anthem by a band which the local Austrian Consul had thoughtfully provided to awake His Highness, and ended with an excellent dinner and the usual toasts after a rousing cross-country gallop on horseback. Maximilian thought afterwards how pleasant the day had been. " I was twenty years of age and had arrived at an important period of my life ", he recalled afterwards ; " notwithstanding my youth, many grave and solemn thoughts dwelt in my mind on that morning. To outward appearances the attainment of my majority would cause but little change in my life, as before it

I was already, so far as my position would allow, my own master, and even in material affairs had not been fettered by the usual restrictions upon minors. If there be any prophetic warning in the manner in which one's birthday is spent, then the year to come will indeed be gay, bright and free from care, for never did I pass this anniversary in so joyous and so enchanting a manner."

Looking back on his brief career, the Archduke Ferdinand Max had to admit that he had not fared so badly ; in fact things had come easily for him. Now for the first time he was to experience unhappiness, for, contrary to his expectation, the twenty-first year of his life which opened so auspiciously contained the seeds of discord and tragedy. Nor were they the last which he was to suffer.

3

For Maximilian the most significant part of the cruise on which the *Novara* took him in that happy and carefree summer of 1852 was his visit to Lisbon and the Portuguese Court. Twenty years before this time Queen Maria da Gloria of Braganza, who was Maximilian's first cousin and was then a girl of fifteen, had been finally established on the throne of Portugal as Maria II after a bitter period of civil war. Her reign had hitherto been a continual struggle between two rival military cliques for power—the reactionaries led by the Duke of Terceira and the Count of Thomar and the Liberals headed by the Duke of Saldanha.

At the time of Maximilian's visit the Liberals were in control of the government, but to all intents their rule was the dictatorship of their leader. " He is now the virtual sovereign ", wrote Maximilian, who was received by Saldanha on arrival at the royal palace of Necessidades ; " he unites within himself the offices of Prime Minister, Commander-in-Chief, and Minister of War. In short, he is all in all. He is a stout man covered with stars, has curly snow-white hair, moustache and beard, a dark-brown Portuguese complexion, and wears steel-rimmed spectacles. To the Queen and the young Princes he is the most odious of flatterers." The Archduke, it may be added, took an intense dislike to this Portuguese dictator, which was confirmed by the subsequent discovery that he was in the habit of cracking jokes with the Queen and her consort during Mass. "What an impression must not this unworthy example have made on the people!" Maximilian noted disapprovingly. "How can obedience and respect towards earthly majesty exist if that earthly majesty does not know how to bow with reverence before the Majesty of Heaven?"

Maximilian was particularly anxious to make the acquaintance of his royal cousin, whom he had never met before. He subsequently had to admit that he was a little disappointed. "I cannot express the eagerness with which I met the sovereign of Portugal," he wrote, "for she had always inspired me with interest — as a near relative, as a female sovereign, more especially as a woman whose lot has been so exciting, as the mother of her family, and also for her outward appearance. She stood before me in a graceful morning dress, surrounded by her husband [1] and their three eldest sons. Maria da Gloria is tall, has a well-set head, noble expressive features, the blue eyes of the house of Hapsburg and delicate hands, but unfortunately the corpulence of a Portuguese to such a frightful degree as I had never witnessed before." To this unfortunate physical disability Maximilian attributed the Queen's lack of energy and perseverance. As a woman and a mother, however, the visitor was pleased to observe that "she sets a rare example of domestic virtues in vitiated Portugal . . . and that in her dress, in her manners, and in the way in which Necessidades is ruled, she follows much of the German style".

As a near relative of the reigning monarch Maximilian received a warm welcome at the Portuguese Court and was introduced to everyone of consequence. "The most amiable and indisputably also the most intellectual person" he found there was Maria da Gloria's stepmother the Dowager Queen-Empress Amelia, who was then living with her only daughter in a small villa at Bemfica, near the capital. Maria da Gloria's father, Dom Pedro, who had been Emperor of Brazil as well as King of Portugal, was twice married. His first wife, the Archduchess Leopoldine of Hapsburg, was a daughter of the Austrian

---

[1] Prince Ferdinand of Saxe-Coburg, King Consort. He was a nephew of the Belgian King Leopold I.

Emperor Francis, and thus Maximilian's paternal aunt. His second wife, Amelia Princess of Leuchtenberg, was a granddaughter of the first Napoleon's Empress Josephine through the latter's son Eugène de Beauharnais,[1] whom Napoleon had created Prince of Leuchtenberg and Viceroy of Italy. As Maximilian truthfully wrote, " harsh Fate has persecuted this Princess with its blind strokes from her earliest youth ". Torn from her family at the age of seventeen and sent out to Rio de Janeiro to marry the dissolute and unpopular Emperor Pedro, she was obliged to contend with his reigning mistress. She had then gone through the revolution which had unseated Pedro from his Brazilian throne and returned to Europe, where she nursed him through the last stages of consumption. Their only child was born in Paris shortly before his death.

The young Princess Maria Amelia of Braganza was now twenty years old, and a girl of striking beauty as well as cultivated intelligence. Maximilian described her as " amiable and distinguished . . . a perfect Princess such as one rarely meets ". He fell in love with her at first sight, and in this new joy the painful memory of little Pauline von Linden gradually receded. One evening they made an excursion to the castle and park of Lumiar, a property which belonged to the Duke of Palmella. It was in these luxuriant gardens with their fragrant flowers that Maximilian declared his love, to which the young girl responded becomingly. They resolved to be secretly betrothed. And yet on this eventful evening Maximilian felt strangely melancholy. He gazed on the serried terraces of enchanting flowers and smiled sadly. It may have been a premonition of death, for Princess Maria Amelia's fresh and alluring beauty was deceptive — she already bore the germs of the fatal disease which had carried her father to the grave.

It was a quick courtship, for Max spent barely two weeks in Lisbon, but there was no doubt about their feelings towards each other. For the time being, however, they decided not to announce the engagement until after the Emperor's permission had as a matter of course been obtained. Meanwhile the elder Amelia gave the couple her blessing.

[1] By Josephine's first husband, Alexandre Vicomte de Beauharnais.

On the traveller's return to Vienna the situation was accepted by the imperial family, although some of its members thought the Archduke might have done better for himself. Still, after all, Maria Amelia was a princess and her mother had once been Empress of Brazil, even if she herself did not belong to a reigning house. It was understood that the wedding would take place sometime during the next year. Max was delighted, and he returned to the dockyard at Trieste with renewed zest for his work. He had almost forgotten Pauline now. Then something happened which suddenly reopened the old wound.

Franz Joseph and Maximilian were invited by their aunt the Queen of Prussia to spend Christmas and New Year with her and King Frederick William IV in Berlin.[1] It was the first time that a Hapsburg had set foot in the Prussian capital, since Austria had for centuries been Prussia's enemy on the battlefields and in the council chambers of Europe. As one of the accompanying entertainments on this occasion a magnificent Court ball was held in honour of the imperial guests. Dancing was preceded by a reception at which the ladies stood in a respectful half-circle waiting to be introduced to the Emperor and his brother. Amongst this gay assembly were the Countess von Linden and her daughter, on whom the Emperor's glance chanced to alight in his search for someone he knew. Franz Joseph came over and greeted them pleasantly, but Pauline noticed that he felt embarrassed and that the pleasantries which he repeated seemed forced and learnt by heart. Maximilian, on the other hand, did not come near either of them, although he watched Pauline closely. Whilst she was dancing she looked at him with an air of reproach, their eyes met, he returned her gaze for a moment, and then turned away sadly, " as if ", wrote Pauline when recalling the incident many years afterwards, " he wished to escape a temptation ". He disappeared into an adjoining room and she never saw him again.

Maximilian returned to Trieste feeling very miserable. Almost immediately he received the shattering news that his beloved Maria Amelia was dead. In the mistaken but at that

---

[1] The Archduchess Sophie's sister, Princess Elizabeth (Elise) of Bavaria, married King Frederick William IV of Prussia.

time generally prevalent belief that sea air was beneficial for consumptives, the ailing girl had been taken by her mother to spend the winter in Madeira. There on February 4, 1853, in Maximilian's anguished words, " she departed, a pure perfect angel to go from this imperfect world to her true home ". Maximilian was overcome with grief, and for days on end he could think of nothing else.

Exactly a fortnight after the tragic death of his affianced bride, Maximilian suffered a further shock. Whilst taking a walk in Vienna the Emperor Franz Joseph was stabbed in the neck by a Hungarian tailor named Libényi who hoped to avenge his down-trodden countrymen. The would-be assassin's dagger was turned aside by the buckle on the Emperor's cravat, with the result that the wound was not as serious as it might have been and Franz Joseph was actually able to walk home to the Hofburg. Although he was confined to bed for three weeks, the succession was never really in danger. Nevertheless, the Emperor's adjutant, Count Grünne, thought fit to ask whether Maximilian, who was then at Cattaro in the extreme south of the Empire, should be sent for. Franz Joseph said "No" firmly. However, Maximilian, who was thoroughly alarmed by the news, came to Vienna on his own initiative. The Emperor was annoyed with his brother for thus interrupting his naval duties, and his annoyance was only partly nullified by the public appeal for subscriptions issued by Maximilian to erect a memorial as a thanksgiving to the Almighty for His Imperial Majesty's happy escape. The appeal was a success, and a stately Gothic church, the Votivkirche, eventually commemorated the attempted assassination.

Notwithstanding this example of fraternal solicitude and devotion, the dark shadow of jealousy had, for the first time in their lives, fallen between the two brothers. Unfortunately for Maximilian, the fault lay with the Emperor.

4

Austrian foreign policy had recently undergone an important change in regard to what was known as the Eastern Question, or the problem of Turkey in Europe. In the eighteenth century Austria had encouraged the expulsion of the Turk from his European possessions, but during the long period of Metternich's sway which followed the Congress of Vienna this policy had been abandoned in favour of the legitimist one of preserving the Ottoman Empire in its integrity. But the Ottoman Empire had lately shown increased signs of breaking up, and the Sultan's Christian subjects looked hopefully to Austria and to Russia, whom they regarded as their natural protectors, the former of the Catholics and the latter of the Orthodox members of the faith. Towards the end of 1852 the small but rugged territory of Montenegro, which was subject to the Sultan's suzerainty, was threatened with a punitive expedition by its overlord which appeared as if it might exterminate its inhabitants. Franz Joseph immediately despatched an ultimatum to the Porte and at the same time massed troops on his southern border. The result was that Turkey withdrew her forces and this hardy Slavic people was saved from annihilation.

The Russian Tsar Nicholas I was naturally delighted at this turn of events, which he felt would strengthen his hand in future negotiations with Turkey. He promptly demanded of the Sultan effective recognition of Russian protectorate over all his Orthodox subjects. The Sultan refused. Thereupon a Russian army crossed the river Pruth into Turkish territory and occupied the two Danubian principalities which now form the kingdom of Rumania. From Vienna Franz Joseph, who realized with uneasiness that other powers might be drawn into this conflict, contented himself with the bare announcement of protectorate over the Sultan's Catholic subjects.

Reports of the persecution of the Catholics in the neighbouring Turkish territory of Albania had reached the Emperor's ears ; he was advised that an investigation could best be carried out on the spot. Franz Joseph decided that his brother Maximilian should undertake the task, and the Archduke was accordingly despatched to Albanian waters in the armed corvette *Minerva*, of which he was put in command. The account of this mission, which Maximilian, who was barely twenty-one

39

at the time, kept in his diary and later revised for publication, is among the best which he wrote.

Albania had been subject to the authority of the Porte since the end of the Middle Ages ; and, although the country had enjoyed a certain measure of political freedom, the fact that many of its inhabitants had been converted to the Moslem creed did not make the lot of the remaining Christians any happier. " On the boundaries of civilization ", as Maximilian put it, " is a wilderness which bears the euphonious name of Albania. In its woody confines, Turks, boars and many Catholic Christians live in contention and strife, chasing each other in wild pursuit. As in the time of Diocletian, Mass is celebrated in anxious fear, and the altar candles serve, as then, to illuminate the dark meeting-places of the faithful. . . . Although near in point of distance Albania is separated from our country by a chasm as wide as an ocean, for it is situated within the territory of the decaying Crescent, where civilization has not yet found an entrance and where all is abandoned to the despotism of the Pashas and their hordes." The object of Maximilian's mission was " to give these poor Catholics moral support " and to report back to the Emperor on their conditions of life.

" This mission ", wrote Maximilian afterwards, " would have been an effective one had the means and circumstances of that time permitted us to act energetically." As it was, there was little which could be done beyond reconnaissance, since Maximilian had been warned before setting sail not to become embroiled with any local Turkish authorities, and in any event the expedition was not able to penetrate very far into the interior of the country. Nevertheless, the mission did not return home without achieving some success. It also had its lighter moments. At Antivari, which was the first port to which the *Minerva* put in, the party was fired on from the customs house, and when remonstrated with later for this inhospitable welcome by the Austrian consular agent, the officers concerned stated that they had mistaken the *Minerva* for a Turkish vessel. A little later, when the corvette dropped anchor off the wild wooded coast near Cape Rodoni and the officers and crew went ashore, the leader of the small local community, whom Maximilian jokingly nicknamed Scanderbeg [1] — he was a fugitive from justice who had killed two men some years previously and had fled to these remote parts to escape vengeance — organized some excellent boar-hunting for the ship's company.

Whilst enjoying the pleasures of the chase in Rodoni woods Maximilian and his companions were surprised by an armed band of mounted police who had been sent by the neighbouring governor to find out who the visitors were and what they and their ship were doing on his stretch of little-inhabited coast. Clad in a white burnous which he had acquired in Algiers the year before, the young commander of the *Minerva* received the official delegation seated under a canopy which he had rigged up and which was designed to impart a fitting atmosphere of Oriental ceremony to the occasion. When he had ranged his guests in a semicircle round the canopy and offered them pipes which they accepted with alacrity, Maximilian told them who he was and showed them the Austrian flag, " which unfortunately they did not seem to know ". He then assured them that he and his friends were on the best of terms with their Padishah, and that the purpose of his visit was hunting, at which moment he produced a dead sow as evidence. This explanation completely satisfied the police, who now settled down comfortably to their pipes and, much to Maximilian's consternation, showed no inclination to leave. Finally, Maximilian hit on the ingenious expedient of telling them that " it was the time of day when we made our ablutions in the Sea ", which to the faithful followers of the Prophet had the desired effect. Their only wish now was to visit the corvette, to which they were duly despatched with a note from Maximilian to his chief officer to see that the visitors were given plenty of wine and coffee. " When they were fairly crammed ", noted Maximilian gleefully, " they were taken ashore in a boat, whilst we who had just entered the sea turned in all directions, making ' salaam aleiks ' as if zealously performing our religious duties. The Moslems were much edified by our devoutness and waved a friendly farewell."

As the *Minerva* was preparing to continue her voyage the

[1] After the great Albanian leader who defeated twenty-three Ottoman armies in the fifteenth century.

huntsman Scanderbeg suddenly appeared on board and threw himself howling at the captain's feet. Between sobs he conveyed to Maximilian that the great potentate, the Pasha of Tirana, had arrived with two hundred men, had seized his son, and threatened to have him beheaded if the corvette should depart before he had been able to visit her. Maximilian immediately despatched an officer ashore with instructions to seek out the Pasha and assuage his wrath. On his return the envoy reported that Scanderbeg had somewhat exaggerated the facts, due to his having taken too much to drink on the previous evening, but that the Pasha had in fact arrived and had expressed a desire to visit the *Minerva* in an extremely peremptory tone. However, in conversation with Maximilian's representative the Pasha had considerably moderated his language, and in these circumstances the Archduke decided to comply with his request.

The description which Maximilian wrote of the subsequent reception is in his happiest vein.

August 6, 1853

At half-past nine a.m. one of the corvette's boats brought the formidable but now tamed Bimbashi on board. Like all Osmanli aristocrats, the lion of Tirana was a fat, delicate little mannikin with bandy legs, a quivering paunch, and a thin pagoda-like countenance. He wore a fez on his round shaven head, a dressing-gown about his panting body, and dirty pantaloons covered his shanks.

A lazy nod from me told him that he might be seated, and we offered him watermelons and champagne to refresh his soul, if by chance the infidel had one. Some meaningless hollow phrases and a somewhat stern admonition from me in regard to Christians formed the subjects of our diplomatic conversation, while his unintelligible roaring or rather grunting nearly made me laugh openly in the face of this blood-thirsty tyrant. When His Highness had refreshed himself, he was dismissed with a few bottles of stale champagne and was honoured with a salute from our thirty-two pounders which rather shook his nerves.

The *Minerva*'s most important port of call was Durazzo, which was then the principal town and chief seaport in the country. Here the mission achieved its greatest success. Maximilian discovered that the local Roman Catholic Archbishop had for the past year been imprisoned by the Turks in his house, which was about twelve hours' ride from the town. He immediately despatched an armed posse " with orders to free the unhappy apostle from custody and conduct him to us and his diocese ". This task was executed without apparent difficulty, and Don Ambrosio, the Archbishop, arrived on board the *Minerva* just in time to join in the Emperor's birthday celebrations, which were fittingly enacted on August 18 by Maximilian and the whole ship's company in addition to most of the native Christian population who were invited to attend.

Awning was spread out over the main and quarter decks and every flag on board was flown. A canopy of purple silk and an altar were erected before the mizzen-mast where the Archbishop duly celebrated Mass, and the German cabin-boys improvised a choir and sang a Te Deum " very well ". The religious service was followed by a banquet on deck at which the Archbishop sat on Maximilian's right hand " and enjoyed the gifts of God with thankful heart ". When every glass had been charged with champagne Maximilian rose and proposed the Emperor's health, a salute of guns was fired, and the whole ship's company stood up and sang an Austrian national air which had been carefully rehearsed beforehand both in German and Italian. " The moment was full of dignity and emotion ", wrote Maximilian in his description of the scene ; " and the song coming from so many vigorous throats and rendered with such heartfelt emotion made a grand impression which did not fail in its effect on our guests."

The mission concluded its investigations into the state of Catholic Christianity in Albania with a brief visit to the port of Avlona in the extreme south of the country. Here the local Bey, " a tractable young man " who had been educated in Constantinople, received the visitors on his divan, and introduced them to a centenarian Turk who remembered Trieste " when it was in the midst of woods, surrounded by swamps, and notorious as the nest of robbers and resort of pirates ". Maximilian noticed that the part of the Bey's palace obviously designed to be a harem was disused and decayed. He was informed that the Bey was not married and that he preferred instead " to have a European liaison with the wife of a Frenchman who does not object, as by this means his position here is rendered more advantageous". The Bey was evidently as generous with his material gifts as with his affections, for when the party had returned to their ship word reached them that the Bey was preparing to despatch a herd of oxen as a present to the commander. However, Maximilian did not wish to be under any obligation to the Bey, who could do little for the Catholics in the neighbourhood since there were so few of them ; he therefore weighed anchor and set the *Minerva*'s course for home as the cattle were still lowing on the shore.

If the voyage was to a great extent politically unproductive, at least it confirmed Maximilian in his love of the sea and of his country's navy. It was his first command and it must be admitted that he discharged it well. "I strove as much as possible", he said looking back on it, " to make life agreeable to my subordinates. . . . A commander, who understands his position and considers himself a true sailor, loves his subordinates and only feels at home among the sailors trained by himself. After a time there is a bond that unites the whole crew. Dangers are experienced together, pleasures enjoyed together, seas are crossed in pleasant company, and everyone feels that on the wide ocean he belongs to a little world linked together by the common occurrences of daily life."

5

While Maximilian was celebrating his brother's birthday with becoming ceremony on board the corvette *Minerva*, the Emperor himself had chosen this the twenty-third anniversary of his birth to take an important step. He announced his engagement to be married to his cousin Princess Elizabeth of Bavaria. The Archduchess Sophie originally intended that Franz Joseph should marry her sister Ludovica's elder child Helen, and she was at first somewhat surprised when the Emperor made up his mind in favour of the younger sister. However, she quickly accommodated herself to this change, as she was quite determined to exercise the full measure of her maternal control over both young people.

Although a mere slip of a girl at the time of her engagement (she was not yet sixteen), Elizabeth, or Sisi as she was known in the family, already showed signs of that radiant beauty which very soon as a woman was to make her famous. Maximilian was enchanted with her, and he envied his brother his good fortune. In particular, he shared with Sisi her love of horses and the open air ; they were both good riders, indeed Sisi's equestrian skill was quite remarkable. Since Max had become a sailor he saw little of his brother, and after the wedding, which took place in April, 1854, he saw less of the Emperor than ever. Of the unhappiness which marked the beginning of the marriage by reason of the Archduchess Sophie's unkind behaviour to her daughter-in-law he knew nothing, although from time to time talk reached his ears that the new Empress had outraged Court etiquette by demanding beer for her luncheon, insisting on wearing old shoes, and ordering a bath to be installed in the imperial palace.

Franz Joseph's mind was not free from worry as he stood before the altar in the Augustinian Church in Vienna with his lovely bride. Only a few weeks previously England and France had joined Turkey in declaring war on Russia. Each side was looking to the Austrian Emperor for support. Franz Joseph mobilized two armies at immense expense to his country's exchequer, but he could not decide which side to join. He did not want to ally himself with the Tsar and confirm the Russians in possession of the Danubian principalities as well as antagonize the French Emperor Napoleon III, who he suspected might seize his opposition as a pretext to assist his Italian subjects in obtaining their independence. On the other hand, he had only recently become the protector of the Catholics in the Balkans, and he could hardly range himself on the side of their oppressor. In the end he did nothing, or rather contented himself with mediating between the combatants, a tortuous and expensive form of diplomacy which was not calculated to enhance his prestige in Europe.

In looking to his country's defences at this time, the Emperor Franz Joseph made one appointment which was to have valuable and far-reaching results. The Danish Admiral Dahlerup had been retired from his command of the Austrian Navy in 1852 as the result of the intrigues of the Emperor's camarilla of military advisers. His successor, Baron Franz Wimpfen, was a much-defeated general of artillery who knew nothing whatever of naval matters. Under his unfortunate command the efficiency and morale of the service had deteriorated noticeably. At last, partly as the result of his brother's remonstrances, the Emperor decided on a spectacular change. On September 10, 1854, he published a decree transferring Wimpfen to the command of an army corps and nominating in his place as *Marineoberkommandant* the Archduke Ferdinand Maximilian with the rank of Rear-Admiral.

At the time Maximilian joined the navy as a cadet in 1850, the Austrian battle fleet consisted of only three sailing frigates — the *Novara* of 1,500 tons armed with 30-pounder guns, the *Bellona* of 1,260 tons and the *Venus* of 1,000 tons, both with 18-pounders — six corvettes, two armed steam cruisers and some other small craft. During the period of the Danish Admiral Dahlerup's command, which coincided with Maximilian's naval apprenticeship, two new 1,500-ton frigates were laid down, the *Schwarzenberg* and the *Maria Anna,* and also twelve armed sloops in addition to a corvette and a steam cruiser. The *Maria Anna* was, however, lost in the storm which the fleet encountered between Venice and Trieste in March 1852, when Maximilian and his brother, who were on board another vessel, narrowly escaped with their lives.

By none was Maximilian's new appointment more warmly welcomed than by that brilliant young naval officer Wilhelm Tegetthoff. "I am convinced that the Archduke Max is full of energy and has the interests of the service at heart", he wrote shortly after hearing the news. At the same time he noted that Wimpfen and his adherents were doing all they could to crab the appointment on the grounds of the Archduke's youth and in-experience. "However that may be", remarked Tegetthoff, "the firm determination to get something done, which certainly inspires the Archduke, will compensate for much". A week later he wrote : "The Archduke is displaying the greatest activity and altogether he arouses the most encouraging expecta-tions. He goes into every detail, and through his love of business and determined zeal I feel he will at last bring about a thorough reorganization of our service, which Dahlerup and Wimpfen merely bungled through their superficial policy."

Immediately after his appointment as Commander-in-Chief was gazetted, Maximilian set to work to overhaul the fleet and to build new vessels. He immediately put in hand the construction of three gunboats, and at the same time he acquired a steam frigate from the English Government which was renamed the *Radetzky*. He had already introduced German as well as Italian orders when he was in command of the corvette *Minerva* on her voyage to Albanian waters in the previous year, and he now extended this practice throughout the service. He tried to recruit cadets for the service from the Dalmatian rather than the Italian parts of the Empire. Above all he strove to make the navy a national one, and he insisted, as far as possible, that the ships and their crews and equipment should be Austrian in character. Considerable progress in the general efficiency of the navy was apparent by the summer of 1855 when the young Commander-in-Chief led out a fleet of fourteen ships-of-war on exercises in the Mediterranean. It was the largest Austrian squadron which had ever put to sea, and when it anchored off Alexandria and later off Toulon its appearance provoked favourable comment in both those ports.

During this cruise, it may be noted in passing, Maximilian made a number of extended shore excursions, visiting Suez, the Pyramids, Jerusalem and other places in the Holy Land, which were then under Turkish rule. At Haifa he noticed the French flag flying from a Franciscan monastery, and, mindful of his country's recently enunciated role of protector of the Sultan's Catholic subjects, he called at the monastery and boldly asked the Father Superior to substitute the Austrian red and white in its stead : he was, however, met with a positive refusal, an action doubtless not unconnected with France's current successes in the Crimean War. In Jerusalem, on the other hand, his sense of national pride as well as his spiritual devotion was gratified by the bearing aloft of a cross through the streets of the city in a religious procession held on the occasion of his visit, which was the first time such a spectacle had occurred since the Crusades six centuries before. " I did not know how to tear myself away from the Holy Sepulchre", he said afterwards ; " the comfort which it instilled in me continually drew me to it. Religion which is full of love has its spirit in Rome, its heart in Jerusalem."

Later in the course of his voyage Maximilian spent three hurried days in Rome, where he was able to report his impressions of the Holy Land to Pope Pius IX. "In the course of these three days", he recalled afterwards, "I was three times in the Coliseum, three times in the Vatican, three times in St. Peter's, visited all the churches, museums, and monuments, examined the chief books in the splendid library at the Vatican and have now a vivid recollection of the individual gems among the statues and pictures. . . . During these three days I visited the Holy Father twice and received the Holy Communion from his hands, accompanied him twice to Mass and breakfasted with him afterwards, attended a long High Mass in the Sistine Chapel, and also went to several large dinner parties, and found time to pay and receive a multitude of official visits. Certainly my labours began about five o'clock in the morning, and, thanks to the full moon, were continued until one o'clock at night."

Meanwhile revolutionary changes were taking place in the principles of naval strategy and the construction of ships-of-war. Ten months before Maximilian assumed command of the Austrian navy, the deadly effect of shell-fire upon unprotected wooden vessels had been proved for the first time in action, when a Turkish squadron which lay under the guns of a small Russian battery in the Crimea was practically annihilated. The British and French Admiralties now began to build floating batteries with armour, and so the age of the ironclad was ushered in. In the autumn of 1855 a combined Anglo-French squadron of ironclads, which appeared before Kinburn in the Crimea, drew heavy fire from the Russian guns which scarcely even dented their hulls and caused the Russian shore commander's surrender. There was no doubt how they would affect the future of naval warfare. As the French Admiral wrote in his official report of the engagement before Kinburn, " everything may be expected from these formidable engines of war ".

Maximilian was quick to realize the superiority of armour to

wood in fighting vessels as well as that of steam to sails which
had already been apparent to him for some years. He now
constructed and fortified an excellent new dockyard and arsenal,
choosing as its site the Adriatic port of Pola, with its traditions
of imperial Rome, which henceforth superseded Trieste as the
chief Austrian naval station. During the next two years several
ships were built here under Maximilian's supervision ; they
included an ironclad steam battleship, the *Kaiser*, of 91 guns,
two large screw frigates and two screw corvettes, all with
4½-inch armoured plating of Styrian iron. At the same time
the frigate *Novara* and the other warships of older type were
converted into ironclads. He also founded a Naval Museum
and a Hydrographic Institute there. In all these reforms the
Commander-in-Chief had the energetic support of his fellow
officer and friend Tegetthoff, whose prospects in the service
he was fortunately able to advance at the same time.

By the time the armistice was signed in the spring of 1856,
and the Crimean combatants assembled round the Congress table
to argue out the peace terms in Napoleon III's Paris of gaslight
and crinolines, Austria was on the way to possessing a navy of
some size and efficiency. This was a comfort to Franz Joseph,
and to some degree it offset the unpleasant fact that Austria's
prestige had fallen considerably in the eyes of the European
nations as a result of her Emperor's vacillating and even treacherous policy. It was in an endeavour to correct this unfortunate
impression and at the same time emphasize his political feelings
that Franz Joseph now decided to send his brother on a tour of
the principal neighbouring Courts in Europe. The Archduke
was to begin with France.

6

In Paris, which he reached on May 17, 1856, Maximilian
found the Second Empire was well into its stride. Over four
years had passed since Napoleon III had seized absolute power,
and during this period it had been the new Emperor's constant
object to distract popular attention from the despotic character
of his rule by maintaining a glittering Court and carrying through,
regardless of expense, an ambitious scheme of town-planning in

the capital. " It would hardly be believed ", wrote Maximilian, " what transformations Napoleon has effected in the outward aspect of Paris within a short time. The enigma is solved only when one finds out how little consideration has been paid to economizing expenditure either by the State or the City. New streets, new boulevards, countless new buildings, all of gigantic dimensions, have sprung up under the present Government. Paris is not the capital of an emperor but of an *imperator*, hence the deification of art which prevails here, the wealth of monuments, columns, and so forth. Just as the First Empire took as its model the Rome of the Caesars, so the second edition takes pleasure in a stiff imitation of the same style. On all sides one has the impression of the transitory ; it is all very brilliant, but unmistakably intended for the moment alone."

Maximilian wrote a number of confidential letters to the Emperor Franz Joseph describing his visit and the impressions which he gained. Fortunately these letters have been preserved, since they show a remarkable insight into the character of Napoleon III and his Court as well as establishing the unqualified success of the Archduke's mission.[1] Franz Joseph became quite enthusiastic when he read them. " You have managed the Emperor most cleverly and also with much tact," he told his brother, " and have thus essentially improved our relations with France as also indeed our future position."

Maximilian found the going far from easy, particularly at the beginning. The Emperor's nephew Prince Napoleon, who had been delegated by the Emperor to receive his guest at the railway station (a special train had brought him from Strassburg to the Gare de l'Est), discharged his task " in such a cold stiff manner " that Maximilian, by way of reprisal, " felt bound to behave with great reserve ". This " strange bearded figure ", who was popularly known as Plon-Plon and whom the Emperor disliked intensely, struck Maximilian as being completely devoid of amiability and having " absolutely the look of a worn-out basso from some obscure Italian opera-house ". Maximilian's

---

[1] Selections from these letters, which are preserved among Maximilian's private papers in the *Staatsarchiv* in Vienna, were first published in 1924 by Count Egon Corti in his *Maximilian und Charlotte von Mexiko.*

annoyance at this casual and unfriendly welcome was increased by the fact that the carriages which were to drive him and his suite to the imperial residence at St. Cloud had not arrived, and he was obliged to wait for some time for them — " a curious and typical detail ", he added in his report to his brother.

The Emperor, who was standing to receive his guest at the top of the steps before the château at St. Cloud, made a most unfavourable first impression on Maximilian. He was dressed in military uniform with large gilt epaulettes, the coveted Spanish Order of the Golden Fleece dangled on his chest, while his bow-legs were tightly encased in bright red pantaloons which were strapped beneath his ankles. His short unimposing stature, " his exterior which is utterly lacking in nobility ", his shuffling gait, his hairy plump hands which trembled as he grasped his guest by the arm, the sly enquiring glance of his lustreless eyes, all these features reminded Maximilian not so much of an Emperor with a sceptre as a circus-master with a riding-crop. The lovely Empress Eugénie, whom he visited immediately afterwards in her room, Maximilian discovered " in a state of great weakness and lassitude ". However, she went to considerable pains to be pleasant to the visitor, but at the same time she appeared " uncommonly embarrassed ", as also did her consort. " Her beauty, which is undeniably great though it owes a good deal to art ", noted Maximilian, " reveals no trace of the Spanish type.[1] She is quite a thoroughbred, but essentially lacking in the august quality of an Empress." To Maximilian's eyes she was by no means as handsome as his sister-in-law the Empress Elizabeth in Vienna.

As Eugénie was not well enough to appear at dinner, Maximilian dined with Napoleon alone. The meal was badly served, and in Maximilian's opinion every nicety of good breeding on the host's part was lacking. " At the table the Emperor was so ill at ease that the conversation was never entertaining," wrote his guest, " and it was all I could do to infuse a little life into it. . . . The reckless way in which he speaks in the presence of his servants is most remarkable ; he often lets fall the most incredible

[1] Eugénie's father, Count Montijo, was a Spaniard, while her mother was Scottish by birth.

statements before them. This seems to me typical of a parvenu, utterly lacking in that *esprit de corps* which makes one careful not to expose oneself before those in subordinate positions."

Next morning they had their first diplomatic conversation. Maximilian was taking a turn in the garden after breakfast, when the Emperor, who thought that this would be a good opportunity for a talk, came out to meet him. So as to have a topic with which to introduce the conversation, Napoleon took his guest into the " famous orangery of the 18th of Brumaire ",[1] which provided him with the opportunity of talking about his own *coup d'état*, which he did " with much archness ". He then proceeded to compliment Maximilian on his imperial brother, saying what great things he had already accomplished in spite of his youth. He was not, however, quite so complimentary about Franz Joseph's Foreign Minister, Count Buol, whom he was inclined to blame for Austria's not having joined in the Crimean War. To this complaint, which was not altogether unexpected, Maximilian replied that " our most material interest in the war with Russia would have been the security and freedom of the Danubian principalities ; had we drawn the sword, the war would have been endless ". Napoleon is stated to have been somewhat taken aback by his answer, but probably more on account of its ingenuousness than its logic. At any rate the Emperor went on to say that at the recent peace congress it might have been preferable to partition the Ottoman Empire instead of maintaining it, in which case Austria could have enlarged her frontiers by annexing Albania and Herzegovina. He met Maximilian's remonstrance that Turkey had displayed far more vitality in the course of the war than she had generally been credited with by saying half-banteringly that " after all it was a sorry business to have to bolster up the Turks, the stupidest people in the world ".

" At any rate ", said the Emperor, " Europe has now got peace. It is not a durable achievement, but it will last at least a few years." The aim of the war, he went on, had been to thrust

[1] The Council of Five Hundred of the Directory of revolutionary France met here on the eve of their overthrow on November 9, 1799 (18th Brumaire), by Napoleon I, who proclaimed himself First Consul.

Russia back within her limits, and this aim had been achieved. Napoleon expressed obvious satisfaction at the Tsar's recent humiliation, and he spoke of Russia's part in the complications of the Eastern Question " with a contempt ", admitted Maximilian, " in which I joined within suitable limitations ".

In discussing Austrian affairs, Maximilian was astonished by the incredible ignorance which Napoleon displayed. For instance, he did not know how long the ex-Emperor Ferdinand had reigned, nor where he was then living. For the rest Napoleon was inclined to look with favour on Maximilian's proposal of an alliance between their two countries, but without the addition of England, which Maximilian had originally suggested.

The same evening the Emperor gave a state dinner for his guest at St. Cloud at which all the leading officials and dignitaries of the Second Empire appeared in Court dress, but which seemed to Maximilian to lack the quality of an imperial entertainment. "The Emperor's incredible lack of ease was particularly obvious ", observed Maximilian on this occasion ; " it occurred to me that he still feels ill at ease in the presence of a prince of more ancient lineage. When he gets over this constraint, he displays great frankness, and the more closely I get to know him, the more solidly does his confidence in me seem to be established. In general there appears to be the most excellent intention of giving a proper setting to the Court, but the whole machinery does not as yet work smoothly. In spite of the unconstrained manner which they try to affect at Court, the parvenu etiquette keeps coming through everything. So far it is my impression that the Emperor of the French is respected by many but loved by none. . . . One can see, moreover, that his suite has formerly been that of the president of a republic : it is often hard for them to maintain themselves on a fitting level. The bearing of the Court ladies towards the Empress, too, their shaking hands with her, their hearty friendliness, are a little shocking to our conceptions of imperial etiquette. The whole impression is, so to speak, that of a make-believe Court, the various offices of which are occupied by amateurs who are not very sure of their parts. There can be no question of a good or bad tone here, for this Court is absolutely lacking in tone."

The next few days were spent in sightseeing, which included a review of the imperial troops near Versailles and an instructive tour of parts of the capital, newly laid out for the Emperor by Monsieur Haussmann, " the whole arrangement of which is mainly dictated by military aims — witness the macadamized roads which are very pleasant to drive along and have also the advantage of doing away with what used to be material for barricades ". Maximilian composed a glowing account of the review as well as of the personalities of the Emperor and Empress, and he addressed it to his brother through the open post, so that it was intercepted by the secret police and its contents reported to Napoleon, as indeed Maximilian intended they should be, " for it was framed for the express purpose of being read in high quarters here ". In a confidential letter, which like his others he entrusted to a reliable Austrian courier, he gave his true impressions. " The Empress's horsemanship, about which such a fuss is made, is nothing out of the way. In spite of my profession as a naval man, I appeared by Prince Oscar's [1] side on my fiery Andalusian by no means to my own disadvantage, and I look back with gratitude to the riding-lessons we took together. The review was very fine, the line marching in particular being a great success. The march past, with the cheers of the units as they went by, had to my eyes an absolutely praetorian character — it was the *Imperator* among his hordes to the life." Maximilian could not help noticing, however, that the Empress's name was " conspicuous by its absence from the soldiers' plaudits ".

Various other entertainments were arranged for the Archduke.[2] One evening a theatrical performance was given at St. Cloud to which an audience " of an incredible character " was invited. " A very improper piece was performed ", observed Maximilian, " which according to our ideas ought not to have been played before ladies." On another evening the Emperor and Empress gave a state ball at which Maximilian

---

[1] Prince Oscar of Sweden, who was also staying at St. Cloud. " Le dernier ", wrote the Austrian Ambassador Count Hübner, " est complètement éclipsé par le prince autrichien dont tout le monde est enchanté ".

[2] In spite of his religion Maximilian is believed to have become a Freemason at this time and to have been admitted to several degrees of Scottish Rite masonry in Paris.

proudly led his hostess into the ballroom. " The entertainment was opened ", he told Franz Joseph, " by all the guests filing past the imperial family, which really produced an irresistibly comic effect upon me. The society was inconceivably mixed and distinguished for its disgusting dress and tactless behaviour. Adventurers swarmed, which is a leading characteristic of this Court." Among them Maximilian noticed Countess Castiglione, wife of the Sardinian Minister, who reminded Maximilian, " not only by her costume and coiffure, but also by her free and independent bearing, of some dancer of the Regency period come to life again ". She was reputedly the Emperor's mistress. Indeed it was not long before Maximilian remarked that Napoleon had a wandering eye for the ladies. " The Emperor's assiduity for all the pretty women is unpleasantly conspicuous, and detracts greatly from his sovereign dignity."

But, judging from what Maximilian said, Eugénie could get her own back on her husband. Each day throughout his visit the Archduke used to lunch quietly with his host and hostess alone at St. Cloud. The conversation was apt to be marked with " great candour " on these occasions. " The Empress's gaiety and naïve vivacity", remarked Maximilian, " do not always seem to please her imperial husband, who sometimes casts reproving glances at her." On one occasion she recounted how, whilst out riding in the park, she had passed a " quite delicious sailor boy ", whom she had recognized as one of the crew of the imperial yacht, and that she had been " stricken so agreeably " by his attractive appearance that she had made her groom turn and ride back with her so she could have another look at this Adonis. " A very pleasant story this for a third person" was Maximilian's dry comment ; " but rather painful for the host, who pulled a long sour face and fidgeted and haw-hawed in his seat."

Both Napoleon and Eugénie were completely captivated by their guest's charm and good-nature. During their final interviews Maximilian informed his brother that the French Emperor " had quite shaken off the lack of ease which is usually characteristic of him, and its place was taken by a cordiality which may perhaps not be unconnected with that report which I sent Your

Majesty from Paris by the post ". On Maximilian's last evening, when a conjuring performance was given by the artiste Houdini before a large company in the château at St. Cloud, Napoleon repeatedly drew the Archduke into an adjoining room, a proceeding which appeared to arouse the jealousy of some of the other guests. Maximilian chose this occasion to tackle the Emperor on the thorny subject of Italy. In their previous conversations Napoleon had hedged when it was introduced, but this time he assured Maximilian that " his desire was always to act in agreement with Austria " and that he " would not allow this question to grow into a cause of dispute between the cabinets of Vienna and Paris ".

When the moment came for the Archduke to leave, Napoleon surprised everyone by personally investing all the gentlemen of Maximilian's suite with orders. At the same time he escorted his guest to his carriage and kept repeating that he and the Empress hoped to see him soon again. " We are like old friends," the Emperor said with more than a touch of emotion in his voice as he finally shook Maximilian by the hand. The visit had indeed been a success.

7

The French Emperor had been so pleased with Maximilian's visit that he put his yacht *La Reine Hortense* at the disposal of the Archduke to take him on the next stage of his tour to Belgium. On landing on Belgian soil Maximilian was met by the Crown Prince Leopold, Duke of Brabant, who conducted him to Brussels. His first impressions contrasted strongly with those of the country he had just left. " The Court is well ordered ", he observed ; " in all the Belgian cities Court carriages were ready for me. On the other hand, the arrangements in the palaces are wretched : Laeken is a delightful residence, but for the rest the palace in Brussels has not even stone staircases. Yet a certain dignity is to be noticed in everything, a *ton de bonne compagnie* and the accustomed formality of a Court ; and by comparison with Paris I was impressed here with a comfortable sensation of being once again among my own kind, for Brussels has for me that pleasant feeling, which I missed in France, of well-bred existence and of being at home."

Leopold I, King of the Belgians, was now sixty-six years old. As Prince of Saxe-Coburg he had been elected to the Belgian throne in 1831, and during the quarter of a century of his rule his small kingdom had come to be regarded as an ideally governed state. " I travelled through the whole of Belgium, which can be managed without difficulty in a few hours ", reported Maximilian to his brother. " It is indeed the most lovely blooming land that I have yet seen ; a country possessing all the elements of prosperity and plenty ; a fertile soil, rich cities crowded closely together, harbours, the sea, a well laid-out network of railways, commerce and factories. On all sides is manifest a feeling of well-being in which the traveller involuntarily shares ; on all sides one sees happy friendly faces ; the whole country is well cultivated ; forests of factory chimneys, industrial establishments, on a scale which I had never seen before, cover whole stretches of the landscape. Belgium fully deserves the self-chosen name of a model country ; this it undoubtedly owes in the first place to the prudent procedure of the King. . . ."

In the field of foreign affairs Leopold liked to be regarded as the Nestor of rulers, to whom the heads of the other European states instinctively turned for guidance. Here he had been immeasurably assisted by the numerous dynastic connections of the house of Coburg, many of which he had arranged himself, and which strengthened the hand he contrived to play in most of the principal international events of his time. At the English Court in particular he was credited with wielding considerable influence, for his niece Victoria was Queen of England, his nephew Albert was Prince Consort, while he himself had at one time been married to Princess Charlotte, only daughter of King George IV, and had lived in that country for many years. Latterly, it is true, Leopold's remarkable political influence had shown unquestionable signs of decline. He had married as his second wife the Princess Louise of Orleans, daughter of the French King Louis Philippe, and had cemented the alliance by marrying off a Coburg nephew and a Coburg niece to two of that monarch's children. However, the events of 1848, which dislodged the house of Orleans from the French throne in favour of the Bonaparte Napoleon III, dealt his family prestige a severe blow. Napoleon also got the better of him during the Crimean War, and now Leopold was afraid that the new Emperor might possibly follow Bonapartist tradition by launching an attack upon his own kingdom. He could not afford, therefore, to relax his exertions as a political mentor, and with increasing age his shrewd sense of values remained unchanged. " In everything he says and does ", observed Maximilian at this time, " the fox peeps out unmistakably."

Leopold certainly lived up to his reputation in his reception of Maximilian. After dinner on his first evening in the palace at Laeken the King drew his guest into a window-embrasure and involved him in a long political lecture, repeating the hackneyed description of himself as " the Nestor among monarchs and that all of them might learn from him ". He promised to come and see Maximilian next day and continue his lecture on the concert of Europe, " an offer ", said his guest, " which I received yawning in spirit". True to his word, Leopold appeared in Maximilian's rooms on the following morning just before luncheon, with the result that the other members of the royal household had to wait an hour for their meal. During the interview the monarch displayed what appeared to Maximilian to be " very shrewd if not quite novel ideas ", overflowing with phrases about " good Austria " and the like and constantly repeating how much could be learnt from his own political wisdom. " He tried to scare me about Italian affairs ", Maximilian told his brother, " in order to assume a sort of paternal authority. If I may use such an expression, he would jolly well like to play the part of a political pope before whose pronouncements all the rulers of Europe must bow." On this occasion it must be admitted that Leopold interpreted the French Emperor's plans with remarkable foresight when he informed his visitor that Napoleon was not at that moment in a position to satisfy the territorial and nationalist desires of the Sardinian King Victor Emmanuel, but that in a few years' time Napoleon would " make a great war " and until then he intended to put off Victor Emmanuel with promises. " It is possible that there is

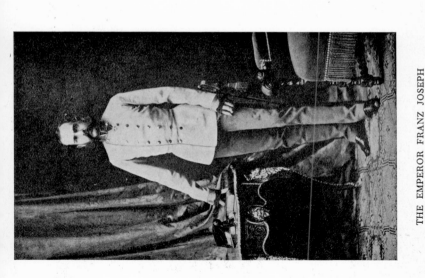

THE EMPEROR FRANZ JOSEPH

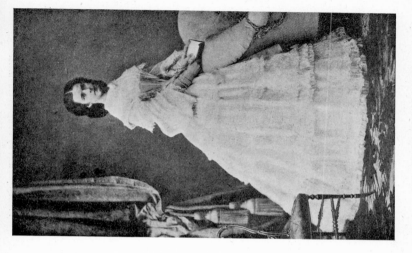

THE EMPRESS ELIZABETH

From photographs taken about 1861

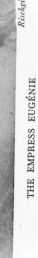

THE EMPEROR NAPOLEON III

From a contemporary photograph

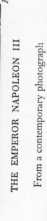

THE EMPRESS EUGÉNIE

From a portrait by Franz Winterhalter

some truth in this," remarked Maximilian dubiously, " but one must never forget that the King's phrases are not much to be trusted."

The Archduke had to confess that he found Leopold's political soliloquies decidedly boring. But there was another feature of the Belgian Court which greatly attracted him, although he did not mention the matter to anyone until after he had left. This was the monarch's sixteen-year-old daughter Charlotte, a pretty young girl with brown hair and eyes who showed promise of great beauty to come. " I think she will be the most beautiful princess in Europe," remarked Leopold at this time. " If only it might bring her happiness ! "

III. *Honeymoon in Italy*

CHARLOTTE was the fourth child and only daughter of the Belgian King Leopold and Queen Louise. Her father was fifty years old when she was born and her mother twenty-eight. Their eldest son had died in infancy; the second son, Leopold, Duke of Brabant, who became Crown Prince, was born in 1835; and the third, Philip, Count of Flanders, had followed two years later. As a child the Crown Prince proved extremely delicate, and in order to protect the succession adequately the parents determined to have another child and Leopold hoped for a son. On the morning of June 7, 1840, a salute of twenty-one guns informed the loyal inhabitants of Brussels that Her Majesty had been safely delivered of a daughter in the royal palace at Laeken. Leopold was quite disappointed at first, and to placate him the Queen displayed a touching devotion in calling the baby Charlotte after the King's first wife, daughter of the English Prince Regent (later King George IV), who, so Leopold confessed towards the end of his life, had given him in their short year of marriage such bliss as he never subsequently knew. For a long time, however, he did not care very much for his infant daughter.

Thanks to the combined efforts of Queen Louise and her mother, Queen Marie Amélie of France, Leopold's dislike of his daughter was gradually conquered. " Charlotte has become a great favourite with Leopold, as you prophesied she would ", wrote the Belgian Queen to her mother on the child's fourth birthday. " She is to dine with us this evening, surrounded by all her presents and crowned with roses. Poor child ! She will probably never have such a happy birthday as this." Charlotte's upbringing and education were to prove that there was some measure of truth in this statement. Prolonged and intensive lessons inclined her to be precocious, while the emphasis placed on religion in her *curriculum vitae* made her serious far beyond her years. At the age of five she was said to be able to follow the prayers in church " like a grown-up " and to have read the

office for Holy Week " with an imperturbable air of *sang-froid* ".
For Charlotte there were no lighter moments in the schoolroom
or even in the nursery. Her games with her dolls were played
in deadly earnest. When she was eight she wrote to her cousin
Queen Victoria of England : " I have received the beautiful
dolls' house you have been so kind as to send me, and I thank
you very much for it. I am delighted with it ; every morning
I dress my doll and give her a good breakfast ; and the day
after her arrival she gave a great rout at which all my dolls
were invited. Sometimes she plays at drafts (*sic*) on her pretty
little draft-board, and every evening I undress her and put
her to bed."

When she was ten years old Charlotte got whooping-cough.
Unfortunately, whilst nursing her, the Queen also caught the
malady. About the same time Louise received the news that
her father, Louis Philippe, who had recently been evicted from
his kingdom by the events of 1848, had died in exile. This
combination threw her into a decline, with the tragic result that
she followed the late King of France to his grave a few months
later. For Charlotte the consequences were doubly unfortunate.
She lost a devoted and saintly mother, and she was now thrown
more than ever into the society of individuals much older than
herself who filled Leopold's pedantic Court.

Her lessons increased in their intensity and severity. A most
rigid training of the mind was inculcated, and at the end of each
day her father, as he had also done with her cousin Queen
Victoria, made her " recapitulate the events of the day and the
motives which made one act oneself, as well as try to guess
what might have been the motives of others ". With practice,
her father pointed out, she would easily perceive if her motives
were good. " Persons in high positions ", observed Leopold,
" must particularly guard themselves against selfishness and
vanity. An individual in a high and important position will
easily see a great many persons eager to please the first and to
flatter and encourage the last. . . . To learn to know oneself,
to judge oneself with truth and impartiality must be the great
objects of one's exertion ; they are only attainable by constant
and cool self-examination. The position of what is generally

called great people has of late become extremely difficult. They are more attacked and calumniated and judged with less indulgence than private individuals. What they have lost in this way, they have not by any means regained in any other. Ever since the revolution of 1790 they are much less secure than they used to be, and the transition from sovereign power to *absolute want* has been as frequent as sudden. It becomes, therefore, necessary that the character should be formed so as not to be intoxicated by greatness and success, nor cast down by misfortune. To be able to do so, one must be able to appreciate things according to their real value, and particularly avoid giving to trifles an undue importance."

The corps of governesses and teachers which her father provided never had a more willing pupil than Princess Charlotte. When she was thirteen she confessed that Plutarch was her favourite author, while she zealously devoured Nicolas's *Philosophic Studies in Christianity* which was published about this time. "I have not wasted my time this year as I did last year", she wrote to her governess Countess Hulst at the end of 1853. "I studied my history and drawing lessons and practised the piano, which I like better now. I know all the Kings of England and their dates without a single mistake and, most remarkable of all, my arithmetic is progressing well ; I do as many as three problems in a day sometimes, and they are not easy problems. The languages are not progressing too badly either. I hope that when you return you will find me completely changed both physically and mentally, since I am now working better and have grown a great deal and am less awkward than before."

She showed a certain talent for dancing, but when she was admitted to the ballroom her appearances were carefully regulated. Only those male partners of royal blood were allowed to lead her on to the floor, and none but her brothers were permitted to embrace her in the waltz. She liked music, but it had to be good music of a serious character. The kind of music affected by her sister-in-law the Hungarian Archduchess Marie, who had married the Duke of Brabant, irritated her. "Marie is very kind," she wrote, "but her education is so poor that she has not developed a taste for more serious things. I am being saturated with concerts. Marie has arranged concerts with opera singers every two or three weeks. It is so uninteresting ; all day long one hears nothing but ' Mademoiselle Sforlanconi will write ' or ' Mademoiselle Sforlanconi is coming ' ! Everything centres round these singers. I am bored to death. It seems frightful to me to have nothing in one's bones but music."

Although Charlotte was still very young, the time was approaching when her father would consider the important question as to whom her hand should be given in marriage. That he should be a prince of a reigning house went without saying. When Maximilian arrived in Brussels he found that there were already two candidates in the running. One was the twenty-four-year-old Prince George of Saxony, and the other was the late Portuguese Queen Maria da Gloria's eldest son, who had recently ascended his country's throne as Pedro V : he was just nineteen. During his short visit Maximilian completely won Charlotte's heart, and as soon as the Archduke had made known his intentions to her father, which he did on his return to Austria, Leopold began to weigh the merits of the respective suitors. He wrote to his niece the Queen of England and asked her opinion. Victoria was strongly in favour of Pedro. " He is out and out *the* most distinguished young Prince there is," she wrote back, " and besides that, good, excellent and steady according to one's heart's desire, and as one could wish for an *only and beloved daughter*. For Portugal, too, an *amiable* well-educated Queen would be an immense blessing, for there *never* has been one. I am sure you would be more likely to secure Charlotte's happiness if you gave her to Pedro than to one of those innumerable Archdukes or to Prince George of Saxony."

The youthful Portuguese monarch had visited Brussels shortly before Maximilian, but Charlotte did not fancy the prospect of settling in Lisbon. Her friend and late governess Countess Hulst was also against the idea. " The Portuguese are only ourang-outangs ", she told Charlotte. " They have no resources, not even a priest capable of understanding you." Nor was Charlotte any more taken with Prince George ot Saxony. Fortunately Leopold saw that it would be unwise to force her hand. " My object is and was ", he told Queen Victoria,

" that Charlotte should decide as *she* likes it and uninfluenced by what I might prefer. I should prefer Pedro, that I confess, but the Archduke has made a favourable impression on Charlotte ; I saw that before any question of engagement had taken place." The English Queen still hoped that Charlotte had not finally made up her mind, " as we both feel so strongly convinced of the immense superiority of Pedro . . . besides which the position is so infinitely preferable ". Compared with Portugal, Maximilian's country had little to recommend it in Victoria's eyes. " The Austrian society is *médisante* and profligate and worthless," she wrote to Leopold, " and the Italian possessions very shaky. Pedro is full of resource, fond of music, fond of drawing, of languages, of natural history and literature, in all of which Charlotte would suit him and would be a real benefit to the country. . . . I would give any of my own daughters to him were he not a Catholic."

But Charlotte had made up her mind to have Maximilian, and negotiations were accordingly opened through the intermediary of Leopold's nephew Count Mensdorff, who was then in Vienna. These negotiations continued throughout the summer. At one stage Maximilian was inclined to hold back, as he thought he detected in the Belgian King's attitude some subtle move of statesmanship or diplomacy. However, he finally satisfied himself and put forward a formal request for Charlotte's hand. Leopold replied reassuringly on October 31, 1856. " In May you had already won my confidence and goodwill, quite apart from all political considerations ", he informed his prospective son-in-law. " I soon noticed that my little daughter also shared my views ; it was therefore my duty to proceed with circumspection. And now we have the fine result that my daughter chooses this alliance and prefers it to all others that offer themselves, and that I joyfully consent to her choice."

At the same time the Belgian King sincerely hoped that Franz Joseph would do something substantial for Maximilian in the way of political employment. " If the thing takes place," Leopold wrote of the proposed marriage to his niece Victoria in England, " the Emperor ought to put him at the head of Venice ; he is well calculated for it." To Leopold's intense satisfaction this hope was realized precisely as he had expressed it. Charlotte, on the other hand, contented herself with confiding her secret to her priest and confessor and taking Communion as an act of thanks. " I can see the hand of God in this," she said.

2

Meanwhile Maximilian was back in Trieste preparing to receive his brother, who had planned a tour of imperial naval establishments. The Commander-in-Chief had arranged an elaborate programme of receptions and dinners, but the Emperor was fussy. " Be sure that the festivities as set down are adhered to ", he warned Maximilian, " in order that the forenoons may be kept free for inspecting institutions, receiving officials, etc." However, everything went off quite well. Franz Joseph spent four days in Trieste, and then, accompanied by the Empress and Maximilian with " the beautiful fleet of steamers ", he went on to Venice. Their reception in this place was " very reserved " and the people did not show much enthusiasm, although later popular feeling seems to have been modified, owing largely to the efforts exerted by Elizabeth. Some days afterwards an excursion was made by sea to Pola, where the Emperor laid the foundation stone of a new naval arsenal. Franz Joseph was quite impressed with what he saw and realized how much was due to Maximilian. On December 4, 1856, he wrote from Venice to his mother : " I was very pleased that the navy has made such good progress under his direction both here and in Trieste ". Before leaving, the Emperor promoted Maximilian to the rank of Vice-Admiral.

In Venice Franz Joseph found that local feelings were still running high by reason of the severe aftermath of the events of 1848, which had not been forgotten. The overt activities of the neighbouring kingdom of Piedmont-Sardinia in favour of a United Italy also worried him. He therefore decided to adopt a conciliatory policy, or rather the time-honoured one of the iron hand in the velvet glove. He immediately pardoned seventy political offenders and rescinded all sequestrations of property. He decided that the governorship of the provinces of Lombardy and Venetia must also be changed. The Governor was the veteran martinet Field-Marshal Radetzky, and happily at this moment he requested to be relieved of his post on the ground of age — he was ninety! After some thought Franz Joseph sent for Maximilian and offered him the job less the military command, which he was informed would be assumed by the senior military officer on the spot, General Count Gyulai.

Maximilian accepted with feelings of some trepidation, but Franz Joseph was quite confident in his choice. " I know of no one who would be more suitable to the post," the Emperor told his Foreign Minister, Count Buol, " in a country moreover where the most requisite thing is to have a decorous Court such as can deal firmly with the unruliness of these people, and thus administer the cure." To his mother, the Archduchess Sophie, the Emperor wrote : " You need have no worry about his success in his appointed post. I have not the slightest doubt of it myself. I consider him eminently suited to deal firmly and no less courteously with the people here who still need a lot of schooling, to educate them too, and to teach them to treat the Court with the respect which is its due. Here in Venice it should be comparatively easy as there has been a great improvement generally during our short visit, but his task in Milan will probably be a difficult one. The fact that Max is a little afraid of it I consider a good sign, as he is fully conscious of the seriousness of his work which I am convinced he will carry out the more assiduously." There was only one thing which worried the Emperor, and that was that the good relations which he had been at some pains to establish between his brother and the military Commander-in-Chief Count Gyulai might be interrupted at some future time. " The lack of such an understanding was the cause of our disaster in 1848," he added, " and I have impressed this on Max very seriously and I shall repeat it a hundred times."

As soon as this matter had been settled, Maximilian left Venice for Belgium to see his betrothed. He reached Brussels two days before Christmas, and was met by Charlotte's two brothers at the Gare du Nord, where he appeared wearing his Vice-Admiral's uniform for the first time. For some days Charlotte had been uneasy that there might be some jealousy on the part of the Crown Prince, who, she said with sisterly candour, " so readily belittles everyone and who is particularly zealous in the severity of his judgment of princes ". She was greatly relieved when she saw that quite a friendship appeared to have sprung up between them. In fact the younger Leopold went so far as to tell her that in his opinion " the Archduke is a superior person from every point of view. Had I had a single thing to say against him, I would have done so, but you may be sure that there is absolutely nothing."

As soon as she saw Maximilian, Charlotte was certain she had chosen wisely. He had already sent her his portrait, and now he loaded her with Christmas presents — a bracelet containing some of his hair, a pair of earrings, a diamond brooch, and also a " lovely portrait of the Empress ". He also lent her the diaries of his travels which he had kept. Charlotte was enraptured. " The Archduke is charming in every way," she wrote from Laeken on December 29, 1856, " and you may imagine how happy I am to have had him here for the past week. Physically I find him more handsome and morally there is nothing further to be desired. He comes to lunch every day and remains until three or four and we talk happily together." They made lots of plans for the future and he showed her a sketch of a castle which he proposed to build by the sea near Trieste and call Miramar. " There will be a terrace with a fountain, and a Moorish pavilion in the garden furnished in Oriental style. He also intends to have a winter garden stocked with every kind of bird. He has promised me Mass every day at Miramar, where he intends to construct the chapel in such a way that the servants will be able to hear everything from the vestibule." As for the governorship of Lombardy and Venice, added Charlotte, " I find the prospect appealing. However, it will be a difficult undertaking. It is a mission of good which we must fulfil. I can feel the thorns already, but I can also foresee the satisfaction to be derived from doing something good."

An exhaustive round of official functions was arranged for Maximilian, since the Belgian people expected to have a good look at the man their Princess was going to marry. On Christmas Eve the Archduke visited Antwerp and inspected the docks ;

several days later he appeared at the Opera House in Brussels with his fiancée to see a performance of Verdi's new opera *The Sicilian Vespers*, and on New Year's Day there was a tedious reception at the royal Court where, Maximilian reported privately to his brother, " for nearly five whole hours I had to swallow all the hackneyed phrases ground out to each other by the constitutional ruler and the various authorities and corporate bodies ". The fact that it was the twenty-fifth anniversary of the founding of the Belgian Government gave the speakers a welcome opening for much pompous self-glorification — references to the country's good fortune and strong position in Europe, " all due to nothing but Belgium's wise Constitution and its wise administration by their wise Sovereign ", were repeated on every side. The scene so affected the Duchess of Brabant that she only half succeeded in stifling her laughter behind the large bouquet she carried. " The King's gentle honeyed speeches did not produce a very enlivening effect ", at any rate not on his future son-in-law. " They were not addressed to the spokesman of each delegation, but as the royal orator spoke, he kept gliding to and fro with his characteristically slinking shuffle, nodding his head amiably. . . . The whole affair was calculated to inspire the unprejudiced observer with a profound disgust for constitutional shams."

A few days later Maximilian was treated to another characteristic spectacle, " a constitutional Court ball ". On this occasion he accompanied the Princess, who was wearing a simple white dress which attracted general attention, particularly when they waltzed together. Otherwise the company did not impress the Archduke. " Since the Belgian regime has not consented to establish a hard-and-fast rule for presentation at Court, so that it is not easy to reject any application," he noted, " it may be imagined how mixed the company at such a ball must be. The higher nobility of the land rubs shoulders with its own tailors and cobblers ; all the English shopkeepers who have retired to Brussels on grounds of economy have access to the ball with their respective families. The crowd is enormous, and was increased on this occasion by the circumstance that everyone wanted to see the Princess's future husband."

Shortly before his departure Maximilian raised the important question of a dowry. He sent Leopold a note couched in the pleasantest terms in which he reminded the King of his own words, " how necessary it is that the princely household should be comfortably established ". He took care to add that it could only arouse the worst impression in Austria " if it were to become known that the King could not bring himself to put his hand in his pocket for the benefit of his beloved daughter ". To this he received no reply until he was on the point of leaving, when Leopold's Chamberlain, Vicomte Conway, came to him with the news that " the King had resolved to do something, but he could not yet name the sum ", and that this contribution should not figure in the marriage settlements. After his return to Austria Maximilian sent an envoy, Baron von Gagern, to arrange the details. Eventually the matter was settled to the satisfaction of all parties.

In addition to her trousseau, jewellery and gold and silver plate, the Belgian Parliament voted Princess Charlotte a dowry of 100,000 gulden. An equal sum was added by the Emperor Franz Joseph with an extra 30,000 gulden as a wedding present. At the same time Leopold agreed to make his daughter an allowance of 20,000 gulden annually as pin-money. This latter item was only reached after considerable argument with Baron Gagern, who wished to make the figure as high as possible so as to impress the King that Maximilian was a good business man and a sound domestic administrator. " The Archduke runs no risk of my misunderstanding him ", observed Leopold wryly. " I am glad to save him the experiences which I had to go through as son-in-law of two of the most powerful Kings. To say nothing of poor Louis Philippe, who granted me by the marriage settlement only a prospective dowry which I did not actually receive for years, my admirable English father-in-law handed over to me as marriage portion with Princess Charlotte nothing but her debts from as far back as 1809, with the comment that this would make some impression on the Princess. This prediction was indeed fulfilled, but the impression was an unpleasant one and remained so."

Maximilian felt that he had scored a personal triumph. " I

was rather pleased with myself ", he wrote to his brother, " for having at last wrung from the old miser something of what he has most at heart." As for Charlotte, she would hear nothing against her future husband. " Max's entire visit confirmed my good impression of him and inspired me with the highest regard for his qualities", she told her friend Countess Hulst. " He was charming to me ; so attentive and thoughtful."

3

" The Italian provinces ", said the Emperor Franz Joseph at this time, " have been allowed to go on too long feeling the conditions of 1848–49." Hence his desire for a more lenient administrative policy which found expression in his intention to nominate his brother Maximilian to the civil governorship of Lombardy and Venetia. Something indeed had to be done to allay the general feeling, not only inside Austria but in Europe at large, against the scandalous misrule of these provinces which had been proceeding since the young monarch's accession. The reaction which followed the suppression of the revolt in 1848 by Radetzky's whitecoats had been practically unparalleled in its brutality. The Austrian army of occupation regarded the natives as a conquered people to be plundered and crushed at will. Hundreds were shot or hanged for being in possession of arms, a professor of the University of Padua expired under the lash, and when the Milanese population hissed a garrison prosti-tute for displaying the Austrian colours on her balcony, Marshal Radetzky had fifteen of the demonstrators flogged, including two young girls. Under this cruel and barbarous regime of martial law nearly 4,000 of the inhabitants were convicted of political offences in two years.

An abortive rising which took place in Milan in 1853 had been followed by an imperial decree providing for the sequestra-tion of property without judicial enquiry at the discretion of the Commander-in-Chief. Nearly a thousand Lombard families were involved, many of whom had become Piedmontese subjects, in spite of treaty rights which secured to these families quiet possession of their properties. The enforcement of this decree led to a breach of relations between Turin and Vienna and gained for the able Piedmontese Foreign Minister, Count Cavour, much sympathy in Europe, particularly on the part of Great Britain and France, which was increased by Piedmont-Sardinia's entry into the Crimean War, and still more by Cavour's brilliant propaganda at the peace table, where he succeeded in convincing the Congress that the cause of Italy " was before the bar of public opinion " and that his little country was her advocate. Franz Joseph might well feel concerned for the future security of his Italian provinces.

As has been seen, the milder policy was determined upon during the Emperor's visit to Venice at the end of 1856, when a number of political prisoners were freed and all the sequestrations rescinded. Of course Franz Joseph did not wish it to be generally thought that his hand was being in any way forced. " It is my desire ", he told his Foreign Minister, Count Buol, " that this action on my part may be regarded as one of mercy and not merely as a measure taken to pacify Piedmont." Unfortunately for him, he deluded himself. At the same time he was conscious of the effect which the inflammatory Piedmontese press was having on the neighbouring province of Lombardy. " It is unbelievable the way the authorities in Piedmont organize and stir things up so as to ruin our visit to Milan ", he wrote on December 27, 1856. " The threads of all these machinations find their centre in Cavour's Ministry. All kinds of horrors are persistently spread abroad concerning Lombardy so as to prevent that poor country from ever settling down in peace."

Franz Joseph and Elizabeth arrived in Milan early in the New Year and remained there for six weeks, being joined towards the end of their stay by Maximilian, who had meanwhile been in Belgium. Their reception in the Lombard capital was frigid in the extreme, and all the charm which the beautiful Empress exerted was powerless to produce the slightest popular reaction in their favour. Bunting was displayed from the houses by order of the authorities, but not a single cheer was heard in the streets, although the authorities had paid the peasantry from the surrounding countryside a lira a head to come into town. The nobility ostentatiously avoided all the Court functions, and to prevent their boxes in the Scala Opera House being filled with Austrian troops in their absence, they sent their servants in their stead. At times Elizabeth was in tears, and her husband clearly showed signs of distress. The sense of depression which Maximilian experienced in these surroundings was aggravated by the fact that he suffered acute attacks of toothache during this visit.

A few days before they were due to depart, Franz Joseph played his final card. On February 28, 1857, he announced in an imperial rescript from the royal palace his brother's appointment as Governor of the Lombardo-Venetian portion of his dominions. The necessary arrangements to implement this change were only concluded, so he told his mother, " after prolonged and arduous toil " on his part. But all the Emperor's work was destined to be fruitless ; for, although Maximilian's reputation for liberalism had preceded him, the appointment could find no favour in the eyes of the Italian nationalists so long as Maximilian remained his brother's representative. Franz Joseph tried to persuade himself that under the new beneficent rule things would eventually right themselves, although it could not be said that he was altogether happy even about that prospect. " I feel a little easier in my mind but not quite relieved," he wrote to the Archduchess Sophie, " since the set-up here is about the most difficult to be found anywhere. It is so hard to be constructive when one meets with incredible cowardice and treachery at every turn. However, time and the Lord will help and Max's tact should do a great deal."

Immediately after this Maximilian had to return to Trieste to attend to some naval matters, so that it was not until nearly a month had passed that he was able to begin his new duties with a visit to the Venetian branch of his kingdom. Here his welcome was not exactly encouraging, but he determined to persevere. " I am glad to know that you are in Venice and at work," wrote the Emperor to him early in April, " for any further interregnum would have been detrimental to affairs. As I had expected, your own good sense has not allowed the frigid reception at Venice to discourage you ; and, if you are able to go your ways without taking much notice of such matters, things will improve. These illegal demonstrations, however, and this unruly behaviour must cease. The perpetrators will have to be run to earth and punished. Severity must be exercised, yet with justice and without any trace of rancour. The coldness of the Venetians seems to have been principally due to the jealousy of the Milanese. Is it true that a Tricolor flag was flying from the Arsenal ? How could it have been possible for this to have been run up on the Piazza San Marco with the gas lamps alight and the sentries about ? And how does it come that it was not hauled down till so late ? "

In Milan, where he arrived later the same month, Maximilian found people more friendly, but there was still a strong undercurrent of hostility and he could not help feeling that such amicable advances as he did receive were more on account of his personal qualities than by reason of his official role. The truth was that the majority of natives felt with the aged Italian patriot Manzoni that Austrian rule merely gave them " the choice of being fried or boiled ". However, Maximilian had hopes of being able to overcome this passive resistance, and at least he made a good start by abolishing some of the vicious practices of his predecessor, such as the sale of exemptions from military service and then conscripting recruits regardless, with which old Radetzky had lined his pockets for many years.

Maximilian only stayed a week or two in Milan, as his wedding had now been fixed to take place in July, and he was anxious to pay a round of private and semi-official visits in various European Courts before that date.

He began by presenting his respects to the Pope, who was on a tour of his temporal dominions and was at that moment enjoying the air at Pesaro on the shores of the Adriatic. Maximilian found the septuagenarian Pius IX " as merry as a grig, looking better than he did two years before, encouraged by the homage of the provinces ", yet to some observers at least still cramped by memories of the year 1848. *Pio Nono*, perhaps it should be added here, had been chosen by the Cardinals of the Church as supreme pontiff two years before the revolution broke out which shook Europe, and at first he had gained the reputation of being a reforming Pope to whom all who had the cause of Italian nationalism at heart looked hopefully. For a moment it had appeared in 1848 as if he might throw in his lot with the nationalists against Austria, but eventually, to their intense disappointment, he had declared a policy of neutrality, and as the revolution spread to his own papal states he had taken fright and fled to Gaeta, where he was comforted by other temporarily dispossessed sovereigns, including the iniquitous " Bomba ". Here he had remained for eighteen months until restored to his dominions by foreign arms, a process which had changed him into a confirmed reactionary. He was now surrounded by Jesuit advisers, and in fact was so afraid of being poisoned that he even brought his own supply of sacramental wine and wafers with him.

Maximilian spent an exhausting but to him not unsatisfactory day with His Holiness. After breakfast, which he took alone with Pius, the Archduke was invested with a sacred Order, and he then accompanied the sovereign pontiff " in an antediluvian carriage with patched-up harness and variegated stage liveries " to the Cathedral for High Mass, which was marked, so he noted, by " the free-and-easy behaviour of the clergy with their incessant chatter and snuff-taking ". More conversation followed with Pius and four cardinals. " I then partook with them of the Pope's dinner," wrote Maximilian, " a gruesome repast only fit for a parish priest served by Monsignori of the Papal household, which was none the less cheered by the good-tempered chat of the well-fed fathers of the Church." The Pope's condescension went so far that he helped his guest to ices and coffee with his own hands. Finally, after the usual foot-kissing and genuflections, Maximilian, who had been in full dress from seven in the morning until four in the afternoon, got into his carriage " half dead " to return to the steamer *Elizabeth* which was to take him on the next stage of his journey.

After a brief stop at Lisbon, which enabled him to see the Dowager Empress Amelia, who had missed becoming his mother-in-law four years before, the *Elizabeth* steamed up the Channel into the Thames. Leopold was anxious that his niece Victoria's prejudices against Maximilian should be removed, and he had persuaded the English Queen to invite him to spend a few days in Buckingham Palace. Both Victoria and her consort

THE ARCHDUKE MAXIMILIAN
AS COMMANDER-IN-CHIEF OF THE AUSTRIAN NAVY

From a contemporary photograph

MIRAMAR

From a photograph

Prince Albert, neither of whom had previously met him, were completely won over by his charm and good manners. Albert was particularly impressed by the young man's " religious tolerance " and his liberal-minded political views." On June 16, two days after his arrival, Maximilian attended the christening of the Queen's youngest daughter Princess Beatrice,[1] and led his royal hostess into the Palace chapel. At the luncheon which took place afterwards in the ballroom the Queen sat between him and Prince Frederick William of Prussia, who was also a guest.[2] The conversation was in German, and Maximilian made a remark which pleased Victoria greatly. " *Ich hoffe*," he said to her, "*dass es von guter Bedeutung für die Zukunft ist, dass bei dieser Gelegenheit England zwischen Oesterreich und Preussen sitzt.*"[3]

Victoria wrote off enthusiastically to Leopold the same day, completely revising her former opinion. "I cannot say how much we like the Archduke ; he is charming, so clever, natural, kind and amiable, so English in his feelings and likings, and so anxious for the best understanding between Austria and England. With the exception of his mouth and chin he is good-looking, but I think one does not in the least care for that, as he is so very kind, clever and pleasant. I wish you really joy, dearest Uncle, at having got such a husband for dearest Charlotte, as I am sure he is quite worthy of her and will make her happy. He may and will do a great deal for Italy."

4

The wedding was a splendid affair. Punctually at a quarter to eleven on the morning of July 27, 1857, Princess Charlotte, leaning on her father's arm, entered the Blue Room of the Royal Palace in Brussels where Maximilian was waiting with his younger brother Karl Ludwig, and a fair sprinkling of

---

[1] She married Prince Henry of Battenberg in 1885 and was the mother of Queen Ena of Spain. She died in 1944.

[2] Later Emperor Frederick of Germany and father of the late Kaiser William II. He married Queen Victoria's eldest daughter, the Princess Royal, in 1858.

[3] " I hope it is a good omen for the future that on this occasion England sits between Austria and Prussia."

relatives from both their families. Here the civil ceremony was performed by the Burgomaster of the city. The bride looked lovely in a gorgeous white satin dress embroidered with gold; her nervousness was largely concealed by her veil of finest Brussels lace. Maximilian appeared particularly handsome in his Vice-Admiral's uniform as he took her hand after the Burgomaster had finished, and led his bride into the chapel of the palace, where they both listened to a homily on the holy and blessed state of matrimony from the Cardinal-Archbishop of Malines. The remainder of the day was taken up with a magnificent wedding breakfast followed by a reception, and then a dinner and ball. " Brussels was in a great state of excitement and the popular feeling excellent ", wrote Prince Albert, who had come over from London. " Uncle was greatly moved and distressed by the imminent separation from his daughter. I have never seen him show so much emotion. Bride and bridegroom were happy."

More festivities followed during the next two days, and it was not until July 30 that the newly married couple were able to leave Brussels on the first stage of their honeymoon. Arriving the same day at Bonn, they took a steamer up the Rhine to Mainz, whence they continued overland through Würzburg and Nuremberg to Ratisbon. Thence they sailed down the Danube to Nussdorf, being met there on August 8 by the Archduchess Sophie. The same day they reached Vienna, and stayed the night at Schönbrunn, where they were welcomed by Franz Joseph and Elizabeth. Charlotte was extremely pleased with her reception by the imperial family. Sophie she found " *bien maternelle pour moi* ", while both the Emperor and Empress were equally charming in their turn. " I already feel an Arch-duchess by blood," she told her husband, " for I like them all very much and from the first moment I felt ' at home ' among them." Fortunately for Charlotte she did not remain long enough at the Austrian Court to see its seamy side, nor does she appear to have been conscious of the tone of domestic discord and intrigue there which should have been noticeable to the shrewd observer.

" From Schönbrunn ", wrote Charlotte to her friend Countess Hulst, " we went to Trieste to spend a week in our delightful villa which is a perfect jewel set in this magnificent southern climate, facing one of the most beautiful gulfs in the world. In the north one has no idea of a really blue sea, and when I first saw it I was enchanted. From Trieste, after a very disagreeable crossing, we arrived in Venice on August 16. I do not believe there is a finer sight anywhere in the world than the entrance to the canals. Venice, with its present full of poetry, its past full of memories, its half-oriental character, its majestic calm, its canals, churches and palaces, and its indescribable charm, has made the deepest impression on me. . . . There is something which attracts and fascinates to such an extent that you have the impression of having always been there and wish to stay for ever. Added to this we were there at the best time of year with a beautiful Italian sky and sun every day. . . . I went about as much as possible seeing all the monuments and churches. The churches are so many museums of paintings, sculpture and mosaics."

On September 6 they made their state entry into Milan. Accompanied by Count Gyulai, the military governor of the provinces, the Archduke and Archduchess were welcomed at the eastern entrance to the city, the Porta Venezia, by the mayor, the officer in command of the garrison and all the civic officials, who escorted them along the Corso to the Royal Palace, while the artillery fired off rounds of salvos and military bands played alternately the Austrian and Belgian national anthems. Outside the palace the new Governor reviewed the troops and there was a march past. In the evening the town was illuminated. So far as the native populace was concerned, the reception accorded the viceregal party could not be described as unfriendly. The marked absence of large masses of Austrian troops to control the crowds made a particularly good impression among the people, whilst the knowledge of the native language which both the Governor and his bride displayed also commanded widespread approval. With one or two exceptions, however, the nobility and upper classes showed by their staying away from the receptions and other functions, as they had done during the imperial visit six months previously, that they would have nothing to do with the latest regime, liberal though it might be.

Such great Lombard families as Adda, Maffei, Dandolo, Borromeo, Casati and Litta simply ignored their new rulers.

At first Charlotte was so engrossed in these surroundings and at the same time so completely in love with her husband that she did not realize that in fact they were both living in a fool's paradise. " I could not be happier ", she wrote to Countess Hulst at the end of ten days in Milan. " Max is perfect in every way, so good, so devoted, so gentle. I am experiencing the most perfect happiness. As you can imagine, my former life holds no regrets for me. This life has everything heart and soul could desire. Today we are going to Monza to live a more retired and regular life and to escape from the whirlpool which has engulfed us for nearly two months now. I am going to organize my time somewhat, though up to the present I have not wasted it. I shall engage drawing and music teachers, and shall spend a little time on religious as well as worldly reading. . . . I do not know whether it is a special grace which I have received from God, but I must confess that receptions, drawing-rooms and dinners amuse me without ever becoming tiring. Perhaps when I am a little older all this will bore me, but I am still at that happy age when everything is new and charming."

The viceregal court was accordingly established in the Governor's palace at Monza, some eight miles from Milan, while the older palace in the capital was used for business and official receptions, Maximilian making it a custom to drive in there on most days. Charlotte, who now liked to be known by the Italian form of her name, Carlotta, was extremely pleased with Court life, and unlike her sister-in-law the Empress Elizabeth seems to have got on admirably both with her mother-in-law, who shortly paid them a visit, and also with the ladies-in-waiting whom the Archduchess Sophie had selected for her with considerable care. " The festivities are over and the quiet of a more retired life has taken their place without, however, being lonely ", she wrote early in October. " Monza is a charming place, and we are comfortably lodged in the midst of our Court which is composed of people of great merit and many qualities. . . . Dear Max is always the same to me and I love and admire him more every day. I am enjoying the most real and wonderful happiness, although I am afraid I cannot be of much assistance to my husband who has so much business on his hands. But this is inevitable." They also stayed at the Villa d'Este, her father's celebrated and beautiful house on the shores of Lake Como.[1]

The close of the year 1857 found Carlotta still jubilant and supremely happy. " I am happy in my home," she wrote, " happy to live in this country where all is congenial to me and everything goes to my heart. I do not know how to thank God who has given me everything. Until now there has been no shadow over the picture I have painted. I know that life cannot always be rosy, but the years that are passing now will always be dear memories of perfect happiness."

5

No Viceroy could have been more anxious to improve the lot of his kingdom by a liberal and enlightened government. In his diary he strongly condemned the theory which had been so strikingly adumbrated by King Louis XIV of France that rulers were responsible to God alone and not to their subjects. " This despotic Prince had his axiom to thank for his severe losses of fortune ", wrote Maximilian. " Only those who have not followed it, and who have adhered firmly to the honourable path of political rectitude, stand unendangered." For one in authority who could express such views as these there was indeed great hope. Maximilian further proved it in his correspondence with his brother. In these letters the Archduke advocated a large measure of home rule for Lombardy-Venetia with its own army and representative institutions, and extensive reforms in the fields of taxation, education and other branches of local government. The adoption of such a liberal programme in Vienna might possibly have secured the Italian provinces to the Empire, but Franz Joseph, who simply regarded every sign of nationalist feeling as revolutionary mischief, threw cold water on all Maximilian's schemes.

[1] King Leopold of Belgium acquired the Villa d'Este through his first wife Princess Charlotte of England, whose mother, Queen Caroline, wife of King George IV, had purchased it during her wanderings in Europe in 1815.

A few of the native intellectuals responded to Maximilian's overtures and were entrusted with various tasks under the new administration. The revolutionary writer Cesare Cantù undertook the reform of the Lombard educational system, the economist Stefano Jacini reported on the distressed area in the Valtelline which Maximilian personally visited, the jurist Lanfranchi revised the legal code, and the archaeologist Selvatico prepared a list of historical monuments worthy of preservation in the kingdom. Maximilian was himself an intelligent patron of the arts, and during his viceroyalty he endeavoured to improve the architectural beauties and other amenities of the Lombard capital. The Piazza del Duomo was enlarged under his direction, a public park was laid out on his instructions, and he entrusted the restoration of the famous Biblioteca Ambrosiana to Schmidt, the architect of Cologne Cathedral. In fact Maximilian did everything within his limited powers to improve the lot and secure the goodwill of a people to whom he felt genuinely drawn. When the great Lombard poet Manzoni was seriously ill, Maximilian made enquiries of his progress every day. " As head of the Lombardo-Venetian kingdom ", said Maximilian at this time, " I should remember that Italian blood flows in my veins and I must promote the interests of a nation whom my renowned great-grandfather [1] loved so much and from whom I myself derive such benefits."

In all major matters of reform Maximilian's hands were tied by the government in Vienna, whose emissaries in the form of *Geheimpolizei* (secret police) swarmed throughout the Italian provinces and reported on the Viceroy's doings to Franz Joseph. The Emperor himself had always taken a keen interest in the activities of this body, which had been divorced from the Ministry of the Interior since 1853 and now fell under Franz Joseph's personal direction. Indeed he personally attended to every detail of police administration in his extended dominions and was to be found working at his desk in the Hofburg or at Schönbrunn shortly after four o'clock every morning. For this reason he insisted that the control of what he termed " this important branch " of the Administration should be centralized in Vienna.

[1] Leopold II (1747–92), Holy Roman Emperor and Grand Duke of Tuscany.

He resented his brother's criticisms of its doings in the Italian provinces where they largely acted as *agents provocateurs* and the Emperor's personal spies, and he kept repeating to Maximilian its advantages in the reinforcement of the local police bodies. " This is a time of great unrest everywhere ", he wrote to him early in 1858. " I would therefore advise you to have recourse to severity in the event of even the smallest revolt. The Venetians are once more becoming somewhat impudent — for all that they cannot be particularly dangerous. These demonstrations in the theatres should therefore not be tolerated any longer, since they serve as good practice for movements on a larger scale, and in a city which is so greatly frequented, this sort of thing shows up the prevalent rowdiness and the all too indulgent attitude of the authorities. That demonstration of the students at Padua ought to have been prevented, for it should never be possible for some 300 students to arrange a thing of that kind without the authorities getting to know about it. Let me know the result of the enquiry, and make sure that the ringleaders do not escape their just punishment."

On the subject of Maximilian's ambitious proposals of constitutional reform the Emperor was adamant. There must be no change except in the direction of intensified repression. In spite of the isolated position in which his Foreign Minister's unfortunate diplomacy had placed Austria — " Buol gets more and more bungling ", said Maximilian frankly — the Emperor clung with characteristic obstinacy to the selfish territorial and dynastic view. " There can be no thought of an independent administration of the Italian provinces ", he bluntly told his brother, " or one freed from the central control at Vienna, such as would be connected with that centre by no more than a Minister for Italian Affairs. . . . In the present day a complete severance of the Italian Provinces from the Monarchy — and that, moreover, at a time when all that is bad clings so closely together, — would mean a weakening of the Government's power of resistance against the Revolution and those who are in its favour. Besides which, in dealing with these Provinces and with our interests in Italy, it is not merely a matter of keeping the view-point as to Italy before our eyes. We have also to take into consideration the condition of the entire Monarchy, never forgetting that the power and influence of our position in Italy depends less on the importance and development of these Provinces than upon the stability of the Monarchy as a whole."

Maximilian, who was already disgusted with this line of imperial policy, was now called upon in his capacity of Governor to implement two decrees which surely equalled each other in their fatuous folly and undid at a single stroke all his good work in the kingdom. The currency was depreciated by making it uniform with the rest of the Empire ; and the law of compulsory military service was extended and coupled with a proviso that no one liable to conscription could get married before the age of twenty-three. The two divisions of the community most favourable to Austrian rule, the merchants and bankers, and the peasantry, were thus alienated irretrievably. Maximilian could not conceal his reluctance to carry out these decrees, and when the news reached Vienna it provoked a sharp rebuke from the Emperor. "I cannot expect that you will see eye to eye with me in all my decisions," wrote Franz Joseph to his brother, "yet I must be able to rest assured that what I have finally decided on will be zealously carried out, and that any possible opposition which may arise shall not be encouraged to take heart by thinking that you too are not in agreement with the measures laid down by me. Of course, this need not preclude you from raising objections to me on what may seem inexpedient, but it would be as well that the foreign press should not be so ready to give publicity, even where general matters are concerned, to every step taken by you, even before it is known here."

No wonder Max began to feel bitter and disillusioned. In the autumn of 1858 he poured out his heart in a long letter to his mother :

. . . If it were not for my religious duties, I should have long since left this land of misery where one is doubly depressed by having to act as the representative of an inactive Government with no ideas, which one's judgment tries in vain to defend. It was with a feeling of profound shame that I recently entered Milan, doubly depressed and weighed down by the friendly manner in which we were both personally received, as it were like respectable private persons. This private friendliness combined with public repudiation is what shows me most clearly how things stand ; it shows how powerless I am, but also shows how irresponsibly the Government trifles with the good-will of the masses. . . .

Only one voice is now heard, that of indignation and disapproval ; it pervades the whole country, and before it I stand alone and impotent. I am not afraid, for that is not the way of the Hapsburgs, but I am silent and ashamed. . . .

If things continue to grow serious at the same rate as they have done, I shall soon begin to think about sending Charlotte back to her father in Brussels, for I have no mind to let her be sacrified to weakness and irresolution ; and where there is danger, it is no place for young and inexperienced women. . . .

We are at present living in a complete chaos, and only the perfect calm which I try to affect in spite of my twenty-six years keeps the whole thing from going to rack and ruin. All those around me have lost their heads and their courage, and I am accordingly beginning to ask myself whether my conscience will allow me blindly to follow instructions from Vienna ; Radetzky disobeyed through loyalty, and monuments are justly set up to him out of gratitude. . . .

Things went from bad to worse, while all Maximilian's pleas and protests had no effect except a purely negative one in the Hofburg. He particularly felt that his authority suffered from the divided command which he shared with Count Gyulai in Verona, but his request for the supreme military authority to be vested in himself met with a blank refusal from the Emperor. To add to his troubles, the navy, which he described as " the thing dearest to me for years ", began during his absence from active duty to be the subject of unjustifiable interference on the part of Franz Joseph's military clique of advisers. " Those whom I praised were usually passed over," he remarked sadly, " and those whom I removed received conspicuous marks of favour." To crown everything Carlotta was insulted by the people during a visit to Venice. " It is horrible to see enterprises that have cost so much pains nipped in the bud," he wrote to his father-in-law, " never to know how any day will end, to be hemmed in by hostile parties, never to be sure whether you will be approved by the vacillating centre,[1] in constant fear of hearing that your innocent wife has been insulted or injured, never to

[1] Vienna.

be sure that you will not be hissed at the theatre, or whether you will return alive from your walk."

At the beginning of 1859 Maximilian sent his wife for safety to their villa in Trieste. Meanwhile he determined to stick quietly to his post " in spite of every mockery and calumny ", and to restrain " as far as possible the rash measures arising from fright and nerves ". He might as well have tried to restrain the Niagara Falls. He realized that he was powerless either to stem the growing tide of nationalist feeling or to check the head-strong course of repression which the Emperor fondly hoped would curb it. " I sit here unable to move and as lonely as a hermit in the great palace at Milan ", he wrote to his mother during the Shrove Tuesday celebrations. " Before me dances and whirls the Carnival, but in my apartments it is as silent as Lent, and the old Countess Lützow [1] takes the place of the mistress of the house at table. I am the prophet at whom they laughed and who has now to experience to the uttermost, word for word, all he foretold to deaf ears, and upon whom they all now want to hammer in order to make people forget the causes of it all, as though it were he who had conjured up all the trouble by his false mildness or sugary amiability. The world is a funny place ; it entirely forgets that the poor prophet begged them to do all the things which now in their mortal terror they want to do. . . . Only he desired it when things were quiet, and the measures could have been represented as part of a systematic plan. . . ."

The Viceroy had already packed up his silver and other valuables in readiness for a rapid departure. His opinion, which he did not attempt to disguise at this time, was that " Austria could exist very well without Lombardy."

6

For Franz Joseph the prospect of war loomed closer. At the French Emperor's reception on New Year's Day 1859 Napoleon III brusquely told Count Hübner, the Austrian Ambassador, that he regretted " the relations between the two Empires were

[1] Grand Mistress of the Court.

not as good as they had been ". A few days later King Victor Emmanuel informed the Piedmontese Parliament in his speech from the throne that he " was not insensible to the cry of woe that reached him from so many parts of Italy ". During the previous summer Napoleon had met Cavour secretly in the Vosges Mountains, and had agreed, in return for the cession of Nice and Savoy and some other advantages, to attack Austria at the fitting moment. Both Piedmont and France now began to hasten their preparations. On January 12, 1859, the Austrian Emperor, who knew nothing of the meeting between Napoleon and Cavour, wrote to Maximilian : " I seem to think that hitherto Turin has placed her hope on Paris. If the Emperor Napoleon understands his own interests he can hardly desire war, but I fear that he is too much given to playing with fire and that *malgré lui* he might go so far as not to be able to escape a war." He therefore sent another army corps to Lombardy. " The additional increase of troops should have a good and salutary effect ", he reassured his brother. " Indeed any outbreak in Lombardy and Venice need hardly be expected now, yet it is our duty to be prepared for all emergencies in order that any revolutionary movement may be nipped in the bud."

Napoleon was not altogether happy as to where his obligations to Victor Emmanuel and Cavour might ultimately land him. He suggested as a way out of his difficulty that the whole Italian question might be referred to a Congress of the powers. However, before the Congress could meet, Franz Joseph, egged on by the militarist party in Vienna which was for teaching Piedmont a sharp lesson, instructed the Foreign Minister, Count Buol, to despatch an ultimatum to Turin demanding under threat of war that Piedmont should within three days disband the volunteers which she had been raising. At the same time Franz Joseph determined on another drastic step which he felt military considerations demanded. He suddenly removed his brother from the governorship of the Italian provinces. " Circumstances having made it necessary for me to take extraordinary measures in defence of my Crown and for the maintenance of order and internal security," he wrote stiffly to Maximilian on April 19, " I have felt bound to reunite under one hand the civil and military authority in the kingdom of Lombardo-Venetia, and consequently I have decided to relieve you of your duties as Governor-General, which you have fulfilled with the greatest devotion and prudence, and in so far as they concern the civil administration to entrust them to General Count Gyulai as Commander-in-Chief."

Immediately he received this letter the Archduke left Milan for Venice to take command of the Austrian fleet which was stationed there. But even in Venice among his beloved ships a further humiliation awaited him. He found that he was placed in a subordinate position to the fortress commander, General Alemann, although this officer was actually junior to him in rank. It was an ill-concealed slight, and he was furious with the Emperor, particularly as he knew that he was not responsible for such measures as the new recruiting law and the depreciation of the coinage, both of which he had opposed and which had so inflamed popular feeling. At least, he protested, his brother might preserve his " good name " and the respect due to an Archduke. Cavour, on the other hand, was delighted that Maximilian had been removed from his post, for so long as the Archduke remained Governor of Lombardy and Venetia, the Piedmontese Foreign Minister felt that there was a real chance that the provinces would become reconciled to Austrian rule. " This gives me life again ", he said on learning the news that Maximilian had left Milan.

Meanwhile, no answer having been received from Turin, Austria had declared war on the kingdom of Piedmont-Sardinia, and Napoleon, who could not escape his obligations now, had come to Victor Emmanuel's assistance and had begun to move troops across the Alps in the direction of Lombardy. The incompetent Gyulai crossed the Ticino with an army of 100,000 men to face an enemy of only half that strength, but instead of pushing forward to Turin he wasted three weeks in a series of fruitless operations and then withdrew to Lombardy, where he eventually met the French sixteen miles west of Milan at Magenta and was defeated. This reverse left the road open to the Lombard capital which Napoleon entered at the head of his troops early in June. Gyulai was now superseded in the chief command of the Austrian forces by the Emperor in person, but the change made little difference to Austria's strategy. Exactly three weeks after Magenta the Austrians again engaged the enemy at Solferino in the hills bordering Lake Garda near Verona, and were driven back across the Adige. " Great things were done," wrote Franz Joseph to his wife, " but fortune did not smile upon us. I am the richer by many experiences and have learnt what it feels like to be a defeated general." As for Gyulai and the other generals like him, such as Wimpfen, Maximilian openly stated that they should all be shot out-of-hand for cowardice.

While the Franco-Sardinian armies were conducting their successful campaign in the plains of Lombardy, a French fleet was lying off the Lido and blockading Venice and bottling up the Austrian navy and its commander there. " For the past month ", wrote Carlotta from Trieste, " I have spent many painful hours trembling for the man to whom I belong so completely and who is there aboard his ship surrounded by enemies, though up to the present they have made no hostile move. Every separation from the Archduke is painful to me, but how much more so now ! " Maximilian considered carefully whether he should lead out his ships and engage the French, but in the end he decided not to take the risk on the ground that if the fleet " should be lost Austria would never sanction its being replaced ". His plan was to prevent the French approaching close enough to the city for effective attack, and with this aim in view he prepared to sink his largest battleship in the principal lagoon in order to block the entrance to the channel. Fortunately for himself and his officers he was not called upon to execute this plan, as before any definite move could be made by the French Admiral, Maximilian heard the astonishing news that a peace had been agreed and that Venetia was to remain under Austrian sovereignty.

There is no doubt that if he had persevered the French Emperor could have reduced Venice, and this would have enabled his army to push on into Austria. But his nerve failed him at the last moment. He was worried by unfavourable reports from home, by the unfriendly attitude of Prussia, and by the semi-independent position of Victor Emmanuel's army —

besides which he felt unwell and irritated by the tropical heat. On July 6 Napoleon's messenger arrived at Franz Joseph's headquarters at Verona with proposals for an armistice, and three days later the two Emperors met at the neighbouring town of Villafranca to discuss the terms of peace. Napoleon proposed that Venetia should form an independent kingdom under Maximilian ; but the Austrian Emperor said he was willing to fight on rather than surrender the province for this purpose, and so this project was dropped. Franz Joseph did, however, lose the rich province of Lombardy which was annexed to Piedmont. For the rest, Parma also went to Victor Emmanuel, and although Tuscany and Modena were restored to their Hapsburg overlords, it was generally felt in Europe that this restoration, like the retention of Venetia by Franz Joseph, was only temporary and that the dawn of Italian unity was not far off.

Franz Joseph's much vaunted " system " of centralization, Germanization and police repression had broken down. In spite of the premature conclusion of the war at Villafranca, Austria now stood humiliated and without friends in Europe. Maximilian for one pondered over the position gloomily. Indeed he was very conscious of the shameful position into which the Emperor's folly and that of his newest advisers had thrust his country. All his own worst prophecies were now being realized. " It is so wretched ", he wrote to his father-in-law, " to see our fine and once powerful monarchy sinking lower and lower through incompetence, misunderstanding, and conduct difficult to explain."

7

Maximilian was in obvious disgrace with Franz Joseph. It is true that he was retained in his command of the navy, but it certainly looked as if his political career was over, at any rate in the Austrian Empire. Forgetting the difficult circumstances in which he had assumed office in Milan, the Emperor openly blamed him for the course events had taken in the Italian provinces and accused him of favouring Cavour's revolutionary designs in a bid for popularity with the Lombards and Venetians.

Relations were clearly strained between the two brothers, and there was nothing for it but for Maximilian to retire with as good grace as he could muster and devote his energies to professional and private affairs. The next few months found him busy in Trieste writing two monographs on the Austrian navy with a plan for its reorganization. He subsequently published the first of these anonymously as the work of " an Austrian sailor ". He also produced a useful study of the French fleet which, profiting by the success which the newly invented iron-clads had achieved during the Crimean War, had been reconstructed so as to become the most powerful in Europe.

In the disappointment and disillusion which he underwent during this summer " replete with anxiety ", Maximilian began to ponder the example of the ancient Roman Emperor Diocletian, who, after a reign of twenty years, abdicated his sovereignty and retired to a favoured spot on the neighbouring Dalmatian coast to grow cabbages and live the quiet life. " I thought to myself that wise old Diocletian was right ", he wrote in his journal at this time. " He had the equanimity to renounce fame and he never repented it. He, the wise deep-thinking Prince, who had tasted to the dregs of all that human passion could give, preferred to lead in retirement the self-sufficing life of a philosopher far removed from deceit, meanness and fraud. He had tasted of all. To him there was nothing new under the sun. What, therefore, could be of greater value to him than removal from the odious throng of men, a genial serene climate, the study of the arts and sciences — those inexhaustible sources of consolation — and his plants which grew and throve under his hands ? "

Maximilian's new-found desire for solitude impelled him to hurry forward the completion of Miramar which he had begun to build three years before about the time of his engagement to Carlotta. With walls of white limestone which gleamed in the sunshine, the castle stood high on a rocky promontory washed on three sides by the waves of the Adriatic. The view was superb across the Gulf of Trieste where the outlines of the city could be clearly recognized. The owner took great trouble with the interior decoration and the lay-out of the park. His private study was an exact replica of his cabin on board the frigate *Novara*, and the main saloon, which was hung with blue damask embroidered with the pattern of anchors, preserved the nautical atmosphere. The gardens contained many tropical plants which Maximilian had ordered or had himself collected in the course of his travels. " Now that the Archduke has almost no business," wrote Carlotta to a friend in August 1859, " he occupies himself to a great extent with the building of Miramar which is his creation. I assure you that the house and gardens will be of remarkable beauty. I do not think one could find anything like it anywhere else, particularly in so picturesque and well chosen a location."

Two months later they found another architectural interest. In October 1859 Carlotta bought the beautiful island of Lacroma off the Dalmatian coast. This " evergreen fairy isle ", with its ericas, myrtles and oleanders, lay about half a mile to the south of Ragusa and was just a mile long by a quarter of a mile broad. It boasted a pine wood, a lake and a disused monastery which owed its origin to the fact that the English King Richard Cœur de Lion was shipwrecked on this island when returning from the Crusades in the Holy Land at the end of the twelfth century. Maximilian and Carlotta immediately set out from Trieste to inspect their newly acquired property. They were both delighted with it, and Maximilian lost no time in putting a band of workmen on to the task of making the monastery building habitable. " I ordered walled-up windows to be opened," he wrote in his diary, " doors to be broken through, pointed out walls which this winter would certainly destroy, and revelled in the rubbish of a century. We dived into a large cistern, into subterranean vaults, and into an arched tomb in which we found there were still many bones. To the spirits of the departed monks it must have been very strange once more to hear all this life, this hammering, these blows resounding in their forsaken halls. It was delightful to see how, with the progress of the work, the view of the warm sky and the golden sun penetrated through the reopened windows."

While these new interests appeared absorbing, in reality Miramar and Lacroma only afforded Maximilian a temporary distraction from the intense fits of depression which he had undergone since being ousted from his Governor-Generalship of the Italian provinces. " My shoulders are no longer free and unburdened ", he wrote at this time. " They have to bear a weight from the bitter past." It was this weight which now induced him to take a long sea voyage to Brazil in an endeavour, as he put it, to " seek the peace which excited Europe can no longer give the troubled soul ". Carlotta, who decided to accompany her husband as far as Madeira, was more reserved. " One must know how to make the most of present leisure ", she said simply. " I do not know what the future holds in store for us."

IV. *The Call of the New World*

TOWARDS the end of November 1859, Maximilian and Carlotta with their attendant ladies and gentlemen-in-waiting left Ragusa on board the imperial steamer *Elizabeth* bound for Brazil. The party included the Archduke's old sailing companion Wilhelm Tegetthoff, who had now advanced considerably in the service and for the purpose of this voyage became Maximilian's Flag Captain.[1] After brief calls at Messina and Malaga the *Elizabeth* steamed into the Bay of Algeciras, to find the powerful English Mediterranean fleet riding at anchor as well as a large French squadron and a number of Portuguese men-of-war. " The sight of the French squadron ", wrote Maximilian the same day in his diary, " cut me to the heart, for I had known some of these ships only too well at the blockade of Venice." However, he cheered up somewhat when he received a friendly welcome from the English Commander-in-Chief Admiral Fanshawe. " The fleets ", added the Archduke dryly, " have the task of watching the movements of the Spaniards with regard to Morocco in order, as always happens under certain circumstances in political affairs, to make the existing confusion still greater."

War had broken out between the Spaniards and the Moors some weeks earlier as a result of a frontier dispute, and a Spanish expeditionary force had recently landed under the personal command of Queen Isabella's Prime Minister, Marshal O'Donnell. However, the British Foreign Secretary, Lord John Russell, had exacted a promise from the Government in Madrid that Spain should acquire no fresh territory as a result of the conflict — hence the presence of the English fleet to secure the observance of this undertaking. " All Englishmen unanimously set down this war as a farce," noted Maximilian, " but surely they laugh from anger, for they would hardly order their whole fleet to come from Malta for a farce." With the aid of a telescope which

---

[1] The interesting reports of this voyage which Maximilian sent the Emperor Franz Joseph are stated by the editor of Tegetthoff's posthumously published correspondence to have been from Tegetthoff's pen : A. Beer, *Aus Wilhelm von Tegetthoffs Nachlass*, at p. 28 (Vienna, 1882).

he found at the signal station on Europa Point, Maximilian was actually able to follow the course of the combat which was proceeding off the opposite shore, and could even distinguish the "victorious banner of the Catholic Queen" waving on a hill above Ceuta amid the smoke from the guns of the Moorish batteries.

The Archduke noticed a number of significant changes in Gibraltar since his last visit of eight years before. For one thing, there were many more guns on the "Rock". "The English never rest in Gibraltar," Maximilian remarked; "they are continually finding some place to fortify anew, and the countless military workmen live in unceasing activity." In fact he felt that the French comic *Journal pour Rire* might well soon advertise "a reward for those who can find a spot in Gibraltar on which to dispose of one additional gun". The Governor of the fortress, too, had changed. Sir Robert Gardiner had given place to Sir William Codrington, a veteran general of the Crimean War who had commanded the famous Light Brigade. Maximilian found him "a large handsome man with silver-white hair and kindly merry eyes, the true type of an English gentleman with all that unaffected friendliness which takes a like response for granted". The Archduke called on Lady Codrington, but he did not enjoy the atmosphere as much as he had on the occasion of his first visit to the Convent. "We found her with her two pretty daughters and a company of officers and official ladies at her tea party", he wrote afterwards. "People shook hands according to custom, then seated themselves in a semicircle like the Roman Senators when they received the Gauls, and sipped tea. The company were naturally strangers to us, and had less of the grave, simple, dignified character of a Court than in the time of my kind friend Sir Robert Gardiner. The building itself has altered to its disadvantage. Formerly in its complete all-pervading simplicity, it possessed a character of grandeur; now, the modern arrangements do not tend to its advantage."

On the neutral ground lying between the fortress and the Spanish frontier post of La Linea there were about 1,700 Jews encamped in tents; they had fled from Morocco on the first news of the Spanish landing. Maximilian and his party strolled over to look at this curious colony. " The whole scene of the camp impressed us deeply ", he wrote. " We saw one Jew eagerly occupied in reading the Talmud in his tent ; he was seated before a board holding the large book in front of him, and he cut marks on the board, probably the number of the verses. It was a picture such as Rembrandt might have painted. Everywhere countless children were swarming. . . . The English, who know how to unite humanity with policy, feed the encampment ; we saw soup distributed from time to time. If these Jews return to Morocco after the termination of the war, they will become English propagandists."

Maximilian and Carlotta also attended a Jewish wedding in the town, at which the Governor and most of the officials were present. The master of ceremonies was the Chief Rabbi of Tangier who had " a pale handsome countenance and fiery red beard, and a turban with a violet-coloured veil on his head — a genuine Old Testament apparition ". The bride, who was only fourteen, lay on a divan " like a motionless wax image on which the glowing colours of art have breathed a fresh living transparency ". The bridegroom was " a very horrid young fellow like an Egyptian goat ". A long ritual took place which included prayer-chanting, drinking wine and dancing to cymbals. " All these ceremonies ", noted Maximilian, " delighted the numerous and vastly merry Englishmen and Englishwomen, who unceasingly followed every motion through their monocles and lorgnettes and made the most comical observations. Thus an elderly lady, who sat in the armchair next mine, told me that the bridegroom would have no claim upon his new wife for eight days, during which time she must remain seated on the throne in the house of her parents to receive her relations and friends : further, she said that as the marriage was only a matter of form the wife possessed the right of separating from her husband at the end of a year. She assured me that in the circumstances, if she were this young wife, she would immediately decide upon this course as she thought the bridegroom so horribly ugly."

Before leaving Gibraltar Maximilian and Carlotta both collected samples of rock plants and shrubs, and they made copious botanical notes for the benefit of the gardens at Miramar and Lacroma. The Archduke also did some necessary shopping with Messrs Saccone and Speed, " who provide all the ships of these well-known Straits with stores ". Maximilian bought a host of delicacies for the *Elizabeth*. " In this point also the English stand pre-eminent ", he noted at the time. " Here one learns of culinary treasures after whose discovery one does not understand how it was possible previously to have done without them. I bought jams made of all imaginable fruits, excellent Scotch salmon in tins and all the most pungent sauces possible. By these means one exalts an ordinary breakfast to a pinnacle of gastronomic enjoyment." While he liked the English and admired their way of life, Maximilian could never quite understand their paradoxical character. For instance, while he called on Admiral Fanshawe, who received him " with the genuine hearty friendship of a true English sailor ", and while he found his flag-ship " an unsurpassed model of cleanliness and seaworthiness ", Maximilian could not help noticing at the same time that " the English fleet was represented in the streets of the town by sundry intoxicated sailors ".

A few days later the *Elizabeth* steamed past the Loo Rock into Funchal Harbour. The sight of Madeira, where Maximilian had spent such a happy twentieth birthday, now filled him with depression and a deep sense of foreboding. He hastened to the scene of his first fiancée Maria Amelia's final tragic illness and death and found that her mother had founded a hospital close by for " twelve men and women suffering from diseases of the chest " to serve as a memorial of the sad event, on whose sixth anniversary some months previously the institution had been opened. " She has named the handsome building after her daughter ", he noted, " and seeks in it to console herself in her own sorrow." From the hospital Maximilian wandered to the house " from which the lovely angel winged her flight ", and after lingering there a while " in grief and sadness ", hurried away and " wrote minute details to the afflicted mother of the visit " he had made.

For a young man of twenty-seven who had recently married a beautiful and intelligent woman, and who had, moreover, the prospect of a full and useful life before him, the thoughts which

Maximilian experienced at this time, and which he was careful to record, were indeed strange. They show how truly the iron of disappointment and unhappiness had entered into his soul. Since his previous visit, he wrote, "seven years had passed over my head, seven years full of pain and joy, full of fortune's storms with few of its blessings, a school of experiences and of many bitter illusions, in which the wheel had turned often and swiftly, and in the course of which many variations of brightness and of sorrow had been experienced and endured. These had been my years of education and of wandering, these years which had swept past since I had joyously celebrated my twentieth birthday in this place. Now I was standing here once more, the restless pilgrim, the modern Ahasuerus, the sole remaining individual from that formerly gay and merry party. . . . Melancholy steals over me when I compare that time with the present. Then I was awaking to life and advancing towards the future with a cheerful heart. In my present coming there lies something of the wearisome."

From this date — December 11, 1859 — on which he visited the hospital for consumptives in Madeira, the Archduke Ferdinand Maximilian of Austria may be said to have finished with the Old World.

2

"That which is unknown and far off interests man", wrote Maximilian in his diary as he passed the Equator, "and when he views life from a distant point, he is immediately attracted hither. . . . The *Elizabeth* is the first Austrian steamer that has crossed the line since steam has ruled the world ; and, though a lady of my country has shown us the road to the New World,[1] I can rejoice in being the first man of my house to enter the southern hemisphere. . . . It seems to me to be a legend that I should be the first lineal descendant of Ferdinand and Isabella to do so, to whom from childhood upwards it has been a daydream to visit this Continent now holding so important a place in the history of mankind." But even when he beheld "the

[1] Maximilian's paternal aunt, the Archduchess Leopoldine of Austria, married the Emperor Pedro I of Brazil as his first wife.

sun-lit wave-washed shore of the new continent ", he confessed it was with a curious feeling — " the feeling ", as he put it, that I had not yet arrived at my ultimate destination ".

At precisely a quarter to eleven in the morning of January 11, 1860, the *Elizabeth*'s small boat, which bore Maximilian and his friends into the harbour of Bahia, grounded on the shingle. " It had scarcely touched the landing place ", wrote Maximilian enthusiastically, " when with feelings of joy rarely experienced I sprang on the soil of the new continent. With a stroke of the magic wand I was placed in the New World. All around breathed life and beauty. If during our voyage we had in those winter months found spring, now the warm delicious perfumed air of luxuriant summer was shed around us. The atmosphere had that elasticity, that fragrance of vegetation, that balmy softness, which is only accorded to us Europeans in the very height of summer."

On landing the party found that they had just missed the Emperor, who had paid one of his rare visits to this portion of his dominions, having been able to save up enough money for the journey. For the past twenty years Brazil had been governed by Pedro II, Maximilian's cousin and also half-brother of his first love, Princess Maria Amelia of Braganza. Scholarly and demo-cratically-minded though he was, Pedro faced a formidable task in ruling this vast slave-owning empire, into much of which his writ did not run. Maximilian was inclined with some truth to attri-bute this state of affairs to lack of communications with the interior. "Brazil above all countries needs railways", he wrote at the time. " A few iron rails laid down wisely and expeditiously in this magnificent country would bring every material blessing, and with but little trouble. As the plough prepares the earth for produce, so would colonization on a grand scale, communica-tion and intercourse between isolated parts of the country, the building of towns, extensive trade, an immense increase of revenue and increased wealth of private individuals, all follow the track of the steam engine. Railways would even alleviate slavery, that ruin and curse of Brazil. . . . So long as Pedro II cannot proceed by railway into the interior of his empire, so long will he remain not an Emperor, but only the master of some custom houses in a few seaports and lord of the small districts around them. For in the interior of the provinces of São Paulo and Minas — only a day's journey from the coast — no more is known of the Emperor and the great Empire of Brazil than we know of the Dalai Lama and its cloud-covered theocracy. Pedro II might have made many discoveries on these subjects if the slave oligarchy that surrounded him had allowed him to investigate for himself."

Maximilian and his companions decided to appear incognito on shore as they considered they would be able to appraise their new surroundings with a greater degree of truth if they went about as ordinary tourists. After eating an indifferent meal at a second-class hotel, they eventually persuaded one of the waiters to guide them to a more reputable establishment where foreign languages were spoken. Here Maximilian was eventually run to earth by the Austrian Consul, who somewhat to his amazement discovered the Archduke " dressed in an exceedingly plebeian manner ", and smoking a cigar quietly in the billiard-room. Meanwhile, news had reached official quarters in the town that a prince from the other side of the Atlantic had landed from the strange-looking paddle steamer in the harbour and the Mayor had already gone on board to pay his respects, supported by members of the local guard consisting, as Maximilian put it, of " large black clowns or monkey-like mulattoes who were lounging about in a melancholy manner in their gay uniforms which had evidently, in consequence of the impoverished state of the treasury, not been made for them ". The Mayor, who thus had " to no purpose sought in his French dictionary for complimentary phrases ", was exceedingly disappointed when he saw that the bird had flown, and by way of reprisal he inspired some acid articles in the local newspaper which appeared several days afterwards. However, Maximilian was more amused than perturbed at this conduct. " The good people ", he said, " ought to have felt flattered that the impulse to rush to their shores should have been so strong."

3

During the next few days Maximilian found himself most hospitably entertained by a number of prominent Bahians as well as by members of the German colony, who both pleased him greatly by respecting his incognito. A botanical expedition was made to the neighbouring island of Itaparica, and a rich sugar plantation was visited up-country. What impressed the visitor most wherever he went was the fundamental slave-owning structure of society from the wealthy sugar planter with several thousands of negro slaves to the impoverished white native who let out two or three slaves as palanquin carriers for hire. " With an inheritance of two or three negroes ", noted Maximilian, " a free constitutional Brazilian citizen can remain idle, can obtain a respectable competence and can talk of the rights of man, for be it understood the Brazilian makes a distinction between the rights of white and coloured working men."

On the controversial subject of slavery as carried on in Brazil Maximilian expressed himself very forcibly :

. . . True progress and real prosperity can never be spoken of in this giant empire so long as slavery exists. Slaves and respectable immigrants cannot live side by side ; slave owners cannot be just. To break through slavery, therefore, should be the first act of modern Brazil. It could not be done without pain, but all natural vigour begins in pain, and certainly it is preferable to idleness and sickliness.

What revolting reasons do not cold-hearted sophists give for the continuance of slavery sanctioned by the State ; they maintain that if slavery were abolished by law a large number of owners would be ruined as they could not cultivate their immense properties without these human machines. In order to leave the idle luxury, the moral indolence of a large number of proprietors untouched, generations of unhappy beings must pine away in slavery.

The blacks are men and Christians, and by the law of God they are born free. That they are regarded as such is proved by their being baptized, also by the fact that their owners frequently have negro wives and children whom they sell again in the market. What an insult to morality and logic ! What a denial of every human principle lies in this circumstance! Why do not the local liberal newspapers, the courageous champions of right, comment upon such deeds ? Perhaps because the traffic in slaves is embodied in a liberal democratic constitution, and the government by pure dint of saying so is deemed enlightened. But who compose this government ? The owners of the black slaves. Even the Emperor himself possesses a large establishment of them in Santa Cruz near Rio.

At the sugar plantation, which he thought was well managed, and where the slaves were well cared for, Maximilian could not help noticing the effect which his human possessions seemed to exercise on the master of this establishment. " The owner of numerous slaves, raising himself to affluence by their means," he observed, " must, in order to reign supreme over such turbulent elements, live in a state of continual uneasiness. He must be incessantly on the watch and be ready at any moment of day and night, so long as he lives, to quell the slightest symptom of insubordination with the lightning flash of his eyes. If this glance fail of effect, the strong arm must be raised and the *chicoto*, the sole sceptre of Brazilian aristocracy, must do its stern duty. Be it observed in passing that the *chicoto* is a long whip made of two pieces of ox-hide, which the keen observer may see lying close at hand in the principal apartment of every Brazilian house. . . . What is most repulsive is the shamelessness and the mirth with which these instruments are shown and talked of. In the eyes of this wealthy man one may discern the necessity for these things at the same moment that one reads in them the most courteous amiability. The searching glance resembles a shuttle ever hurrying from one extreme to the other. These eyes could be soft, intellectual, amiable and even have a look of humility ; but, whilst sparkling with apparent friendliness, they sought with eager restlessness to spy from behind their dark fringes whether all was going on right and whether each inferior was doing his duty, and deep within there seemed to be tiger glances ready at any instant to dart forth in anger upon some victim."

An amusing incident, which was not devoid of significance, occurred during a meal to which Maximilian had invited the rich sugar planter on board the *Elizabeth*. For a long time the planter was seen to stare at a plate of soft white sugar which stood on the cabin table, and then when he thought nobody was looking he suddenly took a spoonful which he hastily ate and then

scooped up a larger portion into an improvised envelope of paper which he placed in his pocket. The Austrian Consul hastened to explain to Maximilian the meaning of this peculiar behaviour. The planter had, " for the first time in his life, met with his deadly enemy. What he had dreamed about during hot tropical nights, the vision which had caused beads of agonized sweat to stand out on his brow, had become a reality. The owner of broad unfailing sugar plantations, whose wealth consisted of slaves and the sweet pulp of the green cane, had tasted free-grown Austrian beet sugar ! One may imagine the blow it was to him. What wicked newspapers had often threatened him with, the hideous nightmare, had sprung into veritable existence, and the thing that endangered his wealth had crossed the ocean to meet his lips in mockery and must indeed have tasted to him most bitter."

From Bahia the *Elizabeth* steamed slowly south in the heat of the tropical summer putting in next at the small port of Ilheos, about 120 miles distant. From here the party made its way up the Cachoeira River to a point where they struck out on foot to explore the primeval forest, the *mato virgem* which Maximilian had made up his mind at all costs to see. For this excursion the Archduke wore a suit of white merino wool made according to his own design and also " an immense straw hat with a veil such as I had seen worn in Egypt by the English ". One night in the jungle was, however, quite enough for the explorers, who, severely bitten by insects, were glad to return to their ship laden with every species of flora and fauna, not to mention pheasants, parrots and other specimens of wild life. In the middle of the jungle they suddenly came upon a settlement hewn out some years earlier by a member of a noble Italian family who was tired of the Old World. At the sound of his name, wrote Maximilian, " I felt my heart prick me. Beautiful Milan, Lake Como, the yearning for fair Lombardy, thoughts of exile and of leaving, all rose before my mind in a moment, the scarce-healed wounds burst open afresh and sadness overspread my heart."

The last port of call was beautiful Rio de Janeiro, which Maximilian felt could not be omitted from their itinerary in order to see the imperial family. He found the serious-minded Emperor and his ugly lame spouse living simply with their two daughters in the near-by mountains at Petropolis. The imperial summer palace in this place was altogether a much more modest establishment than the houses of many of the monarch's subjects, but it enjoined a healthy routine into which the guests from Europe gladly entered. The Emperor would rise at six and take a cold bath in a public bathing establishment near the palace ; he would often stroll or ride about the neighbourhood unescorted, conspicuous in his tall hat and frock-coat and carrying the inevitable umbrella. He particularly liked to watch the trains coming in from the capital, of which there were two daily, and his somewhat austere figure could be easily detected on most days amidst the brightly-dressed country folk who thronged the station platform. The family retired punctually every evening at nine o'clock except when they attended one of the weekly dances at the local hotel, on which festive occasions they stayed up till midnight.

Izabel, the elder of the two girls, was nearly fourteen and Maximilian immediately saw in her a possible future bride for his own youngest brother, the eighteen-year-old Archduke Ludwig Viktor, who was then wasting his time in most undesirable surroundings at home. The Emperor had no male heirs, so what could be a better vocation for Ludwig Viktor than founding a new Hapsburg dynasty in this great South American Empire ? Pedro seemed agreeable, and so Maximilian lost no time in putting the matter to Franz Joseph. " All who know my brother well ", he wrote, " must desire that he should be removed from the aimless existence which he has led hitherto in the atmosphere of Vienna, which is not good for him, and be made a man of. I am convinced that under the strong and judicious though possibly cold and selfish governance of the Emperor of Brazil, his character might be given a healthful direction and his decided abilities and lively intelligence turned to a profitable purpose."

When this piece of business had been put in train, Maximilian bade his cousin farewell and sailed back to Europe. But he did so with a certain measure of reluctance, for he felt very strongly that the New World was beckoning him to stay. "America presents an admirable asylum," he wrote in his journal, "especially for those who have come to a resolution to break with the stormy past and to work their way to a blameless future ; for the ocean is wide, very wide, a lake of oblivion, and whoever sails across it can as by a second baptism wash even the stains of blood from his hands. As in a monastery, so also in America, no one asks a newcomer whence or wherefore he has come. Let him have been ever so wicked in Europe, he may by diligence and perseverance become in America a thoroughly respectable man."

4

Maximilian and Carlotta returned to Trieste in the spring of 1860 to find the castle at Miramar ready for occupation, so they moved in and resumed their former placid existence. "We are still living the same quiet life and we are trying to forget", wrote Carlotta to Countess Hulst when they had been there some weeks. "Miramar will be our town house and Lacroma our country house. In this way our modest way of living works out as well as possible. We have relegated past grandeurs to our memories and we are calmly enjoying what the present has to offer. Providence has done so much for us that in taking away some of her gifts she has left us enough to be happy in another and perhaps more lasting manner." Now that the castle was completed, Carlotta considered it quite charming as well as comfortable. "We have splendid apartments," she told her friend, "warm in winter, cool in summer, from which can be seen the many little fishing boats sailing by which dot these waters. . . . All the foreigners who come here — and there are many — are surprised at what the Archduke has made of Miramar, and it is the object of general admiration. Every Sunday the gardens are thrown open to the public, and a tremendous crowd turns up. There is music on the lawn in front of the castle, and we dine on a balcony from which we can see everything and watch all the people."

As soon as he could get away, Maximilian paid a short visit to Vienna. He returned home greatly depressed by everything he had seen there. He was still on strained terms with his brother, and such comments as he had to offer on domestic policy were not particularly welcome. Franz Joseph, it is true, had got rid of many of his old advisers, but the newcomers did not seem to Maximilian on the whole to be much of an improvement. In particular Count Bernard von Rechberg, who had succeeded the incompetent Buol at the Foreign Office, though considerably more able than his predecessor, was a political reactionary who fervently believed in the perfection of the European pattern of states as planned at the Congress of Vienna in 1815. Maximilian now felt that the collapse of the Empire was fast approaching, and he saw no hope for the future. " As I expected," he wrote to his father-in-law in Brussels, " I found the condition of our poor country tangled and gloomy. Corruption on the one hand and unrest on the other are growing stronger and more disquieting every day. As in the days of Louis XVI, irresolution and inaction prevail. Men do not and will not grasp the situation. There is storm and stress on every side, but in face of it all men close their eyes and ears more and more."

In fact Maximilian was so apprehensive of evils to come that he considered selling the Hungarian bonds in which a great part of his fortune was invested, and he also requested the Belgian King to become the nominal purchaser of Miramar and Lacroma, so that in the event of the intervening strip of the Adriatic coast becoming part of a united Italy these properties would not be lost to him and his family. Leopold strongly advised him not to panic : if the worst happened in Hungary, Leopold pointed out, whatever government was established would be bound to accept responsibility for the bonds, whereas the German Confederation within whose territory Miramar was situated would certainly guarantee the security of this estate and the surrounding country. As for Lacroma, the Belgian monarch was prepared to accede to his son-in-law's request, but it was less out of any real fear for its safety than " because it might serve to set the young people's minds at rest ". Such contemplated arrangements in Maximilian's domestic affairs were not without significance, for they showed clearly in which direction his mind was working and how, as he put it, he was "making all preparations for a crisis" in the internal affairs of his country.

Maximilian had a further anxiety at this time in that he was drawn into the differences which threatened his sister-in-law's married happiness. By the beginning of 1860 the beautiful Empress Elizabeth bade fair to become a nervous wreck, and she not unnaturally appeared most eager to escape from the worrying atmosphere at Court for a prolonged rest. Although Sisi was only twenty-three years old, three confinements in the space of four years, coupled with her constant battles with the Archduchess Sophie, as well as the excitement of the war in Italy, had aged her beauty considerably ; and it looked as if she might suffer a complete breakdown, should she not find it possible to get away. She developed an alarming cough and often would shut herself up in her room crying. Mainly she was unhappy. Unable to sleep, she sat up at night, and in the daytime spent long hours in the saddle which completely exhausted her. "Your present alarming mode of life makes me quite desperate," wrote Franz Joseph to her, "for it is bound to ruin your dear health. I implore you to give it up at once and try to sleep at night, which Nature intended after all for sleeping and not for reading and writing. And do not ride too much or too hard either." The Emperor was eventually reconciled to the idea of her taking a long holiday, but he wished her to go to some sunny resort on the Adriatic coast or to some other place within the confines of the Empire. But Elizabeth insisted in going "far, far away, right out of the country", and on Maximilian's advice it seems she chose Madeira.

There was no Austrian vessel immediately available for the Empress's use, but Queen Victoria of England kindly lent her the royal yacht *Victoria and Albert* for the voyage. She spent the next five months very quietly in a pleasant villa near Funchal, and when she returned to Trieste in the early summer of 1861 both Franz Joseph and Maximilian, who met her, were struck with the evident improvement in her appearance and general state of health. On May 18 the *Victoria and Albert*, flying the English white ensign, dropped anchor off Miramar, and the party was rowed ashore in the yacht's launch to the landing-steps before the castle, where Carlotta was waiting to welcome them, and the Court artist in attendance carefully recorded the scene for the benefit of posterity. After a few days beside the blissful Adriatic, the Emperor and Empress returned together to Vienna and the daily round of official life. A week or two of this life was enough for Sisi. She made up her mind to stand it no longer, and she suddenly announced that her health had again given way and that she must go abroad. Franz Joseph consented unhappily and asked Maximilian to escort the Empress to Corfu, where she had touched on her homeward voyage from Madeira and to which she had now taken a fancy. Maximilian accordingly accompanied his sister-in-law to this island, which was then under British administration, and saw her comfortably installed in the house which the High Commissioner had placed at her disposal. Thus began the series of travels and separations of the Empress Elizabeth from her husband, which were to continue throughout her life. In this particular instance they were inspired largely by Maximilian's own love of travelling in foreign parts, and as the passion grew on the Empress, Franz Joseph was inclined to blame his brother at least in some measure for her apparent restlessness.

Even Maximilian's own married life with Carlotta, which had begun so promisingly, was not unclouded. Although their relations were to all outward appearances entirely harmonious, the truth was that Maximilian no longer cohabited with his wife. The origin of this estrangement may be found in the fact that, although they had now been married for four years, they had had no children. In some quarters it was suggested that Carlotta was barren, in others that the Archduke was impotent. It is certain, however, that their childlessness was not of their own desiring, and that Maximilian indulged in some extra-marital activities which, unfortunately for him, came to Carlotta's notice in a peculiarly unpleasant manner. The authority for this conclusion is Maximilian's valet Antonio Grill, who was with the young couple from the beginning of their residence at Miramar, and whose reliability there is no reason to doubt. In the early days at Miramar, said Grill, " they had seemed to be still enamoured and were always together, but afterward during a trip to Vienna something had happened which alienated them from each other. From that time, although their mutual attitude before the world remained affectionate and loving, privately there was no such affection or confidence." They no longer slept together in the same bed, and the valet attributed this separation to Carlotta's discovery of one of her husband's infidelities " having wounded her pride as a beautiful woman ". She had therefore decided to adopt this attitude towards Maximilian " naturally without seeking to create a public scandal ". The incident during the trip to Vienna to which Grill refers is now known to have been a venereal disease, which Maximilian contracted from a prostitute and which he subsequently communicated to his wife.

At Miramar Carlotta spent her time writing and painting, and when she went to Lacroma she would bathe, ride, sail and stroll through the beautiful woods of her fairy island. All the while, however, she was inwardly consumed by a strong ambition to participate again in more worldly affairs, although she would not admit it even to her closest friend. " The life I am leading is not what I thought it would be," she told Countess Hulst at this period, " but I assure you I thank God for it, for in times like these one is better off far away from this world, and the less one has the less one can lose. I have no idea what the future holds in store, but should the world return to normal, I believe the day will come — and this without any ambitious notions on my part — when the Archduke will again occupy a prominent position. By this I mean a position where he will govern, for he was made for that and blessed by Providence with everything necessary to make a people happy, and it seems impossible to me that these gifts should be buried forever after shining for a brief three years."

These words were strangely prophetic. Even as Carlotta wrote them events were happening in another part of Europe to shape her husband's destiny and her own in the direction of her fondest wishes and ambition. The immediate result of these events became apparent towards the middle of October 1861, when the Austrian Foreign Minister, Count Rechberg, arrived in Miramar to enquire whether the Archduke Maximilian was interested in the idea of becoming Emperor of Mexico.

5

When the intrepid *conquistador* Hernando Cortés crossed the ocean early in the sixteenth century and with a mere handful of men conquered the once mighty Aztec Empire and took prisoner its ruler Montezuma, he assured the rich and glorious land of Mexico to Maximilian's Hapsburg ancestor Charles V and his successors on the throne of Spain for the next three hundred years. The Spaniards became the governing race, and exploited the vast mineral resources of this new colony to the utmost, while the Inquisition dispossessed the native Indian priesthood, their sun worship and human sacrifices, and enforced the observance of the Catholic faith with the customary vigour of the Holy Office. The struggle for Mexican independence did not begin until the Napoleonic Wars, when Napoleon's action in setting aside the ruling dynasty in Madrid showed Spain's inherent political weakness and at the same time encouraged all the Spanish colonies in the New World to throw off the yoke of the mother country. Eventually, after much bitter fighting, an ambitious Spanish officer who had espoused the nationalist cause, Don Augustín Iturbide, effectively proclaimed the independence of Mexico just forty years before it was suggested to the Archduke Maximilian that he might become the country's sovereign.

Iturbide wished to make Mexico an independent monarchy, and by one of history's interesting coincidences he despatched a deputation to Vienna in 1821 to offer the crown to Maximilian's grand-uncle, the Archduke Charles, brother of the Emperor Francis. The Archduke, however, turned down the offer, whereupon Iturbide, who was ambitious as well as valiant, promptly had himself proclaimed Emperor. This was the signal for the outbreak of civil war which continued intermittently for the next forty years and drained the country of man-power, material resources and, as it turned out, extensive territory. It was during this period that the states of Texas, New Mexico, California and southern Arizona — an area equal to about one-sixth of Europe — were ceded to the United States. By the time Maximilian appeared on the scene, the country was virtually bankrupt.

Iturbide's disgruntled supporters had forced him to abdicate and flee the country, but his inability to withstand the temptation of returning to Mexico shortly afterwards led to his capture and execution at the hands of his opponents. His successor, who had been his lieutenant, Antonio López de Santa Anna, became first President of the Mexican Republic, a post which he contrived successfully to occupy no less than six times during the next thirty years. Santa Anna, who ruled as a dictator with the support of the reactionary clerical and Conservative elements in the country, was a picturesque figure, like so many of Mexico's subsequent Presidents. In 1838, whilst personally directing military operations against the French, who had sent a fleet to Vera Cruz to enforce payment of compensation claims of French nationals arising out of the prolonged civil war, Santa Anna lost a leg. He caused the amputated limb to be conveyed to the capital and there solemnly interred beneath a handsome monument which for a short spell became a kind of national shrine. Such, however, were the vicissitudes of Mexican national politics, that when Santa Anna fell from power some years later his political opponents dug up his leg and dragged it through the streets of Mexico City. Yet the wheel came full circle, for the passing of another decade found the irrepressible Santa Anna once more installed in the presidential palace.

Santa Anna eventually retired for good in 1854, taking with him his wooden leg and the title to a large fortune which he had amassed in the course of his long political career and which he had had the foresight to deposit with a banking house in Cuba. His Liberal successor, President Comonfort, antagonized his supporters as well as his opponents by attempting unsuccessfully to reconcile the two conflicting parties in the state, and he was forced to resign after a brief uneasy rule. Under the terms of the constitution he was succeeded by the fifty-year-old Vice-President Benito Juárez, who led the radical element among the Liberals. Juárez was of pure Indian stock, and at the age of twelve had been unable to read or write or even speak a word of Spanish. His adoption by a wealthy tradesman enabled him to become a lawyer and later drew him into politics, where his outstanding intellectual gifts, exercised in the extreme Liberal cause, raised him eventually to the first post in the state. The Conservatives, however, refused to recognize Juárez as the rightful President and established their own candidate in Mexico City in the person of Felix Zuloaga, who retired in 1859 in favour of the extreme Conservative General Miramón. Meanwhile Juárez set up his headquarters in Vera Cruz, and, like the medieval papacy, Mexico treated the world to the unedifying spectacle of two rival warring Presidents each endeavouring to extend his jurisdiction over a land which was fast lapsing into anarchy and chaos.

In many ways Miguel Miramón presented as striking a figure as his principal Liberal antagonist. His career is particularly worth mentioning because its later and final phases were destined to be fatally interwoven with Maximilian's own life. He was born in the same year as the Austrian Archduke, so that at the time of his succession to the presidency of the Republic he was only twenty-six years old. His rise in the troubled firmament of Mexican politics was truly meteoric. He entered the military academy at the age of twelve and as a cadet took part in the war against the United States in 1847. He rapidly attained commissioned rank and in 1855, at the age of twenty-four, he was given command of a brigade. His participation in the internal struggles which Comonfort's government provoked was on the clerical and reactionary side ; it was so successful that it eventually led Zuloaga to nominate him as his successor in the National Palace. Although personally very ambitious and but an indifferent general, Miramón was a brave man at heart as well as an honest one, and he served his party faithfully even though as its titular leader he could hardly be said to represent the mass of the Mexican people.

The struggle for supremacy between Miramón and Juárez lasted for the next four years. Since he was established on the coast, Juárez was much better off financially than his rival, for he controlled the customs houses in the Gulf ports which, owing to the trade with Europe, provided the greater part of the country's revenue. On the other hand, Miramón, although he enjoyed the support of the clergy and the well-to-do landowners, was in constant financial straits. Amongst other expedients to raise funds he signed a contract with a Swiss banker named Jecker for a loan of 750,000 dollars, in return for which he was to hand over Mexican Government bonds to the value of fifteen million dollars redeemable at fixed intervals. In November 1860 Miramón had no money left with which to pay his army, and in his extremity he broke into the British Legation, where he knew that the agents for the bond holders of Mexican state loans were accustomed to deposit the sums by way of interest which they collected from time to time, and carried off no less than 660 pesos from the strong-room. But Miramón was at the end of his tether. A month later he was decisively defeated in the field by Juárez's forces and he threw up the sponge and fled to Cuba. Early in 1861 Juárez entered the capital and the unfortunate dual presidency came to an end.

Juárez signalized his accession to power by promulgating a series of drastic laws aimed at the Church. All Church property was nationalized, religious houses were suppressed, and the privileges of the clergy were abolished. These reforms were naturally not carried through without bitter opposition on the part of the remaining Conservative elements in the country. Although Juárez was now President in fact as well as in law, the latent opposition to his measures, particularly among the clergy and landowners, which he had to encounter, added to the difficulties which he was having in his relations with foreign powers, made his position by no means secure. When the first Jecker bonds were presented for payment, he disavowed all previous financial agreements and suspended for two years all payments due on foreign loans. The principal foreign creditors were Spain, France and England, and the prospect of intervention which Juárez's moratorium suggested was made more inviting by the knowledge that the United States, from whom opposition to such a move might otherwise have been anticipated, was now embroiled in a bloody civil war. Spain at first proposed to despatch an expedition to Vera Cruz on her own account, but on representations being made to her by the other two powers she eventually agreed to the principle of joint intervention.

The possibility of armed foreign intervention in Mexico seemed a heaven-sent opportunity to the opponents of the Juárez regime, particularly those Mexican exiles and so-called patriots who congregated in Paris and other European capitals and conducted endless discussions on the subject of the restoration of the monarchy. Most prominent amongst the Mexican *émigrés* was the sixty-year-old José María Gutiérrez de Estrada who had dedicated his whole life to the cause of monarchist restoration in his native land. As a young man he had been a member of the delegation which had offered the Mexican crown to the Archduke Charles in 1821, and later had served as Mexican Minister in Vienna, where he married the daughter of the Marquise de Saint Laurent, who as Countess Lutzow subsequently became Mistress of the Household at Maximilian's Court in Milan. Gutiérrez was a verbose Conservative reactionary and clericalist — he once wrote a letter of eighty-four pages on his pet subject — but he was also a man of considerable financial means which he devoted with all his mental and physical energies to the political cause which he had most at heart. Time and again he worried the Foreign Ministers of England, France, Spain and Austria with his views, and although several times in the course of twenty years he thought himself on the verge of success, " unforeseen circumstances ", as he put it, " have always intervened and rendered all my efforts vain ". In 1854 President Santa Anna had even invested him with plenary official authority to seek a monarch amongst the European Courts, but as before nothing came of his overtures.

Gutiérrez had two energetic supporters of his plans in the persons of Juan Almonte and José Hidalgo. Former aide-de-camp to Santa Anna and afterwards Mexican Minister in Paris, General Almonte was believed to be the illegitimate son of Morelos, the priest who had been one of the national leaders in the Mexican War of Independence and had subsequently been executed. Hidalgo, on the other hand, was an elegant young Spaniard whose father had served under Iturbide when the latter was fighting on the Spanish side ; he had filled diplomatic posts in the Mexican Legations in London, Madrid and Paris, where his endearing manners made him particularly popular with ladies of rank and substance. Among those whom he thus courted in Spain was the lovely Eugénie de Montijo who married the French Emperor Napoleon III.

Hidalgo kept up his acquaintance with Eugénie after her marriage, and he used to be invited to stay with the Emperor and Empress at their various places in the country. It so happened that he was at Biarritz with them in September 1861 when the news reached him by letter that Juárez and the Mexican Assembly had suspended the payments on all foreign loans. This was the first that his host had heard of the subject, since at that time the transatlantic cable was not in operation and posts took six weeks or more to arrive from Mexico City. The Emperor's interest in the New World dated from the days when he was a prisoner of King Louis Philippe in the fortress of Ham — had the French King at that time been willing to release him, Louis Napoleon would have accepted the presidency of Ecuador which had been offered him. He had also played with the idea of leading a commercial enterprise for the purpose of cutting a canal through the isthmus of Nicaragua to join the two oceans. For some years past Hidalgo had been pressing him to intervene in Mexico, but the Emperor had not unnaturally been unwilling to act alone. Now the ideal moment seemed to have arrived.

" Sir," said Hidalgo to Napoleon after he had imparted the latest news from Mexico, " England together with France and Spain is now irritated by Juárez's policy, and they are all going to order warships to our ports. And so, Your Majesty, we have what we needed : English intervention. France will not be acting alone, which was what Your Majesty always wished to avoid. Spain has long been prepared. . . . The United States are in the throes of war ; they will not move. Besides, they would never oppose the three united powers together. Let the allied flag once show itself, Sir, and I can assure Your Majesty that the country will rise as one man and rally to the support of this beneficent intervention."

Although the Emperor had not seen the latest despatches from Mexico to the French Foreign Office, he immediately replied that if England and Spain were prepared to act, the interests of France demanded that she do likewise. " If the country declares that it desires to organize itself with the support of the European powers," he added, " I will lend a hand."

" Sir," rejoined Hidalgo, who saw the realization of his wildest dreams not far distant, " whatever may happen, we shall have only France to thank for it. Will Your Majesty allow me to ask whether you have a candidate for the throne in view, for the Mexicans would accept him from Your Majesty as if it were their own idea ? "

So far the Empress had said nothing. Napoleon replied that he had no one in view, whereupon all three fell to discussing the merits of possible candidates. After a number of individuals had been mentioned and dismissed on account of one objection or another, Eugénie suggested the name of the Archduke Maximilian but immediately added that he " would not be willing ". The others agreed that Maximilian would not be willing.

After a moment's silence the Empress turned round and suddenly exclaimed : " Well, I have a presentiment that tells me he will accept ! "

" We can but try," said Hidalgo, " and I might write to Gutiérrez de Estrada to go to Vienna and sound His Imperial Highness."

V. *Acceptance of a Crown*

THE proposal officially put forward to Maximilian by Count Rechberg on behalf of the French and Austrian Governments met with an immediately favourable reaction at Miramar. In his considered reply the Archduke dwelt on the glory of the Hapsburg dynasty for which he was prepared to exert himself at any personal cost. " I shall always and in every circumstance of life ", he told Rechberg, " be found ready to make every sacrifice, however heavy it may be, for Austria and the power of my house. In the present case the sacrifice would be doubly great for both me and my wife, for it would involve tearing ourselves away from Europe and its life for ever. I do not by any means underestimate the advantage this would be to Austria in reviving the lustre of my house. . . . Owing to the pressure of contemporary conditions the pristine glory of our house has become dimmed. While the Coburgs gain throne after throne and spread their growing power abroad over the whole earth, our family has in quite recent times lost two sovereignties.[1] None sees more clearly than I that it is the duty of our house to wipe out this stain ; and so I cannot fail to see what an impression would be made upon the world, and above all upon an enfeebled Austria, if the proposition in question were carried into effect."

At the same time Maximilian and Carlotta consulted the Belgian King, " our dear wise father " whose " enlightened counsel " the Archduke sought " in this critical moment ". Leopold, who had himself been offered the Mexican crown thirty years before, replied that the project had decided possibilities but that everything depended on " what the country itself would do ", and until then they should keep themselves free " without, on the other hand, rejecting the proposition ". Meanwhile Gutiérrez had been busy with pen and paper and had already written a memorandum on the subject to Maximilian in which he made it clear that if the Archduke accepted the crown he

[1] The Grand Duchy of Tuscany in 1859 and the Duchy of Modena in 1860.

would owe it to the Mexican *émigrés*. This last sentiment was too much for Maximilian, who agreed with Leopold that if he accepted the crown it should be at the will of the country as a whole and not of a minority group not even resident within its frontiers. " I should never have decided to accept the crown ", he told Rechberg, " at the sole invitation of the Mexican exiles, however many honourable men they may include within their ranks. Nothing but the clear and distinctly expressed will of the country itself can make me determine upon it."

Gutiérrez was now most anxious to come to Miramar and meet the Archduke. Maximilian was, however, against this course at first as he felt it might compromise him publicly. Instead he sent his confidential private secretary, Sebastian Schertzenlechner, to meet Gutiérrez in Paris. This individual had originally been a valet in the imperial household where his zeal and quickness of mind had compensated in Maximilian's eyes for his lack of education. The result of their meeting was that Gutiérrez requested that he should be appointed the Archduke's confidential agent at the French Court, thus to some extent cutting the ground from under Hidalgo's feet ; and thanks largely to his mother-in-law Countess Lützow's activities behind the scenes at Miramar where she still kept her old position as Mistress of the Household, Maximilian relented and invited the Mexican to spend Christmas with him. Gutiérrez came hot-foot to Trieste, and Maximilian fell completely under the spell of his flattery and deferred to his wishes in everything.

The Emperor Franz Joseph, who may have seen in the scheme a method of getting rid of his embarrassing " free-thinking " brother, had already signified his consent to it in principle. The details remained to be discussed, and Maximilian took advantage of his brother's presence at this time in Venice, where the Emperor was on one of his customary tours of inspection, to seek an interview with Franz Joseph. Maximilian left Miramar for Venice as soon as Gutiérrez had departed, and the two brothers met on the last day of the year 1861.

Franz Joseph and Maximilian sat down together and examined the project carefully. The Emperor agreed that Maximilian should have leave of absence from the navy and that when the time came he should make the journey to Mexico in an Austrian warship. The effect which acceptance of the Mexican crown would have on Maximilian's family rights and expectations was postponed for later discussion. On the financial side Franz Joseph agreed to advance the sum of 200,000 gulden out of the family funds to meet the preliminary expenses of the candidature; this was to be repaid out of Maximilian's appanage together with the sums which he had borrowed for the building of Miramar. Miramar was eventually to become State property while Lacroma was to be similarly disposed of. To start off the new government on a solvent basis a loan of 25 million dollars was to be raised, preferably through the house of Rothschild, and guaranteed by the powers which had assisted in the establishment of the throne. On the military side the Mexican army was to consist at first exclusively of foreign troops and only gradually to be reinforced by native recruits. Finally, if Europe recognized the independence of the Confederate States of the North American Union, the new state was to be asked as a reciprocal condition to respect the integrity of Mexico. Until the arrival of Maximilian the government of the country was to be in the hands of a regency of three members, of whom it was hoped that the one-legged Santa Anna with his wealth of experience and local connections would be one.

The Archduke communicated the substance of these conclusions to the French Emperor in a most flattering letter which he well knew how to pen. Napoleon sent his reply by the safe hand of General Almonte, who he proposed should proceed to Mexico directly and put matters in train for the inauguration of the new rule. " The ideas which Your Imperial Highness is good enough to communicate to me seem very just," wrote Napoleon," and when the time comes I will do all that is in my power to facilitate their carrying into effect. Your personal qualities and the illustrious house to which you belong are causes which ought to ensure the success of the task which you are undertaking. Never in my opinion will any task produce greater results. For it is a question of rescuing a whole continent from misery, of setting an example of good government to the whole of America, and lastly of raising the monarchist flag, based upon a wise liberty and a sincere love of progress, in the face of dangerous Utopias and bloody disorders."

2

Mexico was now experiencing the uncongenial effects of foreign intervention. By a convention signed in London on October 30, 1861, Spain, France and England had agreed to occupy the port of Vera Cruz jointly and simultaneously. Owing to the fact that Spanish troops were stationed in Cuba, which was then a colony of Spain, this power succeeded in establishing a foothold ahead of her two neighbours. Six thousand Spanish troops arrived in the middle of December ; some weeks later about a third of that number of French marines and zouaves appeared ; and later still the English landed several hundred marines, a mere token force intended to show that Britain did not wish to be left out of the demonstration.

Difficulties immediately beset this combined expeditionary force. In the first place, Vera Cruz was a hot-bed of yellow fever, and none of the troops naturally displayed any inclination to remain there for long. Then the allied leaders made the unpleasant discovery that they were by no means unanimous on what they intended to extract from the government of Señor Juárez. The French Ambassador quickly threw the cat among the pigeons by proposing such a huge sum (12 million pesos) as compensation for France's claims that nothing would have been left to satisfy the claims of the other two powers if it had been paid. The Mexican people were merely informed by a proclamation that the visitors had come to give them " a friendly hand ", but nothing was said about debt-collecting. Juárez replied that Mexico was not in need of foreign assistance, and fruitless discussions between the allies dragged on in the healthier atmosphere of Orizaba, to which the troops had moved from the coast. Eventually in April, 1862, deadlock was reached ; and Spain and England decided to withdraw their forces, leaving the whole burden of the enterprise to be shouldered by France alone.

The country showed no signs of rising to welcome the invader as the Mexican exiles had predicted and fervently hoped. On the contrary, the French were roundly defeated by the Juárist troops outside Puebla on May 5, thereby adding another national holiday to the already full Mexican calendar. Napoleon was not disposed to turn back now, for, like all dictators, his foreign policy was designed to dazzle his subjects. Reinforcements under a new commander-in-chief, General Forey, were poured into the country. Eventually, early in 1863, after a long delay on the coast, Forey advanced and overwhelmed Puebla, and the way to the capital lay open.

Meanwhile the castle of Miramar was the scene of constant activity. Visitors kept coming and going, some warmly advocating and others with equal vehemence opposing Maximilian's candidature for the Mexican throne. Egged on by his wife, the Archduke had only ears for the ayes. He would not listen to Count Rechberg, who counselled the utmost reserve in view of England's lukewarm attitude to the project. Nor was he much impressed by the picture drawn of the country by Mr. Bourdillon, the recently returned correspondent of the London *Times*, who, although he personally favoured the establishment of a monarchy (primarily because he was interested in a mining concession and Juárez had expelled him before he could exploit it), pointed out there was not the slightest trace of Liberal ideas to be found in Mexico on paper, education was non-existent, thieving and corruption were general among all classes of officials, and the nation as a whole was rotten to the core. Maximilian and Carlotta were, in his judgment, altogether " too good " for it. As for the late English Minister in .Mexico City, Sir Charles Wyke hoped that the Archduke would not run his head " into such a hornets' nest " as he undoubtedly would do if he were to accept the crown from the clerical party in the Mexican capital, which did not in his opinion represent the majority of the nation and only existed in certain areas between the capital and the coast where it was in effect supported by French bayonets.

England indeed was most reluctant to see the Austrian Archduke involved in this venture, and the English Foreign Minister, Lord John Russell, now came forward with the offer of another throne in an endeavour to direct Maximilian's attention from

Mexico. In consequence of a revolution King Otto of Greece had recently been obliged to leave the country with his spouse, and the English Foreign Minister had been searching for a suitable successor. But Maximilian rejected the offer almost angrily. " I can only explain to myself such a lack of tact on the part of the man at the head of the English Cabinet as is to be found in this almost offensive proposal," he wrote at the time, " by the embarrassment in which he has been placed by the repeated refusals of the throne of Greece. Even if it had been lawfully vacated by the death or abdication of King Otto and had not, moreover, every kind of objection against it, I should indeed be the last to feel inclined to accept a crown which has been hawked round unsuccessfully to half a dozen princes. Moreover, I am too well acquainted with modern Hellas and its present corrupt state not to have been convinced for a long time past that the crafty and morally degenerate people is incapable of offering a firm foundation for an independent State."

It is a pity that Maximilian did not possess some first-hand knowledge of the country whose crown a reactionary minority was now preparing to invite him to accept. After Forey's occupation of the capital, a national assembly consisting of the most Conservative and clerical elements which had supported Santa Anna in the days of his dictatorship proclaimed the introduction of a hereditary monarchy which they proposed that deputation headed by Gutiérrez should request the Archduke to assume. "I am happy at this first result," telegraphed Napoleon to Miramar, " and hope that the whole of Mexico will soon follow the capital and summon Your Imperial Highness to regenerate her." In Vienna Franz Joseph was considerably less elated. He called his brother to Schönbrunn, and warned him that the Austrian Government's attitude to the venture must remain purely passive : as for the deputation, since the assembly which nominated it had not been recognized by Austria, such a visiting body " could not well be recognized as possessing an official character ". At the same time the Empress Elizabeth did everything within her power to dissuade her brother-in-law and his wife to drop the whole idea. Indeed Sisi was quite at a loss to

account for their anxiety to possess a crown : in her opinion
they should have been only too glad not to have one.

3

Shortly after this Carlotta paid a visit to Brussels to see
her father and obtain his advice. For hours they talked together
of the Mexican project. Leopold promised to use his good
offices at his niece's Court with a view to modifying Britain's
attitude. He doubted, however, whether any guarantee would
be forthcoming, although he thought Victoria might perhaps
furnish a frigate to escort his son-in-law and daughter to their
new kingdom. " Guarantees are rather illusory ", he told
Carlotta, " and they are only obtained from England when it is
clearly and obviously to her interest. A good quality of English
guarantees is their trustworthiness ; hence they are not very
lavish with them." Leopold thought that England's attitude
was bound to change, as he felt (quite wrongly, as it turned out)
that England would soon be forced into war with the northern
states of the American Union, and for that reason would wish
to create a bulwark for herself on the North American continent.
The Belgian King also discussed every aspect of the venture
from questions of civil establishment to methods of government.
" Take only a small household," he advised his daughter, " no
more than three or four manservants. The Emperor Napoleon
had far too many ; he found himself forced to have them in
order to reward those who had served him." On the whole
Leopold strongly advised Maximilian to accept the Mexican
crown, and he made it clear that it was Carlotta's duty to accompany her husband. " Above all things ", he said, " I recommend
a good administration and justice, since these two things together
are certainly the things to which the Mexicans are least accustomed and which they value most."

Unfortunately Leopold's judgment, which in most matters
was extremely sound, was in this instance clouded by dynastic
ambition — the desire to see his daughter on a foreign throne,
thus adding another name to the already impressive Coburg
hierarchy. Like Napoleon he hedged on the all-important

question of guarantees, and like the French Emperor too he placed more faith in a benevolent despotism backed by force than in a constitutional rule supported by popular acclaim. " When once the country is physically and morally pacified," wrote Napoleon to Maximilian at this time, " Your Imperial Highness's Government will be recognized by all, and the guarantee which is so hard to obtain from the naval powers would scarcely contribute towards its stability. . . . A state which is sunk in anarchy is not to be regenerated by parliamentary liberty. What is wanted in Mexico is a *liberal* dictatorship. I mean a strong power which will proclaim the great basic principles of modern civilization, such as equality before the law, civil and religious liberty, an honest administration, and an equitable system of justice. As regards the Constitution, that must be the work of time, and I believe that even if it has been promised and elaborated, it should not be really applied until several years have passed, the country is pacified, and the Government in good working order."

Meanwhile the deputation conveying the offer of the crown to Maximilian was on its way to Trieste. The party, which consisted of four Mexicans resident in Europe, among them Hidalgo, and five who had come over from Mexico, including a priest named Miranda, arrived at Miramar on October 3, 1863. They were received by Maximilian alone, who listened patiently while their leader Gutiérrez let fall a seemingly interminable flow of honeyed phrases from lips which, he said, " have never been stained with flattery ", bewailing the unhappy state of republican Mexico and begging a Catholic Prince of such enlightenment and perfection as the Archduke to come and rule over the country. " We who are but feeble interpreters of the hopes and prayers of a whole nation ", said Gutiérrez, speaking in French, " come to present in that nation's name to Your Imperial Highness the crown of the Mexican Empire which the people offer you, Prince, freely and spontaneously by a solemn decree of the assembly already ratified by many provinces and which soon will be, as everyone says, by the entire nation."

Maximilian replied briefly in Spanish. After expressing thanks that the Mexican people should turn to a Hapsburg descendant

Rischgitz

LEOPOLD I, KING OF THE BELGIANS

From the portrait by Franz Winterhalter in Buckingham Palace

By gracious permission of His Majesty the King

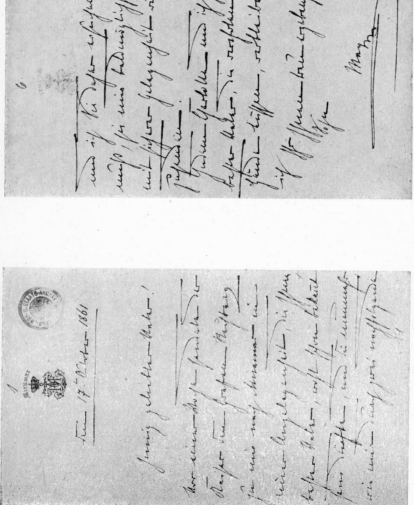

TWO PAGES OF A LETTER FROM THE ARCHDUKE MAXIMILIAN TO KING LEOPOLD I

From the original in the Austrian State Archives in Vienna

This was the first letter in which Maximilian consulted his father-in-law on the Mexican venture. It is quoted briefly on page 115

of the Emperor Charles V for a monarch, the Archduke stated that he could not accede to the wishes of the delegation " unless the whole nation expressing freely its will would wish to ratify the wishes of the capital ". He also mentioned in general terms the " indispensable guarantees " which would be necessary in order to place the country " under protection from the dangers which might threaten its integrity and independence ", but he did not indicate the names of the powers who were to implement them. Provided these two conditions were satisfied, Maximilian informed the visitors that he would be ready " with the consent of the august chief of my family and confiding in the support of the Almighty, to accept the crown ".

The Archduke's prevarication on the subject of the guarantees provoked a sharp rebuke from his brother in Vienna, prompted no doubt by Rechberg. " From your reply to the deputation and from Napoleon's letter ", Franz Joseph telegraphed to Miramar, " I see that you do not explicitly adhere to the guarantee of the three powers, particularly England. I must remind you in the most decided manner of this condition as originally stipulated between us. You cannot place yourself in a state of dependence upon France alone."

Maximilian excused himself feebly on the ground of the English Foreign Minister's " touchiness ". The truth was that, come what might, the Archduke was too deeply engaged in the enterprise to withdraw now. It might have been worse, but not much. " I am only glad ", said Leopold to his daughter, " that Max was not called upon to rule over Poland. That would have been terrible, for Russian sentiment would never allow it, and Prussia has never given back what she possesses." Nevertheless, even the Belgian monarch could not be blind to the dangers of the project. " The undertaking is a perilous one," he wrote to Queen Victoria in England, " but if it succeeds it will be one of the greatest and most useful of our time." Leopold felt that much depended on his daughter's energy and initiative. " She is very venturesome and would go with Max to the end of the world ; she will be of the greatest use to him ; and, if success there is to be, much will be owing to her."

4

Although he realized that he was so much involved in the Mexican scheme by this time that he would find it extremely difficult, if not actually impossible to stand aside to the satisfaction of his honour, the Archduke Maximilian still hesitated before the prospect of taking the plunge and accepting the crown. There was the vexatious question of the guarantee from England, which seemed as far away from achievement as ever and which he was gradually coming to see would have somehow or other to be dropped if he was ever to get to Mexico at all. Then there was the matter of popular support in the country itself for his assumption of the monarchy. As yet only a relatively few towns and localities between the capital and the coast had declared for Maximilian as Emperor, and even a considerable number of their " acts of adhesion " emanated from places which, in the words of the former English Minister, Sir Charles Wyke, " were possibly inhabited by two Indians and a monkey ". General Bazaine, who had now succeeded Forey as Commander-in-Chief of the French Expeditionary forces, was accordingly instructed by Napoleon to obtain without delay the necessary plebiscites to justify the new sovereignty.

Bazaine proceeded to carry out his master's orders and at the same time to engage Juárez's rapidly disintegrating army at every point. The French General had a force of 40,000 French soldiers in addition to 13,000 Mexican auxiliaries, whereas his opponent possessed only 20,000 men. For the gallant little Indian the odds were overwhelming. In November Juárez lost one of his ablest commanders, the former President Comonfort, who was killed in action, and shortly after this two of his best generals, Vidaurri and Uraga, went over to the interventionist side. By the spring of 1864 Almonte's prophecy to Maximilian that Bazaine would succeed in pacifying the whole country seemed to have come true, with the exception of one district in the south where the brilliant young Juárist General Porfirio Díaz still held out, and a few points in the far north near the United States border where the titular President himself was established.

Almonte was anxious that Maximilian should lose no time in going out to Mexico, and Napoleon now began to press the Archduke in this sense. But Maximilian still held back, perhaps on account of the discouragement which he encountered in the Hapsburg family circle. Both his parents and his grandmother the Dowager Empress Caroline were strongly opposed to his acceptance of the Mexican crown, and although he told his brother Franz Joseph that he considered the older people had been " led astray " and were infected with " prejudiced views " on the subject, it seems that for a time at least their objections did carry some weight with him. His hesitation was also increased by the fact that his youngest brother, Ludwig Viktor, refused to fall in with his wishes. It will be remembered that during his visit to Brazil Maximilian had sought to promote a marriage between this somewhat aimless and dissolute young man and one of the Brazilian Emperor's daughters. He now spoke of making Ludwig Viktor his heir as Crown Prince of Mexico, and he cherished wild dreams that this arrangement, coupled with the Brazilian marriage and the absorption of the weak republican states adjacent and lying between Mexico and Brazil, would one day result in the establishment of a vast Hapsburg empire stretching from the Rio Grande to the River Plate. But Ludwig Viktor told " Montezuma," as he playfully called his brother, that he could not " imagine an existence for himself beyond the ocean " and that he would only go out to Brazil " as a martyr " if expressly commanded to do so by Franz Joseph. Thus, as the Emperor felt that he could not rightly give such a command to the young Archduke, the scheme came to nothing.

Meanwhile Napoleon was growing uneasy at the delay and for the first time began to show signs of impatience and a desire to clinch matters. " I realize that I have got myself into a tight place," he admitted to his intimates, " but the affair has got to be liquidated." There was nothing for it but to try to force the Archduke's hand. The French Emperor therefore let it be known to Maximilian through devious channels that he had a rival candidate in view who was prepared to come forward if the Archduke did not make up his mind very soon. This was the forty-five-year-old Prince de Joinville, who was a younger son of the late French King Louis Philippe, and thus an uncle of Carlotta's. This candidature naturally commanded support among the Orleanist party in the French Chamber, and it particularly commended itself to Napoleon's Finance Minister, Achille Fould, who realized that if it materialized it would facilitate raising part of the Mexican loan and also possibly troops in Spain, whose Queen was already closely connected with the Orleans family.[1]

The reception of this news at Miramar had precisely the effect desired by Napoleon. "It is impossible to keep the Mexicans in suspense any longer", Maximilian told his brother the Austrian Emperor on December 26. " I cannot with honour continue to put forward conditions which I now know to be unattainable." The Archduke accordingly despatched a trusted agent, Kint von Roodenbeck, to Paris, and there, in the Tuileries Palace on January 3, 1864, this emissary conveyed his master's definitive acceptance of the Mexican throne subject only to the receipt of the French Emperor's own guarantees. Napoleon promptly replied by assuring Maximilian that the French army would not leave Mexico until it could do so without endangering the existence of the new Government, and even then it would leave the Foreign Legion behind for another six or eight years. He went on to say that on the question of the loan and the expenses of the French Expedition the most favourable conditions possible would be granted, but he urged Maximilian's presence in Paris soon so as to reduce their understanding on this and other matters to a formal basis.

5

Austria had experienced a drought of unparalleled severity in 1863. "There is no glory in the grass nor verdure in anything", wrote the American historian John Lothrop Motley, who then occupied the post of United States Minister in Vienna. " In fact we have nothing green here but the Archduke Maximilian

[1] Joinville's brother, the Duc de Montpensier, was married to the Spanish Queen Isabella's younger sister, the Infanta Luisa.

who firmly believes that he is going forth to Mexico to establish an American empire, and that it is his divine mission to destroy the dragon of democracy and re-establish the true Church, the Right Divine, and all sorts of games. Poor young man ! " Motley added with perhaps a greater sense of justice that the project was not generally regarded with favour in Austria. " That a Prince of the House of Hapsburg should become a satrap of the Bonaparte dynasty, and should sit on an American throne which could not exist a moment but for French bayonets and French ships, is most galling to all classes of Austrians. The intrigue is a most embarrassing one to the Government. If the fatal gift is refused, Louis Napoleon of course takes it highly in dudgeon. If it is accepted, Austria takes a millstone round her neck in the shape of gratitude for something she didn't want, and some day she will be expected to pay for it in something she had rather not give."

Maximilian and Carlotta set out for France at the beginning of March. On the eve of their departure from Miramar a memorandum arrived from Franz Joseph on an unpleasant subject which had been raised at the first discussion of the Mexican project between the two brothers more than two years before and to which Maximilian's attention had been drawn more recently by Rechberg. This was the contingent renunciation of the Archduke's right of succession in Austria. Maximilian determined to postpone dealing with this thorny question until his return, and he did not in any way allow it to spoil his enjoyment of the visit to Paris.

A hectic week in the French capital was devoted to a round of entertainments at which the guests, somewhat to their embarrassment, were received with imperial honours. At table Carlotta and Eugénie conversed together only in Spanish. Napoleon was in the best of spirits, and he painted a glowing account of the state of Mexico, declaring that Maximilian would find the country entirely pacified and that the loan would serve mainly for building railways and other public works. In reality he inwardly rejoiced that the Archduke had been deceived into thinking that his election was due to the expression of the Mexican national will, and he hoped that the arrangement would soon enable the French forces to be withdrawn with consequent commercial and financial advantages for France. The formal agreement, which was drawn up between Napoleon and Maximilian and initialled by the latter before his departure, reflected this feeling on Napoleon's part and did not bode altogether well for the future Emperor. It looked, for instance, as if in military matters Maximilian would be subject to the will of the French Commander-in-Chief. Also the financial stipulations, which were inserted by the crafty Finance Minister Fould, were sufficiently onerous. Mexico had to pay approximately 270 million francs for the expedition to date, 1,000 francs annually for each French soldier thereafter, as well as compensation in full on account of all claims for financial loss put forward by French subjects in the country.

To some extent Maximilian's mind was set at ease by the secret articles in the agreement which provided that the French forces in Mexico should be withdrawn only gradually according to a fixed scale, and that " however events in Europe might turn out, the assistance of France should never fail the new Empire ". But in this, as indeed in most of his other dealings with Maximilian, the French Emperor was thoroughly deceitful. " It is a bad business," Napoleon admitted to Duke Ernest of Saxe-Coburg at the time. " If I had been in his place, I should never have accepted the crown." But to both their guests the French Emperor and Empress overflowed with words of honeyed sweetness. As they were leaving Eugénie gave Maximilian a small gold medallion with the image of the Virgin. " It will bring you luck," she said. Napoleon added that Maximilian could invariably rely on him. " I beg you to count on my friendship always," he told him. " You may be sure that my support will not fail you in the fulfilment of the task you are so courageously undertaking." To his kinsman the Duke of Saxe-Coburg Maximilian bade good-bye uneasily and with tears in his eyes. " Unless you come over to me," he said, " I shall never see you again."

From Paris Maximilian and his wife crossed over to London, where they were joined by Carlotta's father and spent three days. They had the most friendly reception from Queen Victoria, but her Ministry let it be known politely but firmly that they could do nothing for the young couple beyond wishing them well. One day was spent at Claremont in Surrey, where Carlotta's grandmother the Dowager French Queen Marie Amélie was living in retirement. Carlotta found the leave-taking somewhat unnerving. As she and Maximilian embraced the old lady for the last time, the Queen Dowager burst into tears and, as if in a moment of prophetic insight, exclaimed : " They will be murdered ! They will be murdered ! "

In Vienna, whence they proceeded directly from London, a further shock awaited Maximilian. He received the following letter from his brother the Emperor :

Vienna, March 22, 1864.

Sir, my dear Brother, Archduke Ferdinand Max :
        Since, according to the information I have received, you are disposed to accept the throne of Mexico, which has been offered to you, and to found an empire there, God helping you, I find myself compelled, as supreme Head of the House of Austria and after the most mature and earnest consideration of the duties which are incumbent upon me as sovereign, to notify you that I can grant this grave and momentous act of state only on condition that you previously draw up and solemnly confirm the deed, of which I enclose a copy, renouncing your and your heirs' right of succession and inheritance in Austria. Should you be unable to consent to this and prefer to refuse the crown of Mexico which is offered you, I would take it upon myself to notify foreign countries of your refusal, and in particular the Imperial Court of France.   Franz Joseph.

Maximilian was furious on reading this letter. His reaction was immediate. He returned to Miramar, and announced his intention of declining the Mexican throne and setting out as soon as possible for Rome to explain matters to the Holy Father.

6

The consternation which the news of Maximilian's abrupt change of plans caused when it reached the Tuileries can be imagined. Napoleon routed the Austrian Ambassador, Prince Metternich, out of his bed at two o'clock in the morning of March 28 to remonstrate with him. " I really must say that I have no luck with Austria," he stormed at the Ambassador. " It looks as though I were being purposely left in the lurch at the last moment." The Emperor thereupon telegraphed frantically to Miramar. "Your Imperial Highness has entered into engagements which you are no longer free to break," he protested to Maximilian. "What would you really think of me if, when Your Imperial Highness had already reached Mexico, I were suddenly to say that I can no longer fulfil the conditions to which I have set my signature? It is impossible for you to give up going to Mexico and admit before the whole world that family interests compel you to disappoint all the hopes that France and Mexico have reposed in you. In your own interests and those of your family the matter must be settled, for the honour of the House of Hapsburg is in question."

In thus appealing to Maximilian's honour Napoleon struck at the Archduke's weakest point, for he knew that Maximilian was more than anything else anxious not to disgrace it. At the same time the French Emperor despatched a trusted agent in the person of General Frossard to Vienna to see the Austrian monarch and try to effect a solution of the difficulty. Franz Joseph remained firm. "Yes," he told Frossard, "it is a question of honour for us all ; it must be satisfied. I am making every effort. My brother must submit to the consequences of the new situation in so far as they concern his own native land." The utmost to which the Austrian Emperor would go was to write Maximilian a vague and non-committal letter in which he stated that, "in the event, which God forbid, either of your voluntarily renouncing the throne of Mexico or of circumstances arising which should decide you to leave that land again", he felt impelled by his brotherly love to assure the Archduke that "it shall remain my care to take all such measures to safeguard your position in my Empire as I shall find compatible with its interests". His brotherly care, Franz Joseph added, would also in such circumstances be extended to the Archduchess Carlotta.

This letter was dated March 31 and it arrived at Miramar on April 2. Maximilian discussed its contents carefully with his wife, and to neither of them did it appear satisfactory. On the same day the Archduke wrote to his brother requesting an assurance in some form or other than in the event of the monarchy in Mexico failing to prove of long duration, he should be reinstated in his rights. He gave this letter to his wife to take personally to Vienna, whither Carlotta hurried off on the following day.

In this crisis in Maximilian's life it must be admitted that the Archduchess stood out as by much the stronger character of the two. For three hours on April 4 she harassed her brother-in-law in the Hofburg and in her own opinion " forced him to abandon all his arguments ". Owing, however, to the fact that, as she put it, the Emperor " grasps things with difficulty ", she failed to move him in any material particular except in securing his agreement that in the event of Maximilian returning from Mexico his full financial allowance from the family exchequer should be restored to him.

Next day Carlotta received a letter from Brussels in which her father offered advice which was intended to be fortifying but which in fact tended to confuse her. " Give up nothing ", wrote Leopold. " Do not consent to any proposal of the kind." On the other hand he added these significant words. " Do not abandon the enterprise, since to do that would create grave problems." Carlotta immediately returned to the attack and at first seemed to move her brother-in-law, who she told Maximilian " had a strong sense of justice " and, " moreover, is very anxious for you to go to Mexico ". But any signs of giving way which Franz Joseph may have shown were momentary. His opposition hardened, although he showed Carlotta personally no ill-will. He told her that he would even come to Miramar himself to try to persuade Maximilian to acquiesce.

On the evening of April 6 Carlotta received a telegram from her father which had obviously been sent after Leopold had been in touch with Napoleon. " It is now almost impossible to break with the Mexicans ", wired the Belgian King. " To do so would cause the most appalling confusion. We must attempt to reach a compromise." It seems that it was this message which broke down what remained of Carlotta's determination to resist the renunciation proposals. Unfortunately, too, the Archduchess Sophie, with whom her personal relations were excellent, declined to interfere, as she was by no means convinced that the Mexican venture would bring her son good fortune. Seeing that nothing further was to be gained in Vienna, Carlotta prepared to bow to the inevitable and assumed Maximilian's acquiescence as a foregone conclusion. Before leaving on April 8 she therefore telegraphed her father that the Emperor would come to Miramar next morning and that she and Maximilian would sail for Mexico two days later.

Back at Miramar she found Maximilian a prey to the most gloomy thoughts and a picture of abject misery. A short talk, however, convinced him that he must yield to his brother or else yield the crown which was almost within his grasp. He immediately wrote both to Napoleon and Franz Joseph informing them of his decision. " I have kept my plighted word ", he told the French Emperor, " by which I undertook, out of sincere attachment to your person, to make every sacrifice compatible with my honour. My conduct in this whole affair has always been upright and straightforward."

At eight o'clock on the morning of April 9 the Austrian Emperor Franz Joseph stepped out of the special train which had brought him from Vienna to the private station at Miramar. Maximilian led his brother straight to the library, where a long and not unemotional interview took place. No one knows exactly what transpired at this meeting, but when the two brothers emerged into the great hall of the castle, where other members of the family and various officials were assembled, it was plain that both men had been deeply affected. Then in the presence of seven Hapsburg Archdukes, including his two younger brothers, and the chief Ministers of State, the Archduke Ferdinand Maximilian signed the document which deprived him of the rights which he had inherited at his birth.

As soon as this ceremony was over the Emperor returned to the imperial train. Maximilian accompanied him on to the platform for a final leave-taking. As Franz Joseph was about to enter his carriage, a strange presentiment appeared to come over him. He suddenly turned round and, walking quickly towards his brother, stretched out his arms to him. " Max," he said, and his voice broke with tears. The two brothers embraced for the last time. It was indeed the last time they were to see each other in this world.

7

On the following day, which was a Sunday, the Mexican delegation which had come to make Maximilian the formal offer of the crown arrived from Trieste and were received by Maximilian and Carlotta in the presence of a large gathering, including members of their future imperial household as well as the principal notabilities of Trieste and Napoleon's representative, General Frossard. Gutiérrez de Estrada made one of his usual flowery speeches which suggested that in this role he represented the united people of his country. Pale and restless from worry and lack of sleep, the Archduke stood beside a table in the great hall on which lay the various " acts of adhesion " to the new Empire which the French Commander-in-Chief had secured. " Now I can comply with the conditional promise which I made you six months ago," he said, " and declare here, as solemnly I do declare, that with the help of the Almighty I accept from the hands of the Mexican nation the crown which it offers me." When this speech ended, the Abbot of Lacroma stepped forward and administered the imperial oath by virtue of which Maximilian swore to " promote through all the means within my power the welfare and prosperity of the nation, to defend its independence, and to preserve the whole of its territory ". With this the Mexican flag was run up on the castle tower, the Austrian frigate *Bellona* which lay in the roads fired a salute of twenty-one guns, and the spectators cheered lustily, " Long live the Emperor Maximilian ! Long live the Empress Carlotta ! " It was the last occasion on which Maximilian's consort was to be addressed in the former Italian style. Henceforward she was no longer Carlotta but Carlota, the name by which she was to be known among her new subjects and by which she now subscribed herself.

A Te Deum was then sung in the chapel of the castle, and this was followed by the signing of the convention which had previously been initialled by Napoleon and Maximilian in Paris. " Maximilian has accepted ", Carlota telegraphed to her father. " Give us your blessing." The Emperor-elect next proceeded to make various appointments. Almonte was to act as Regent until his arrival in Mexico, Hidalgo accepted the post of Mexican

Minister in Paris, and another member of the delegation, Velásquez de Léon, was entrusted with the formation of a ministry. Gutiérrez de Estrada, however, declined the Mexican Legation in Vienna which was offered him, preferring not to risk the possibility of suddenly being summoned to his native country, which he had not seen for a quarter of a century.

These ceremonial and official proceedings proved too much for Maximilian, who was now on the verge of a nervous collapse. Towards evening he withdrew to his private apartments in the so-called " garden house " in the castle grounds, where his physician, Dr. Jilek, found him sitting at a table with his arms stretched out and his head buried in his hands. " If someone were to tell me that the whole thing was broken off," he said, " I should jump with joy. But Carlota ? " He shrugged his shoulders. A little later he made a pathetic effort to pull himself together for the state banquet which he was expected to attend that night, but the doctor, who feared a complete breakdown, absolutely forbade him to appear. The young Empress accordingly represented her husband on this occasion and did the honours without showing the slightest signs of fatigue. At the same time their departure, which had been arranged for April 11, was postponed for several days.

During this period when the new Emperor was under medical observation his wife deputized for him with untiring energy. She received innumerable visits of congratulation, welcomed deputations and attended to the details of the forthcoming journey, which was to take place in the warship *Novara*. Whilst he was at lunch alone with Dr. Jilek in the garden house on the 11th Carlota brought him a congratulatory telegram from Napoleon. He waved her away. " I tell you," he said, " I don't want anyone to talk to me about Mexico now." Although he proceeded to draft a letter in reply to the telegram, its contents did not satisfy Carlota. She redrafted the letter with her own hand. Thanks to Maximilian's trust in Napoleon's friendship, she wrote, he hoped to bring to a happy issue " the noble mission " with which the Mexican people had entrusted him. " Your flag and its civilizing influence will help me in this work," her pen ran on, " while for my part I shall be happy to see drawn closer the bonds of mutual friendship which unite us to one another and will unite our two empires."

By April 14 Maximilian had recovered sufficiently to be pronounced by his doctor fit to set out on the long voyage across the Atlantic. He spent the morning wandering sadly through the rooms of the castle and taking a last look at the terraces and gardens, all of which he had planned and laid out with such care. He went through the painful business of saying good-bye to the household staff, and for the first time for four days he felt strong enough to receive the Mayor of Trieste, who expressed the genuine feelings of that municipality for the departing Archduke. " Miramar, your cherished retreat, is reflected in the waters that bathe Trieste. Between Miramar and this city exist bonds of affection that can never be broken. This affection runs in the blood of the people and will be transmitted to our sons." Maximilian was deeply touched. He gave the Mayor the sum of 20,000 florins to endow a fund for the poor of Trieste, and he expressed the hope that its people should always continue to enjoy the gardens of Miramar. " On abandoning Europe ", he said, his voice choking with sobs, " I know how dear are the recollections of gratitude which link me to that city. This recollection will follow me abroad as a powerful consolation and a happy augury for the future."

By now an immense throng had gathered on the jetty in front of the castle to watch the Emperor and Express embark. At two o'clock in the afternoon Maximilian with Carlota leaning on his arm walked down the marble steps amid salvos from the castle cannon, shouts of " *Auf Wiedersehn* " and the strains of special Mexican music composed for the occasion and played by the band of the Trieste garrison. At the last moment a telegram was put into Maximilian's hand. It was from his mother. " Farewell ", it read. " Our blessing — Papa's and mine. Our prayers and tears accompany you. May God protect and guide you. Farewell for the last time on your native soil where, alas, we may see you no more ! We bless you again and again from our deeply sorrowing hearts."

Maximilian was visibly affected. As he stepped aboard the gaily-bedecked boat, with its red-and-gold embroidered canopy, which was to take him and the rest of the imperial party to the *Novara*, tears streamed down his cheeks. " Look ! " said Carlota to one of her ladies-in-waiting. " Look at poor Max. How he is crying ! " For the first time the Mexican flag was flying from an Austrian vessel. Meanwhile the guns boomed, the band played on, and the rowers dipped their oars in the smooth water. It was a great send-off. Maximilian and Carlota were on their way at last to their new empire beyond the seas.

VI. *Imperial Mexico*

ONCE surrounded by his native element, as he regarded the sea, Maximilian soon recovered his old self, and on the day after the *Novara* had set sail the new Emperor was seen on deck talking cheerfully to members of his suite and the crew. He was particularly pleased on passing the island of Brioni and the end of the Istrian peninsula to see the fishing fleet in those waters which had assembled to give him a great ovation. On April 18 the ship dropped anchor off Cività Vecchia, where a special train was waiting to convey the imperial party to Rome. Arrangements had been made for them to stay as Gutiérrez's guests in the Palazzo Marescotti. Night had fallen by the time they had installed themselves in this luxurious residence, but, showing no signs of fatigue, they immediately hurried off to see the Coliseum by moonlight and did not return until the small hours.

Next morning, after an early Mass at St. Peter's, the ladies put on the customary high-necked black dresses with long sleeves and veils and, accompanied by the gentlemen in uniform, drove to the Vatican for the audience which had been arranged with the Holy Father. Pope Pius IX walked through several rooms to greet the imperial couple and their retinue, and after everyone had knelt to receive the papal blessing His Holiness conducted the Emperor and Empress to his private study. Here the Supreme Pontiff proceeded to admonish his visitors in what Carlota described as " a touching allocution ", observing that although " the rights of the people are great and it is necessary to satisfy them, the rights of the Church are greater and more sacred ". After listening to this homily the new sovereigns received Communion from the Pope's hands and remained to luncheon as his guests.

In the afternoon they drove out to see the ex-King and Queen of Naples, who were living as exiles in the Eternal City. That night Gutiérrez de Estrada gave a magnificent banquet and reception in his Palazzo to which three hundred guests were invited. Carlota looked radiant with a crown of diamonds and won all hearts by her beauty. Led by the almost youthful figure of Cardinal Antonelli, the Papal Secretary of State, whose " clever, sharp finely-cut face " also attracted attention, the guests included a great number of dignitaries of the Church. As she studied them one of Carlota's ladies-in-waiting, Countess Paula Kollonitz, asked herself how many of these well-fed clerics " were induced by the love of God, by humility, self-sacrifice, anxiety for the welfare of their own souls and those of their fellow men to follow this calling ", and she regretfully came to the conclusion that they betrayed " scarcely a single trait which could give evidence of such feelings ".

Next morning the Pope returned the imperial couple's call. Maximilian and Carlota received him on their knees at the top of the staircase in the Palazzo Marescotti, and the ultramontane old Gutiérrez literally wept for joy that such an honour should have fallen to the lot of his house. After the usual benedictions His Holiness took his leave and was escorted to his carriage by the Emperor, who promptly fell on his knees once more in the street, which by this time was packed with interested spectators. Pius was seen to embrace Maximilian effusively. " The Pope never blessed any prince with such emotion ", wrote the German historian Gregorovius, who was living in Rome at the time, " nor dismissed one with such fervent good wishes ". Later the same day the imperial party returned by train to Città Vecchia and resumed their voyage. But the Roman wiseacres shook their heads, and one of them in the guise of Pasquin issued a solemn warning. He observed ironically that " the French knew very well what they were doing in rigorously closing the streets and guarding the Emperor's lodging, for they would not find anyone else to accept the crown of Mexico in a hurry ". The pasquinade ran thus:

> Maximiliano, non te fidare
> Torna sollicito a Miramare ;
> Il trono fradicio de Montexuma
> E nappo gallico, colmo di spuma ;
> Il " timeo Danaos " a qui non ricorda ;
> Sotto la clamide trova la corda ! [1]

---

[1] " Beware, Maximilian ! Return promptly to Miramar. The frail throne of the Montezumas is a Gallic snare — a cup full only of froth. He who does not remember the ' timeo Danaos ' shall instead of the purple find a halter."

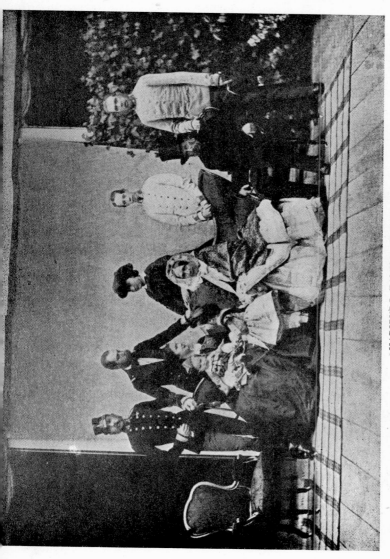

HAPSBURG FAMILY GROUP

From a photograph taken about 1864

Standing, from left to right: Emperor Franz Joseph, Archduke Maximilian, Archduchess Carlota, Archduke Ludwig Viktor, Archduke Karl Ludwig. Sitting, from left to right: Empress Elizabeth with her children Crown Prince Rudolf and Archduchess Gisela, Archduchess Sophie, Archduke Francis Charles

DEPARTURE OF MAXIMILIAN AND CARLOTA FROM MIRAMAR, APRIL 14, 1864.

From the water-colour by Cesare Dell Acqua in the National Library in Vienna

On April 24 the *Novara* steamed into Algeciras Bay where a pleasant surprise awaited the imperial couple. From the Spanish as well as the British shore royal salutes of guns were fired, "thereby", remarked Carlota, "putting us on official terms with those powers". Both the Emperor and his consort were particularly touched by this attention from the fortress cannon in Gibraltar, which made some slight amends for Leopold's failure to obtain any substantial assistance for the new Empire from his niece's Government. General Sir William Codrington was still Governor of the "Rock", and he received Maximilian and Carlota as old friends. The "galleries" and gardens were again inspected, and later they all went to the races which were being held that day. Here the Emperor enjoyed himself wandering about among the spectators, but Carlota remained in the Governor's carriage. After the Governor and his family had been entertained to dinner on board, anchors were again weighed to the accompaniment of loud salvos from the shore batteries.

A day was spent in Madeira which Maximilian felt he must see once more. Thence the *Novara*'s course was set for Martinique. This part of the voyage does not seem to have been particularly agreeable. For one thing some rough weather was encountered ; nearly everyone suffered from sea-sickness, which copious draughts of sherry and curaçoa apparently did little to alleviate. A somewhat humiliating incident also occurred. The *Novara* had been fitted with auxiliary steam-engines, but unfortunately by the time she was ten days out of Funchal the supply of coal ran so low that she was only able to make three knots an hour. There was nothing to be done but for the French warship *Themis*, which had ample supplies of coal in her bunkers, to take the *Novara* in tow, and in spite of the grumblings of many of the *Novara*'s passengers and crew that they should thus be "under the necessity of begging French assistance", the Austrian vessel arrived within sight of Fort de France in this manner.

While the *Novara* was bunkering in Fort de France harbour, the Emperor and Empress were entertained by the courteous Governor, Rear-Admiral Maussion de Condé, and his strong-minded wife, known for her overbearing ways as the *Gouvernante*. The latter struck the visitors as " a small plain lady who rejoices throughout the colony in a quarrelsome and violent character and whose name is mentioned with but little love — the tenderer feelings of her bosom she appears to lavish on dogs and parrots ". A somewhat exhausting excursion to the lower slopes of Mount Vauclin was undertaken, while in the evening the Savane with its statue of Napoleon's Josephine was illuminated and the natives danced the bambula for the diversion of the imperial guests.

The next port of call was Port Royal in Jamaica, which in those days contained the principal British naval establishment in the Western Hemisphere and was the headquarters of the Commander-in-Chief of the North America and West Indies station. The Commander-in-Chief, Admiral Sir James Hope, saluted from his flagship and subsequently conducted the Emperor and Empress to Kingston, where they were received by the Governor, Mr. Edward Eyre. This remarkable British pro-Consul had become famous some years before as an explorer in opening up Central Australia, and he was shortly to raise a storm of controversy on account of the manner in which he suppressed the negro rebellion which broke out in Jamaica in the following year. The party later made an excursion into the interior of the island and, after partaking of an excellent lunch at Government House, returned to the *Novara* and continued the voyage.

During this period, and indeed throughout their whole time at sea, the Emperor and Empress worked hard making plans for the new government and Court and also practising their Spanish. Maximilian assembled the various members of his suite every day for several hours and discussed his proposed arrangements with them. He drafted instructions for the imperial chancery, which he divided into two sections — a civil cabinet and a military cabinet — to deal with their respective affairs of state. The taciturn forty-five-year-old Belgian Felix Eloin, a civil engineer who had been strongly recommended by King Leopold, was appointed head of the civil cabinet, much to Scherzenlechner's annoyance, as the ex-valet coveted this post for himself. The Emperor further appointed a Master of Ceremonies and a Lord Chamberlain, and he personally sketched out the heads of a work on Court ceremonial which he intended to complete in Mexico as a standard authority on the subject.

One other document to which Maximilian set his hand on this momentous voyage was a declaration drafted by Carlota to the effect that he had been made to sign the renunciation of his rights of succession in Austria without previously having read this so-called Family Pact and " subject to the most notorious moral pressure ". This recorded protest was witnessed by Eloin and Schertzenlechner who confirmed its contents, and copies were set aside for deposit in the Archives in Mexico City and for despatch to the Mexican Legation in Vienna. There is no doubt that Maximilian's mind was seriously troubled by the renunciation, which he felt had been forcibly extracted from him at Miramar, but this protest was an unfortunate method of setting his mind at rest. For one thing, he had actually seen a copy of the renunciation document before he signed it, as his brother Franz Joseph had sent him the draft with his letter of March 22. Furthermore, the policy of bringing such underlings as Eloin and Schertzenlechner into this delicate and controversial matter was very questionable.

Four days after the *Novara* left Port Royal the coast of Yucatan came into view and Maximilian had his first glimpse of the empire which he had been called upon to rule. Carlota's lady-in-waiting, Countess Kollonitz, watched him on deck as " quietly and cheerfully he gazed into the distance ".

2

Towards noon on May 28, 1864, the *Novara* steamed past the fortress of San Juan de Ulloa into the harbour of Vera Cruz. The *Themis*, which had gone on ahead, was lying with several other French men-of-war in the roads, but Maximilian purposely gave his Flag Captain instructions not to go among the French fleet so as to avoid identifying, in the minds of the Mexicans, the Austrian vessel with those of the dominant foreign power. Eventually anchors were dropped some distance away.

An ominous silence followed in the harbour. The heat of the day was then at its height, but this could scarcely be considered a valid excuse on the part of the local authorities for neglecting to welcome their new ruler immediately. At length, after some considerable time, the French naval commander, Admiral Bosse, came aboard the *Novara* in an extremely bad humour, which he was at no pains to conceal, because the Austrian vessel had not anchored among the French ships. Showing " an unparalleled want of consideration and propriety ", the Frenchman informed the Emperor that the *Novara*'s present position was undoubtedly the most contagious spot in the harbour : if they were to remain there a single night they would certainly all catch yellow fever. He also painted a lurid picture of the dangers which beset the traveller on the road from Vera Cruz to the capital, and he went on to say that a plot had been formed among Juárez's supporters to ambush and capture the Emperor and Empress while they were on their way.

In the face of this unfriendly reception Maximilian maintained what Countess Kollonitz characteristically described as " a sarcastic tranquillity ". Unfortunately there was a considerable element of truth in what the Admiral said, although out of pique he had made the prospect as unattractive as possible. The roads were notoriously unsafe and yellow fever was endemic in the port. In fact, General Almonte, who as Regent was naturally expected to meet his sovereign, had been waiting some distance inland at Orizaba so as to escape the contagion, and the municipal authorities at Vera Cruz were all absent, as they willingly seized the opportunity which the Regent's presence at Orizaba provided to go and fetch him there. It was therefore not until evening that Almonte came hurrying on board, profuse with apologies and respects. The decision was then taken to remain where they were for the night and not to begin the difficult and dangerous journey inland until the following day.

After hearing an early Mass on deck, the imperial party were rowed ashore at five o'clock in the morning. There were few people about to welcome the new rulers. Here and there a triumphal arch had been hastily erected and some paid hands fired off several rockets. Otherwise, to quote a member of the imperial suite, the reception was " excessively chilling ". The Emperor and Empress drove through practically deserted streets to the Plaza, which was then the terminus for the railway which the French had hurriedly constructed a short distance inland with a view to conveying their troops as rapidly as possible out of the fever zone. It took some time to install everyone in the rickety carriages with their seats of plaited straw and venetian blinds, since the imperial entourage consisted of eighty-five persons in all, together with over five hundred pieces of luggage.

At Soledad, about twenty-five miles along the line, a stop was made for breakfast. A considerable crowd of natives had collected, a band hired by Almonte played appropriate airs, and Maximilian made a short speech in Spanish. The reception, though warmer than that accorded by the Veracruzanos, could not be described as exactly cordial. However, the atmosphere improved progressively as the party got further into the interior. At Loma Alta, twenty miles beyond Soledad, the railway came to an end, and the travellers changed into carriages and cumbersome *diligencias*.

Carlota's introduction to Mexican roads was almost terrifying. On the first day she confessed that " things looked very queer and I should not have been surprised if Juárez himself had appeared with some hundreds of guerrillas ". Fortunately this did not happen, " thanks to the skill of the French generals ", said the Empress, " but we passed through many most suspicious-looking spots where several thousand partisans lay concealed ". In the middle of a dense forest near the river Chiquihuite they encountered a heavy rainstorm amounting almost to a cloud-burst, and to add to their troubles a wheel of the imperial carriage broke, so that the Emperor and Empress were obliged to continue the journey " in a republican stage-coach " to Córdoba, which they did not reach until two o'clock in the morning. There they learned that the regular mail-coach plying between Mexico City and Vera Cruz had just been held up by Juáristas and robbed. " That day's journey has left a strange impression on my mind ", wrote Carlota afterwards. " The Mexicans kept apologizing for the road — we had passed through half a dozen gullies with rocks several yards long — and we kept assuring them that we did not mind in the least, but as a matter of fact it was beyond description and we needed all our youth and good-humour to escape being crippled with cramp or breaking a rib. . . ." During this remarkable journey " one of the coaches following us completely upset with six gentlemen in it, among them M. Velásquez de Léon who had to get out of the window, and that merely because it had been raining for less than a quarter of an hour ".

Popular sentiment for the visitors seemed to improve with the appearance of the country. Flowers and triumphal arches were in generous evidence at Orizaba, " as pretty a place as one might see," said Carlota, " reminding one of Italy and the southern Tyrol ". The steep ascent of the rocky plateau above Orizaba was made on horseback, and during this part of the journey they were met by General Brincourt, who commanded the French garrison in Puebla and who had ridden out from that town to meet them. The French General informed the Emperor and Empress that the brilliant Juárist General Porfirio Diáz had been to the neighbourhood with a body of guerrillas hoping to ambush the imperial suite but that fortunately he and his band had been dispersed.

At Puebla they met with quite an ovation which had been carefully staged by the French military authorities, and this was repeated at Guadalupe on the outskirts of the capital, where a visit was paid to the famous Shrine of the Virgin. The reception on their arrival at Guadalupe was such as Carlota said she had never seen before. " On the following day ", she wrote, " a most affectionate demonstration took place in the great plaza, which was thronged with people. It was in the evening ; we had been on the balcony for a few moments when shouts were heard of ' Let our Emperor come out ! ' We returned, and then there was such applause that one heard nothing but a confused and inarticulate noise." The sight of the image of the Virgin of Guadalupe also touched the Empress greatly. " It was ", she added, " as it were a great act of historic reparation that homage should be rendered to the protectress of the Indians by a descendant of Charles V on the point of ascending the throne of Montezuma."

What particularly impressed Maximilian and Carlota on this journey was the realization that of the eight millions of their subjects who inhabited the 767,000 square miles of the empire nearly five millions were of pure Indian stock, about two millions were of negro or of mixed descent and barely a million were white. " Nearly all the Indians can read and write ", noted the Empress ; " the people are in the highest degree intelligent, and if the clergy instructed them as they ought they would be an enlightened race. We have seen very advanced schools in which the children knew things they certainly do not know in Austria, others in which we were questioned as to whether God had hands or ears or as to what was the difference between the real Holy Virgin and the one in the Church — and that at Puebla, the clerical city *par excellence* ! " It must be admitted that the Indian elements of the population evinced the greatest interest and curiosity in the person of their new Emperor, for there was a legend among them that one day a fair-haired prince would come from the east to restore peace, liberty and happiness to their race, which had previously been so oppressed by the white peoples. One of the ablest Mexican Generals, Tomás Mejía, who had been a partisan of Miramón's and had later declared for the Empire, was a pure Indian.

The journey to the capital also convinced the Empress that Mexico was ripe for imperial rule. " From all that I have seen ", she wrote to the Empress Eugénie in Paris, " there is room for a monarchy in this country, and it meets the general requirements of the population ; none the less, however, it remains a gigantic experiment, for one has to struggle against the desert, the distance, the roads, and the most utter chaos. . . . Things will go on well here if Your Majesties stand by us, since they must go on and we mean them to go on; but it is an appalling task, for when a country has spent forty years of its existence in destroying all that it possessed in the way of resources and government, it cannot be put right in a day."

3

From Guadalupe Maximilian and Carlota made their state entry into Mexico City on Sunday, June 12. There an abundance

145

of triumphal arches, flowers and red carpet greeted them. The streets through which Their Majesties passed were packed with people, who, at the prompting of the joint efforts of the Conservatives and the French, combined to give the impression of a great popular demonstration in favour of the new rulers. The imperial cortège was led by a certain Colonel Miguel López at the head of a Mexican regiment of lancers, then followed a French regiment of Chasseurs d'Afrique, then came the state-coach flanked by the French Generals Bazaine and Neigre. The imperial attendants, occupying no less than sixty coaches, brought up the rear.

At the entrance to the capital the Emperor and Empress were received by the Municipal Prefect, who handed Maximilian the customary keys of the city. The sovereigns next proceeded to the Cathedral, where they were received by Archbishop Labastida and a Te Deum was sung. Surrounded by an immense throng of spectators and escorted by the Cathedral clergy, they then walked across the Zocalo to the *Palacio Nacional*, which was henceforward to be their principal town residence. This was a long, rambling, two-storied building which looked more like a fortified barracks than an imperial palace. During the recent years of civil struggle it had fallen into sad disrepair, which the news of the Emperor's impending arrival had done little to remove. Everything had an air of hasty improvisation. The members of the imperial suite, who had come on in advance of the main party several days before, found nothing ready. Builders and decorators were still hammering away in the imperial apartments which now gave the impression of having been most hurriedly renovated. There was no large hall or reception room : all the rooms opened off from each other and were low and narrow like corridors. The floors were of stone covered with tiles over which carpets had been laid. The Empress's drawing-room reminded her lady-in-waiting, Paula Kollonitz, of a tastelessly decorated room in a European hotel. Her bedroom, which had been done up in a shade of dark blue, was rather better, and it contained a pretty silver dressing-table which was stated to be the gift of the ladies of the capital. Generally speaking, the place gave the impression of inexpressible dreariness, not to mention discomfort. Maximilian, however, professed himself quite contented with his new dwelling, as indeed he was with his reception generally, and as for Carlota she declared she was " enchanted " with everything. " Our reception everywhere was cordial and sincere," wrote the Emperor, " free from all pretence and from that nauseating official servility which one very often finds in Europe on such occasions."

The Emperor lost no time in getting down to work. He reviewed the personnel of the provisional government which had been established by Almonte and made some significant changes. Señor Arroyo, the Minister of Foreign Affairs, had granted Napoleon III a mining concession in the wealthy province of Sonora. Before leaving Europe Maximilian told the French Emperor he could not agree to this exploitation, which he envisaged as the preliminary step in the handing over of the province to France. Maximilian now formally cancelled the arrangement and dismissed Arroyo. He entrusted the portfolio of Foreign Affairs to José Fernando Ramírez, a Liberal, who was politically so closely affiliated with Juárez's party that he had refused to join the junta which had offered Maximilian the crown. Almonte himself the Emperor shelved with the sinecure appointment of " Grand Marshal of the Court and Minister of the Imperial House ". The fact was Maximilian intended to rule as little as possible with the aid of foreigners. He wished, as he told Velásquez de Léon, " to be before all things a Mexican and to place the interests of his people above all others ". Accordingly he issued a general amnesty to all political prisoners, including those already under sentence, and he recommended the prefects to behave as conciliatorily and deal as leniently as possible with any of the monarch's opponents who came within their jurisdiction. He also decreed that he would grant public audiences to suitors regardless of rank and position every Sunday in the National Palace.

Carlota viewed everything through rose-coloured glasses, and she saw the Mexicans as a simple, docile people who had been led astray by unscrupulous military adventurers. " They have great confidence in Max, and they expect everything of him ", she wrote to her grandmother a few days after her arrival in the capital. " Max has chosen as Minister of Foreign Affairs a distinguished man who possesses the sympathy of all parties ; indeed we frequently have at our table those who have formerly served Juárez. What is so surprising here is that for the first time the Government is taking its task seriously. Proclamations are no longer issued in the public squares with a grand rumble of words ; instead there is hard work and unremitting efforts to improve the general lot of the country. The people understand this, and as they have never been accustomed to anyone's goodwill in the past, their enthusiasm is growing all the time and has already developed almost into idolatry." The Empress did not realize, nor for that matter did her husband, that the political elements which counted for anything in the country were more guided by personal interests than popular welfare, and that they consequently regarded Maximilian's initial proceedings with either alarm or suspicion. The Conservatives were amazed to see Almonte shelved and Ramírez and others like him elevated to posts of importance in the State. The Liberals, on the other hand, looked on with few exceptions with feelings of distrust or even hostility.

After a week in the National Palace, Carlota decided to move out to the castle of Chapultepec, which was situated on a hill in a delightful park in the suburbs of the capital. The castle had been built for one of the Spanish viceroys towards the end of the eighteenth century on the spot where the Aztec Emperor Montezuma's palace had once stood. It commanded a splendid view of the city and indeed the whole valley with the mountains beyond. The building itself, however, in spite of a hasty renovation, left much to be desired. Its interior presented an unpleasant picture of dirt and neglect which its new tenants determined to correct without delay. On their first night in this new abode they were so troubled with vermin that the Emperor had to get up and continue his slumbers on a billiard table, while Carlota and other members of the household had their beds carried out to the terrace. The Empress kept asking her ladies-in-waiting for supplies of insect powder.

Despite this unpromising beginning, both the Emperor and Empress quickly came to like Chapultepec, and in fact they greatly preferred it to the uncomfortable and stuffy National Palace. Maximilian particularly enjoyed working there and would think nothing of rising at four o'clock in the morning to begin his labours. "You may well imagine", he wrote to his younger brother Karl Ludwig, "that I am overwhelmed with work of every sort, but one is glad to work when one has an end in view and one hopes to be useful to one's fellow men ! . . . The surroundings of the capital have quite the character of our unforgettable Lombardy, glorious pastures, fine trees and abundance of water. We live by turns in the vast *Palacio Nacional* in the city, an old and venerable building with eleven hundred windows, and at Chapultepec, the Schönbrunn of Mexico, a fascinating country residence on a basalt crag, surrounded by Montezuma's famous giant trees, and offering a prospect the like of which for beauty I have seen perhaps only at Sorrento." About this place Carlota echoed her husband's feelings. "We are enchanted with Chapultepec, where we are already living," she wrote to the Empress Eugénie on June 22 ; "the view is perhaps one of the finest in the world. I think it surpasses Naples. The air here is excellent and suits us well. All this offers us ample compensation for the patience we shall have to exercise in other respects."

Carlota continued to talk and write in a vein of unbridled optimism. On August 10 she wrote to her grandmother in England : "When I think that we have only been here since May 28, I see we have not wasted our time. More than anything else the government is distinguishing itself by its great forethought and it is that which impresses the people, accustomed as they have been to seeing laws passed one day and repealed the next." On the same day as the Empress wrote these lines Maximilian left the capital for a two and a half months' tour of the interior of his kingdom. During his absence Carlota was designated to act as regent, and with marked alacrity she took his place at the council table and deputized for him at a variety of functions, including the Sunday audiences to the public, thus following the "good example" of the Empress Eugénie, as she took care to tell her. She also busied herself visiting schools and charitable institutions.

Maximilian's tour was satisfactory as well as instructive to himself, although the favourable reception he generally met with was undoubtedly encouraged by the successes which the French army were enjoying at the same time. While he detected many abuses on the part of various officials and in fact speedily became convinced that " the whole administration must be placed on a new footing " by getting rid of the dead-wood, on the other hand in his private letters to various members of his family in Vienna he never lost an opportunity of reminding them that " all the stiffness and trumpery with which we uselessly hamper ourselves in Europe, and shall continue to hamper ourselves for years, has long been got over here ". September 16, which was Mexican Independence Day, found him in the village of Dolores whence the patriot priest Hidalgo had set out to raise the standard of revolt in 1811. The Emperor, who felt extremely nervous, addressed a vast multitude in Spanish from a window in Hidalgo's house. " It went off well, thank God," he wrote afterwards, " and the enthusiasm was indescribable." During the journey he met Uraga, a former Juárist General who had recently come over to the Imperialist side. " *Olvidemos las sombras pasadas*," [1] said Maximilian as they sat down to dinner together.

" At Morelia, the most dangerous and politically trouble-some city in the Empire," continued Maximilian in the account which he gave Napoleon, " I was received with enthusiasm such as I have never before seen in my life ; I could hardly get my horse to go forward, and when I was on foot, the crowd pressed close round me." Only one misfortune befell the Emperor during the journey : for part of the time he was laid up with an inflamed throat which developed into an attack of quinsy. His recovery left him in somewhat low spirits for a short while, although by the time Carlota came out to meet him at Toluca on the final stage of his journey he felt quite fit again. " During this tour through a part of the country remark-able for its wealth ", he wrote on his return, " I was able to see that the inhabitants of the provinces are better able to appre-ciate noble motives and are more devotedly patriotic than those of the capital, who have unfortunately been under the bad

[1] " We will forget the shadows of the past."

influence of the foreign element which has for too long past been used to taking advantage of disorder and revolution to make their fortune by any means."

Both the Emperor and his consort appeared quite content with their role at this time, and did not regret the vital decision taken at Miramar earlier in the year. " We both feel quite comfortable in our new position ", wrote Maximilian to his family in Austria. " We trust in God and are very contented. We are helped on every side with touching affection. Neither Carlota nor I wish ourselves back again. . . . I do not regret the present. The peaceful joy of life may be lacking, but there is a deep satisfaction in the thought that one is serving humanity, and that I can now contribute a few drops of oil to the great lamp of enlightenment, that it is granted to me to take part in that work of improvement at which men of goodwill have been working for hundreds, nay, thousands of years. Though here I no longer have the breezes of the Adriatic or the air of Lacroma, I am living in a free country, where principles prevail of which you at home cannot even dream."

As for the Empress, she was likewise full of confidence and ambition for their common work. " Our task is great for there is everything to be done ", she wrote about the same time. " However, progress is already considerable and the country is with us. I feel perfectly happy here, and so does Max. A life of action suits us ; we were too young to do nothing."

4

At the conclusion of his first tour of the provinces the Emperor remarked that the worst features of the country which he had so far encountered were three classes in the community — the judicial functionaries, the army officers and the greater part of the clergy. " None of them are familiar with their duties and they live for money alone ", he said. " The judges are corrupt, the officers have no sense of honour and the clergy are lacking in Christian charity and morality." He had therefore appointed commissions to reorganize the judicial and military branches of the Government. " As regards the clergy,"

Maximilian felt that " if they are to be improved, what is necessary is a good concordat and a nuncio with a good Christian heart and an iron will. Only thus will the clergy be reformed, made Catholic (which they are not at present), and acquire the good influence which they have hitherto not possessed."

Of the various problems which confronted Maximilian at the outset of his rule none was more difficult and vexatious than the position of the Catholic Church. The Conservatives and clericals who had been mainly responsible for calling the Emperor to the throne were naturally anxious that the ecclesiastical policy of Juárez, which had found expression in the secularization of Church property and the suppression of religious orders, should be reversed and that the property seized should be handed back to the clergy. Maximilian, on the other hand, who held a liberal outlook in ecclesiastical matters, was in favour of complete freedom of worship and, far from reversing the secularization law, wished to see the process completed, thereby hoping, as he put it, to pull off a " splendid stroke of business " for the national exchequer.

At their interview in April the Pope had promised Maximilian that he would accredit a nuncio to the Mexican Court without delay. It was not until two months after Maximilian had arrived in Mexico that the papal curia announced the appointment of Monsignore Meglia, a pompous prelate who had been Archbishop of Damascus, to the post of nuncio. But even then His Holiness appeared in no hurry to despatch his representative to Mexico. Eventually Maximilian became impatient and made Ramírez, the Foreign Minister, inform the Mexican Minister in the Vatican City that if the nuncio did not put in an appearance very soon he (the Emperor) " would act on his own initiative and take such measures as the situation demanded ". The truth was, of course, that the Mexican clergy, led by Archbishop Labastida, had been complaining volubly to Rome, and although he took steps to hasten his nuncio's departure, the Pope at the same time informed Maximilian with marked bitterness that so far the hopes of the Church in the new Empire had been thoroughly disappointed.

The nuncio eventually arrived in Mexico City at the begin-

ning of December, " without demonstration of any sort,—
arrangements had been made to prevent them if any had been
intended," to quote Carlota, who now shared her husband's
ecclesiastical views. He duly presented his credentials to the
Emperor and at the same time delivered a letter from the Supreme
Pontiff which contained a number of drastic demands, including
the annulment of all the reforming laws, the restoration of the
Catholic to the exclusion of all other denominations, and the
removal of all restrictions which subordinated the Church to
the State.

At this audience the Emperor submitted his own suggestions
in the shape of counter-proposals which he hoped would form
the basis of a concordat, and which were in fact very different
from those put forward by the nuncio. They included liberty
of worship and the abandonment of Rome's claims to the
nationalized Church property. Since, however, Maximilian was
convinced that the question could be settled " in an entirely
Catholic but also perfectly liberal sense ", he further proposed
that the Catholic faith should become the State religion and
that the State should assume responsibility for payment of the
clergy's stipends.

Monsignore Meglia said nothing at the time but immediately
reported what had happened at this meeting to the Archbishop.
They thereupon summoned a meeting of the clergy at which
it was agreed that the Emperor's views were utterly opposed
to His Holiness's wishes. Two days later, being pressed by
Maximilian for a reply to his proposals, the nuncio stated coldly
that he had received no instructions to comply with such
demands but that the Pope had clearly defined his point of view
in the letter which he had brought with him.

Maximilian and Carlota were thunderstruck. It was now
painfully evident that the Empire had lost the support of the
clergy and the Vatican, and that there was no longer any hope
of concluding a concordat in the present circumstances. Furious
beyond words, the Empress irreverently suggested to Bazaine
that all he could do now was to throw the nuncio out of the
window, for his obstinacy and pigheadedness were beyond comparison. " In addition to this ", she wrote to the Empress

Eugénie, " he ventures to maintain that the country, which is simply steeped in hatred of theocracy, wishes the property of the clergy to be restored to them. It is just as if someone were to come up in blazing sunshine and declare that it was night ; but unfortunately — and I admit that it is humiliating for us Catholics in this century — such is the stuff of which the Roman Curia is made."

The Emperor was fully determined to promulgate his ecclesiastical reforms whatever line was followed by the nuncio. However, he wished to give the Monsignore a final chance to change his mind. He felt too angry to see him himself, so he asked his wife to do so in his stead. The meeting took place on December 23, and lasted two hours. " Nothing has given me a better idea of hell than that interview," Carlota wrote afterwards, " for hell is nothing but a hopeless impasse. To try to convince someone, knowing that it is a complete waste of time and that you might as well be talking Greek since he sees things black and you white, is a labour fit for the damned. Everything slid off the nuncio as though off polished marble." Carlota made every possible representation with all her eloquence, but Monsignore Meglia brushed aside her arguments like dust.

Finally, the nuncio remarked that it was the clergy who had set up the Empire.

" One moment," exclaimed Carlota, interrupting him. " It was not the clergy. It was the Emperor who did so on the day of his arrival."

With these words the Empress rose, signifying that the audience was at an end. " Monsignore," she said as she dismissed him, " whatever happens, I shall take the liberty of recalling this conversation to you. We are not responsible for the consequences. We have done everything to prevent what will now happen, but if the Church will not help us, we shall serve her against her will."

The Empress kept her word. Four days later, in a letter to Pedro Escudero, the Minister of Justice, Maximilian confirmed the principle of freedom of worship and the nationalization of Church property, and an imperial decree to this effect was published shortly afterwards together with a further decree

THE EMPRESS CARLOTA
By Albert Graefle

THE EMPEROR MAXIMILIAN
By Joaquín Ramírez

From the portraits in the National Museum of Mexico in Chapultepec Castle, Mexico, D.F.

By courtesy of the Government of Mexico

THE NATIONAL PALACE, MEXICO CITY

From a lithograph by M. C. Rivera in the possession of the author

designed to prevent the unauthorized promulgation or execution of papal bulls within the Empire. On this the nuncio sent a vigorous letter of protest to Maximilian which Escudero, through whose hands it passed, considered so insolent that he returned it to the sender without disclosing its contents officially to the Emperor. " In his playful way ", observed Carlota, " the Holy Father says that he himself has the evil eye ! Well, it is a fact that since his envoy set foot on our soil we have had nothing but trouble and we expect to have more in the near future."

The Empress's foreboding proved unpleasantly accurate. A short time afterwards, in 1865, a certain Abbé Alleau appeared in Mexico in the declared guise of a secret agent whose mission appears to have been to report to Rome on the situation and stir up trouble amongst the clergy. On his arrest, which was provoked by his indiscreet conduct, a letter wishing him well in his mission was found on him from Gutiérrez which did much to shatter the Emperor's faith in this long-winded and reactionary ultramontane. Also amongst the Abbé's papers was found a memorandum which stated that the Empress Carlota " was wearing herself out by her restless craving for activity because she was unhappy at having no children ". The reason for her childlessness was stated to be her husband's impotence, caused by his having contracted a venereal disease from a Brazilian woman during his travels. Unfortunately this statement was largely true ! [1]

Meanwhile the Pope let it be known to the world in an encyclical what he thought of affairs in Mexico. This particularly annoyed the Empress. " The Holy Father is doing us a pretty service in Europe with the encyclical ", she wrote to Eugénie. "If I might allow myself a slight irreverence, I should say that if it comes from any spirit at all, I do not think it is the Holy Spirit. Our Lord gave peace to His Apostles and did not address them in any other terms. Nowadays it is trouble they are trying to spread."

This difference with Rome could only lead to one result — the recall of the nuncio, whom the Pope could hardly expect to look on impotently while the Church in Mexico was being despoiled of her possessions. He remained to participate in the Easter celebrations of 1865 and then left for Guatemala. Neither

[1] See above, p. 107.

Maximilian nor Carlota was sorry to see the last of this " stiff-necked priest with his brusque, hot-tempered and not very diplomatic ways ", although as good Catholics they regretted the withdrawal of the Pope's representative. " He had some cards up his sleeve," said Carlota, " but he played them badly. He proudly supposed that we should take the trouble to wait until his black period was over, instead of which we took him at his word and all his calculations went astray. Chickens always come home to roost."

5

Although José Fernando Ramírez was an able and enlightened Minister, the foreign policy of the Empire was, like its ecclesiastical counterpart, beset with difficulties from the outset. The ship on which the unfortunate Monsignore Meglia sailed from Europe also carried representatives of the other powers. With the exception, however, of the British Minister, Sir Peter Campbell Scarlett, whom he was genuinely delighted to see, the Emperor confessed that he expected little good would come from " the tiresome diplomatic corps " who he knew would involve him in " odious " receptions and dinners. The new Austrian Minister, Count Guido Thun, was particularly unwelcome, for it had come to Maximilian's ears that he carried secret instructions from Rechberg to confine his mission to seeing that the Family Pact was strictly observed by the monarch to whom he was accredited.

As a result of Maximilian's feeling on this delicate family matter his relations with his brother's Court in Vienna began to deteriorate rapidly. Towards the end of 1864 Franz Joseph had submitted the Family Pact to the Austrian Reichsrat for approval, and this publication of what Maximilian considered a private proceeding, whose validity in any event he questioned, infuriated the Mexican Emperor. He retaliated by attacking his brother in the French press, and at the same time he despatched notes to Great Britain, Belgium, France and the Vatican as well as to Austria denouncing the Pact. Napoleon was obliged to reply to the Austrian Ambassador's protest that he had instructed his ministers to regard Maximilian's act as if it had never taken place. Besides straining his relations almost to the breaking-point with the Court of Vienna, " this unheard-of step on the part of the Emperor Maximilian ", as Prince Metternich put it, foolishly played into the hands of the Juáristas, who naturally lost no time in proclaiming that Maximilian merely regarded his sovereignty in Mexico as a step towards a better position in Europe.

Despite the fact that his Empire was unconsolidated and internally far from secure, Maximilian began to look abroad in the hope of extending its frontiers. It will be remembered that whilst still in Europe he had dreamed of creating with his youngest brother Ludwig Viktor's assistance a vast Hapsburg dominion in Latin America which would extend as far south as the river Plate. The frivolous Ludwig Viktor's refusal to cooperate had caused Maximilian to modify his schemes somewhat, but he still seriously entertained the idea of annexing the whole of Central America as far as the Panama Isthmus to the Mexican Empire. With this aim in view he despatched his friend and former brother officer in the Austrian navy, Count Ollivier Rességuier, on an exploratory mission to this area. Rességuier talked the matter over with Tallien de Cabarrus, the French Consul-General in Guatemala City, and they decided that the simplest thing would be for General Carrera, the Conservative President of Guatemala, to unite Central America into a single state over which he would then rule as Maximilian's viceroy. However, Carrera's death, which occurred shortly afterwards, added to the increasing seriousness of the Empire's domestic problems and caused the reluctant abandonment of this fantastic scheme.

To Maximilian perhaps the most disquieting feature on the foreign horizon was his relations, or rather the absence of relations, with Mexico's neighbour north of the Rio Grande. The United States continued to accredit its representative to Juárez's government, which it recognized as the only lawfully constituted " supreme authority " in the country, and when shortly before Maximilian's arrival the House of Representatives in Washington declared its resolute opposition to the recognition of a monarchy which had been erected on the ruins of the Mexican Republic, Secretary of State William Seward notified Juárez through his

Minister that this was the " unanimous sentiment " of the people of the United States. A little later Maximilian made an attempt to open the way to relations by despatching a consul designate to Washington, but Seward bluntly refused to receive him, giving as his reason that the United States made it " a fixed habit to hold no official intercourse with agents of parties in any country which stand in an attitude of revolution, antagonistic to the sovereign authority in the same country with which the United States are on terms of friendly diplomatic intercourse " and " to hold no unofficial or private intercourse " with them. At the same time the Secretary of State told John Bigelow, the American Minister in Paris, that Maximilian might be informed through the French Government that no exclusion of American consular agents from Mexico would have any influence in inducing the United States to change its political attitude towards that country.

So long as the Civil War continued to rage north of the Rio Grande, Maximilian felt that Lincoln's government would be much too occupied to attempt to undermine his Empire by declaring war on France, and indeed throughout this period Seward contented himself with transmitting from time to time mild and respectful protests to Napoleon. But early in April 1865 there came a significant change. After suddenly evacuating Richmond, the southern General Robert E. Lee capitulated at Appomattox Court House, and the Confederacy was at an end. For a few days it was thought in the Mexican capital that President Lincoln, who had declared that there would be no more wars under his administration, might now recognize the Empire. But any hopes of this kind which Maximilian may have entertained were suddenly doomed by the news of the President's assassination in Washington's National Theatre. With the new President, Andrew Johnson, Maximilian fared no better. He wrote him a letter of condolence in which he politely raised the question of refugees from the southern states crossing into Mexico, and he entrusted it to a special agent for delivery. But President Johnson refused to receive either the agent or the letter.

Seward could now afford to stiffen his representations to Paris. French intervention all along had been a violation of the Monroe Doctrine, but at no time did the Secretary of State specifically invoke this celebrated Presidential pronouncement, since he was conscious that it formed no part of international law, and he rightly preferred to stress the gravity of the intervention from the American point of view in his own language. On the contrary, Seward hoped to get the French out of Mexico by peaceful means, although as a last resort he was prepared to go to war, and he made no attempt to restrain the movement of a considerable body of troops which General Grant had ordered to the Mexican border. Congress was, moreover, inclined to the use of arms.

Seward's diplomacy was masterly. Throughout the summer of 1865 he kept priming Bigelow with instructions to apprise Napoleon of the rising state of American feeling on the question. Finally, in November he came out with a warm despatch to Bigelow asking him to inform Napoleon's Foreign Minister, M. Drouyn de Lhuys, that the intervention was " disallowable and impracticable " and that there was not the slightest chance of the United States recognizing the monarchy in Mexico. When the Foreign Minister replied that he " derived neither pleasure nor satisfaction from the contents " of this communication, Seward knew that he had won his case and that intervention in Mexico was doomed. " You can pass whatever resolutions you want now," he told the House Foreign Affairs Committee in Washington. " I am ready for anything."

A few days later Bigelow was instructed to demand in polite but firm language the withdrawal of French forces from Mexico. The prospect for the Empire could not be called happy.

6

At first the campaign against the titular republican President and his partisans had met with a certain measure of success, and to those in Europe who followed the fortunes of the new Empire from the newspapers the achievements of the French forces under the command of Bazaine, who had now received a marshal's baton from his master, seemed positively encouraging. By the end of 1864 Juárez had retired to the province of Chihuahua in the far north of the country ; early in the following year his ablest General, Porfirio Díaz, surrendered in Oaxaca to a French force along with four thousand men ; and later in the same year the Liberal leader himself crossed the United States border into Texas, where he settled down to await the turn of events and rally American elements to his side.

The trouble was that Juárist bands kept springing up everywhere, and no sooner had the French forces defeated a detachment in the field than others would appear to harry the Imperialist ranks. Communications between Mexico City and Vera Cruz were quite unsafe for travellers, and mail-coaches were liable to be held up and robbed by Juárist flying columns. Indeed the enemy even penetrated to the outskirts of the capital, so that when the Court was in residence at Chapultepec it was necessary to introduce a system of alarms. " Life here is almost like the Middle Ages ", wrote Carlota in February 1865. " We are gay, contented and calm, and yet there is nothing to prevent a band of guerrillas from falling upon us at any moment. Up here we have cannon and a system of signals for communicating with the city. But that does not prevent us from always being on the look-out." It was little wonder that both she and Maximilian in their letters to Paris kept harping on the need for reinforcements. Yet early in 1865 Bazaine, who appeared to resent Maximilian's natural desire to be master in his own house, deliberately weakened the French expeditionary force by despatching a portion of his more experienced troops back to Europe. As a result of this move the relations between the Court and the French Commander-in-Chief, though outwardly cordial, in fact began to deteriorate seriously.

François Achille Bazaine, Marshal of France, was now in his fifty-fifth year. " A plain-looking man, short and thickset, whose plebeian features one might search in vain for a spark of genius or a ray of imagination," so a contemporary at the Imperial Court [1] described him ; " and yet under the commonplace exterior dwelt a kindly spirit and intelligence of no mean order." However, it is doubtful whether his acknowledged military and mental merits compensated in Maximilian's eyes

---

[1] Mrs. Sara Yorke Stevenson. See below, p. 170.

for the circumstances of his birth and lack of breeding. His father had been an obscure engineer from Lorraine who subsequently migrated to Russia, leaving his wife and children to fend for themselves. Indeed Marshal Bazaine was only too conscious of his family past. " I cannot deny my humble origin," he wrote shortly after his most recent promotion ; " and no doubt it is because I have risen from the common people and the ranks that the envious pursue me and the officers who have graduated from the recognized military academies cannot forgive me."

The Marshal's professional career had been fairly spectacular and his rise in the military hierarchy had been in the best traditions of the first Napoleon. Enlisting as a private soldier in a line regiment thirty-four years before, he had soon transferred to the Foreign Legion, where he quickly achieved a commissioned rank. He had served first in Algeria, later in Spain (where he mastered the language), and then back to North Africa, where as an up-and-coming colonel of thirty-six he had fallen in love with the pretty seventeen-year-old daughter of his Spanish landlady. This damsel, whose name was María de la Soledad Tormo, appears to have been in every sense the favourite of the regiment, and, as her education in other respects also seems to have been somewhat lacking, Colonel Bazaine had been obliged to send her back to school as well as overcome the objections of the French War Ministry before he was finally able to lead her to the altar. A year or two later he took his young bride out to the Crimea (he was a General of Brigade now), where she seems to have been as popular as ever with the troops, particularly with Marshal Pélissier, whose calls upon her attracted general notice during her husband's temporary absences on duty from headquarters.

The frail young Madame Bazaine had also accompanied her husband on his next campaign, which was in northern Italy, where he had fought beside the Piedmontese troops against the Austrians at Solferino and had subsequently been decorated by King Victor Emmanuel. But when General Bazaine was appointed to the Mexican command she had stayed behind in France, for the new terrain was not considered suitable for her health. About a year after his arrival in Mexico he received the distressing news of her death.[1] For a while he was prostrate, but then of a sudden he began to cheer up. He was in love again. This time the object of his affections was a seventeen-year-old Mexican brunette, María Josefa de la Peña y Barragán y Azcárate, who had no money but whose uncle, in whose house she was living, had once been President of the Republic.[2] She was known as Pepita.

The Marshal was coy and at first refused to admit that there was anything between him and the young lady, although tongues buzzed at a fancy-dress ball in the capital where they danced together two quadrilles, the lancers and the habanera, after which " the Marshal then escorted her to the buffet ". In some quarters his intentions were not accepted as being strictly honourable, " but ", said the Empress, " I think he is a man of too much heart and honour to trifle in this way with the simplicity of a young girl before the whole of Mexican society, and even in his own house ". Carlota was right. With a woman's unerring instinct for what was really going on, she finally wrung the secret from the love-lorn Bazaine, and in return she promised to plead his cause with Eugénie. " Josefa Peña is seventeen years old ", wrote Carlota to the French Empress, informing her of the engagement. " She has a pretty face, infinite grace and simplicity, beautiful black hair and a most expressive type of Spanish beauty. She is an only child, her mother is a widow; she belongs, they say, to a very good family and has been very well brought up. She speaks French with a good accent, and it is to her credit that although she is the object of a marshal's attentions, and consequently of those of the whole French army,

---

[1] She is said to have committed suicide on learning that her lover's wife, an actress in the Comédie Française, had sent the proofs of their liaison, in the shape of a bundle of compromising letters, to Bazaine. After an unsuccessful attempt to stop the package by Napoleon III, whose aid was invoked by Mme. Bazaine, the letters are supposed to have arrived in Mexico during Bazaine's temporary absence from his headquarters. The story goes that they were burnt without his knowledge by two of his staff officers who opened and read them first.

[2] Manuel de la Peña y Peña, a former chief justice of the supreme court, was President during the negotiation of the treaty between Mexico and the United States in 1848 which terminated the two-years war between the two countries and ceded the territories of Texas, New Mexico and Upper California to the U.S. in return for a cash payment of $15 millions.

she has not lost her naturalness for a moment nor seemed conscious of the admiration of which she is the centre or of the great future opening before her."

The marriage ceremony was celebrated with considerable splendour in the National Palace on June 26, 1865. At the wedding breakfast the Emperor sat beside the bride and the Empress next to the Marshal. When dessert was served, Maximilian rose and proposed the healths of bride and bridegroom. "May God bless the union", he added fervently, whereupon Carlota got up and embraced Pepita with a marked show of affection. At the same time Maximilian presented the seemingly enchanted couple with the title-deeds of the Palace of Buenavista as their future residence. "We never fail to think of any attention, small or great, which may give him pleasure", wrote Carlota to Eugénie with a certain naïveté. "I do not want to mention our wedding presents, but Your Majesty knows that both the Emperor's and my presents to the Marshal were not unworthy of the gratitude felt by Mexico to the Commander-in-Chief of the French troops."

In reality relations between the Marshal and the Court were very far from the standard of perfection which their outward behaviour suggested. While Bazaine in his letters to Napoleon complained that the Emperor was not settling any of "the grave questions by which the country is disturbed", Maximilian accused the Commander-in-Chief of "laziness and lack of organizing power coupled with jealousy and discontent with others". Bazaine, according to the Emperor (who in this instance spoke with some truth), invariably opposed all attempts to organize a national army. "He has thwarted everything we have wanted to do", grumbled Maximilian. "The older Mexican generals have been astonished — they think I do not want an army — whereas it is the Marshal who will not give me anyone to organize it." Another source of friction was the position of the Austrian and Belgian volunteers who had been recruited in their own countries for military service in Mexico. Bazaine was naturally unwilling to concede the separation of commands, and this caused strained relations from the outset with consequent deplorable effects on the current campaign.

" I tell Your Majesty frankly ", wrote Maximilian to Napoleon towards the close of 1865, " this situation is a difficult one for me. I add as a good and true friend that it is dangerous both for you and for me ; for you, in that your glorious reputation suffers by it ; for me, since my intentions, which are, moreover, yours too, cannot be carried into effect. . . . I can do nothing lasting with a population whose confidence is shaken at every moment by such very questionable protection, for everybody knows that if the *guerrilleros* return, everyone who has declared for the Empire will be hanged or shot without mercy, and people are naturally careful not to express their sympathy for a government which is unable to protect its subjects."

About the same time as Maximilian was writing these lines the Marshal, against whom they were primarily directed, was reading a most revealing letter from his master. " The Emperor Maximilian must understand that we cannot stay in Mexico for ever ", wrote Napoleon. " He ought to realize that a government that has done nothing to enable it to live on its own resources will be more easily abandoned than supported through thick and thin."

7

It is worth while noticing, however briefly, some of the other individuals who composed the Imperial Court and Government as well as a few details of their administration. Theoretically the Emperor ruled through a Cabinet or ministerial council composed of nine members, although in practice he was often guided, particularly in the latter part of his reign, by his intimate advisers and favourites of the moment. It has already been seen how Maximilian, greatly to the disgust of certain of the reactionary elements which had helped him to the throne, leaned heavily on the side of the Liberals. Indeed, for the first two years of his reign the majority of the Cabinet was composed of Liberals, and its two ablest members, Ramírez, who held the portfolio of Foreign Affairs, and Castillo, the Finance Minister, were both of this political persuasion. Almonte, the most influential Conservative in the country and the General who had headed the Provisional Government before Maximilian's arrival, was given a high-sounding Court appointment to keep him out of politics, while the two other leading Conservative Generals, Márquez and Miramón, were sent abroad on ostensible missions for the same reason. " These missions cost enormous sums of money," wrote a member of the imperial staff some time later, " but this was considered to be unimportant on the theory that, first, it was worth it to have possible traitors out of the country, and secondly, that the presence of the pair in Europe, travelling and living on an ostentatious scale, would impress upon observers abroad that the Empire was stable."

The organization of his own chancery or secretariat took the form which Maximilian had planned on board the *Novara*. The Belgian Eloin, in spite of the eloquent testimonial which he had earned from King Leopold, was not the most fortunate choice as head of the civil cabinet. He disliked the French intensely, he showed a profound ignorance of American affairs in general and those of Mexico in particular — he could not even speak Spanish — and on the whole he was responsible for a good deal of mischief. He eventually fell a victim partly to his own folly and partly to an intrigue on the part of the French. The Emperor became convinced that his office was becoming virtually a powerful central government, which was to some extent true, besides which Maximilian complained of the administrative details with which Eloin continually bothered him. After a little more than a year Maximilian resorted to his favourite remedy for dealing with inconvenient advisers. Eloin was sent abroad on a special mission, and the office was placed under Colonel Loysel, a French officer, who also headed the military cabinet. At the same time the Emperor, far from divesting himself of details, took more and more administrative matters into his own hands. He went so far as to decline to see any members of the two cabinets officially and he gave orders that the doors connecting them with his private apartments should be walled up. Like his brother Franz Joseph, who communicated with his ministers and even with his son by letter, Maximilian gave as his reason for this arrangement that " it can no longer be alleged that the Emperor has said or desired this or that ; everything is written and signed ". Such a method of carrying on business could never be really satisfactory.

During the early days of the Empire Maximilian's chancery seems to have been run in a most haphazard manner, and the household officials whom the Emperor had brought from Austria were constantly interfering in its affairs either because they were jealous, like the former valet Schertzenlechner, or because, like the wife of the Imperial Treasurer Kuhacsevich, there was no one else to do the work. " The disorder is still great ! " wrote Frau Kuhacsevich at the beginning of 1865. " Günner[1] ought to have a dozen heads ; he has to do everything, for there is nobody here. . . . I am in the same position. Günner and I are telegraphing all day ! " For the first ten months of his reign Maximilian relied greatly on Schertzenlechner, who on account of his cow-like demeanour was nicknamed " the great Moo " at Court. " The great Moo governs ", added the Treasurer's wife, " and says everything is going on splendidly — where nobody is sure of his life. His Majesty is always running to him for advice as to what he ought to do." At last the ex-lacquey overreached himself. A furious quarrel which he had with Eloin in the Emperor's presence led to his disgrace. In revenge he spread the extraordinary and totally false rumour that seven thousand Indians were marching on the capital to demand his reinstatement. For this he was allowed to return to Europe after narrowly escaping a court-martial.

The Emperor was in the habit of rising punctually every morning at four o'clock whether in the capital or in the country. When he had finished dressing he would ring for his secretary and commence work. At first the principal private secretary was an Austrian named Poliakovitz, but after a few months he met with a serious riding accident and the Emperor replaced him by a young Mexican named José Luis Blasio whom he had discovered working in Eloin's office as an interpreter. Blasio was barely twenty years old, but he had a good memory and a lively intelligence and Maximilian took a strong fancy to him. Furthermore, he kept a record of most of what he saw, and it is by reason of this fortunate circumstance that there exists today one of the most instructive and entertaining

---

[1] Prefect of the Palace.

memoirs of Maximilian and his Empire.[1]

About eight the Emperor would don the picturesque native charro costume and ride out for an hour with Carlota or his secretary " to enjoy the glorious morning air ". He would then, if at Chapultepec, drive to the National Palace, where the remainder of the morning and early afternoon would be spent either in attending council meetings or giving audiences to ministers and others. As a rule he would return to Chapultepec in time for dinner at four, when Carlota and any guests there might be were joined by him. Generally there were not less than twenty present, including members of the household, on these occasions. Except in State festivities, these gatherings were on the whole easy and informal, and everyone was encouraged to speak Spanish. At first the meals were very ordinary — " Have you ever eaten so badly as here ? " the Emperor asked one of his wife's ladies-in-waiting — but gradually things improved until early in 1865 Maximilian was able to report to Vienna that, " thanks to great efforts, our cuisine at least is one of the best that exists at present and so are the imperial cellars ". While Maximilian himself ate and drank most sparingly, it was otherwise with many of his official guests. " The diplomatists ", he wrote to his brother, " gorge and swill to such an extent that as a rule after dinner they can only mumble inarticulate sounds."

After dinner the Empress and her ladies would withdraw to their apartments, while the Emperor would as a rule lead the gentlemen into the smoking-room, where the company would remain standing while His Majesty smoked and chatted for half an hour or so. He actually retired to bed about eight o'clock after he had done a little more work with his secretary. " Business is piling up as the Government becomes consolidated," he wrote at the beginning of 1865, " and I am kept on the go from five in the morning till eight in the evening." This remained the normal routine throughout his reign. He disliked balls and receptions as they kept him up late.

At this time the National Palace could only be reached from

---

[1] *Maximiliano intimo. El Emperador Maximiliano y su Corte*, Paris and Mexico, 1905 (English edition, *Maximilian, Emperor of Mexico*, edited by R. H. Murray, New Haven, 1934).

Chapultepec Castle by a roundabout route. For this reason the Emperor conceived the idea of constructing a two-mile avenue from the castle to the equestrian statue of the Spanish King Charles IV, known as the Iron Horse, there connecting with the Zocalo by a road about a mile long. The result was a magnificent highway called the *Calzado del Emperador*, now known as the *Paseo de la Reforma*. It remains perhaps the finest and most beautiful in Mexico. Within the palace itself Maximilian also made drastic alterations. He had the plaster stripped off the ceilings, thereby revealing fine cedar beams, and all the small rooms overlooking the Zocalo in the left wing were on his instructions thrown together so as to form one large reception room, which the palace then lacked. He restored the interior throughout where it had fallen into decay, paying particular attention to the exquisite tiles in the patios.

In the cultural field Maximilian did much for Mexico, for he liked to see himself above all an enlightened Humanitarian. On the first anniversary of his acceptance of the throne he founded an Academy of Science and Literature. About the same time he purchased from the well-known Mexican book collector José Maria Andrade a magnificent library of printed books and manuscripts relating to Mexican history and culture. He intended that this library of nearly 5,000 volumes should form the nucleus of an Imperial Library for the use of the nation. Shortly after this he established a national theatre under the direction of the poet José Zorrilla, and to stimulate interest in the drama he offered substantial money prizes from his private funds for the best plays to be written. He commissioned Mexican artists to paint portraits of himself and Carlota, and he endeavoured to collect the portraits of the country's former rulers which had become scattered during the political troubles of previous years. He also sought to regain for the National Museum various Mexican relics which had found their way into the imperial collections in Vienna. Although Franz Joseph refused to surrender everything, Maximilian did succeed in recovering Montezuma's shield as well as the original manuscript of a report from Cortés to Charles V on the conquest of the country.

On the more ornamental side of government, the Emperor

took a great interest in Court etiquette, and in fact became an expert on this subject. " Our *Court Ceremonial* ", a thick printed book, a gigantic piece of work, " is at last complete ", he wrote to his younger brother in February 1865. " I may flatter myself that in this sphere I have achieved the most finished piece of work that has ever been done." This so-called *Reglamento para el Servicio y Ceremonial de la Corte* was an astonishing production bound in green and stamped with the imperial crown in gold, which contained no less than three hundred quarto pages and twenty diagrams. Every conceivable degree of Court procedure was set out in its voluminous and detailed pages from the reception of a Cardinal to the Court mourning prescribed on Maximilian's death. It might just as well have been issued for Ruritania, as it bore as much relation to the realities of Mexican life, and though it might have served its purpose at the Hofburg and Schönbrunn, it was strangely out of place at Chapultepec and the *Palacio Nacional* in Mexico City.

Maximilian's interest in cultural and aesthetic subjects tended to increase his idealistic outlook on life and at times made him hopelessly impractical. For instance, he wished to organize the educational system throughout his Empire on such a scale as would enable Mexico to " take its place by the side of the leading nations of the world " without pausing to consider the cost of this ambitious programme or the suitability of his subjects for its reception. Particular emphasis was to be placed on " that too much neglected science " philosophy in the curriculum, since " it trains the understanding, teaches men to know themselves and to develop the moral order of society out of themselves as an inner necessity ". The Minister of Education, to whom Maximilian proposed these ideas, simply shook his head, for he considered them out of this world.

Furthermore, his anxiety to acquaint himself fully with the working of his Government led the Emperor to interfere in person far too much in its details. When he complained of his chancery and other departments, which he said required " funda-mental " reorganization, he was in reality censuring himself, for he ought to have been able to control these instruments effectively in the interests of the State. Like the Caliph Haroun al-Raschid and Louis XI of France, Maximilian liked to wander through the streets of his capital incognito to see that everything was in order. In one instance at least — the laudable desire to investigate working conditions in the bakeries — his popularity was scarcely enhanced. After being refused admittance to several bakeries by the occupants, who declined to believe he was the Emperor and even threatened to have him arrested if he did not leave them alone, he eventually succeeded in penetrating one such establishment, only to find that the workmen had nothing to complain about. " What kind of a ruler is this ", people asked, " who wants to find out everything for himself instead of sending some subaltern to do it for him ? Doesn't this prove how little confidence he has in his subordinates ? "

On the other hand, it must be admitted that wherever he went the Emperor won adherents by his disarming manners and personal charm. Blasio relates how on one occasion Maximilian visited a hospital in the provinces where one of the younger doctors, an ardent Liberal, had refused to participate in the reception which the town had given him on the previous day. After a few minutes' conversation the doctor was completely won over, and he entered with zest into a discussion on the needs of the hospital and the money necessary to meet them. The Emperor informed him that the requisite sum would be supplied from his own privy purse, and he then invited the doctor to dinner, to which the young Liberal promptly came, a complete convert to the Imperialist cause.

The American archaeologist Mrs. Sara Yorke Stevenson, who as a young girl lived in Mexico during the whole of the Empire and frequently appeared at Court, has borne witness to Maximilian's striking charm. In spite of the weakness and indecision which his features revealed, " he looked and was a gentleman ", she wrote in her reminiscences of the period.[1] " His dignity was without hauteur. His manner was attractive ; he had the faculty of making you feel at ease ; and he possessed far more personal magnetism than did the Empress."

---

[1] *Maximilian in Mexico. A Woman's Reminiscences of the French Intervention, 1862–1867.* New York, 1897.

CHAPULTEPEC CASTLE

From a photograph

THE BORDA GARDENS

From a photograph

He also possessed in abundant measure another quality which his wife lacked, a sense of humour. Blasio gives several good examples of this. A certain count laid siege to the affections of the wife of a colonel about the Court. As usually happens, the affair was common knowledge except to the lady's husband. Maximilian happened to be looking up a date on the calendar in his study when he said to his secretary : " Don't forget to congratulate the Colonel on September 15. That's his Saint's day." On consulting the calendar himself, Blasio discovered that the saint whose martyrdom was celebrated on that day was Cornelius, traditionally the patron of cuckolds.

On another occasion the Emperor's attention was drawn to the fact that one of the Court officials and his wife were the proud parents of a dozen children. Maximilian said that " it was obvious that they made excellent use of their time and toiled so patriotically to increase the population of the Empire ", and in these circumstances he had decided " never to permit the official to accompany him on any of his journeys and thus compel him to lose precious hours which might be employed more agreeably and profitably ".

Besides his wit that endeared the Emperor Maximilian to all who came into touch with him was his seemingly inexhaustible cheerfulness. He refused to be discouraged by the turn of events, but his unwillingness to see anything but the rosy side of the picture was in the end to prove a two-edged sword. To Bazaine, who came out to meet him at the conclusion of his first tour of the provinces, he made a remark which summed up at once himself and his rule : " The present is gloomy, but the future will be splendid ".

VII. *Decline*

EVERY Monday evening the Empress Carlota used to give a reception in Chapultepec at which a band played and there was dancing. The Cuban singer Concha Méndez would also perform, her most popular number being " La Paloma ", a haunting song which became the Empress's favourite. These occasions were known as " the Empress's Mondays ", but although Maximilian described them as " a great success and very animated " and his roving eye did not fail to notice that they were attended by " a bevy of the loveliest women " who joined in the dance, the Emperor did not as a rule himself appear. Maximilian, who disliked evening entertainments since they kept him out of bed, was content to leave the honours to his wife. Carlota certainly was a good hostess and did her duty conscientiously — too conscientiously perhaps — but she did not exercise the strong personal charm which came so easily to the Emperor. Competent observers such as Sara Yorke (later Mrs. Stevenson) found her reserved and somewhat lacking in tact and adaptability. " A certain haughtiness of manner, a dignity too conscious of itself, at first repelled any who were disposed to feel kindly toward her." Thus wrote young Miss Yorke, but at the same time she admitted to the view, which Marshal Bazaine shared, that the Empress's strong intellectual face, although a trifle hard at times, had the advantage over her husband's features and " her determined expression impressed one with the feeling that she was the better equipped of the two to cope intelligently with the difficulties of practical life ".

Apart from the social duties which she was naturally expected to perform in her position, there is no doubt that Maximilian's consort, as time went on, began to interfere more and more with matters of state which were, strictly speaking, outside her immediate concern. There is evidence that many of the official letters and state papers which bore his signature and approval were drafted by her, but whereas Maximilian's own letters, particularly those to Napoleon, were always courteous and considerate, they frequently betrayed feelings of irritation and discontent when Carlota had a hand in their composition. She defended herself on the ground that having no children she felt she must help her husband in any way she could, and in any event what she did was solely " at Max's wish and for his good ". She felt, furthermore, that as she and Maximilian were " so closely united on policy ", there could be no danger of any attempt to drive a political wedge between them.

That Carlota was not conscious of the criticisms which her conduct evoked in Europe as well as Mexico is evident from a letter which she wrote her grandmother at this time.

Chapultepec, September 29, 1865

. . . It is being said that I have influence and that I do or advise certain things. Since Max is far superior to me in every way, I hardly see how I could persuade him to do anything whatsoever, and furthermore I am much too loyal to seek any personal influence. What Max does not tell me I do not ask him, and I am much more scrupulous about this now than before we became sovereigns because I respect the dignity of his position. I help him where I can ; at the moment I am doing the work of a " *chef de cabinet* " on special duty, but I am only facilitating the work and saving Max's time ; we are the only ones who work here, and regardless of whether or not I succeed in what I do, I never brag about it to anyone. It seems only natural to me that in a position such as ours a woman who is not a mother should be of direct assistance to her husband. I assist him only because he wishes me to, and because I enjoy doing useful work for which I have always longed, and not because of any personal ambition. Occasionally the wife of a farmer helps him till his fields ; this is a vast uncultivated field and two are hardly enough for the work, and, having neither children nor anything better to do, I do not see why I should not help.

I am only telling you this, dear Grandmother, in order that you may judge how much truth there is in the remarks passed in Rome and elsewhere in which I am represented as being a virago. Actually I am exactly as you knew me and less interested in my person and having my own way than ever, having found that vanity, egotism and ambition are very useless activities. Possibly I am ambitious to do good, but not in order that it should be talked about, simply to see that it is done. I make known only that which is necessary as Max's wife who must have the people's respect, but I consider that this respect reflects on Max's wife and not on me as a person. . . .

Apart from her preoccupation with the charge that she was

interfering rather than assisting in the Emperor's work, this remarkable letter from Carlota throws an interesting sidelight on the private domestic relations between husband and wife. It shows, for one thing, that the Empress was resigned to being childless. The fact that they had ceased to live together in the physical sense a few years after their marriage has already been noticed. This separation continued in Mexico, and, although to all outward appearances they were careful to give the impression that they were in the closest harmony, the truth could not be concealed from their servants and other acute observers. Blasio, for instance, relates how on one occasion when the Emperor and Empress paid a state visit to Puebla, Maximilian was escorted to the rooms which had been prepared for them in their host's house. At first he displayed marked satisfaction at seeing the grand double bed with its canopy of fine lace and silken ribbons which was waiting for him and Carlota. But as soon as his host was out of the way, he immediately ordered the servants to find a room at some distance from this magnificent marital chamber, and when this had been done he had his special travelling bed, which he had brought with him, put up there. " He did this almost angrily ", noted Blasio, to whom indeed the whole scene was a strange and unexpected revelation of his master's domestic feelings.

" What conjugal drama was concealed by the Emperor's action ? " the Mexican secretary asked himself. " What was it that two young married persons, who in public seemed to love each other, at the age of vigour shared no marital life and the husband appeared irritated at the prospect of sleeping in the same bed with his wife ? " The reasons for this conduct, which have already been explained, Blasio was obliged to admit baffled him at first. " Later ", he wrote, " I was convinced that some estrangement existed between them, something the nature of which for the moment I was unable to decide — whether it was because of reasons of state, because of the Emperor's infidelity or because of some organic defect in Maximilian. For neither in Puebla, nor in Mexico City in the palace, nor at Chapultepec, did they ever sleep together. This could not escape the servants' notice, for the attendants of the Empress slept near her and those of Maximilian in a room adjoining his."

There seems no doubt that Maximilian was interested in women from the physical side and that he sought from various ladies, who were willing to submit to his embraces, the satisfaction which his wife failed to provide in their marriage bed. To his secretary he said of certain ladies about the Court that " he could see their ardour in their eyes and that they ought to be formidable women to love ". That Maximilian made the attempt, apparently with considerable success, is borne out by the testimony of his valet, Antonio Grill, who was in an excellent position to observe what was going on. " You may have seen nothing," Grill told Blasio, " but I saw a good deal. The Emperor's bedroom was visited many times by ladies of the Court, who slipped in and out so mysteriously that only I saw them, and frequently without knowing who they were. How many of them, whom no one would believe capable of it, yielded to His Majesty's desires ! " Nor can it be said that Carlota had no knowledge of these happenings. According to Blasio, " it escaped no one's notice that Maximilian cast desirous eyes upon various beautiful women about the Court, and when discreet mention was made of topics of gallantry the Empress would smile with a sadness that we all observed ".

Carlota did not wear her heart on her sleeve, but she was a woman, nevertheless. She still respected and admired her husband and it gave her some sense of satisfaction to know that she was able to help him in his work, but she was pained to think that, though she was only twenty-five, the time for love and love-making between them had passed. " Today ", she wrote to her grandmother in the letter which has been previously quoted, " I am growing old, if not in the eyes of others, at least in my own, and my thoughts and feelings are in reality very different from the semblance of my outward appearance."

2

At the end of the first year of his reign it was clear not only to the Emperor but to the Court at large and many of the outside public that Carlota could not supply an heir to the throne. Still confident in the future of the Empire, Maximilian now determined to make the necessary arrangements elsewhere to establish the succession. Since his younger brother Ludwig Viktor was unattracted by the prospect of becoming Crown Prince, Maximilian turned to the descendants of the late Emperor Augustín Iturbide for the missing heir. The ill-fated Iturbide had left three sons, Augustín, Angel and Augustín Cosmo, and a daughter, Josefa. Angel, who had died some years earlier, had married an American woman, and they had had a son who was called after his grandfather and was then just over two years old. It was this infant Augustín whom the Emperor wished to adopt as his lawful successor. Carlota described him as " fresh and rosy-looking but not too well brought up at the moment ".

In order to carry out his design it was necessary for the Emperor to come to an understanding with the Iturbide family. Maximilian proposed to confer the title of Prince on little Augustín and also on his cousin Salvador, son of Augustín Cosmo Iturbide. Salvador was of school age and in fact studying under Hidalgo's supervision in Paris. At the same time the boy's aunt Josefa, the late Emperor's youngest daughter, was to be raised to the dignity of Princess and the prospective Crown Prince was to be entrusted to her immediate care. All the other members of the Iturbide family, including the infant's American mother Alicia, who had only recently arrived from the United States, were to leave Mexico and not to return, while the Emperor on his part undertook to continue the pensions they had been receiving from the Government as well as to make certain other payments to them which were certainly not ungenerous. Only Josefa, young Salvador and the infant Augustín were to have the privilege of living within the Empire. According to Carlota, the reason for excluding the prospective Crown Prince's two uncles was that whilst in the United States they had " contracted habits of gambling and drinking which rendered impossible their elevation to princely rank ".

These arrangements were embodied in an agreement which was duly signed by the interested parties on September 15, 1865. Although the agreement was supposed to be secret, its terms soon leaked out, which impelled Carlota to say that its aim was not to ensure the succession, but that it was "simply an act of justice" on the part of Maximilian "to take under his protection the descendants of a dethroned Emperor who was not of royal blood".

The various members of the Iturbide family, who were affected, immediately left the capital for Vera Cruz with the intention of taking the next steamer to Europe. Doña Alicia, who had parted with her child most reluctantly after an unsuccessful plea to Maximilian to let her keep him until his fifth year, stopped at Puebla, and there her maternal feelings overcame her sense of obligation to the Emperor. She appealed to Bazaine to help her and at the same time returned to Mexico City, travelling in the name of Alice Green. On her arrival Bazaine informed her that he had been officially requested to take no action in the matter, so she addressed a long letter to the Emperor which she gave to the Marshal, and in which she said that she had wept so much and had experienced so much bitterness since she had been separated from little Augustín that she could now only beg His Majesty to restore the son who was the charm of her existence. "In my dreams as a mother", she wrote, "I never thought that my son should one day be a prince who would aspire to a crown. My passion was to educate him as a good Mexican who, brought up with good ideas, might one day become useful to his country but very contented with the humble position in which I lived. My happiness knew no limits, and now that Your Majesty honours in my child a national memory, am I to separate myself from him when he stands in need of all my solicitude?"

Maximilian, who considered the mother mentally unbalanced, believed that the child would suffer if he were to give in to her. However, the lady showed no signs of following the rest of the family, and in the end had to be forcibly abducted and transported to Vera Cruz, where she was placed on board the steamer. This vessel touched at a United States port where the irate Alicia disembarked and made her way to Washington. Here she sought an interview with Secretary Seward, to whom she poured forth an account of her troubles which certainly lost nothing in the telling. In reply to the Secretary of State's enquiries she stated " that Maximilian was afraid of the popularity which the infant Iturbide enjoyed and was likely to acquire in Mexico ; that the aunt Josefa, now some fifty-six years of age, was not on good terms with her brothers, hated her, was very ambitious and had been bribed by the title of Princess to lend herself to this unnatural intrigue ; and that Marshal Bazaine treated her very kindly, regretted that he had no authority to take the child, and manifested a willingness to do everything in his power to induce the Emperor to surrender it ".

The Secretary of State informed Señora Iturbide that he could not approach Maximilian as he had no relations with the " so-called " Imperial Government of Mexico. However, as Doña Alicia was on her way to Paris, Seward wrote to Bigelow requesting him to lend his good offices " towards aiding that lady in the accomplishment of her object ", which the Minister duly undertook to do " to the verge of official propriety ". On her arrival in the French capital she called at the United States Legation, and when he had heard her story Bigelow agreed to approach Drouyn de Lhuys, the French Foreign Minister. The latter's official reply was to the effect that he had no competence to deal with the matter since Maximilian possessed a Minister in Paris to whom the lady should address herself. However, the Minister privately warned the Emperor that he would be well advised to terminate the pact with the Iturbides and restore the child to his mother, since there was every likelihood and danger of the American press getting hold of the story and representing Maximilian as unjustly robbing a mother of her son.

This is precisely what happened. Matias Romero, Juárez's Minister in Washington, into whose hands a copy of the secret family agreement had found its way, forwarded the document to Secretary of State Seward, who promptly published it. Indeed the whole affair was to prove a source of acute embarrassment to Maximilian, for it proclaimed his wife's childlessness before the world and was exploited by his enemies and ill-wishers to the full. " As regards the affair of the Iturbide family," he wrote to Napoleon at the end of 1865, " the young prince's mother, a half-crazy American, was suddenly called back to Mexico which she had left quite contentedly, and the two uncles, a pair of drunkards, have been incited to go to Paris and Vienna to stir up trouble and make my government appear ridiculous."

3

In the interests, as he hoped, of his adopted country, Maximilian continued to put in long hours at his desk, in the council chamber and on horseback. "If you were to see your old friend, you would laugh", he wrote to Count Hadik, one of his old tutors ; "your Archduke stronger and more able-bodied than before, with a beard flowing down over his chest, a moustache that would arouse the envy of any Hungarian, a bald spot too, I admit, which is already of Hadikian proportions ; working from ten to twelve hours a day, now at the Ministerial Council, now at the Council of State, now at army organization, now at ecclesiastical meetings, taking the chair in the most fluent and elegant Spanish, occupied for the rest of the time with audiences, or rushing off on wild horses like a regular *ranchero* ; the mistress of the house fresh, gay, faithful and loyal, sharing all her husband's toil and dangers, travelling indefatigably through vast stretches of country. . . . I can truly say that I have chosen the better part, and I would not for anything in the world give up my position and return to the old life. I am struggling with difficulties and obstacles, but fighting is my element and the life of Mexico is worth a struggle."

But during the summer of 1865 Maximilian sounded a discordant note for the first time. He began to reckon with the possibility of the failure of his mission. On August 23 he wrote to his father-in-law : "I am under no illusions as to the possibility that the new edifice upon which we are working may collapse, if exposed to storms, and that I may perish with it, but nobody can deprive me of the consciousness of having worked devotedly for a sublime idea, and this is better and more comforting than to moulder in inactivity in old Europe". Indeed he never ceased extolling the virtues of useful employment in the Western Hemisphere in contrast to the idle existence such as his two younger brothers enjoyed in the Old World.

As he put it, " there is no more pitiable creature than an apanaged prince leading what is called a care-free life ".

Apart from now following any course of action which might compromise the family honour of the Hapsburgs, Maximilian was now more anxious than anything else to prove himself " truly Mexican ". Twice during this summer he made tours of the provinces, where " the people, and the lower clergy in particular, receive me with an enthusiasm which delights me ". On Mexico's Independence Day (September 16) he made a rousing speech in the capital designed to show the country's northern neighbour that her independence would be defended. " Henceforth every drop of my blood is Mexican," he said, pointing towards the Rio Grande, " and if God permits new dangers to menace our beloved country, you shall see me fight side by side for your independence and integrity."

That the Emperor entertained a marked liking for Liberals in the country, many of whose political views he warmly shared, has already been seen. He even wished to join forces, if it were possible, with his opponent the titular President, who had recently through his plenipotentiary in Europe caused a strong hint to be conveyed to the Emperor that he would be well advised to withdraw from his precarious throne while there was yet time. " I wish greatly to come to an understanding with Juárez ", Maximilian wrote towards the close of 1865. " But before everything he ought to recognize the determination of the effective majority of the nation which wants calm, peace, and prosperity ; and it is necessary that he decide to collaborate with his ceaseless energy and his intelligence in the difficult work which I have begun. If, as I believe, he really has in view the happiness of Mexico, he ought to understand very soon that no Mexican loves the country and has its advancement at heart so much as I and that I am working for this in all sincerity and with the best intentions. Let him come to help me sincerely and loyally, and he will be welcomed with open arms like all good Mexicans. . . . I am ready to receive Juárez into my council and among my friends, but for the present I have to defend that which stands above my vanity and my personal well-being, namely the independence of a beautiful country and of eight million people, a task worthy of a prince of my family."

But Juárez was unyielding in his opposition to the Empire and determined to accept no compromise. " With the attitude that the government of the United States has lately assumed," he wrote to an exiled supporter at this time, " Maximilian has now not the slightest probability of cementing his so-called throne. He must see very clearly that even should he arrive at the complete conquest of the country, occupying with his forces even to the utmost limits of the republic and destroying the national government, which, however, will never take place, the United States will never permit him to consolidate his power, and his sacrifices and victories will have counted for nothing. The certain result is already in the conviction of all. It has augmented the increasing discouragement of our opponents and has reanimated the public spirit on our side to such an extent that, in my judgment, without the necessity of the United States taking any direct part in our war, we shall ourselves alone be able to obtain the definitive triumph of the cause of the national independence. Such is my desire, and to such result all my efforts are directed."

Juárez's determined refusal to enter into any relations whatsoever with Maximilian was strengthened by the critical military situation of the Empire at this period. Acting on instructions from Napoleon, who, now that the American Civil War was over, feared that the United States might send troops across the Rio Grande to engage the French army, Marshal Bazaine began to concentrate his forces at a relatively small number of strategic points. This development involved the evacuation of a number of lightly held localities, with the result that the Juáristas proceeded to occupy them and wreak vengeance on any Imperialist supporters on whom they could lay their hands. Pressure was now brought to bear upon the Emperor to authorize drastic measures in the interests of internal security. He began to be reproached on many sides for his weakness or what the Austrian Ambassador, Count Thun, called "misplaced clemency". Bazaine in particular urged him to have recourse to severity. At last Maximilian yielded, and on October 3, 1865, he issued the notorious " Black Decree " to the effect that henceforward any enemy of the Empire caught in arms should be executed after summary proceedings before a court-martial. The decree, which was drawn up by the Ministry of War, was signed by the Emperor in Council and included the signatures of the principal ministers, among them Ramírez and Escudero.

Bazaine, whose major share in the responsibility for this decree has now, despite contemporary denials, been established, instructed all the officers under his command to carry out the decree ruthlessly, telling them that the struggle had now become a war to the knife in which neither mercy could be shown nor prisoners taken. The natural effect of these orders was merely to intensify the partisan strife, and although the decree did not differ materially from one which Juárez had promulgated in 1862, the fact that its legality was in question and that it was applied in districts which had no knowledge of its publication did the Imperialist cause the greatest possible disservice. Two of the first Republican leaders to suffer under the decree were the Generals Arteaga and Salazar who were captured by the cruel Imperialist colonel Méndez, who had them shot largely to gratify a personal grudge. On the eve of their execution they both wrote touching letters which were later widely circulated both in the United States and Mexico and constituted most valuable propaganda for the Juáristas.[1]

Meanwhile the Juárists were regaining ground rapidly, thanks to Bazaine's policy of concentrating his forces. The Emperor repeatedly begged the Marshal to take effective counter-

[1] General Arteaga's letter was as follows :

Uruapán, October 20, 1865

My adored Mother :

    I was taken prisoner on the 13th instant by the imperial troops, and tomorrow I am to be shot. I pray you, mama, to pardon me for all the suffering I have caused you during the time I have followed the profession of arms against your will.

    Mama, in spite of all my efforts to aid you, the only means I had I sent you in April last ; but God is with you and He will not suffer you to perish, and my sister Trinidad, the little Yankee.

    I have not told you before of the death of my brother Luis, because I feared you would die of grief ; he died at Tuxpán in the State of Jalisco about the first of January last.

    Mama, I leave nothing but a spotless name, for I have never taken anything that did not belong to me ; and I trust God will pardon all my sins and take me into His glory.

    I die a Christian, and bid you all adieu — you, Dolores and all the family, as your very obedient son.

José María Arteaga.

Doña Apolonia Magallanes de Arteaga,
Aguas Calientes.

measures, but to no purpose. Indeed Maximilian thought that he was " too much occupied with his young wife " to give the military situation the attention which it plainly demanded. Bazaine, on the other hand, was merely carrying out his master's orders and he now did no more than report to Maximilian the increasing number of risings which were taking place throughout the country. Even in the near-by province of Michoacán, which lay westward between the capital and the Pacific, an undefeated Republican army was in possession. But the Emperor still refused to be cast down or to lose hope. " However troublesome these events may be, and they are indeed grave," he told the Marshal a few days after New Year 1866, " they ought not to discourage us. I know that one cannot extirpate the revolutionary spirit in a day, and I know too that I have undertaken a task of unprecedented difficulty ; but my courage is equal to bearing that burden, and I shall go on resolutely to the end."

In an attempt to get Bazaine to move, the Emperor now tried a policy of appeasement. He asked for the names of all Government officials and ministers whom the Marshal considered objectionable, and as a result a considerable number of prefects and other provincial officials were removed. In addition, Ramírez, who was particularly disliked in Paris as well as in the French Headquarters, had to surrender his portfolio of Foreign Affairs to Martin Castillo, although for the time being he remained a member of the Ministry. To these overtures Bazaine responded by undertaking to pacify the country anew. On January 19, 1866, he wrote to Maximilian : " So soon as the troops have received all the reinforcements from France and are so far organized as to be able to undertake a fresh campaign, it is my intention to despatch them in every direction in the Empire at once, and Your Majesty will then see that it is not the military situation in Mexico which ought to cause the greatest anxiety ".

This undertaking constituted the supreme example of Bazaine's duplicity, or rather that of his master by whose orders he was bound, for the decision had already been taken in Paris to evacuate the French forces. Even as the Emperor read the Marshal's letter, another letter was on its way to him from

Napoleon in Paris in which the French Emperor stated bluntly that the Chamber's refusal to contribute further to the upkeep of the army overseas had forced him " to set a definitive term to the French occupation ". The withdrawals were to begin in the autumn of the same year and to be completed in 1867.

4

To escape for a while from the altitude of Mexico City the Emperor took up his residence at Cuernavaca, about forty-five miles from the capital, along with Carlota, the little Augustín Iturbide and the child's aunt Josefa. It was whilst staying in this idyllic spot that Maximilian received Napoleon's unpleasant letter, but severe as the blow which the news it contained must have been, to outward observers at least his composure appeared little disturbed, and he continued to enjoy for as long as he could the attractions of this beautiful retreat.

" Picture to yourself a broad level valley blessed by Heaven ", so Maximilian described Cuernavaca to a friend, " stretching out before you like a golden bowl, surrounded by a variety of mountain ranges rising one beyond the other in the most glorious shades, ranging from the purest rose red, purple and violet to the deepest azure, some jagged and confused, piled crag upon crag like the legendary coasts of Sicily, others soaring upwards and thickly wooded like the green mountains of Switzerland : beyond them the enormous volcanoes with their snow-clad crests towering up like giants towards the deep blue heavens. Imagine this golden bowl filled at all seasons — or rather all the year round, for there are no seasons here — with a wealth of tropical vegetation with its intoxicating fragrance and sweet fruits, and added to all this a climate as lovely as the Italian May, and handsome, friendly, loyal natives. In this happy valley, a few hours from the capital, we live in a pleasant unpretentious villa set in the midst of a luxuriant garden. . . . On the terrace running the length of our rooms and shaded by a veranda hang our fine hammocks, and with the song of gaily-coloured birds in our ears we lull ourselves to sweet dreams. Here at Cuernavaca for the first time we lead a real tropical life."

The villa and gardens known as La Borda were the work of
a Spaniard, José de la Borda, who had amassed a fortune from
working the Taxco silver mines early in the eighteenth century,
and at the time of their construction were estimated to have
cost upwards of a million pesos.[1] When Maximilian first set
eyes on the place the house had become dilapidated and the
gardens overgrown, but he declared himself enchanted nevertheless, and ordered repairs to be quickly put in hand. The
house, which was a stone building of one storey, with an attractive
veranda running its whole length on one side, was completely
renovated, tapestries were hung on the walls, the gardens were
cleared and the swimming-pool put in order. The interior
furnishings were of chintz " in the simplest style ", and consisted mainly, as one visitor put it, of " that Viennese twisted
cane furniture one sees in arbours and suburban villas ". As
the house was small there was never room for more than two
or three guests at a time. One of the first visitors was the new
Foreign Minister Castillo, " a polite young man with curly
hair and whiskers provoking the Emperor to say that he looked
like a wax figure out of a hairdresser's shop ". At all events
he impressed observers more by his manners than his knowledge
of diplomacy. Another visitor was Archbishop Labastida, who
disgusted everyone by indulging in " the dreadful Mexican
fashion of belching at dinner ". Many other Mexicans visited
La Borda, including the Imperialist Generals Miramón and Mejía,
whose fortunes were later to be tragically linked with the
Emperor's. Most constant amongst the European guests was
the Austrian Professor Billimek, an eccentric naturalist who had
once been a monk and who had been employed by Maximilian
to assemble a natural history collection at Lacroma. " His
equipment included an immense yellow umbrella, a cork helmet
and a linen duster with capacious pockets ", wrote Blasio.
" Occasionally he would take off his helmet and display to us
centipedes, scorpions, flies, grasshoppers and grubs pinned to

[1] José de la Borda (1716–1794) has often been described incorrectly as a Frenchman,
since he spent his later years in France, where he was known as Joseph le Borde and
where he was guillotined during the Revolution in Paris. Authoritative biographical
details are given by Manuel Toussaint in his *Don José de la Borda restituído a España*
(Mexico, 1933).

the lining." Maximilian, who was passionately interested in insect life, would spend hours with the professor, as his secretary put it, " perfectly happy ".

The days were spent riding, walking, picnicking or strolling in the gardens, which abounded in mangoes, coffee, bougainvillea and every kind of tropical plant and shrub. During the day Maximilian liked to wear charro dress with a large grey sombrero bordered with silver lace. As a rule he would work with his secretary on the veranda where the whole household invariably assembled for coffee after dinner. " He was at heart most good-natured," said the Austrian Baron Malortie, recalling these occasions, " a most delightful companion and conversationalist." The household staff was small. The Emperor had one aide-de-camp, the secretary Blasio, and his valet Grill. Grill's wife did the cooking for the household, her favourite fare being Viennese schnitzel and Hungarian goulash. Carlota kept a single lady-in-waiting in attendance, usually Señorita Josefa Varela, a beautiful young Indian who was directly descended from the Aztec poet-king Netzahualcoyotl. The Empress as a rule appeared in white with a bunch of fresh flowers pinned to her dress. It was a simple, gay and natural life for everyone there. The sound of a running stream filled the air and the whole place breathed an atmosphere of complete restfulness. An especially delightful feature was an artificial lake in the gardens to which the members of the household and their guests would come on moonlit nights for a swim in the tepid waters.

Throughout the year 1866, which witnessed the progressive ebb of the Imperialist fortunes, Maximilian went to Cuernavaca whenever he could. He also built a small brick bungalow or " Indian chalet " for Carlota in the near-by village of Acapacingo which was called El Olvido (Forgetfulness), and which, in the Empress's words, was " surrounded by dense groves of oleanders, orange and banana trees scattered in graceful profusion by the hand of nature ".[1] The road from Mexico City, hitherto almost impassable, was now thoroughly repaired, while the bandit-infested woods through which it passed were regularly patrolled

[1] The remains of this property, which lies about half a mile to the south of Cuernavaca, can still be seen, but the place is now completely overgrown and neglected.

by the military, so that the route for the first time came to be regarded as safe for travellers. In fact the Emperor's visits to Cuernavaca became so frequent that people began to say that there was a stronger attraction in the neighbourhood than the good air and low altitude. The story, which has an unexpectedly plebeian ring about it and is hardly in keeping with Hapsburg tradition, was that Maximilian had succumbed to the charms of the pretty seventeen-year-old Mexican wife of the gardener at La Borda and that she had willingly responded to His Majesty's advances. However, it is confirmed by several reliable and independent witnesses, including Colonel Blanchot, an officer on Bazaine's staff who subsequently wrote the history of the French intervention in Mexico. Her name is stated to have been Concepción Sedano y Leguizano and it has been established that she bore the Emperor a son.[1]

The nature of Maximilian's relations with some of the ladies about the Court has already been noticed, and at La Borda it is fairly certain that the gardener's young wife was not the sole object of the Emperor's attentions. Blasio, who spent the greater part of the day at Cuernavaca with him, found it difficult in his youthful innocence to believe that such things could be, until one day the valet Grill enlightened him. " At Cuernavaca ", said Grill, " the guards were so stationed that they could not have seen a woman going in or coming out. Did you never notice a narrow door in the garden wall, scarcely wide enough to let one person through? It was always closed, but that door could tell you many curious things about the people who used it." [2]

To what extent, if at all, Carlota was aware of these interests on her husband's part it is impossible to determine with any measure of certainty. It was commonly said that stories of Maximilian's infidelities had reached her ears and impelled her to pass whole weeks at La Borda in an attempt to find out if they were true. If she did discover anything, she kept the

---

[1] He was born in Cuernavaca on August 30, 1866. For his subsequent history see below, p. 313 *et seq.*

[2] The door, which led from the *zaguán* or carriage entrance into the bathroom of Maximilian's private apartment, can still be seen. It is in the south-east part of the building facing the Avenida Zapata, and it has recently been restored along with the rest of the property by the present tenant, Sr. Eduardo Bollio Rendón.

knowledge to herself. All she would admit was that Maximilian was extremely attached to the place. " The Emperor ", she wrote at this time, " is very fond of Cuernavaca because he can work there more at his ease."

5

The Emperor was at last gradually realizing how serious was the internal condition of the country and how precarious his throne was becoming. He no longer toured the provinces. Towards the end of 1865 he had hoped to visit the peninsula of Yucatan, but he finally decided he could not leave the capital and sent Carlota instead. The Empress met with a good reception on the whole, particularly from the Indian population, but although she constantly told her attendants what pleasure the journey was giving her, she could not effectually conceal her anxiety for the welfare of the Empire.

The Empress left the capital early in November, immediately after her Saint's Day, which was celebrated with considerable pomp. She was attended by a fairly sizable retinue including Ramírez, Eloin, General Uraga, Señorita Josefa Varela and another lady-in-waiting, a chaplain, physician and about fifteen servants. On the morning of her departure two thousand Indians assembled in the main patio of the National Palace, where the Empress and Maximilian distributed silver medals. On one side of each medal was the likeness of the Virgin of Guadalupe and on the other that of the two sovereigns.

The Emperor accompanied his consort for a few miles of her journey, but he turned back before she reached Puebla. Here, as also at Orizaba where stops were made, Carlota's reception was cool, for both these places were dominated by the Conservatives, who felt extremely annoyed that the Empress should be escorted by such prominent Liberals as Ramírez and Uraga. However, it was a different story at Vera Cruz, which had strong Liberal sympathies. There were balls, concerts and illuminations and the Empress was dragged through the streets of the port in a triumphal car.

The next stage of the journey had to be made by sea and, as the Empress did not wish to embark in any but a Mexican vessel, a passage had been arranged in the *Tabasco*, a miserable craft, while most of the rest of her entourage went on board the comfortable Austrian corvette *Dandolo* which served as escort. After two days of choppy seas and misery for the Empress during which she felt, as she put it, " like a sick bird ", the two vessels put in to Sisal, whose white houses impressed Carlota with their roofs made of the dried maize leaves. A deputation was waiting to greet her ; the local priest, who declaimed an address of welcome, referred to the Empress as " the angel of peace who had crossed the seas bringing prosperity in her arms ". Thence she set out for the ancient Mayan city of Mérida in an open landau. The Indians whom she met on the way, particularly the women with their embroidered dresses of many colours, did not seem to her to have changed much since the days of the Aztec Montezuma. She was moved by their almost child-like enthusiasm. " Everyone acclaimed me and threw flowers at my carriage ", she wrote to Maximilian.

It was the same in Mérida, where she passed beneath a decorated arch and received the keys of Yucatan's capital town from the civic authorities. Everywhere garlands and " *Vivas* ". She noticed that the shouts had a peculiarly personal note about them. They were for herself and for the Emperor, and she even heard one for her father Leopold, but there were few " *Vivas* " for Mexico, for, as she explained to Maximilian, everyone was for the dynasty, " the dynasty of the country ". The dark healthy-looking men with a touch of gallantry about them and the beautiful pale women, she felt, were monarchists by nature and had a real respect for sovereign authority. " Since they thus have something to live for," she added, " they occupy themselves little with democratic theories." In this well-ordered population the Church naturally played a conspicuous part. On entering the Cathedral Carlota had been particularly struck by the numerous clergy officiating in their golden vestments before a high altar of solid silver, " which gives you an idea of the wealth of the Church before the spoliation ".[1] She had to admit, however, that the whole structure and background of

[1] This celebrated altar together with the monstrances and Church vestments were stolen during the revolution in 1917.

this society was thoroughly medieval in character and reminded her of the Old World with its conception of sovereign rights. "Everything is exactly like old colonial Spain", as she put it in her account to her husband. "In a word, nothing is American and the Middle Ages are reflected on all sides."

Carlota was greatly taken with the kind, courteous, friendly and hospitable ways of the Yucatecos. She liked their characteristic traits. As she drove along the road to Mérida she noticed telegraph wires which she was told were the first to be erected in the peninsula. At first the local inhabitants were inclined to dismiss this novel method of communication as a device imported from Mexico City which was " no better than the devil ". However, as soon as it was installed the natives proceeded to telegraph assiduously all day, and it became so popular in Mérida that chairs had to be set out in the telegraph office for the convenience of the ladies who came to watch it in operation.

The Empress saw only the good side of this relic of pre-Aztec civilization. She was especially struck by the absence of beggars and the general air of contentment. "No one has asked me for alms ", she remarked in a slight tone of surprise, " and I have not had a single petition for assistance." She was fascinated by the fine houses and clean streets, and above all by the tumultuous welcome she received. The house in which she stayed was surrounded by a cheering mob, and on the night of her arrival she had been obliged to appear on the balcony and deliver a short speech in Spanish appropriate to the occasion. She had seen nothing like it since she was in Venice. "I don't know what people die from here," she told Maximilian, " but it is from neither unhappiness nor chagrin. Life goes on like a perpetual springtime and it is easy to understand how the people love their surroundings."

From Mérida the Empress continued her tour overland as far as Campeche, whence she re-embarked for Vera Cruz. A touching scene occurred in the house of a poor Indian woman where Carlota stopped and at the woman's request joined in the meal which she had prepared for herself and her family. "I like Your Majesty very much ", the Indian told her simply, " because you are very good and because you have an Indian lady of honour, which proves that Your Majesty does not dislike but, on the contrary, loves the Indians."

On the way the Empress also paused to see the two-thousand-year-old Mayan ruins of Uxmal with their emblems of phallic worship and indecipherable inscriptions whose meaning has baffled generations of archaeologists. In this tropical spot, where she confessed that the heat overwhelmed her though it was the month of December, Carlota suddenly became a prey to sad thoughts and an inexplicable feeling of depression. The mood persisted until she returned to Vera Cruz a fortnight later, and a vigorous ride on horseback through the picturesque country-side failed to shake it off. She was particularly conscious of it on December 10 when she felt more in the presence of God than with the people of this world. It was in fact on this date that her father Leopold I, King of the Belgians, passed away in his palace at Laeken. His last thoughts had been of Charlotte and Max in Mexico and the difficulties against which they were struggling. " What counts in America is success ", he had written to them from his death-bed. " Everything else is mere poetic twaddle and waste of money."

A great change became apparent in the Empress as the result of this expedition. She looked worried and drawn, and these distressing features continued long after the period of Court mourning for her late father had terminated. She became more and more depressed and at times irritable, and indeed for a while she was ill. At a later stage the theory was advanced that she had been deliberately poisoned in Yucatan by being given in some fruit a quantity of *toloache*, a herb which in small doses was known to disturb the mind. Others said that the poison was administered out of a sense of revenge by the husband of Maximilian's love at La Borda. There is no reliable evidence for any of these tales, although later in 1866 Maximilian was to receive an anonymous letter in which the writer stated that the Empress had been poisoned in Cuernavaca.[1] The decline in

[1] Frederic Hall, the American lawyer who assisted in Maximilian's defence at his trial in Querétaro, states in his *Mexico under Maximilian* (New York, 1868), at p. 57, that the writer of the anonymous letter, who was apparently a woman, subsequently admitted to an acquaintance of his that " she had heard statements which appeared to her quite satisfactory that poison had been administered to the Empress ".

health seem to have been caused, or at least promoted, by her husband's political troubles which gave her much concern at this time. As for herself, everyone liked her. " Wherever she went ", remarked Blasio, " she attracted regard, especially in Mexico City, where even the most irreconcilable enemies of the Empire admired her magnanimous heart and praised the maternity hospital she founded, which did not cost the treasury a centavo and which still exists as an imperishable remembrance of her." In any event, as most of the Mexican journals subsequently pointed out in denying that Carlota had been poisoned in their country by their people, they did not conquer their foes in that way ; such barbarous treatment, if it really occurred, could only be the work of monsters like Napoleon or Bazaine.

One of the first letters which Carlota wrote, when she felt well enough, was to her old friend Countess Hulst whom she was always anxious to convince that the Mexican venture, to which she was opposed, had hitherto not been in vain. If the Empire were eventually to collapse, it would be through no fault of her own or Maximilian's, for they both were trying their hardest to make it a success. For herself, she was determined to stick gamely to her task as Empress and she was not the person to want to leave the country for the sake of a few clouds or breakers on the horizon. " Put yourself in my place ", she added, " and ask yourself whether life at Miramar is preferable to that in Mexico. No ! I say, a hundred times no ! For my part I would infinitely rather have a job which involves activity and duty and, if you wish, even difficulties, than sit looking at the sea until I am seventy years old."

6

It will be remembered that on Lincoln's death Maximilian had written a letter to his successor in the White House in which he raised the subject of supporters of the Confederacy migrating to Mexico. Although President Johnson had refused to receive the letter, his action had not prevented a Confederate army corps and about two thousand civilians from crossing the Rio Grande after General Lee's surrender at Appomattox. The immigrants included such well-known southern figures as ex-Governor Sterling Price of Missouri, ex-Governor Isham G. Harris of Tennessee, General John B. Magruder, who had commanded the Confederate forces in Texas, and Commander Matthew F. Maury, the well-known hydrographer and meteorologist who had been one of the Confederate commissioners in Europe. They looked forward to establishing new homes in Mexico and hoped that the country's soil might yield its wealth to their experienced southern hands.

Among the Confederate leaders Matthew Fontaine Maury had been known to the Emperor since the time of his appointment as head of the newly created United States Naval Observatory in Washington more than ten years before. Maury had been the first naval authority to encourage masters of ocean-going vessels to make systematic tide and weather reports and observations of marine life. Maximilian had himself been a pioneer in marine exploration. When the *Novara* had been sent round the world on a scientific expedition in 1855, during his term as Commander-in-Chief of the Austrian navy, he had entered into an enthusiastic correspondence with Maury on the objects of the cruise ; and on his return from Brazil five years later he had sent Maury the log of the *Elizabeth*'s voyage. Maury had consequently become a warm admirer of the Archduke, as Maximilian then was, and it was through Maximilian's hands that the Austrian gold medal of arts and sciences had been conferred upon him. When he read in the newspapers that a deputation of Mexican notables had been to Miramar, Maury had publicly expressed the view that the Mexicans would indeed be fortunate in securing " so enlightened a prince and so generous a patron of art to rule over them ". It was quite natural, therefore, that when the Confederate commander appeared in Mexico and offered his services Maximilian should turn them to account. What the Emperor did was to appoint Maury to the office of Imperial Commissioner of Colonization and Immigration, at an annual salary of $5,000, and Director of the Astronomical Observatory in Mexico City.

" If Maximilian is wise and will encourage my plans ", wrote Maury to a friend at this time, " I can assist mightily to make firm the foundations of his dynasty." On September 5, 1865, the Emperor had issued a decree after consultation with Maury in which the colonization scheme was outlined : immigrants were to receive a good title to their lands, were to be tax-free for the first year and were to be allowed to bring in their agricultural tools and seeds without paying duty. Those immigrants who could show that they had lost everything in the Civil War were to receive free passage to Mexico. As part of the scheme a Land Office was set up under General Magruder to survey the lands prior to transfer to the settlers. Under the impetus of these arrangements Confederate colonies were established in the states of Vera Cruz, San Luis Potosí, Jalisco and Chihuahua.

The settlement in the state of Vera Cruz, which was near Córdoba, was called the " Carlota Colony " as a compliment to the Empress, whom, as one of the settlers put it, " we all love and admire and for whom we are ready at any moment to shed what remains of Confederate blood in this and the other country ". Price and Harris and Maury's son Richard were among those who acquired land in this settlement. " In the olden times Córdoba was the garden spot of New Spain ", wrote Maury in describing the foundation of the colony. " There stands on one side and but a little way off the peak of Orizaba with its cap of everlasting snow, and on the other side the sea is in full view. The lands are heavily in debt to the Church, and as the Church property has been confiscated (not by the Emperor, though) Maximilian took possession of these lands for colonization. The railway hence to Vera Cruz passes right through them—and I am now selling these lands to immigrants, as fast as they can be surveyed, at $1.00 the acre at five years' credit. There are about forty of our people already here. . . . By the time these lands are paid they will be worth, even if no more settlers come to the Empire, $20, $30 or even $100 the acre — for they produce everything under the sun and yield perpetual harvests."

Unfortunately the town of Carlota, which it was hoped would soon become as large as Richmond or New Orleans, never developed beyond a few hastily improvised dwellings. Nor did the colonization schemes in the other parts of the country fare any better. There were various reasons for the failure of Maury's plans, the strongest of them being north of the Rio Grande. First, the whole idea of Confederate settlement in Mexico met with a hostile press in the south as well as the north. While the Yankee papers referred to the inhabitants of the Carlota Colony as " seedy southern exiles ", the journals in Richmond and Charleston criticized the Confederate immigrants for leaving their country just when they were most wanted in the work of reconstruction. Secondly, the Federal commanders in Texas and California put every obstacle in the way of would-be settlers leaving these territories. General Sheridan, for instance, refused to let intending immigrants embark at New Orleans since he was determined, so he said, " to break up the Maury nest of Confederates which was agitating the public mind of the south and preventing the people there from quietly sub-mitting to subjugation ". In any event, the civil war which was raging between the Imperialists and the Juáristas in Mexico was not calculated to encourage them to begin a new life in such insecure surroundings. Finally, the title to some of the lands was in question, for it had been necessary to dispossess a number of Indian squatters, who promptly appealed to Juárez's forces for assistance. The result was that those imperial settle-ments which did not die a natural death from lack of immigrants were broken up by the Liberals. Such, in fact, was the fate of the Carlota Colony.

Maury had not been in office long before he found it im-possible to carry out his official business through any of Maxi-milian's ministers. He therefore requested an audience with the Emperor, to whom he explained his trouble, with the result that he was attached to the imperial civil cabinet as a councillor, which gave him direct access to Maximilian. In this role he submitted at the Emperor's request a number of confidential reports on the general state of the country. These documents were extremely outspoken in their criticisms. The ministers were principally distinguished by their greed and untrustworthi-ness, according to Maury ; the clergy were deliberately stirring up discontent against the sovereign, while they themselves were ignorant, hypocritical and immoral ; internal security was shocking, and the army could hardly be said to exist — only a few ill-disciplined units pursued about the country by hordes of women camp followers. Most public officials thought only of themselves and not of the Empire. The Emperor, Maury suggested, should show more energy and fairness and he might be obeyed more faithfully. He should, for instance, wear a uniform and surround himself by a brilliant general staff. The only figure to emerge unscathed from this severe and discouraging conspectus was Carlota, whom the Immigration Commissioner found " very clever, practical and business-like ". On one occasion when he was speaking to the Empress he told her that in his opinion she could do more business in a day than all the ministers put together could do in a week. " I believe I could," she replied.

Early in 1866 Maury obtained leave of absence from the Emperor to visit his family who had left the United States for England at the conclusion of the Civil War and whom he had not seen for several years. He seems to have had an idea that he would not return to Mexico, and so events proved ; for he had hardly reached London before he received a letter from Maximilian stating that it had been found necessary to abolish the colonization commission owing to " motives of economy and convenience". The Emperor begged him to return and continue his scientific work under the imperial patronage, but Maury pleaded that in view of what had happened his presence would only be an embarrassment. However, the pathfinder of the seas did redeem a promise which he had made to Carlota when he paid his farewell respects. He succeeded in obtaining from Clements Markham, the well-known English explorer who was then in charge of the geographical work of the India Office in London, three packets of cinchona seeds which were despatched across the Atlantic and thus made possible for the first time in Mexico the cultivation of the valuable quinine-producing bark.

The rare seeds were first planted in the neighbourhood of Córdoba. The Carlota Colony soon disintegrated and its inhabitants drifted back to the southern states, but the cinchona trees continued to flourish and long remained a meritorious if little-known remembrance of the Empress who promoted their introduction.

7

The opening of the year 1866 brought the imperial pair a host of troubles both private and public. First came the news of the Belgian King Leopold's death. A few weeks later a small mission arrived in Mexico from Belgium to announce the new King's accession. On their return from the capital to Vera Cruz they were unfortunately attacked by a group of bandits in the woods near Puebla ; Baron Huart, a young officer and aide-de-camp to the Count of Flanders, was killed, and three of his companions were wounded. Although both the Emperor and Empress attended young Huart's funeral and made every effort to bring those responsible to justice, the assailants were never captured or even identified. Such a regrettable incident was not calculated to inspire or renew confidence on the part of the European Courts in the stability of the Mexican Empire.

Maximilian's most acute problem was that of national finance and with it the military situation, since if an effective army was to be maintained it had to be paid. The civil war was costing sixty million francs a year in the maintenance of troops and by this time had reduced the State to the verge of bankruptcy. Nor was Bazaine at all helpful in the raising of local units. " I must use soldierly frankness ", wrote Maximilian at this time, " and say that the French marshal has worked day and night by endless intrigues, by orders and counter-orders, to render a good and final organization of our brave troops impossible. French policy has always aimed at keeping Mexico weak in two respects — and these the most important for the existence of the country — namely, military and financial affairs." Napoleon's orders to Bazaine to evacuate the French forces were followed by peremptory instructions from the French Finance Minister Fould to suspend all payments to the Mexican army and " finally to close " the account of the Mexican Government. The Emperor was at his wits' end. In desperation he turned to M. Langlais, the French financial adviser, who had arrived in the autumn of the previous year. Langlais, who was an extremely competent financier, investigated the national balance-sheet carefully and promised to help. "I shall manage it," he said confidently, "but the Emperor must roll up his shirt-sleeves and put his hand to the plough with the rest of us. If he does as I propose, I guarantee to save him. If not, I give it up."

Langlais, in spite of his native allegiance, had the interests of the Mexican Empire very much at heart, and, had he lived, he might have reached his objective. He was fully aware of the atmosphere of graft in which the Mexican loans had been administered by the Paris financiers. In fact he told Maximilian that he knew that considerable portions of each loan had been misappropriated in France instead of finding their way into the Mexican Treasury. He knew too that the ranks of Bazaine's army were by no means incorruptible. There considerable sums were embezzled, and dutiable goods were smuggled into the country as "military stores" by enterprising officers. Even the Marshal himself was reputed to have a controlling interest in a millinery establishment in the capital which specialized in Parisian wares and whose mistress served her principal customer in both senses of the word. But it is doubtful whether the Emperor, who seems to have been as careless of public finances as he was of his private affairs, really appreciated the gravity of what was happening. "My dear General," he said to an acquaintance who had pointed out how his supplies of wine at Chapultepec were disappearing, "everybody is more or less robbed in this world, and I dare say my butler thinks old Hock injurious to my constitution."

Unfortunately the kindly disposed Langlais died of a heart attack before he had an opportunity of putting his schemes into effect, and the management of the national exchequer was governed by those who thought only of French interests and squeezing what they could out of the country before the *débâcle*. It was useless to attempt anything further. The customs receipts from the Mexican ports, the sole remaining sources of national revenue, were now fast disappearing with the isolation of these ports by Juárist forces. In May 1866 the President of the Council of State announced that the loans were now completely exhausted, the troops that had been raised locally could no longer be paid, and the Mexican army would have to be disbanded.

Meanwhile the Emperor had despatched a number of emissaries to Europe with the object of gaining support for his tottering Empire. To Rome on his behalf went Father Augustín Fischer, a Jesuit priest whom the Emperor had met shortly after his arrival in Mexico and to whom he had become attached. Fischer was a plausible adventurer, German by birth and a convert from Protestantism, who had once earned a precarious livelihood as an agricultural labourer and, generally speaking, had led a disorderly life. He had produced a draft concordat which he undertook to get accepted at the Vatican, so that Maximilian had appointed him a Court Chaplain and then sent him off to the papal curia in the autumn of 1865 with a letter of introduction to the Holy Father in which he was described as " one of the most distinguished members of the Mexican clergy ". But Fischer did nothing except send gossipy letters with the latest news about Cardinal Antonelli's mistress and quarrel with the mission headed by the Conservative Velásquez de Léon which was already in Rome for the same purpose as himself. All the while the wily Papal Secretary of State, who knew full well how things were really going in Mexico, prolonged the negotiations on every conceivable pretext.

In the French capital Maximilian fared no better. Eloin, who arrived in Paris with the Emperor's reply to Napoleon's letter announcing the withdrawal of the French troops, was dismissed with scant ceremony from the Tuileries, while Loysel, the head of the military cabinet, who went over at the same time, turned out to be no more than an agent of Bazaine's. But if they did nothing else, Eloin and Loysel at least opened the Emperor's eyes to the negligence and even perfidy of his official representative in Paris, José Hidalgo. The hostile tone which the French newspapers were now adopting towards their country's commitments in Mexico reflected most discreditably on the Mexican Legation in Paris, which had been provided with funds to influence the local press. As for the Minister himself, he thought only of serving his own interests at the Tuileries, and to this end his reports to Mexico were inaccurate and misleading. Maximilian accordingly made up his mind to dismiss Hidalgo and replace him by the veteran Conservative General Almonte,

" the best that Mexico can produce ", as he told Napoleon.

Almonte, who arrived in Paris to present his credentials to Napoleon on May 20, brought with him a draft convention which went beyond the agreement concluded at Miramar in 1864, and in return for an annual payment of twenty-five million francs on the part of the Mexican Government provided that French troops should remain in the country until it was " entirely pacified ". July 15 was set as the limit to negotiations ; and, should the French Emperor not agree to them, Almonte was empowered to request that the French troops be withdrawn immediately. " If this extreme case occur," wrote Maximilian in his instructions to the new Minister, " Almonte shall give the Emperor Napoleon to understand that His Majesty the Emperor Maximilian will never abandon his great work, but, true to the responsibilities which he has assumed for the benefit of Mexico, will remain in the Empire as a good Mexican and share its fate."

Napoleon and his cabinet took little time to reject Maximilian's proposals as quite unacceptable, although they kept Almonte waiting for a fortnight before communicating their official decision to him. Finding it difficult, perhaps, to forget that the French Emperor had formerly been his patron, Almonte felt he dare not now request the immediate evacuation of the French forces in accordance with Maximilian's instructions. Maximilian had therefore to submit to the measure under pressure and in Napoleon's own time instead of insisting, as he had wished to do, on an immediate withdrawal as a sop to his wounded pride.

As a final hope Maximilian turned to Brussels and Vienna, with whose Courts Carlota and himself were linked by family ties. They could at least supply fresh recruits for the Belgian and Austrian Legions then serving in Mexico. But Leopold II, the new Belgian monarch and Carlota's brother, who was dissatisfied at the treatment already accorded the Belgian volunteers, refused even to receive Eloin to discuss the proposal. As for Austria, she agreed to despatch fresh levies, but as they were on the point of embarkation at Trieste, Mr. Motley, the American Minister in Vienna, received a note from Secretary of State Seward instructing him to ask for his passports as soon as the

first Austrian troopship weighed anchor. At the same time Seward told Romero, Juárez's Minister in Washington, that any future intervention in the internal affairs of Mexico by a European power would be regarded as a *casus belli* by the United States. Austria, who was now on the verge of a diplomatic break with Prussia, had no option but to cancel the sailings.

This news was the last straw for Maximilian. He had done everything to save the Empire, but the situation seemed to him now to be beyond saving. Painful as it was, he had to make the admission to himself that his mission had failed and his plans to regenerate Mexico on a firm imperial basis had miscarried. He resolved, therefore, to announce his abdication publicly and leave the country.

When Carlota heard this decision, she immediately reproached her husband for his weakness and, as Napoleon had done so successfully two years before, she appealed to his sense of honour. Just as a brave soldier did not abandon his post before the enemy, she pointed out, so he must not abandon his crown. She herself would go to Europe and plead the Empire's cause in person with Napoleon and the Pope. But Maximilian must remain at his post. "Abdication amounts to pronouncing sentence on oneself and writing oneself down as incompetent," she told him, " and this is only admissible in old men and idiots ; it is not the thing for a prince thirty-four years of age, full of life and hope for the future. I know of no situation in which abdication has been anything but a mistake or a piece of cowardice. Emperors do not give themselves up. So long as there is an emperor here, there will be an Empire, even if no more than six feet of earth belong to him. The Empire is nothing but the Emperor. It is not a sufficient objection that he has no money. One will get it if one has credit, but credit can only be got by success, and success is won by effort."

In the face of this eloquent appeal Maximilian decided to stay where he was, while his consort should hasten across the Atlantic by the next steamer. He felt it was a heavy sacrifice parting with the Empress, particularly as she would have to travel through the yellow fever zone at the worst season of the year, but he gladly made it out of a sense of duty. Besides his blessing he gave her a letter to Napoleon and detailed statements of the financial situation. " Carlota with her sure tact will ascertain how far we can still reckon upon the help of sluggish old Europe ", he wrote at the same time. " If the old continent abandons us entirely out of fear of North America, as Austria has already done, we shall at least know for certain that we must help ourselves by our own efforts alone."

VIII. *Carlota's Voyage*

THE Empress and her suite left Mexico City at four o'clock in the morning of July 9, 1866. Besides the Foreign Minister Castillo, the party included the gentlemen-in-waiting del Valle and Bombelles, the lady-in-waiting Manuela del Barrio and her husband, the Imperial Comptroller Kuhacsevich and his wife, and her personal physician Dr. Bouslavek. She was also escorted by a detachment of cavalry commanded by Colonel López. Maximilian accompanied her as far as Ayutla, and there they bade each other farewell — as it turned out, for the last time in their lives. The Emperor, however, hoped to see her back in the near future. " The months during which we shall be separated by the ocean will indeed be the hardest trial in my life," he said, " but great sacrifices must be made for great objects."

The first night was spent at a hacienda on the route, where they were joined by General Count Thun, commander of the Austrian Volunteers, and his observant aide, Baron Malortie, The host had prepared a table of thirty covers in a spacious gallery overlooking the most beautiful grounds which had been illuminated for the occasion. The Empress was in good spirits, and after dinner held a small circle at which she chatted gaily to everyone, although Baron Malortie noticed disapprovingly that when coffee and cigarettes were handed round some of the older ladies puffed their smoke into her face " without the slightest compunction at this incredible breach of etiquette and good breeding ". Several of the ladies even followed Her Majesty into her bedroom and offered " to put her to bed if she wished it ".

Next day the Empress made a state entry into Puebla, where she was received with fitting ceremony by the Cardinal Archbishop. A bull-fight, banquet and other festivities followed. Carlota stayed the night in Puebla, where, according to the secretary Blasio, a curious incident occurred. About midnight, some time after she had retired, the Empress suddenly reappeared, called for a carriage, and asked to be driven to the house of Señor Esteva, who had been prefect of the town but at that time was occupying a post in Vera Cruz. On arriving at the house she called out until the caretaker opened the door and admitted her. She then walked through the empty rooms until she reached the dining-room, which she pointed out as the scene of a banquet which she had attended some months before. She then returned to her lodgings without explaining to her attendants the reason for this strange visit.

Next day Carlota continued her journey to Orizaba and thence to Córdoba and Paso del Macho, which had by this time become the farthest point reached inland by the railway from Vera Cruz. On the way the cavalcade encountered torrential rain which made the roads almost impassable. Furthermore, there was the constant danger of running into Juárist *guerrilleros* ; indeed on one evening the Empress's carriage mules were driven off by bandits amid shouts of " Adios ! Mama Carlota ! " Carlota's carriage also got stuck repeatedly in the mire, which made her so irritable that she continued the journey for a while on horseback. She astonished her companions somewhat by expressing fear that the French mail steamer at Vera Cruz would not wait for her, and, in her anxiety to reach the coast quickly, she rode through the night, " a truly glorious vision on her splendid thoroughbred charger ", as Malortie remarked, " against the silvery rays of a full moon ". A white dust mantle over her grey well-fitting riding-habit and a large sombrero with a long floating veil contributed to give her, added the Baron, " the appearance of an elf-like fairy queen racing through the night of time in company of a host of faithful retainers ". In an endeavour to shorten the journey she pushed her mount hard as only a nervous and impatient rider can. Otherwise Malortie did not notice anything unusual about her behaviour. In fact her animated looks and conversation reminded him vividly of the happy days he had spent with her and the Emperor at Cuernavaca.

At Vera Cruz, which the party reached on July 13, the strangest incident of the whole journey so far took place, and it was witnessed by the crowd of natives which had collected by the quayside to observe the Empress's departure. When she saw that the launch which was to take her out to the steamer *Empress Eugénie* was flying the French flag, she refused to go on board until the Mexican flag was run up in its place. After some argument the Captain of the Port, not wishing to cause a scene, issued the necessary instructions and the substitution was made. In these circumstances did the Empress embark, shaking hands first with a great number of people who had come to see her off to whom she said : "*Auf baldiges Wiedersehn!*" She now looked quite cheerful and said she hoped to be back in Mexico within three months. The *Empress Eugénie* sailed at six o'clock the same evening.[1]

The voyage to France was uneventful. Sometimes the Empress appeared gloomy and depressed, but at other times she was her old gay self and talked to Bombelles and Manuela del Barrio of the bright future of the Mexican Empire and of her gratification at being able to open Napoleon's eyes to the depths of Bazaine's turpitude. She refused to go ashore at Havana where the vessel put in for two days. On August 8 the *Empress Eugénie* steamed into the harbour of St. Nazaire. Here disappointment awaited Carlota. Of the Mexicans in Paris only Almonte and his wife were there to greet their sovereign, and they brought bad news. Prussia had invaded Bohemia, and within a few weeks the Austrian troops had been overwhelmingly defeated in the field, and the peace for which Franz Joseph had been immediately obliged to sue had confirmed Prussia's hegemony among the German states. At the same time, heartened by an alliance with Prussia, the new Italian monarch had taken up arms against Austria and, in spite of suffering a severe naval reverse at the hands of Admiral Tegetthoff off Lissa, Victor Emmanuel had at last succeeded in wresting the province of Venetia from Austrian domination. It now began to look as if it might be France's turn next.

At St. Nazaire nothing was ready for the Empress's reception, and the Prefect of the Department had not received any instruc-

[1] It is difficult to accept Malortie's statement that the Empress's departure was made secretly with the intention of deceiving Bazaine, since the announcement of her intended journey appeared in the official gazette *Diario del Imperio* published in Mexico City on July 7, and the embarkation from Vera Cruz took place in full view of the public.

tions on the point from Paris. In fact both the Prefect and the Under-Prefect had already made themselves scarce as they feared they might compromise their chances of professional advancement if they participated in any official welcome to the Mexican Empress. Only the Mayor rose to the occasion. There was not even a Mexican flag in sight, for the simple reason that nobody possessed one. However, one of the local inhabitants, who had recently returned from South America, produced the Peruvian national emblem, which was incongruously draped across the Empress's path as she stepped on to the quay and was received by the Mayor. This worthy individual stammered out a few excuses and regrets, and, displaying a remarkable ignorance of protocol, informed Her Majesty that there were two comfortable hotels in the town where she and her suite might dine well and spend the night if they felt so inclined.

Carlota could scarcely contain her anger. She was furious at the Prefect's absence and said so, and she also commented harshly on the fact that there were no troops to present arms and that she would be obliged to traverse the streets of the town without a proper military escort. In fact she had to walk some distance to one of the hotels before she could find a hackney cab to drive her to the railway station. Before entering her carriage she wrote out a telegram to Napoleon which she handed to the Mayor to despatch. " I have today arrived at St. Nazaire ", it read, " charged by the Emperor with the mission of discussing with Your Majesty various matters concerning Mexico. I beg to assure Her Majesty of my friendship and to believe what a pleasure it will be to me to see Your Majesties again." At the same time she sent telegrams to her brother in Brussels and her mother-in-law in Vienna, curtly informing them that owing to the attitude of their Governments she would be unable to visit them. As might be imagined, these latter messages caused the most painful impression in both capitals.

At Nantes, where the train stopped, Carlota was handed a telegram which contained Napoleon's answer to hers. " I have returned from Vichy ill," wired the French Emperor in an endeavour to gain time, " so that I am not in a position to come to meet you. If, as I suppose, Your Majesty is going first to

Belgium, you will give me time to recover." This attempt to put her off only infuriated her. She replied that she was coming to Paris, and she immediately resumed her journey. She arrived during the afternoon of August 9. Napoleon had detailed an aide-de-camp and some orderlies to meet her with the Court carriages, but by an unfortunate mistake they went to the wrong station. There were only a few Mexicans, including Gutiérrez de Estrada whom Almonte had warned. There was no red carpet, no official welcome, and no offer of accommodation in one of the imperial palaces. Deeply hurt, the Empress drove to the Grand Hotel in a hired carriage with her lady-in-waiting. She had scarcely arrived when Napoleon's emissaries came hurrying up with profuse apologies. They enquired politely when it would be convenient for Her Majesty to receive her imperial sister and expressed curiosity as to how long the Empress of Mexico intended to remain. Carlota replied that any hour suited her on the following day and for the rest that she was thinking of staying in Paris, since she " had no family or other interests which were not bound up with others ".

2

The French Empress accompanied by her suite drove up to the Grand Hotel at two o'clock on the following afternoon. Carlota was waiting at the top of the marble staircase with her ladies and gentlemen-in-waiting distributed throughout the building so as " to give a favourable impression of the good breeding of the Court of Mexico ". Castillo, the Foreign Minister, remained with Carlota to emphasize the official nature of the visit as well as his own position as a member of the Mexican Government. Carlota descended to the first step of the staircase and welcomed her distinguished visitor with an embrace and a kiss. The two Empresses then retired to Carlota's sitting-room, where the hostess in somewhat agitated words proceeded to describe the difficult position which confronted her husband in Mexico. Though affecting sympathy for her unfortunate sister, Eugénie said little, but rather attempted to steer the conversation into less serious channels. She asked about the

Court ceremonial and entertainments and expressed particular interest in the imperial villa at Cuernavaca. However, Carlota was not to be diverted from her main objective, and before the interview terminated she made it abundantly clear to Eugénie that, although Prussia might have disturbed the balance of power in Europe, France's work in the New World was far from complete.

Finally, Carlota brought up the delicate subject of when she might return the call.

" The day after tomorrow, if Your Majesty so wishes," replied Eugénie.

" And the Emperor ? " Carlota went on. " Shall I not be able to see him too ? "

" Oh ! " said Eugénie, who had been expecting this request. " The Emperor is still unwell."

Carlota was now afraid that Napoleon would go off to some watering-place and that she would not be able to see him at all. She therefore asked if she might come on the following day, adding that she would insist with all her might on seeing the Emperor. " Otherwise," she said menacingly, " I shall break in upon him."

Somewhat taken aback by these words and by Carlota's obvious excitement when she uttered them, Eugénie appeared embarrassed. But she quickly recovered herself and took her leave when she had assured Carlota that she looked forward to a visit from her at St. Cloud next day. She said goodbye to Carlota at the top of the staircase.

Carlota returned to her room, her cheeks still glowing, and sat down to write an account of the meeting to Maximilian. " What struck me ", she remarked with almost uncanny accuracy, " was that I know more about China than these people here know about Mexico, where they have ventured upon one of the greatest enterprises in which the French flag has ever been involved.[1] I thought I noticed that the Empress has lost much of her youth and strength since I last saw her, and that amid all their greatness any sort of pressure, real or imaginary, is irksome

[1] The Empress Eugénie, who had recently read the account of the conquest of Mexico by Cortés with his handful of followers, naïvely enquired of General d'Hérillier on Bazaine's staff " why so many men were needed to pacify Mexico *now* ! "

to Napoleon and his wife and that they cannot endure it any longer. The throne of France soon ages those who sit upon it, but History teaches that this warlike nation, like the goddess of fortune, smiles only upon the young."

In visiting the Grand Hotel the Empress Eugénie had hoped to spare her husband a painful and unpleasant interview. She now realized that Carlota was determined, come what may, to see Napoleon, and that, if he failed to put in an appearance on her arrival at St. Cloud, she would in all probability carry out her threat and really burst into his private apartments. Eugénie therefore told the Emperor that he had better see Carlota. It was too bad in view of everything, but he would have to go through with it. Napoleon was not at all well and, to add to his worries, the French Minister to Prussia had just arrived from Berlin with the disturbing news that Count Bismarck was determined to go to war with France if Napoleon did not modify his foreign policy in several important particulars. A marked air of uneasiness reigned in the imperial château.

At noon next day, August 11, two open Court carriages drew up before the Grand Hotel to take the Empress of Mexico and her attendants to St. Cloud. Carlota, who looked particularly elegant in a black silk dress and a new white hat which she had bought for the occasion, drove off in the first carriage with Señora Almonte, while del Valle and the faithful Manuela del Barrio followed in the second. Quite a crowd had collected before the hotel and the people cheered her on her way. This unexpected ovation pleased her, for she had lately heard only of the dislike felt by the French for Mexico. Nevertheless, she fingered her lace mantilla nervously and she kept squeezing her companion's arm as if for support. The colour in her cheeks ebbed and flowed. But Señora Almonte succeeded in calming her and by the time they reached St. Cloud she was once more thoroughly self-composed. As her carriage passed through the park gates the guard turned out and she gracefully acknowledged their salutes, and on approaching the château she bowed graciously to the imperial standard which fluttered in the breeze.

The carriage stopped at the foot of the stone staircase leading to Napoleon's private apartments. At the top stood the Emperor and his consort surrounded by members of their household. The Emperor looked pale and ill at ease. The little Prince Imperial, then ten years old, bounded down the staircase wearing the Order of the Mexican Eagle round his neck and helped the distinguished guest out of her carriage. Carlota slowly mounted the steps between two ranks of guards in their bearskins, and after she had been welcomed and had presented her attendants, she was conducted to the Emperor's study, where she remained closeted for the next two hours with Napoleon and Eugénie.

"Monsieur," said Carlota to the Emperor as she sat down, "I have come to save a cause which is your own." With this she handed him Maximilian's letter which she had brought together with other documents, including a number of detailed financial statements. Although she was in a state of extreme nervousness and excitement, she spoke intelligibly and forcefully. The object of her mission was plain enough to the French Emperor, and he listened silently as she developed the familiar and unpleasant theme. With real eloquence Carlota appealed to him not to abandon a cause which was so closely bound up with his dynastic interests, and she drew a truly moving picture of Maximilian's uncomfortable and increasingly dangerous position. France was a rich nation with a population of forty millions, great capital resources and a victorious army, she pointed out, and it was ridiculous to say that nothing could be done for the Mexican Empire. Napoleon must recall Bazaine, he must continue the expeditionary force until the districts threatened by Juárez's forces had been pacified, and he must also renew the pay subsidies for the auxiliary troops. The financial position was extremely serious and the scarcity of money threatened to paralyse the whole domestic administration. In fact, Maximilian was so short of funds that he had been obliged to finance her journey from the cash reserve kept to cover the paper currency.

Carlota's words undoubtedly made an impression on her listeners, and in the case of Napoleon it was a sad one. The Emperor looked helplessly at his wife like a man, as Carlota wrote afterwards, "who knows that he is being ruined but does not know how to act". Large tears rolled down his cheeks and in his debilitated condition the Emperor cut a sorry figure. At last he pulled himself together, and told his visitor briefly that the matter did not depend upon him and that he personally was unable to do anything. "We have done our best by Maximilian," he said in as kindly a tone as he could command, "but all we can do now is to help him to escape from his present danger." Carlota, however, refusing to take no for an answer, declared that she saw where the difficulties lay and that she would take up all the points personally with the Emperor's ministers and talk them round. This moved Napoleon to say that he would have another word with his advisers before the decision could be considered irrevocable. So the long interview terminated.

A curious incident occurred at this momentous conference which subsequently gave rise to the alarming but, as it happened, quite erroneous report that Carlota's life was endangered. During the impassioned conversation which took place the door suddenly opened and a footman appeared carrying a decanter of orangeade on a silver tray. This refreshment had in fact been sent in by one of Eugénie's ladies-in-waiting who had heard that Carlota liked something cooling to drink in hot weather. Both Eugénie and Carlota were rather surprised at the interruption. At first Carlota refused the offer of a glass, but on being pressed eventually was persuaded to drink. The story later received credence in certain quarters that this was a deliberate attempt on the part of the French Emperor and Empress to poison their guest. Needless to say, it was entirely devoid of foundation.

There is no doubt that the meeting was an extremely trying one for Carlota as well as for her host and hostess. Her face clearly showed signs of anguish and nervous tension, and Napoleon realized how deeply hurt she was. There was an embarrassing wait until the postillions, who had wandered off into the park, could be found and the carriages got ready for the return journey. After refusing an invitation to stay to luncheon Carlota walked to her conveyance without assistance, declining the arm of the aide-de-camp who rushed to her side. But the French Empress noticed that on entering the carriage she sank back into the cushions in an attitude of complete despair, languid and exhausted. The carriage drove off quickly, but Carlota seemed momentarily unconscious of her surroundings, and as she passed by the imperial standard she did not repeat the salute she had given on her arrival.

3

The two succeeding days were spent, as Carlota had intimated, in seeing the various French ministers. The unfortunate Empress got precisely nowhere with any of them. Outwardly they pretended to agree with her while thinking otherwise to themselves. The Foreign Minister Drouyn de Lhuys was most accommodating, but he did not mind particularly what he said as, unknown to Carlota, he had his resignation in his pocket. On the other hand, Achille Fould, the clever Jewish Finance Minister, took a hasty leave of her before the discussion had properly ended, as he felt if he remained much longer he would be convinced by the Empress's arguments. He was so impressed by the description of Mexico's mineral wealth which he was given that he exclaimed : " Had I been young, *I* too would have gone to that country."

A more unwelcome caller on the Empress perhaps than any of Napoleon's ministers was Doña Alicia Iturbide, who came to the Grand Hotel to demand the return of her child. Carlota received her coldly, and did not ask her to sit down. The visitor, however, had no compunction in seating herself on the same sofa as Her Majesty and speaking very plainly.

Carlota regarded her with evident displeasure. " I have done you great honour in giving you this interview," she said. " You should not make me regret it. I wished simply to tell you that your child is well and improving every day in person and intelligence."

Doña Alicia interrupted with the remark that the separation was a source of great grief to her.

" I am treating your child with the greatest kindness," said the Empress. " I am supporting it with my own money."

Doña Alicia replied that she asked nothing more than the

privilege of supporting the child herself.

" If we give you back your child," said Carlota, " you should refund the money the Emperor paid to your family."

To this Señora Iturbide answered that what the family had received was in reality a debt due from the Mexican nation, but that they would refund it rather than be deprived of little Augustín.

The Empress thereupon altered her tactics. " What advantage can your son be to me ? The Emperor and I are both young ; we may have children of our own."

" I earnestly hope so," commented the mother, " if that will restore me mine."

" You may have other children," said Carlota.

" I do not know," replied Doña Alicia. " I am sure of this one and I want him."

" For how long are you willing to give him up to us ? "

" Not an hour longer than I am compelled to ! "

This somewhat bickering interview ended with the Empress advising her tiresome caller to write personally to the Emperor.

" I have done so many times," was the answer, " and received no reply."

" Then write again," said Carlota, " and write politely."

On August 13 Carlota paid another visit to St. Cloud, this time privately. She again saw Napoleon, and on this occasion laid before him extracts from those letters of his in which he had undertaken to guarantee the stability and integrity of the Mexican Empire. " You may be sure ", such were the words that Napoleon was reminded he had once written, " that my support will not fail you in the fulfilment of the task you are so courageously undertaking." And again, had not Napoleon once very properly asked Maximilian what he would think of him if he suddenly were to say that he could no longer fulfil the terms of the agreement to which he had set his signature ? It was no use. Napoleon squirmed in his seat and looked most unhappy, but he put off his visitor with evasive replies, saying that everything now depended on the Ministerial Council which was meeting to consider the matter on the following day. At the same time, wrote Carlota in her account of this meeting to her husband, " he spoke a great deal about Mexico, but it is as though he had long since forgotten the affair. He wept more the second time than the first." In fact both Napoleon and Eugénie had taken to weeping frequently. "I do not know whether it leads to anything", Carlota added.

Eugénie succeeded in cutting short the interview, which was obviously of the greatest embarrassment to her husband, by inviting Carlota to her own apartments. Here the visitor, who was already considerably worked up, found the financier Fould as well as Marshal Randon, the Minister of War. Carlota could not contain her anger and she spoke out in no measured terms. What had become of the difference between the nominal amount of the Mexican loans and the sum actually paid to Mexico? "Who are the persons," she said, pointing to Fould, "whose pockets are filled with gold at Mexico's expense?" As Fould tried in vain to defend himself, she turned on the War Minister and proceeded to enumerate all Bazaine's gross errors which had produced such a dreadful military situation in the country. "If those in Paris," she shouted, "had conspired to bring about the ruin of the Empire, they could not have acted otherwise."

By this time Carlota had worked herself up into a state of hysterical frenzy. She had completely lost all self-control, and threw herself sobbing into an armchair. The unhappy woman was later helped into her carriage in a half-fainting condition, and as she was driven away the ministers who had been witnesses of this pathetic and undignified scene shook their heads. They were sorry, but they could do nothing.

Next day the ministers met in council to consider the Mexican situation. The Minister of War argued strongly in favour of the withdrawal of French troops, and Fould spoke with equal fervour against contributing any more money in support of the Empire. It was unanimously decided to abandon Maximilian and Carlota to their fate and to send instructions to Bazaine by the next steamer to get out as quickly as possible.

As the Ministerial Council were in no hurry to inform Carlota of their unfavourable decision, Carlota appealed to the War Minister, who broke the bad news to her. Meanwhile Drouyn de Lhuys had sent for Almonte and requested him to inform Castillo officially. Carlota tried to stave this off by getting the

Mexican Foreign Minister to feign indisposition. She thereby hoped to keep the matter alive on a personal plane between herself and Napoleon. "I take my answers only from the Emperor himself," she told Rouher, the Minister President, "to whom I put the question." She insisted that she was not negotiating with the French Government but with the French Emperor, and that he must see her again.

Napoleon eventually agreed to see Carlota, and on August 19 he called at the Grand Hotel with the intention of telling her quite frankly and clearly that she could hope for nothing more. The meeting was short. Carlota quickly divined the Emperor's intention, and she interrupted him as he was speaking, thereby hoping to avoid a direct refusal. Finally, Napoleon, with a decidedly exasperated air, told her flatly that she had better not indulge in any more illusions. Carlota was beside herself with rage and apprehension.

"Your Majesty is immediately concerned in this affair and ought not to indulge in any either," she said, her eyes blazing with anger.

The French Emperor immediately rose and left the room without another word. Two days later he sent Carlota formal notification that her demands were refused. "It is henceforward impossible", he wrote, "for me to give Mexico another *écu* or another man."

This communication infuriated Carlota more than ever, and she made up her mind to leave Paris immediately for Miramar. Before doing so she wrote to Maximilian. It was a long rambling letter full of vindictive hate for the French Emperor and showing alarming signs of persecution mania. To her disordered imagination Napoleon had become the Devil incarnate, and she asserted that on the occasion of their final interview his expression was so hideous that it would make one's hair stand on end. Bazaine and Fould were his attendant satellites, and the general conspiracy had been joined by Almonte who had thus basely betrayed her.

Paris, August 22, 1866

. . . I have the satisfaction of having upset all their arguments, brought all their false pretexts to nought, and thereby given you a moral triumph which He curtly refuses, and no power can aid us, for He has hell on his side and we have not. It is not the opposition ; He chooses the legislative bodies. Still less is it his anxiety about the United States. He means to commit a long-premeditated evil deed ; not out of cowardice or discouragement or for any reason whatsoever, but because He is the evil principle upon earth and wants to get rid of the good. Only humanity does not see that his deeds are evil and they adore him. . . .

. . . I cannot see clearly whether they want you to abdicate or not here. I think you ought to maintain yourself as long as possible, for if hell is thrown out, it would be in the interest of France and the whole of Europe to make a great empire in Mexico, and we can do this. Things in the Old World are sickening and depressing. He is so near, and one smells him in all the bloodshed, in every nation that is seeking unity. Bismarck and Prim are his agents ; He makes propaganda in every country and laughs over the victims who have fallen. On the other side of the ocean one can defy him.

. . . You cannot exist in the same hemisphere as He, He would burn you to ashes : He can hardly bring himself to mention your name. You must get rid of the financial agents or else master them, and separate military affairs from the French, otherwise you are lost. The whole army question and the amalgamation have been clear proof of this. If you can find support from native elements, the matter is feasible ; but do not trust the French. One never knows whether it is not He who is bringing them. If Europe became aware of your situation, money would come in from every side. All Frenchmen have a material interest in the affair for their trade and power. So soon as you shall send for me I shall be overjoyed, but I think that you cannot exist in Europe with Him and that He fills the whole atmosphere from the North Cape to Cape Matapan. I hope that you will soon summon me if you rid yourself of Him in Mexico. My visit is the heaviest blow he had had for some time, and many people are interesting themselves in me everywhere.

She also wrote that she was inheriting money and jewels from all sides. Unhappily Carlota's mind was showing unmistakable signs of giving way, and she was in fact on the verge of a complete mental breakdown.

4

The Empress left Paris on August 23 with her suite, having come to the conclusion that her most dignified course was to travel through Italy to Miramar and then await news from Mexico. Napoleon showed some consideration in placing a special train at her disposal and in arranging for her to be appropriately received by the prefects and other officials at the principal stops on the journey through France to the Italian frontier. But the agonized and distraught woman only found these attentions " official-looking and contemptible ", and on approaching Italy she thanked God that she was at last leaving the country where " He " lived and " poisoned the atmosphere with his villainy ".

In that portion of the new Italian kingdom through which she went Carlota was accorded a royal welcome. At Turin she was received by the mayor and municipal authorities. Although she felt that the country had suffered much in the recent war, which she attributed to " the hand of the destroyer of men ", on the whole she was pleased with " the national appearance of all things ". She felt that " the red volunteers and the soldiers from all regions united under one flag have a martial air which befits a young nation and is a sign of faith and strength ". It was the same in familiar Milan, where the commanding general welcomed her in the King's name, and also in Como whither she turned aside to spend a few days resting in her late father's magnificent villa on the lake. " The Kingdom of Italy is springing wonderfully into being," she wrote, " and what strikes one is the transformation of the revolutionary spirit into a new and mighty national feeling. There are no longer any constrained and forbidding faces, everything is natural and friendly."

The sight of the Villa d'Este brought back a flood of happy recollections mingled with pangs of sadness. In her bedroom she found her husband's portrait — doubtless placed there on purpose — inscribed *Governatore Generale del Regno Lombardo-Veneto*. Her eyes filled with tears as she took up her pen and described the scene to Maximilian. " In this land so full of memories and happiness and enjoyment of the best years of our life ", she wrote, " I never cease thinking of you. . . . Everything here breathes of you. Your Lake Como, of which you were so fond, lies before my eyes in all its blue calm. All is the same ; only you are over there, far far away, and nearly ten years have passed by ! And yet I remembered it all as if it were yesterday, and Nature here speaks to me of nothing but untarnished happiness, not of difficulties and disappointments. All the names, all that happened, come forth again from some long-unused corner of my brain, and I live once more in our Lombardy as if we had never left it. In two days I have lived over again the two years which were so dear to us. . . . The moon is shining now, and there has been singing ; it is beautiful beyond words."

The rest did Carlota good. Her spirits rose. She was delighted with the attentions she received everywhere, particularly on Sunday when she went to Mass in the Cathedral and the local inhabitants crowded round her. She felt " it was not curiosity but grateful affection ". But in spite of the improvement in her nerves she still suffered from the delusion that she was being persecuted. Whilst out driving with Countess del Barrio she suddenly leaned across the carriage and ordered the driver to whip up the horses and drive back to the villa as fast as they could go. Then, pointing with her parasol to an old peasant who was sitting by the side of the road with a carbine by his side, she said to her lady-in-waiting : " You noticed that old man ? Well, I have recognized him. It is Almonte in disguise bribed to shoot me, but we passed too quickly, and I have escaped him for this occasion. We must leave tonight in all secrecy, otherwise I am lost." She then covered her face with a handkerchief and made the Countess change places with her, remarking as she did so that " that old traitor will never think I am in the carriage when he sees you in the place of honour ".

The imperial physician did not consider it advisable to oppose his mistress's wishes and thus the Empress and her party hurriedly continued their journey. As things turned out, the next stage was, as Carlota herself put it, the most interesting experience she ever enjoyed. At Desenzano Garibaldi's volunteers in their red shirts gave her a thundering ovation, as the Mexican standard fluttered side by side with the Italian tricolour. " They have a brisk and patriotic air," she noted, " the flower of the youth of Italy." The great Italian Liberator was recovering from the recent campaign, as a result of which Venetia had at last been

FRANÇOIS ACHILLE BAZAINE, MARSHAL OF FRANCE

BENITO JUÁREZ, PRESIDENT OF MEXICO

From contemporary photographs

THE EMPRESS CARLOTA IN 1866

From a contemporary photograph

incorporated in the kingdom of Italy, and in his absence the Empress was received by his deputy General Hany. Pointing to the two flags, she was delighted when the General said that " the Emperor Maximilian would carry all Europe with him ". Carlota was delighted, too, that " the revolution in Europe should show its respect and recognition of the young American monarchy. It would not have happened to any monarch over here, for none of them deserves it unless it be in many respects the King of Italy himself." On the opposite shore of Lake Garda stood the Austrian cannon " like a symbol of stiff old traditional Europe " : they also fired off a salute and a band played the Austrian national anthem. From Verona to Peschiera she was escorted by two of Garibaldi's officers and thence to Venice by five Austrians, including a naval officer, Baron Hahn, who had once served under Maximilian's command. " Thus old and new Europe vied with each other in paying attentions to the wife of the Mexican Emperor ", wrote Carlota at the time. " All sovereign honours were shown to me by both Austria and Italy, and the King of Italy came from Rovigo to Padua especially to greet me. Nothing was asked for, but nothing was refused, for it is an advantage that the powers of Europe should bow before an American sovereign." As a monarch Victor Emmanuel impressed her greatly. " He is a man with a heart : he believes firmly in Italy and really plays a part there, more than is supposed. I consider him one of the best sovereigns in Europe, for he loves the people."

Carlota reached Trieste to find Admiral Tegetthoff's fleet riding at anchor in the harbour, and she was loudly cheered by the crews as in pouring rain she boarded the flagship to congratulate the gallant commander on the victorious engagement off Lissa. Tegetthoff replied that the splendid condition of the fleet which had enabled it to overcome an opposing force of superior numbers was largely due to the Emperor's achievements when in command of the Austrian navy. The Admiral had just received a letter from Maximilian which he proudly displayed. " The glorious victory, which you have gained over a brave enemy vastly superior in numbers and nurtured in grand old naval traditions," wrote the Emperor, " has filled my heart with unmixed joy. When I handed over to others the care of the navy, which had become so dear to me, and relinquished the task of making the land of my birth great and mighty by sea amid the clash of contending nations, I looked hopefully to you and the young generation of officers and men whom I had been glad to see growing up and striving in a noble emulation under my command."

Back at last in Miramar, the unhappy Empress wandered from room to room showing quite childish joy at everything she saw. The Mexican arms had been put up in the dining-room, and Maximilian's former physician, Dr. Jilek, who had always been opposed to his master's imperial venture, had with a touch of almost blasphemous irony garlanded the escutcheon with thorns. She wrote a rapturous account to Maximilian of all the improvements in the gardens and added that she appreciated the place to the full for the first time. "Everybody is amazed at these two works of the absent Prince," she wrote to Maximilian on September 9, " the battle of Lissa and the palace of Miramar. These ideas are associated in everybody's speeches and even before their eyes, for today the victorious squadron will pass Miramar in the same order of battle as at Lissa, with Tegetthoff leading in the *Erzherzog Ferdinand Max*. Morituri te salutant. It is the navy's last salute, for it is leaving Trieste and perhaps disappearing from history. It cast the first ray upon your coming power, upon your dearly bought independence ; it saved the coast which was so dear to you ; now it too will leave Austria and your brother to their fate. Its mission is accomplished. So is yours. The honour of the house of Hapsburg crossed the Atlantic with the name of one of their last victories, Novara. It is sinking here with the sun to rise again over there. The motto of your forefathers was ' plus ultra.' Charles the Fifth showed the way. You have followed him. Do not regret it. God was with him."

From this fantasy of dreams Carlota was suddenly recalled to a sharp sense of reality by a telegram from Mexico. It contained bad news. Tampico had fallen, the Juáristas were already fighting near Vera Cruz, and Bazaine was busily evacuating one place after another in spite of his written promise to pacify the country. Maximilian asked her to inform Napoleon of this "detestable military situation" immediately, and he also urged her as a last resort to go to Rome and see the Pope.

Carlota was considerably upset by this news. She wrote to Napoleon and Almonte that on her side Mexico would remain faithful to the French alliance and that the Emperor would not follow any other line of foreign policy. She also wrote to the Belgian Minister in Rome requesting him to inform His Holiness of the desirability of resolving the difficulties between Mexico and the Vatican by means of a concordat. But she could not at first make up her mind whether or not to go to Rome herself immediately and plead her husband's cause there. Finally, she decided to wait for Maximilian's young Mexican secretary, José Blasio, who, according to a further telegram received, was on his way to Miramar with fresh instructions for her.

Meanwhile she wrote page after page to Maximilian begging him to hold his ground and stand firm at all costs. She deluded herself that the abandonment of France's tutelage was really a blessing in disguise, since "when the Liberal party sees that you are staying, it will submit to you in a body, and then no further reason will exist for the United States and Europe to mistrust a monarchy founded upon the will of the people". Maximilian must say plainly to everyone : "I am Emperor". Nobody wanted a President, for "the republic is a stepmother like Protestantism and monarchy is the salvation of humanity : the monarch is a good shepherd, the president a mercenary". The outlook in Europe was bad. There disturbance would break out which would last for years, and Austria would lose all her territory. Only in the New World was there hope, she wrote wildly. "Then we shall be able to alter states and appoint kings at our will ! We on our continent have now such fullness of youth and promise that we need only civilization and men to reach heights unknown upon earth. Everything in Europe, on the other hand, looks like mere playthings. One does not understand the smallness and weakness of it till one has been over there."

As darkness descended on her mind Carlota's mood alternated between insane ambition and abject despair. She had tried so hard in this mission to succeed, but against "Him" one was powerless. " I hope, dear treasure," she wrote in one of her last lucid letters to Maximilian, " that you will be satisfied with me, for I have worked incessantly for the object you have set before me."

5

Blasio appeared at Miramar on September 17 and he was immediately conducted to the Empress's apartments. On entering them the secretary noticed that Carlota was dressed in deep mourning and her face betrayed signs of intense suffering. She eyed him suspiciously as she spoke.

" Why are you so late ? Since you arrived at St. Nazaire we have lived here in the greatest impatience. You should have understood how anxious we were and not delayed a moment in coming to find us."

The young man protested respectfully that he had come as quickly as he could. He had to wait a day in Paris in order to cash a letter of credit, since he had arrived there on a Sunday. Otherwise he had spent all his time in railway trains and hotels. He then handed over the despatches which he had brought.

The Empress tore them open, looking carefully before she did so at the seals. She questioned Blasio again.

" Are you sure that no one has touched the Emperor's letters either on your crossing or on your way through France ? "

Blasio assured her that the papers had been in a small brief-case which had never left him. " Your Majesty can also see," he added, " that the seals are intact and that according to the way-bill not a single document given to me when I left Mexico City is missing. I also believe Your Majesty cannot doubt my loyalty for a moment and my proud devotion to your person."

" I do not doubt you for a moment," replied Carlota, " but you come from America. You are ingenuous and suspect no one. That would not happen if you knew the intrigues of the European Courts. I am always afraid of Napoleon, who is our mortal enemy."

Maximilian had written rather more reassuringly of events in Mexico, but at the same time had urged his consort to proceed to Rome as soon as possible, for their last hope rested with the

Holy Father. Carlota therefore instructed Blasio to go ahead with Kuhacsevich and make the necessary arrangements for her reception on the way. The date of departure was set for September 18. It was decided to make the first stage of the journey overland by way of the Tyrol as cholera was raging in Trieste, and the Italian authorities had declared that all ships clearing from Austrian ports must spend a fortnight in quarantine. On the eve of her departure Carlota presided at a dinner in the castle to celebrate Mexican Independence Day. Blasio thought that she was much more cheerful and he listened to her talking with some of her old animation on the possibility of the Empire holding out without French assistance.

The most alarming symptoms began to make themselves evident in the course of the journey. At Bolzano, where a stop was made for the night, she suddenly announced to Castillo, who had accompanied her, that she felt unwell and could not continue the journey ; she added that she had been poisoned by Napoleon's spies and traitors, by whom she was surrounded, and bade her attendants increase their vigilance. She also imagined she saw Colonel Lamadrid, commandant of the Mexico City municipal guard, playing a street-organ in disguise. A telegram was accordingly despatched to Kuhacsevich and Blasio, who were at Reggio, telling them to return immediately to Miramar. However, when these two got as far as Mantua they received another telegram telling them that the Empress had changed her mind and would proceed with the journey after all. Carlota travelled by post-chaise to Mantua, which was then the nearest town to the Italian frontier, and after an appropriate reception by the Austrian garrison, entered a special train bound for Rome by way of Ancona. During the journey she again sent for Blasio and cross-examined him on his custody of the despatches which he had brought with him from Mexico. At Foligno, where a stop was made in the afternoon of the 25th, the Empress said she was too tired to attend the dinner which had been arranged for her by the civil authorities and dined alone instead with Countess del Barrio in her carriage.

It was dark and raining when the train at last steamed into the principal station in Rome at eleven o'clock the same night.

A delegation of cardinals sent by His Holiness and some members of the diplomatic corps were waiting to welcome the Empress. A company of Papal Guards was also in attendance, and these troops escorted Her Majesty to the hotel, the Albergo di Roma, opposite the Church of San Carlo in the Corso, where the whole of the first floor had been reserved for Carlota and her suite. By this time the Empress was feeling thoroughly exhausted.

Next morning Carlota awoke somewhat refreshed to find the sun shining brightly. After breakfast she went out with her lady-in-waiting to see the principal churches in the Eternal City and later in the day she drove through the beautiful Pincio gardens. In the afternoon Cardinal Antonelli, the Papal Secretary of State, called at the hotel and spent an hour with the Empress. The wily cleric, who appeared in a purple cassock and mantle and was attended by a powdered lackey, informed Carlota that the Holy Father would be prepared to receive her on the following day, but he studiously avoided being drawn into any discussion on the supposed demerits of Napoleon III, for, like his master, the Cardinal was fully conscious that the French Emperor represented the last bulwark which stood between the states of the Church and the kingdom of Italy. His Eminence did not, however, neglect to deliver a lecture on Maximilian's shortcomings with regard to the Church in Mexico which was accepted by Carlota with becoming humility.

Meanwhile a succession of callers had appeared at the hotel to pay their respects to the Empress and sign the visitors' book. A detachment of the Papal Guard and a body of French troops which were still garrisoned in Rome alternated in providing a guard of honour both within and outside the Albergo di Roma. There was also a band which played at stated intervals throughout the day. All this show naturally attracted a crowd of curious sightseers who were intent upon catching a glimpse of the Empress, and they never tired of watching the picturesque charro costume of the Mexican servants.

The Empress's audience with the Pope had been arranged for the following morning, September 27. Shortly before eleven Carlota, accompanied by Count del Valle and Countess del

Barrio, drove into the Vatican in a state coach drawn by four horses and escorted by a corps of Papal cuirassiers. The famous Swiss Guard, resplendent in their coloured uniforms which had been designed by Michelangelo, lined the corridor leading from the stairway to the throne-room. Here His Holiness Pope Pius IX sat in a high gilt chair dressed in a cassock of fine white wool and surrounded by cardinals, bishops and other dignitaries of the Church. As the Empress approached and knelt to kiss the Pope's foot, Pius stopped her gently and extended his right hand for her to press her lips instead to the Papal ring. The Pope then blessed the Empress and her suite and immediately afterwards everyone retired to leave Pius and Carlota alone together.

No one knows exactly what passed between these two august persons at this audience, but it is certain that Carlota handed the Pope the draft concordat which had been despatched by her husband from Mexico. She also no doubt heard from his lips the sad truth, which she had already guessed after her talk with Cardinal Antonelli, that Pius declined to intervene with Napoleon. At all events, Blasio and her other attendants remarked that after the conclusion of the audience, which lasted for over an hour, she drove back to the hotel in gloomy silence. She then dismissed her suite from attendance upon her, asked that the guard of honour be withdrawn and the band stop playing, and finally shut herself up alone in her apartments, appearing only for meals with her suite. The same evening she came into dinner in a bad temper, insisted on Castillo sitting on her right although the place was properly due to Velásquez de Léon ; she refused to have any coffee or sherbet until everyone else had been helped, and she finally had the coffee-pot removed because she thought there was a hole in it.

On the following day Velásquez de Léon was confined to bed with some minor ailment. The Empress sent for him three or four times and eventually ordered him to be brought before her in his bed. As this could not be done, she sent an attendant to find out what was the matter with him, as she felt sure he had been poisoned at her table the previous day.

On the 29th the Empress emerged from her seclusion to

receive the Pope, who came to return her visit. This call, which was remarkably short, passed off without incident. At its termination Pius solemnly blessed her suite. That evening at dinner it was noticed that she ate nothing but oranges and nuts after she had first made sure that the peel and shells were intact. On the following day she ate little and drank nothing at all, fearing that everything liquid set before her was poisoned.

Very early in the morning of October 1 she awoke Countess del Barrio and told her to order a cab. Together they drove to the Fontana di Trevi, Rome's most magnificent fountains, and the Empress quenched her thirst with the crystal water. To her lady-in-waiting's astonishment she then ordered the driver to take them to the Vatican. On arriving at the gates she dismissed the cab and told the driver not to come back for her. She then asked to see the Supreme Pontiff. On this occasion she was dressed in deepest mourning, which included a cloak of black velvet and a small bonnet with black silk ribbons tied under her chin. To the guards her sunken eyes and flushed cheeks presented a strange appearance. However, they hastened to comply with her request and after a short delay told her that His Holiness would receive her immediately.

The Pope had just said an early Mass and at the moment Carlota was announced he was partaking of a frugal breakfast in his private apartment. The distraught Empress threw herself at his feet and amid floods of tears begged His Holiness to have all the members of her suite arrested as they were trying to poison her, adding that in the hotel she was surrounded by the spies and agents of Napoleon. A half-finished cup of chocolate was standing on the Pope's breakfast tray, and as soon as she saw it Carlota dipped three of her fingers into the cup and putting them to her mouth exclaimed : " This at least is not poisoned. Everything they give me is drugged and I am starving, literally starving."

The Pope, who was not unnaturally somewhat alarmed at this remarkable outburst, attempted to calm the distracted woman without, it must be admitted, very much success. Ringing a bell near his table he asked Carlota to allow him to send for another cup of chocolate.

"No, no," she almost shrieked. "They would poison it, knowing it was for me. No thank you ! I prefer sharing Your Holiness's cup." With this she plunged her fingers into the chocolate once more.

It was now clearly apparent to the Pope that Carlota was suffering from some acute form of mental derangement. As soon as a servant appeared in answer to his summons he sent for some paper and ink, and apologizing to the Empress for writing a line to postpone some audiences, he sent a note to Antonelli instructing him to find several doctors but in order to avoid arousing Carlota's suspicions to disguise them in the Papal Chamberlains' uniforms. Antonelli was further instructed to proceed immediately to the Albergo di Roma and have all the members of the imperial suite whom the Empress had named as poisoners transferred to another hotel. Finally, the Cardinal was told to send a telegram to the Count of Flanders in Brussels asking him to come to Rome as his sister was obviously suffering from a brainstorm.

"Your Holiness cannot imagine how good it was," said Carlota, licking her fingers. "A real treat to feel one is safe, and that there is no poison." Although she was now rather calmer, the Empress kept asking the Pope whether he used any antidotes against poison. "Yes," answered His Holiness, who had by this time become a trifle exasperated ; " the rosary and prayer."

It was now the hour at which the Pope was accustomed to give his morning audiences, as Pius tactfully informed his unwanted guest. But Carlota was in no hurry to leave. "Your Holiness need not mind me," she said. "I can sit near a window, and I shan't listen ; but don't send me away just now. The assassins are waiting outside, and I dare not leave before it is dark, when I shall disguise myself and Manuelita."

At this moment Cardinal Antonelli came in, and after a few moments' conversation with the Pope in the Neapolitan dialect which Carlota did not understand, he suggested that she might like to see the treasures in the Vatican Library. To this suggestion the Empress assented, but she insisted that His Holiness should accompany her, as she fancied herself to be only safe under his personal protection. In these circumstances Pius could not do otherwise than follow her, but while her attention was engaged in examining an old illuminated folio the Pope was able to slip away unobserved, leaving her in the charge of Cardinal Antonelli and Colonel Bossi who commanded the Papal Guards. Having satisfied her curiosity here she then asked to be taken into the Vatican gardens, and when she had had another drink of water from an open spring she gave Colonel Bossi a card with the names of three of her suite written on it and begged him to have them arrested immediately. The individuals in question (Count del Valle, Dr. Bouslavek and Frau Kuhacsevich) were subsequently advised not to show themselves in the presence of the Empress, while at the same time she was informed that they had all been put in prison.

Carlota now announced her intention of remaining to luncheon, and to humour her Cardinal Antonelli was obliged to do the honours with Colonel Bossi whom she also begged not to leave her. Throughout the meal she insisted on eating everything from Countess del Barrio's plate. Afterwards she rested for a while in a room which the Cardinal thoughtfully placed at her disposal. Some time later she said she wanted to go out again and a carriage was ordered. Whilst in the Pope's private apartment she had seen a goblet which she had asked his permission to take. With this grasped firmly in one hand she drove once more to the Fountains of Trevi and drank from it. After this she walked round the equestrian statue of Marcus Aurelius in the Piazza del Campidoglio and then bought a glass of lemonade from a street vendor which she drank. Velásquez de Léon, who had now appeared on the scene, persuaded her to return to the hotel, but as soon as she had arrived in her room and found the keys missing—they had been removed by the doctor who intended to lock her in—she asked to be taken straight back to the Vatican. This was done. She reached the Vatican about nine and to the consternation of everyone said she wished to spend the night there.

6

Never before in known history had a woman spent a night in the Vatican, so that the effect which the Empress's astonishing proposal produced among the entire Papal entourage can be imagined. But Carlota was not to be moved on any consideration from the Library, where she firmly announced her intention of staying. " I shall sleep here in this room," she said ; " I cannot leave, for they are waiting for me outside. It would be madness to throw myself into the arms of these hired assassins." She added that it was an honour for the Vatican to shelter a persecuted Empress, that beds could be placed in the Library in ten minutes (for she insisted that her faithful lady-in-waiting should stay too), and that a carriage could fetch her clothes and toilet things from the hotel.

The Pope was consulted, and when he heard that Carlota had wailed that she would sleep on the stone floor in the corridor if she could not have a room, he finally gave his consent. The Library was accordingly transformed into a bedroom. Two bronze bedsteads were carried into the room, and the beds were made up with priceless lace coverlets from the Papal wardrobe, while large silver candelabra lit up this unique and curious scene. Yet in spite of all the trouble which she caused the Papal household the Empress seems to have slept little if at all. Instead, she wrote farewell letters and made her will, still convinced that she was going to be poisoned and being, as she put it in her note to the Pope, " on the threshold of death ". To Maximilian she left all her property and her jewels with the exception only of a few personal mementos for her brothers. She also desired that her body should not be embalmed or lie in state, but should be buried quite simply in the basilica of St. Peter's as near as possible to the tomb of the apostle. Finally, she dashed off a few heartrending lines to her husband :

Rome, October 1, 1866

Dearly beloved Treasure :
  I bid you farewell. God is calling me to Him. I thank you for the happiness which you have always given me.
  May God bless you and help you to win eternal bliss.

Your faithful
Charlotte.

Towards daybreak the Empress dozed off only to awake with a start, exclaiming, " Where am I ? Where have they taken me to — the wretches ? " Countess del Barrio told her she was quite safe and succeeded in calming her. On remembering where she was, Carlota said that she would like to attend Mass in the Pope's private chapel. However, on enquiries being made, the Major-domo sent back word that His Holiness could not leave his rooms, as he had been so upset by the incidents of the previous day, and that at his age the greatest care and precautions were necessary. He added that the Empress was free to assist in the prayers at St. Peter's and that orders would be given for the royal pew to be placed at her disposal. Carlota shook her head on hearing this. " How can I go to St. Peter's, a public place of worship ? " she asked fearfully. " I should be a dead woman before the service was over ; there would be one of those scoundrels behind each pillar. No, I shall do like the Holy Father and say my prayers in camera. They can't get up here. We are too well guarded in the Pope's own apartments."

Shortly after this the doctors who had been dressed up as Papal chamberlains appeared, and having explained that His Holiness hoped to see the Empress again as soon as he felt strong enough, informed her that instructions had been given for Court carriages to be in attendance at her hotel.

" At the hotel ! " exclaimed Carlota excitedly. " But I am not returning. I intend staying here as long as it is unsafe for me to leave the Vatican. I don't wish to be murdered on stepping out of the door. Pray tell His Holiness that ! Perhaps his police may be able to arrest the gang, for I want to see them all hanged before I go back to the hotel."

The disguised medicos retired saying that they would convey this message to the Holy Father. They immediately sought out Cardinal Antonelli and in conjunction with Countess del Barrio they devised another scheme to get the unfortunate Empress out of the building. The Cardinal sent word to the Mother Superior of the Convent of St. Vincent de Paul to come and invite the Empress to visit their orphanage and assist at the feeding of the poor children who were cared for in this establishment. The Mother Superior duly arrived with two of her sisters and played her part splendidly. Carlota at first declined on the ground that, as she put it, private reasons of great importance did not allow her to leave the Vatican for the present. " I know," said the Mother Superior sympathetically. " We have heard of the wretches who want to attempt Your Majesty's life, but Your Majesty would be as safe with us as here, and our children will be so disappointed if you do not come. I have given them a half-holiday, and they have been making garlands since daybreak, all dressed up in their Sunday best. Your Majesty must not refuse — the dear children would be too miserable ! "

On being assured that if the sisters showed themselves at the windows of the carriage she would be perfectly safe, the Empress eventually agreed to the expedition. During the drive, which went off without incident, she was careful to hide her face behind a handkerchief, and from her corner she kept asking whether any of the people outside were looking at the carriage or whether anyone was following it. Arriving at the Convent, Carlota completely recovered her equanimity and astonished everyone by delivering a most appropriate and quite lucid address to the five hundred orphan children who were assembled in the entrance hall to greet her.

The Empress's tour of the convent included a visit to the kitchens, where great cauldrons stood in front of the fire filled with meat and vegetables. Thinking to interest Carlota, the sister in charge offered her some of the stew to taste which was being served for that day's dinner. The Empress suddenly pushed the plate away from her with a look of terror. " You see the poison ? " she said to the Mother Superior, pointing to the knife, which had a speck of rust on it. " They have forgotten to polish the knife." With this she knelt down and, lifting up her eyes, gave thanks to the Almighty for saving her life. She then went up to the sister in charge who was standing near one of the cauldrons and told her she must not worry and that the children must not be kept waiting for their dinner. Immediately after saying this the Empress leaned over the cauldron and plunged her hand and arm up to the elbow into the boiling mass of meat and gravy. Pulling out a piece of meat she began to gnaw it voraciously. " I felt so hungry," she went on to say to the Mother Superior by way of explanation, " and they can't have poisoned this morsel."

In a few moments she began to feel the pain caused by the burn, and as soon as one of the sisters tried to bandage her arm, which presented a ghastly sight of scalded flesh, she shrieked and fainted away. Advantage was thereupon taken of this situation to carry the Empress into her carriage and drive back to the hotel. Whether on account of the pain or the jolting of the carriage, Carlota recovered consciousness as they were crossing the Piazza d'Espagna. On asking where she was being taken she was told that they were going back to the Vatican. However, she was able to pull back one of the carriage blinds with her uninjured hand, and on realizing where she was she suddenly began to shout, " Murder ! Stop the carriage ! They are killing me ! " She continued to shout in this distressing manner until the carriage reached the hotel, into which she was carried kicking and screaming through a crowd of curious bystanders who had been attracted by the noise. She was then put to bed by her maid and no one else was allowed to see her.

Meanwhile His Holiness Pope Pius IX was anxiously enquiring whether the Empress of Mexico was still in his apartments. " Everything comes our way in the end," he remarked philosophically. " Till now the only thing that hadn't happened was for a woman to go crazy in the Vatican ! "

7

The next days were spent by Carlota either brooding gloomily alone in her room at the hotel or else driving about to the various fountains, from which she would drink with the goblet which she had taken from the Pope's apartments. On October 5 His Holiness wrote her a letter in which he returned the draft concordat and begged her to keep the goblet, adding that he prayed to God every day that her peace of mind might be restored and that " He will remove those fits of suspicion which only cause your incessant agitation ". Unfortunately there were no signs of any improvement in the Empress's mental state. On the contrary, her condition grew daily more serious.

She refused to eat any food which was not prepared before her eyes, and for this purpose she had her Viennese maid Mathilde Doblinger procure a small iron charcoal stove, also several chickens which the maid was obliged to kill, dress and cook in the Empress's presence. She also sent for a cat and made it taste every dish before she herself would touch anything. She would not undress at night or go to bed, but would doze for a few hours in an armchair when she was not pacing the room restlessly and talking to herself.

She spent a good deal of time composing formal decrees in which she stated that she dismissed the various members of her suite for sundry crimes ranging from treachery to murder. Young Blasio, who was summoned to her room on October 7 to record several of these edicts, observed that the large four-poster bed showed no signs of having been slept in. He also noticed some eggs and the Pope's goblet filled with water on a table, and on the floor were several hens tied to the table legs. Her face was haggard and her general appearance neglected. The idea of being poisoned scarcely ever left her. On the following day her brother the Count of Flanders arrived, and with him she saw the ex-King and Queen of Naples, whom she solemnly warned to exercise the greatest care in what they ate and drank. That night her brother stayed in her room and she did not go to bed. In an apparent delirium she talked about the palaces she had built in Mexico, about America and its customs and about the religious ideas of the New World. She also asserted that no great person had ever died a natural death and that the ranks of those who had been poisoned included her father and mother, Lord Palmerston, and Prince Albert of England. Next day the Count of Flanders took her back to Miramar.

The homeward journey passed off without anything untoward happening, but on her arrival the Empress said she did not want to stay at Miramar but go at once to Vienna and Brussels and intercede there on Maximilian's behalf. She tried without success to escape, wearing only the clothes she stood up in and without either hat or cloak. She talked repeatedly about her husband of whose plight in her lucid moments she seemed to be fully aware : at other times she thought that even he was conspiring to poison her, because she had failed to give him an heir. On one occasion, when she appeared to be expecting him, she asked a servant why he had not been present at luncheon.

Professor Riedel, a well-known brain specialist and director of a mental home, was summoned from Vienna, and he recommended that the sick woman should see as few people as possible and should in fact be isolated from the outside world. By a tragic coincidence it was decided to install her in the pavilion or garden house in the Miramar grounds where Maximilian had shut himself up with his doctor during the last few days before he embarked for Mexico. Here in a large room, which had the windows screwed down — presumably with the object of preventing her from throwing herself out of them — the Empress spent the greater part of each day. She was encouraged by the doctors to paint and read and play the piano, but she would soon tire of these pastimes and launch forth instead into muddled political soliloquies, when she would constantly refer to the Revelation of St. John and Dürer's gruesome vision of the Apocalypse. While her mental state rapidly deteriorated, her physical condition improved. She began to eat regularly and take long walks, and no doubt as a result of this carefully supervised regimen her suspicions gradually decreased, and, except for her curious topics of conversation, to outward appearances she began to resume her normal demeanour.

For a short time the doctors believed that given time and patience a cure might eventually be effected. But by the end of the year 1866 she had become completely imbecile and her condition was regarded as hopeless. She lived in a world all her own of insane illusions and the wildest dreams of ambition. Maximilian no longer appeared to her troubled mind as a poisoner intent on taking her life : she confessed that this vision was a nightmare of which she was grateful to be relieved, and she now spoke of her husband as the " Lord of the Earth " and the " Sovereign of the Universe ". She was convinced, among other obsessions, that Napoleon had died and that Maximilian would now become Emperor of France, Spain and Portugal. Such a view, said her brother, could probably be traced to her own fundamental desire to be sovereign of "it mattered not what nor where". This ambition had driven her into the mad Mexican venture which had ended in her own madness.

*　　*　　*　　*　　*　　*

Some reference must be made here to an extraordinary legend which has been accepted widely as fact, although there is no shred of evidence beyond hearsay to justify it. The story, for what it is worth, is that shortly before leaving Mexico Carlota became pregnant by her husband and that she gave birth to a son during her unhappy seclusion at Miramar. For obvious dynastic reasons Franz Joseph was anxious that all details of the birth and parentage should be suppressed, and it is supposed to have been a term of the secret family agreement which was afterwards concluded between the Austrian Emperor and King Leopold II that this course should be followed by the latter in return for the transfer of the infant to the custody of the Belgian royal house.[1] The child, who was given his father's principal Christian name, was secretly removed from Miramar to Brussels, where he was brought up in ignorance of his parents' identity ; he joined the French army at an early age and had a brilliant career in the service of the republic which has but recently terminated. All that has been established, however, is that the birth of a male of unknown parents was registered with the civil authorities in Brussels as having occurred in that city on or about January 21, 1867, and that the child subsequently became known to the world as Maxime Weygand.

Whoever his parents may have been, it is difficult to believe that General Weygand was the son of Maximilian and Carlota or indeed that they should ever have had a child at all. It is true that during her stormy interview with Doña Iturbide in the previous summer Carlota referred to the possibility of the Emperor and herself having a child of their own,[2] but from what is known of their private domestic relations it would appear extremely unlikely that one was even conceived by them.

[1] See below, p. 304.　　　　　　[2] See above, p. 213.

IX. *Querétaro*

A FEW days after the Empress had departed on her tragic voyage from Mexico letters arrived for Maximilian from Gutiérrez and Almonte in Europe. Both these staunch Conservatives expressed the unanimous opinion in the strongest possible language — Gutiérrez in a letter forty-four pages long — that, if the Emperor did not ally himself completely with the leaders of the party which had brought him to the country, neither of them could answer for the security of the Empire much longer. After a brief reflection Maximilian yielded, although it wounded his sense of pride deeply to think that his liberalizing policy had landed the Empire in such difficulties. Towards the end of July, therefore, he dismissed his whole Cabinet, replacing it with an entirely Conservative ministry under the premiership of Teodosio Lares, former President of the Assembly of Notables which had originally proclaimed Maximilian Emperor. The new government included two French Generals, Osmont who became War Minister, and Friant who was given the portfolio of Finance.

Buoyed up by the hope that much would come of his consort's mission in Europe, Maximilian confidently announced a new policy of "action" and "energy" in Mexico. With General Osmont's assistance he hoped to raise a native army of forty thousand men by October. He also set to work to correct the gross negligence which seems to have characterized all the departments under the late ministry. According to the Emperor, there was no proper system of archives or protocol, most important papers in the Foreign Ministry were lying about the floor of the Minister's room, none of the officials kept regular office hours, and documents were always getting lost or mislaid. At the same time a number of known traitors to the Empire were arrested. "I have summoned the Conservative elements into the Government," Maximilian told Count Bombelles, "I am appealing confidently to all honourable men in the country, I am acting in a conciliatory spirit towards the bishops, I am patiently enduring the Marshal's malicious intrigues, and to my intense satisfaction I meet with the sincerest and most cordial support from all the members of my Government. If the country does not abandon itself and I do not abandon it, let France withdraw her tarnished banners in defiance of the treaties."

In spite of these well-intentioned changes, difficulties and worries crowded in on the Emperor from every side. The lack of funds presented a most acute problem. Maximilian cut his civil list most drastically, but, though it was reduced to a fifth of the original amount, he was still hard pressed for money for his most urgent needs. The cost of publishing the daily official gazette or *Diario del Imperio* had, for instance, frequently to be met out of the publisher's pocket. About the same time the Emperor was obliged to part with half of the customs receipts from the Mexican ports — the sole remaining source of national revenue — to the French in return for their promise of continued military assistance. This move was simply a ruse on Napoleon's part to squeeze as much as he could out of the country before evacuating his troops. Bazaine, in fact, quickly showed that he had no intention of pacifying the country as he had promised ; instead he began to withdraw his forces from Monterey and other important commercial centres, and early in August the fruits of this policy were seen in the loss to the Juárist forces of the important port of Tampico.

Nor was Maximilian free from private anxieties. His health began to give him trouble. He complained of frequent pains in the stomach and suffered several attacks of dysentery which left him apathetic and exhausted just when the exercise of strength of mind was required in coming to some critical decision. Further, various members of the Iturbide family, who had noted the decline of the imperial fortunes with marked satisfaction, kept pestering the Emperor for the return of little Augustín to his mother and employed the occasion to stir up public opinion in the United States, which was already inflamed by the appointment of the French Generals Osmont and Friant to important posts in the Government of the person who, it was said, " claims to be Emperor of Mexico ".

It was about this time that the first transatlantic submarine cable was opened for regular commercial traffic.¹ Maximilian hailed the invention as " the greatest scientific triumph of the age ", which, so he told the French Emperor, " by bringing us closer to each other will enable us to exchange our ideas most expeditiously and will thus contribute towards the disappearance of all misunderstanding ". In the certainty, as he put it, that " I cannot but be the gainer by this more frequent communication with your Majesty ", Maximilian sent Napoleon a telegraphic code to facilitate their intercourse by this novel means. But the transatlantic cable did not fulfil the Mexican Emperor's enthusiastic expectations. Indeed it was to prove a handicap rather than a help to him, since, apart from its being generally the bearer of bad news from Europe, Maximilian did not at first realize that, as it was connected with United States territory, the cable could be tapped and the messages which it carried intercepted by his enemies.

About the same time Eloin wrote to him from Europe of the " general discontent " which he had observed in passing through Austria. " Yet nothing is done ", added the Belgian. " The Emperor [Franz Joseph] is discouraged, the people are impatient and openly demand his abdication : sympathies for Your Majesty evidently extend throughout the Austrian Empire. In Venetia a whole party is eager to proclaim its former governor." Unfortunately this letter, together with a number of other confidential documents, including a cipher telegram with an *en clair* summary of the text, fell into the hands of Juárez's representatives in Washington, and Maximilian had the mortification of learning of their contents for the first time in the American newspapers. The impression which the publication of this letter caused at the Court of Franz Joseph can be imagined.

In the same compromising letter Eloin alluded to the French Government's refusal to permit Osmont and Friant to continue in their new posts, a fact which had already been made known to Maximilian through Bazaine, and which, to quote Eloin's words, " proves that henceforth the mask is shamelessly thrown

¹ The first transatlantic cable had actually been laid in 1857, but after a few weeks it had ceased to transmit audible signals owing to an operational error on the part of the electrician in charge. It was not until nine years later that the first commercially successful cable was completed between Valentia in Ireland and Trinity Bay in Newfoundland.

aside ". The two French Generals, who really were tackling their jobs efficiently, had in fact been informed that if they wished to continue in Maximilian's service they would be obliged to forfeit their military commissions. The consequence was that they both resigned, and with their action what little hope Maximilian had of bringing a sense of order into the Mexican army and finances finally disappeared.

Eloin advised the Emperor to remain in Mexico until the French forces had withdrawn, when the Mexican people could freely express their views as to whether Maximilian's rule should continue. If the popular vote should be adverse, then Maximilian could return to Europe, where " you will be able to play the role which by all considerations belongs to you ". Maximilian's thoughts now kept recurring to the past and for the first time he began to regret that he had ever left the Austrian navy. The news of Tegetthoff's victory at Lissa gave him a pang. " Old memories revive again ", he wrote ; " the navy with my splendid officers, my beloved Dalmatian and Istrian sailors and the wondrous Adriatic float once more before my mind's eye, and it is only with difficulty that I can control my grief at the fact that it was not granted to me to give the young flag its baptism of fire on board the ship that bears my name. But now all that is past, and nothing remains in my soul save the gratifying feeling that I have done my duty."

The post of October 1 brought a brutally frank letter from Napoleon dated August 29 in which the French Emperor confirmed the unqualified refusal to extend any further the assistance which he had already given Carlota — to whose requests, wrote Napoleon, " it was very painful for me to be unable to accede ". Napoleon posed a crucial problem. " Can you maintain yourself by your own strength or will you be forced to abdicate ? " In the former case the French Emperor promised that his troops would remain in the country until 1867 in accordance with the Convention of Miramar. However, should Maximilian decide to abandon his throne, then advantage must be taken of the French army's presence in the country to summon a representative national body and cause a government to be elected which would offer some guarantee of stability. " Your Majesty will understand how painful it is for me to enter into such details, but we can no longer lull ourselves with illusions, and it is necessary that the Mexican question, in so far as it concerns France, should be settled once and for all."

Maximilian's two most intimate advisers at this time were the iniquitous Father Fischer, who had returned from his abortive mission to Rome and had once more insinuated himself into the Emperor's confidence, and Stefan Herzfeld, a former Austrian naval officer who had served under Maximilian in the *Novara* and had recently come out to Mexico at the Emperor's invitation. Maximilian now had lengthy discussions with these men on the subject-matter of Napoleon's letter. Fischer, who represented the last hopes of the Conservative party and the clergy, was for the Emperor remaining and not hindering the withdrawal of the French troops. Herzfeld, who possessed all the bluff common sense and honesty of purpose to be expected of a sailor, strongly advised Maximilian to abdicate and leave the country.

The Emperor was still undecided as to what to do when on October 18 telegrams arrived from Castillo and Bombelles informing him that Carlota was seriously ill. The telegram from Bombelles, who was at Miramar with the Empress, gave no details but simply stated that the patient was under the care of Dr. Riedel, who had been summoned from Vienna. On learning this fact Maximilian sent for his own physician, Samuel Basch, and asked him whether he knew of Dr. Riedel.

Basch, who had no knowledge of the contents of the telegram, answered innocently : " He is the director of the lunatic asylum."

Slowly the terrible truth dawned on the unfortunate Emperor. He was distraught with grief and anxiety. Meanwhile the sympathetic Herzfeld reiterated his previous advice, and the same night Maximilian made up his mind to follow it. He briefly informed his entourage of his intention to leave the country, and two days later started for Orizaba, where he proposed to wait for further news from Miramar before continuing his journey to Vera Cruz. Instructions were sent to the captain of the Austrian corvette *Dandolo*, which was then lying in this port, to coal his vessel and be prepared to sail with the Emperor at short notice.

Maximilian was on his way to Orizaba within the next forty-eight hours. Before leaving he wrote to Bazaine asking him to suspend the activities of the courts martial and to annul the law of October 3, 1865, the notorious " Black Decree ". During the journey he passed Brigadier-General Castelnau, one of Napoleon's aides, who had been sent out to implement the contents of the French Emperor's fateful letter of August 29 and if necessary to overrule Bazaine's orders in doing so. Maximilian, however, refused to receive him, as he felt unable to face an interview which could only be decidedly unpleasant. A further disagreeable surprise awaited the Emperor at Acalcingo, where a halt was made for the night. The six white mules which drew the imperial carriage were stolen during the night. Such brazen impertinence hurt the Emperor deeply.

The Jesuit Father Fischer was naturally disturbed at this turn of events, particularly as he had not been consulted. He told the Emperor " frankly and unequivocally " that he should not desert the country at such a time, and the wily priest then proceeded to devise a plan with his Conservative friends to keep the wretched Maximilian within their control. The first move was to stage a reception at Orizaba which would flatter the Emperor's vanity and sense of popularity. Although hastily arranged, the welcome which Maximilian received on his entry into this town was quite encouraging and served the Conservative purpose well in that it contributed to a state of mind on the part of the Emperor in which he might more readily be prevailed upon to change his decision. The next step was to get rid of Herzfeld, who had all along been the most ardent protagonist of abdication and return to Europe. This was quite easy. The Emperor was induced to send Herzfeld back to Austria under the impression that he would be following him soon, and Fischer so arranged matters that the trusted Austrian was unable to see his master again before his departure.

After a week or two in the invigorating air and refreshing surroundings of Orizaba Maximilian's spirits and general health began visibly to improve. He went for long rambles with his friend old Dr. Billimek, and their pursuit of butterflies and other objects of naturalist interest was regarded with some amazement by the local inhabitants. Meanwhile Fischer and the Conservatives worked subtly on Maximilian's sense of honour. Lares reminded him of the oath which he had taken at Miramar. " What would the world say, what would history say if it were not fulfilled ? " Another of the Conservative ministers kept pointing to fictitious evidences of personal loyalty to the Emperor and repeatedly expressed his opinion that the situation could be saved by the forces which remained. " If Your Majesty were to leave us," he added, " it would be a terrible misfortune for the people." On the other hand, the English Minister Sir Peter Campbell-Scarlett, whose judgment Maximilian greatly respected, expressed the view that it was by no means certain, in the event of the Emperor following Napoleon's advice and appealing to the country, that the Mexican people would not decide to maintain the Empire, provided that French intervention completely ceased. " It is quite certain," added Scarlett on the other hand, " that after the departure of the French a strong party would prefer to rally round the imperial flag so as to save Mexico from being rent asunder by civil war and its consequences."

Meanwhile the Emperor, though weakening in his determination to abdicate, allowed the preparations for his leaving the country to continue. Case after case of his secret archives and personal valuables were transported to Vera Cruz and shipped on board the *Dandolo*. At the same time he addressed a great number of farewell letters to his friends and advisers most of which began : " On the eve of leaving our beloved fatherland ". He even composed a telegram to his mother which was to be sent at the time of his embarkation. Although his health was daily improving he appeared very different from his old self. Blasio who returned from Europe at this time was particularly struck with the change. " There were none of the jokes and good-humour of former days," noted the secretary sadly, " and his head, which before had been so proud and erect, was bowed as though by the weight of worries and sufferings."

Maximilian's resolution was further weakened by the appearance of the Conservative Generals Miramón and Márquez who had now returned from their European travels, on which they had been sent during the Emperor's flirtation with the Liberals early in his reign. Both these staunch reactionaries begged the Emperor to remain at his post and undertook to raise forces on his behalf. Maximilian was not yet wholly convinced, but he now agreed to put the question of abdication before a full Council of his ministers and other advisers whom he invited to Orizaba for the purpose. All accepted except Bazaine.

The meetings began on November 25 in the house where the Emperor was staying. The Emperor opened the proceedings with a short address in which he stated that " he did not wish to take a definite decision without previously deliberating with his councillors wholly independent of French influence ". After greeting everyone present he retired to his apartments, leaving the twenty-one Conservatives and two Liberals who had assembled to make the decision for him.

The discussions were long and heated. But Maximilian heard nothing of them, for he was out in the fields with Billimek and Basch seemingly happily engaged in chasing butterflies. Eventually the question was put to the vote of the gathering. The two Liberals, who had both formerly served in the Ministry, voted in favour of immediate abdication. Ten of the Conservatives also voted in favour of immediate abdication. Ten of the Conservatives voted in favour of the Emperor's staying. The remaining eleven wished to postpone abdication until their particular partisan interests could be safeguarded. On learning the result of this meeting, which could hardly be regarded as satisfactory, the Emperor announced his intention of convoking a national congress to decide " whether or not the Empire should continue ". All parties were to have access to the Congress " on the broadest and most liberal bases ".

The momentous decision finally to remain in Mexico was reached on November 28. " To abdicate power into the hands of foreigners would be treason and not flight," announced Maximilian. " No Hapsburg would do that — therefore a proclamation and a free Congress." The conditions under which he agreed to stay included an " arrangement for getting out of the toils of the French ", an understanding with the United States, raising of funds, reorganization of the army, and suspension of the law of October 3, 1865.

Bazaine shook his head when he heard this latest news. " The Emperor declares that he will maintain himself by his own resources ", he wrote to Paris ; " Our role is at an end. It only remains for us to withdraw as quickly as possible. Let us then leave Mexico as soon as we can." The Marshal's words were echoed by Carlota's brother, the Count of Flanders. " It appears that Max instead of returning to Europe is going to try the Empire's fortunes by his own means. I think his fall will be more violent than it would have been if he were to leave the country now."

3

The official reaction outside Mexico to Maximilian's decision to stay was one of mingled astonishment and disapprobation. Napoleon telegraphed angrily to Castelnau from Paris ordering him to hasten the evacuation of the French forces as well as all other Frenchmen in the country. The Austrian Minister Baron Lago, who disliked Maximilian intensely, did his best to dissuade his fellow countrymen from joining the reorganized Mexican army and loudly voiced his opposition to the idea of a national congress on the ground that it was beneath the dignity of a sovereign to let himself, as it were, be " balloted for " by his subjects. From Washington Secretary of State Seward had sent Mr. Lewis D. Campbell and General William T. Sherman to negotiate with Juárez on the subject of a new government, but as soon as they arrived in Vera Cruz and learned that Maximilian had changed his mind about abdicating, they immediately returned to the United States, less friendly disposed than ever to the Mexican Emperor.

Maximilian left Orizaba with his entourage on December 12. On the eve of his departure Father Fischer and the Conservative ministers had a champagne supper to celebrate what they regarded as a victory. The Jesuit felt so indisposed next day that he was unable to accompany the Emperor on his journey and was obliged to call in Dr. Basch for a " pick-me-up ".

He also began to be worried that the Emperor would discover what he termed his "immorality". The physician reassured him by saying that the Emperor had as yet not noticed anything untoward about his behaviour, although Basch himself was well aware that the reverend gentleman possessed numerous illegitimate children scattered about the country.

To the faithful Blasio, who was determined to remain by his master's side, it was a sad departure from Orizaba. "The Emperor, sensitive to impressions, was palpably downcast by presentiments, fears and anxieties," noted the secretary, "and seemed to divine that he would never return to the picturesque town which had so many memories for him and where he had spent so many pleasant days." These feelings were increased by the reception with which Maximilian met on the route. Although he was greeted quite cordially, almost everyone in the villages and towns through which he passed expressed the utmost astonishment at seeing the Emperor again, for by this time it was generally thought that he was well on the way to Europe. Sensible persons, remarked Blasio, saw in his return a pretext for a renewal of civil warfare more bloodthirsty than ever and "regarded with affectionate concern the unfortunate Hapsburg who was considered by those of judgment already to be the sacrificial victim of the Conservatives". The whole incident reminded Blasio strongly of the return of "that other luckless sovereign" Louis XVI to Paris after the celebrated flight to Varennes, and he could not dismiss from his mind the feeling that Maximilian was bound for a similar fate to that which befell the late French monarch.

The journey back to the capital was made by slow and easy stages. Long halts took place. A week was spent at Xonaca outside Puebla where the Bishop placed his country house at the Emperor's disposal. There were more botanical expeditions, a good deal of time was spent making fresh plans for Miramar and Lacroma, and pistol practice took place regularly in the garden in which the whole imperial suite was made to join. At Xonaca and later at Puebla various Utopian schemes were discussed between the Emperor and his advisers, which showed that Maximilian had virtually become a partisan instrument in the hands of the Conservatives. He finally consented to see Castelnau, but it was more with the object of humiliating Napoleon's latest emissary than of obtaining any satisfaction from him. Maximilian told him frankly that his mind was made up, he refused to abdicate, and if ever he did relinquish the throne it would only be at the unanimous vote of the national congress which he proposed shortly to convene. The Frenchman listened in silent wonder, while, to reinforce his arguments, the Emperor pulled out of his pocket a telegram which he stated he had received the previous day from Bazaine : in it the Marshal agreed with his decision to stay in Mexico, promising supples of arms and undertaking to give him every support up to the last moment of the French occupation. " I've squashed Castelnau," said Maximilian jubilantly when the interview was over.[1]

That Bazaine was playing a double game at this time only gradually became apparent. There is no doubt, however, that he was guilty of gross treachery towards the Emperor whom he buoyed up with false hopes at the same time as he was in negotiation with his enemies among the leading Liberals. Personal and family interests must to some extent account for this equivocal conduct. His young Mexican wife, who had already borne him one child, was again pregnant, and neither she nor her family, whose fortunes were in a substantial measure linked with the Empire which the Marshal had helped to establish, were particularly anxious to leave the country just then. For a while, encouraged no doubt by Pepita's relations, Bazaine toyed with the

[1] Castelnau's own remarks on the Emperor and this interview, contained in his recently published papers, are worth quoting. " What is needed above all in Mexico is a man of practical common sense and energy. The Emperor possesses neither of these qualities. He is a Utopian dreamer who remains constantly shut up *chez lui*, never mixing in the life of his people whom he does not know, never having any relations with those individuals who could really enlighten him, and spending his time in the composition of decrees which have no force whatever and which are not even published by the prefects charged with their execution. . . . He has no understanding of affairs and no initiative, but he has already acquired from the Mexicans a kind of cunning which makes him conceal his thoughts so that it is very difficult to get a decision or a definite answer out of him. I saw the Emperor at Puebla, I found him quite gracious, chatting away easily and readily, and wishing to appear a strong man in politics and diplomacy, but always reasoning from his imagination and the figments of his brain rather than from realities. A perfect ' gentleman ', gracious and good, he exhibits a dilettantism and an emotional instability which prevent him from enjoying himself in any serious work. He is often in the clouds and only comes down to earth to bother with frivolities." *La Revue de Paris*, August, 1927, at p. 593.

idea of becoming ruler of Mexico himself. But his master's express orders from the Tuileries to hasten the evacuation of the French forces reminded him that after all he was a soldier and it was his duty to obey his superiors. Nevertheless there was nothing to prevent him from enriching himself in the process. He sold everything he could lay hands on, including a carriage which had once belonged to Santa Anna and all the furniture at Buenavista which by rights was the property of the State. He even offered to dispose of large quantities of French arms and ammunition to General Díaz for a cash consideration, and when the Liberal leader refused the offer, rather than turn the *matériel* over to the Emperor, Bazaine gave orders that it should be destroyed.

On January 6, 1867, Maximilian reached Chapultepec. As the castle had been stripped of its furnishings when it was thought he was bound for Europe, the Emperor put up at the neighbouring hacienda of La Teja, whose owner obligingly placed it at his disposal, but " in conditions so unworthy of a sovereign ", wrote Castelnau, " that it astonishes and distresses me that he should have accepted them ". Here Maximilian was acclaimed enthusiastically by a crowd of Conservatives who had assembled in carriages and on horseback. But most people already regarded the imperial cause as lost. Among those who were there to greet the Emperor were the two prominent Liberals Ramírez and Escudero, who had formerly served in Maximilian's cabinet. Feeling that it was only a matter of time before their erstwhile partisans must triumph and knowing that they could expect no mercy at Juárez's hands, they had come to say farewell before leaving the country. At the same time they vainly tried to persuade the Emperor to follow their example. Maximilian shook his head. " Ramírez wept on leaving me," he told his physician afterwards. " As he prayed that his sad forebodings would not be realized, tears came into my eyes also."

Maximilian might well weep too, for the wisdom of Ramírez's advice was very soon to become only too apparent. Indeed that same night a telegram arrived from Cuernavaca with the disquieting news that the town had been attacked by the Juáristas and the beautiful villa where the Emperor had spent such happy hours had been ruthlessly pillaged. Young Colonel Lamadrid, the Commandant of the city guard, happened to be present when the telegram was opened — the same Lamadrid who formed the subject of Carlota's first weird hallucination in Italy. He asked that he might take a body of troops and dislodge the Juárists from the town. Permission was granted and the young colonel hurried off. Next day came news that the counter-attack had been successful and the Juáristas had been dislodged from Cuernavaca, but that Lamadrid while riding back on his tired horse to the town from a point some miles distant, whither he had pursued the enemy, had been ambushed by some stragglers and killed. For the second time within twenty-four hours Maximilian's eyes were filled with tears.

The Emperor persisted with his idea of a national assembly, although he now realized that any such styled gathering could not be regarded as national in any sense of the word. What actually happened was that a Conservative junta assembled in Mexico City consisting of the ministers and a number of their clerical and reactionary supporters. Bazaine, who appeared before this gathering at its request, expressed his opinion in the most emphatic language that the survival of the Empire was impossible and that in the interests of his honour and personal safety Maximilian should resign his power into the hands of the nation. On the other hand, General Márquez, who had been appointed to command the capital garrison, easily swayed the assembly with the view that the recent deterioration in the military situation was really due to popular uncertainty as to the Emperor's plans and not to Juárist successes in the country. He was supported by the Finance and War Ministers, who advanced optimistic and deceptive figures to prove the need for the continuance of the campaign and the Empire. Finally, out of a quorum of thirty-three persons present seventeen voted in favour of Maximilian's remaining, eight against and eight abstained from voting. The Emperor pronounced himself satisfied with this decision : indeed in his present frame of mind it was exactly what he wanted.

Towards the end of January a significant incident occurred

at La Teja. The police guarding the hacienda discovered two unauthorized men in the gardens. The intruders, who were promptly arrested, stated that they were thieves, but it was generally thought at the time that they were spies from the Liberal camp who had been commissioned to report on what was going on in the imperial counsels and if possible abduct the person of the Emperor. As a result of this unpleasant discovery Maximilian and his suite left the hacienda and took up their residence in the National Palace in Mexico City.

About the same time Lares as Minister-President of the Government addressed a letter to Bazaine in which he asked what form French assistance would take in the event of an attack on the capital, pointing out that in the recent Juárist attack on the town of Texcoco any such assistance had been conspicuously absent. On receipt of this letter the Marshal immediately wrote to Maximilian stating that in view of the tone of Lares's letter he could hold no further communication with the ministry and warning him against this " perfidious section of a party " which was rapidly leading him to disaster. The letter was returned to Bazaine with a note from Father Fischer that the Emperor had instructed him to say that His Majesty would not permit such language to be used about his ministers, and if Bazaine did not withdraw his words the Emperor would hold no further communication with him. The Marshal responded with a request for an audience but this was refused. The Conservatives had won their battle, and the Emperor was virtually their prisoner.

The French expeditionary force, which consisted of about two and a half divisions and was concentrated in the area of Mexico City, was now ready to leave together with the majority of the Austrian and Belgian volunteers. At dawn on February 5 the French troops began to march out of the capital with Bazaine at their head. Their bands played appropriate military music as the men stepped out and the French flags fluttered in the chill morning air. The populace greeted the departure with silence or indifference. There were no friendly farewells.

The route of the departing troops lay past the National Palace. As a mark of imperial disapproval the doors and windows of the palace remained tightly closed and even the guards were withdrawn inside the palace walls. Watching the marching men surreptitiously from behind a parapet on the roof stood a tall man with a fair beard, wrapped in a long grey cloak and wearing a wide felt sombrero. It was the Emperor. As he saw the end of the long column disappearing in the distance, he is reported to have turned towards a group of Mexicans who attended him near by and said : " At last we are free ! "

4

The Juáristas were now beginning to close in on the capital and the Emperor once more turned pathetically to his cabinet for advice. Lares and the other ministers had come to realize at last that the Empire as such could not be expected to hold out much longer, and if there was to be any hope for their own particular interests and those of the clergy, Maximilian must endeavour to secure them by coming to terms personally with the Republican leaders. Only in this way they felt could an amnesty for Imperialist partisans be obtained. But in order to achieve this object the Emperor must represent a power with which Juárez and his supporters would be willing to enter into negotiations, and accordingly the ministerial council advised Maximilian to put himself at the head of his armed forces and accompanied by as brilliant a staff and as many troops as possible to establish his headquarters in some provincial town known to be devoted to the imperial cause. Márquez suggested Queré-taro about 170 miles north of the capital. Maximilian would have preferred to reach a compromise with the Liberals without assuming the duties of Commander-in-Chief in the field. On the other hand, the suggestion appealed strongly to the romantic side of his character and so he gradually allowed himself to be convinced of the necessity of undertaking a journey which was ultimately to lead him to his Calvary.

Meanwhile the struggle between the two opposing forces continued with increasing bitterness and even ferocity. Juárez had now moved his government to Zacatecas, less than 450 miles from the northern gates of the capital, and General Miramón took advantage of this development to attempt a knock-out blow at the Republican headquarters with the object of raising the Emperor's prestige in the country which was badly in need of support. Miramón even hoped to capture the person of President Juárez, and as the event turned out he nearly succeeded. With nearly half a division which he disposed skilfully the Imperialist General managed to surround the town and launch an attack which came as a complete surprise to its inhabitants. A large number of prisoners together with guns and some important documents were captured, and Juárez only contrived to escape in a carriage and elude the pursuing cavalry with the utmost difficulty.

Unfortunately this success, which was enthusiastically proclaimed in the capital, was followed a week later by a shattering reverse. The Republican General Mariano Escobedo met Miramón at the Hacienda San Jacinto near Zacatecas and put the Imperialist army to flight. Most of Miramón's artillery was captured, his war chest fell into enemy hands, and he also lost 1,500 prisoners, including over a hundred Europeans, mostly French, as well as his own brother, General Joaquín Miramón. The fate of the prisoners was exemplary. A few days after their capture they were given some spirits and told that they were going to be transferred to another place but that, as they had to pass through the Liberal lines, it was necessary for their eyes to be bandaged. Having marched blindfold for half an hour, they came to a halt and the bandages were removed. To their horrified surprise they found themselves standing against a wall in a courtyard in San Jacinto and facing a firing party of Liberal infantrymen. When they had been informed that they had been sentenced to death by court-martial they were executed in batches of ten while their comrades looked on. A little later the captured General Miramón, who was so severely wounded in the feet that he had to be dragged to the place of execution in a chair, was shot by candlelight. Such scenes of butchery were part of a policy of terrorism whose effect Juárez intended should not be lost on the remaining adherents to his opponent's Empire.

The news of Escobedo's victory reached Bazaine whilst the latter was on the way to Vera Cruz to embark his troops. The

Marshal immediately sent a message to Mexico City informing the Emperor that he would still be glad to offer him any assistance he could to return home if he would avail himself of it immediately. But the message never reached Maximilian. By the time it had been received in the capital the Emperor had already departed for Querétaro.

Maximilian had originally planned to set out on February 12, but at the last moment the journey had to be postponed until the following day, since the Conservative ministers had failed to provide the funds which they had so boastfully promised. As it was, only about 50,000 pesos were forthcoming. Moreover the date was taken as a bad omen by the superstitious-minded who remembered that it was on the thirteenth day of the month that the Empress Carlota had set forth on her unlucky voyage to Europe.

Lares and the other ministers had succeeded in persuading Maximilian that this expedition should be a wholly native one and that the Emperor should not take any foreign troops with him or indeed any foreigners at all on his staff. The Austrian and Belgian levies were, therefore, kept in the capital, and as they were much more reliable and experienced than the Mexicans, this arrangement deprived the Emperor of a valuable military support and at the same time contributed to the security of the ministers, who likewise remained behind in Mexico City. Apart from two servants, Grill, the Italian valet, and Tudos, the Hungarian cook, the only other foreigner who accompanied the Emperor from the outset was his German Jewish physician Samuel Basch. Prince Felix Salm, a Prussian soldier of fortune who had commanded the Eighth New York Regiment in the American Civil War and had later joined the imperial Mexican army as a staff officer, particularly begged to be included in the expedition, but the Emperor regretfully refused his request. However, the intrepid Salm, who did not lack resourcefulness, succeeded without much difficulty in attaching himself to the forces of General Vidaurri which joined up with the Emperor's contingent shortly afterwards.

Attended by General Márquez, the Emperor rode out of Mexico City in the grey light of the dawn at the head of two thousand infantrymen including the "Empress's Regiment", which was commanded by the treacherous Colonel Miguel López. Only a few early risers saw what was happening, for Maximilian had kept his plans a deep secret. At Tlalnepantla, about eight miles distant, a halt was made for breakfast at which everyone toasted the success of the expedition in champagne. Immediately afterwards Maximilian underwent his baptism of fire. His force was attacked by a body of Liberal *guerrilleros* who were forced to retire after several hours' fighting. The Emperor deliberately put himself in the thick of the fray and seemed to take an insensate joy in exposing himself to the enemy bullets. "What do you want me to do?" he said to one of the Generals who remonstrated with him. "Run away the first chance I get?"

The *guerrilleros* were pursued for ten miles past the old Aztec town of Cuauhtitlan. Here an unpleasant sight met the Emperor's eyes as he rode into the main plaza. The body of an Imperialist soldier, probably one of the vanguard which had followed close on the heels of the enemy, was hanging head downwards from a tree: it had been practically hacked to pieces with *machetes*. This might be Juárez's way of fighting but it was not Maximilian's. About the same time a Liberal soldier was discovered by some of the women camp followers hiding in a ditch. He was brought before the Emperor and, although in response to interrogation he furnished some information on the enemy troop dispositions, Márquez and the other Mexican commanders wished to have him shot immediately. Maximilian, however, insisted that his life should be spared and the man was subsequently drafted into one of the cavalry regiments.

On February 16 the enemy again attacked, and this time the imperial force not only took a number of prisoners but also captured a substantial dinner which had been prepared for the Liberals in a neighbouring village and to which the Imperialists now did full justice. After this engagement Maximilian issued a general order of the day to the army in which he himself was appointed Commander-in-Chief with Márquez Chief of the General Staff, while Miramón commanded the infantry, Mejía the cavalry and Méndez the reserves. These were the five

" magic M's " round which the ensuing tragedy was to be played out. " We trust in God who protects and will protect Mexico ", so ran the imperial order, " and we shall fight under the sacred slogan, ' Long live Independence ! ' "

Three days later Maximilian reached Querétaro. The Emperor and his escort were loudly cheered as they made their way through the narrow streets of the town. The ladies threw flowers from their balconies. " Posterity ", said the town Prefect as he greeted Maximilian, " will bestow upon Your Majesty the title of Great." Everyone shouted " *Viva Maximiliano! Viva la Independencia* " as the Emperor went off to the Cathedral for the traditional Te Deum. On the whole it was a heartening reception. " In spite of the two clashes which we had with the dissidents, my journey has ended fortunately," wrote Maximilian to Eloin on his arrival, " and the welcome which I have had from the people here has been most gratifying and enthusiastic. It has been the same with my reception from the troops, who are full of courage and devotion and are determined to fight for the principles we hold sacred."

As the Emperor entered the town his horse was seen to stumble, which Prince Salm took for a bad omen. But in the excitement of the moment the incident was not generally noticed.

5

Querétaro was a picturesque old Spanish colonial town of some 30,000 inhabitants to which were now added the imperial armies consisting of about 9,000 men. Lying in the midst of a fertile valley and divided by the waters of the fast-moving Rio Blanco, the place was entirely surrounded by hills from which every house below could be reached by gun-fire. For this reason Querétaro was a most unfortunate choice of location at which to make a stand, since it could only be effectually defended by an army numerous enough to occupy the surrounding hills which Maximilian's forces were not in a position to do. Its principal merit in the eyes of the Emperor's Conservative supporters was that it was a great Catholic stronghold and for that reason strongly partisan. It was also a textile manufacturing centre of some importance.

It would have been difficult enough for this terrain to be defended by a brilliant general staff, but unhappily Maximilian's command was neither united nor particularly strong. The forty-seven-year-old Chief of Staff, General Leonardo Márquez, was a cunning, cruel and insincere adventurer of sinister appearance, known throughout the country as the " tiger of Tacubaya " because he had massacred a number of medical students who had come to succour the wounded at the engagement which took place in that suburb of the capital during the civil war which had preceded Maximilian's assumption of the crown. In spite of his ferocity, Márquez was but an indifferent soldier and was, moreover, at daggers drawn with the infantry commander Miramón. The latter, although he had little talent for generalship, was at least a straightforward brave man and a former President of the Republic. At a banquet held on the night of the Emperor's arrival Márquez proposed a toast in which he referred ironically to the youthful temerity of Miramón (he was only thirty-six) as displayed in his recent defeat. Miramón kept his temper, though white with rage. At the same time the young ex-President had another bitter enemy in the person of General Ramon Méndez, a plump, good-looking little Indian like Mejía, but ruthless as well as courageous ; he deeply distrusted Miramón who, he said not altogether without truth, " cared little either for Empire or Emperor, but only for himself and his ambitious plans ". Such unhappy rivalries as these, which neither Maximilian nor the other Generals could resolve, were ultimately bound to produce disastrous effects on the imperial cause.

As soon as he had reviewed his troops the Emperor, who had taken up his residence in the Casino, summoned his staff to a council of war. Three Republican corps commanders, Escobedo, Corona and Riva Palacio, with a combined force of about twenty-seven thousand, were advancing on Querétaro from different directions, while the most brilliant of all, young Porfirio Díaz, who had escaped from prison after his defeat at Oaxaca, was moving towards Puebla. Miramón advocated a strong offensive before the Juárist armies could effect a junction, but as might be expected he was warmly opposed by Márquez who represented that the enemy forces should be permitted to concentrate freely so that the imperial army might eventually annihilate them " at a blow ". Unfortunately these dilatory tactics prevailed with the Emperor who still secretly cherished the hope of being able to negotiate with Juárez. The Republican leader once again made it clear that as far as he and his party were concerned the issue could only be decided by the sword, but at the same time he was careful to keep Maximilian's agent in play until his main armies had united round Querétaro.

The first days which the Emperor spent in the town were comparatively quiet and uneventful. Maximilian would rise as usual at five and would work for several hours with the secretary Blasio mostly answering letters which contained requests for money. Afterwards the Emperor would go about the streets on foot dressed sometimes in civilian clothes or, if on horseback, in charro costume ; at other times he wore a plain blue uniform. He would mingle freely with the people and, as he was invariably smoking, would often ask a passer-by for a light or offer one himself. The rest of the day was spent in conversations with his staff and receiving visitors in the Casino. After an early dinner, at which he usually invited a number of guests, he would play billiards for an hour and retire to bed at nine.

Meanwhile the Liberal armies were rapidly approaching, and on March 6 General Mariano Escobedo, who had been appointed to the supreme command of the Republican troops, joined forces outside the town with General Corona. Maximilian was now confronted with a besieging army of 25,000 strong as against the 9,000 under his own command. To pay the imperial troops and provide funds for other purposes the inhabitants of Querétaro cheerfully consented to a forced loan which was levied on their collective financial resources.

As the Republican Generals were massing their troops around the town the Emperor and his staff rode out to the rocky Hill of Bells (Cerro de las Campanas) to the west of the town. There was a dense fog at first, and as it gradually cleared and the sun came out Maximilian could see the long enemy columns with their bayonets gleaming. Shouts of " *Viva el Emperador !* "

from his own men greeted him as he surveyed the scene. The spirits of the Imperialist troops were excellent. Miramón fervently hoped and begged to be allowed to attack. But as usual he was opposed by Márquez, who insisted successfully on leaving the first offensive move to the enemy in accordance with the original decision of the council of war. This was unfortunate, for the beleaguering force was at this time but a mere screen, and there is no doubt that Maximilian's troops could have broken through at any point and probably turned their flanks. However nothing was done, and at dusk the Imperialists withdrew towards the town while the Emperor established his field headquarters on the Hill of Bells, where he was to sleep under a blanket in the open air each night for the next week.

Early the following morning Blasio arrived at the hill with the latest despatches to find trenches and parapets being constructed. Soldiers were clearing away the brush and cactus, and the inhabitants who lived near by were gladly lending a hand and dragging the cannon into position. " Come to my office ! " said Maximilian, and led the secretary to a hollow cleverly concealed in the rocky side of the hill by bushes and brush. Blasio sat down and together they dealt with the correspondence, exactly, said the secretary, " as we used to do in the good old days at Chapultepec or Cuernavaca ". Occasionally they would hear a shot in the distance, but little noise interrupted them save the chirping of birds. At ten o'clock a servant appeared with breakfast consisting of roast turkey, cold meat, eggs, cheese, bread and a bottle of wine, which, in spite of the Emperor's air of deprecation, provided an excellent meal. After breakfast Maximilian lit a cigar and lay back on a rug at the entrance to the dug-out and studied the enemy camp which could be clearly seen in the distance.

During the next few days some skirmishes took place when small bodies of Imperialist cavalry attacked the Liberal positions and took a few prisoners. At the daily council of war held in the Emperor's rocky retreat Miramón invariably advocated attack and was as often overruled in the face of Márquez's opposition. Meanwhile the enemy took the opportunity of reviewing their forces and improving their positions : they also succeeded at this time in cutting the aqueduct on which the town was largely dependent for its water supply. At the end of the week, seeing that the enemy seemingly were not intending to attack, the council of war decided to withdraw to the town and set up general headquarters in the old Spanish convent of La Cruz, a massive building whose thick walls made it a miniature fortress. It was situated in the eastern part of the town and within sight of the enemy lines. Blasio noted that they arrived there on the 13th, " the Emperor's unlucky day ".

Maximilian chose for his personal quarters one of the cells in the convent. A table, two or three chairs, washstand, clothes-rack, and the iron camp bed which he always carried round with him, comprised the furnishings of this spartan apartment. Basch, Blasio and the other imperial aides lived in adjacent cells, all of which overlooked a large patio where a battalion was quartered amongst the trees. Other soldiers occupied the corridors and the remainder the cells. Sleep was difficult owing to the incessant " *Alertas* " of the sentinels and the rattling of arms as the guard was changed. The defence of the building had, of course, been entrusted to Márquez, and the foolhardy Chief of Staff had failed to fortify two prominent outbuildings consisting of a chapel and pantheon or burial-place of the convent. He gave as the astonishing reason for this neglect that the Emperor and the rest of his staff " did not know the enemy with whom they had to deal " and that the Liberals were " nothing but a worth-less rabble ".

Early next day, March 14, Escobedo launched his first serious attack on the town. The main assault was directed against the convent, the Alameda gardens to the south of the town and the bridge crossing the Rio Blanco to the north ; at the same time in a feinting movement against the Hill of Bells an attempt was made to draw off a body of Imperialists in that direction. At first dense columns of infantry advanced against the convent from the east, and thanks to the lamentable negligence of Márquez the pantheon and chapel were occupied by the enemy, who were thus able to fire directly into the convent from the chapel roof. At the same time the Imperial General Headquarters were the target for the enemy's withering artillery fire from the conveniently situated hill known as the Cuesta China to the south-east of the town. The Emperor took up his position in the plaza in front of the convent where he encouraged his forces and appeared completely oblivious to the rain of projectiles to which he was exposed. Mejía begged him to take cover. " Consider, Your Majesty," he said, " if you are killed, all of us will fight each other for the presidency." But the Indian General's entreaties were of no avail. Maximilian insisted on staying where he was while the fighting continued.

Towards evening the Imperialists, who had retreated to the patios of the convent and were in imminent danger of losing their headquarters and with them the whole town, made a determined sally, and after a fierce hand-to-hand struggle succeeded in driving the Liberals from the pantheon and the chapel and even pursued them for some distance outside the town. At the same time the enemy were repulsed at the other points of attack. Prince Salm, who commanded a regiment of Chasseurs, particularly distinguished himself during the engagement by the bridge over the Rio Blanco, when he made a brilliant charge at the head of his men and captured a cannon which had been responsible for severe havoc in the Imperialist ranks.

The enemy was thus beaten off with heavy losses, in fact suffering over 2,000 casualties as against 600 Imperialist lives. Under the influence of Salm, who was immediately promoted to the command of a brigade and became a kind of personal aide to the Emperor, Maximilian was anxious to attack while the Liberals were still disheartened and disorganized. Two days later Maximilian in fact ordered an attack, although the Generals were opposed to it. However, Miramón, who was to lead off with the infantry, overslept, so that when his troops finally took up their positions the Liberals were waiting for them, and so the offensive had to be abandoned. The Emperor was furious, but he could do nothing except confine to barracks the two staff officers whom Miramón blamed for failing to wake him.

Nothing further of consequence occurred until March 21 when a long council of war took place at which two important decisions were reached. First, it was unanimously agreed that the defence of Querétaro should be continued and that no major offensive operation should be undertaken for the present. Secondly, support was forthcoming for the Emperor's proposal to send one of the leading Generals to Mexico City to obtain reinforcements of men and supplies and generally to set matters to rights in the capital. Maximilian wished to despatch Miramón for this task, but as might be expected his rival Márquez objected on the ground of Miramón's proved temerity in the past and offered to go himself. Eventually the choice of Márquez was agreed to, and the Chief of Staff gave his word of honour to the assembled company that he would return to Querétaro within a fortnight, cost what it might.

About forty-eight hours later, whilst Miramón distracted the enemy's attention by launching an attack to the east of the town, Márquez, accompanied by Vidaurri and 1,100 cavalry, rode unhindered through the Liberal lines between the two hills to the south and soon was well on the road to the capital. He carried in his pockets letters from the Emperor dissolving his cabinet and appointing a new team with Vidaurri as Minister-President. He himself was charged, in Maximilian's words, with plenary powers as the imperial deputy or *lugarteniente* " to re-establish order among the old women, raise morale, and rally my true friends ". The Emperor also asked for some books, maps, decorations, another good telescope and a supply of burgundy. " We are content and in good spirits despite our difficulties," concluded Maximilian, " but we are extremely annoyed with the old fossils in Mexico City who are openly betraying us through sheer funk and feebleness."

As Márquez rode along the road to the capital the Emperor's parting words rang in his ears : " Do not forget, General, that the Empire today depends on Querétaro." The Chief of Staff knew that he was the last hope of the beleaguered force. " Rest assured, Sire," he had replied. " Before a fortnight is out I shall be back."

6

The prospects facing the Imperialist army were now far from bright. On the same day that Márquez and Vidaurri forced their way out of the city the Liberals received substantial reinforcements, including a unit under the command of the able and cultured General Riva Palacio, which brought their total strength to roughly 40,000 men and eighty guns. On the other hand, the Imperialists were reduced through casualties and the withdrawal of the cavalry which accompanied Márquez to less than 7,000 men with only forty guns. Powder and ammunition were running short in the city, but this deficiency was to some extent corrected by the ingenuity of the artillery commander General Arellano, who confiscated all the available sulphur and saltpetre and stripped the theatre and churches of their lead and bells which were melted down into shot. Food and water were also getting scarce and, despite a few wells which were in use, the loss of the main water supply through the cutting of the aqueduct was a great handicap. As rations the garrison were gladly devouring horse and mule flesh, while cat pie even made its appearance at the imperial table.

General Severo Castillo, a brave and reliable soldier and perhaps the best educated of all the Mexican Generals who surrounded the Emperor, took Márquez's place as Chief of Staff. He was also probably the best strategist in the country, but unfortunately he could not in himself compensate for the military defects of his colleagues. Time and again during the siege tactical successes were gained by the Imperialist commanders which they neglected to follow up. The successful diversion on the part of Miramón which marked Márquez's departure resulted in the capture of a great quantity of ammunition, equipment and prisoners at the Liberals' outpost to the east of the town. Miramón did not, however, press home his victory, and as soon as the Liberals had recovered themselves they began to bombard the town vigorously.

Meanwhile the Emperor did not spare himself ; indeed he was altogether careless of his personal safety throughout the siege. In the afternoon for exercise he used to walk in the square opposite the convent with Blasio and, as he did so, he would dictate additional material for a new edition of his work on Court Ceremonial which he hoped one day to bring out — a proceeding which considerably astonished the secretary in view of " the critical circumstances that prevailed ". From the enemy lines his tall figure did not escape the searching eyes of the Liberals behind their field-glasses, and the result was that as soon as he began his daily walk the Emperor became the principal object of interest on the part of the Liberal artillery. Although the plaza was perpetually bombarded in this way, the enemy invariably aimed too high, so that the cannon balls as a rule buried themselves in the brickwork of the adjoining houses. Eventually in response to urgent entreaties from Miramón the Emperor consented to abandon these hazardous afternoon strolls and his literary activities were consequently interrupted. On the other hand, Maximilian continued to visit the front lines, and as he was well aware that Mexican officers frequently ill-treated the men under their command, he would always enquire whether the men were getting their pay and rations regularly. This conduct endeared the Emperor to the common soldiers in the Imperialist ranks, who had hitherto been quite unaccustomed to such solicitous treatment. He was also assiduous in his calls on the sick and wounded in the hospitals whose management had at his suggestion been taken over by Dr. Basch, which had resulted in a marked improvement in the Mexican surgery in those institutions.

Maximilian received a most striking tribute from his army at this time. On March 30 he ordered his staff and all officers and men recommended for decorations to assemble in the convent square. He stood under an awning which had been decked out with flags and flowers, and to the accompaniment of a military band decorated all those who had distinguished themselves in the recent fighting. When the Emperor had distributed the awards and was about to leave, Miramón approached holding the bronze medal for valour in his hand and said : " Your Majesty has decorated your officers and men as an acknowledgment of their bravery, faithfulness and devotion. In the name of Your Majesty's army, I take the liberty of bestowing this token of valour and honour to the bravest of all, who has always been at our side in all dangers and hardships, giving us the most august and brilliant example, a distinction which Your Majesty deserves before any other man." With these words the General pinned the medal to the Emperor's uniform and at the same time gave him the Mexican *embrazo*.

The troops applauded and cheered enthusiastically as Maximilian, who had been completely taken by surprise by this spontaneous act, expressed his thanks. He was indeed deeply touched, and he wore the decoration with pride for the remainder of the siege. The same day he received from his staff a finely illuminated testimonial inscribed on vellum to commemorate the incident. " No monarch ", so ran this document, " has ever descended from his throne in similar circumstances to endure with his soldiers, as we here see it, the greatest dangers, privations and hardships which do not find their equal in the world — with soldiers to whom Your Majesty has understood how to give such striking examples of self-denying patriotism and endurance in suffering. Both the nation, whom Your Majesty is endeavouring to save and enhance, and the verdict of history will one day do justice to the monarch of Mexico — Maximilian I."

Unfortunately admiration for their Commander-in-Chief was about the only subject on which the imperial staff were united. With the departure of Márquez, Miramón had transferred his animosity to the Indian Méndez. The quarrels between these two leading Generals grew more bitter every day, and each urged the Emperor to have the other arrested. There is no doubt that Maximilian leaned towards " the young General " as he called Miramón, while he was inclined to believe that Méndez, " the little stout one ", as he called the Indian, took " too gloomy a view of our affairs ". Now Méndez, though ruthless and cruel like so many of his fellow countrymen, was utterly devoted to the imperial cause, and it galled him greatly to witness what he regarded as a most wasteful series of skirmishes with the enemy carried on by his rival. He accordingly begged the Emperor to let his Indian colleague Mejía and himself cut their way out with him to the Sierra Gorda mountains to the north-west, which was an Indian stronghold where they would all three be safe and have time to plan a new campaign. But Maximilian, who believed that Márquez was on his way with reinforcements from the capital, turned down this proposal, whereupon Méndez retired to his quarters sulking and pleading illness.

April 5, the latest day by which Márquez had undertaken to reappear in Querétaro, passed without any news from the *lugarteniente*. Maximilian was convinced that Márquez would turn up and that some unavoidable accident must have delayed him. However, when another week went by and there was still no news, the Emperor began to get anxious, and after several more days he decided to despatch a trustworthy officer to find out what had happened to him. Prince Salm was chosen for this hazardous mission and, as ugly rumours of treason had reached Maximilian's ears, he was given authority to arrest Márquez should he consider this step necessary. Salm and a small body of men set out from the Hill of Bells on the night of April 17, but as soon as they crossed the Rio Blanco they saw the Liberals firing rockets which suggested that the enemy was aware of their movements. Dense columns of infantry soon blocked their path, and with the exception of a handful of men who succeeded in getting through to the Sierra Gorda, the party including Salm were compelled to retrace their steps to the town. Salm strongly suspected treachery, which was quite possible, and he also blamed Miramón for bungling the preparations for the expedition on the ground that he was naturally far from eager for Márquez's return.

After this unsuccessful venture the Emperor refused to let Salm risk another attempt to break through the enemy lines. Instead he sent out a number of messengers, but they were invariably captured and their bodies would be exposed on a pole from the Liberal trenches with a placard bearing the following inscription : " The Emperor's Courier ". These gruesome apparitions did not encourage volunteers to come forward for the role.

On April 22 an imperial courier from Mexico City succeeded in reaching the Emperor's headquarters. He brought the crushing news that Márquez had marched on Puebla to relieve the garrison which was besieged there by Porfirio Díaz ; ignorant that relief was so near, the garrison had capitulated before Márquez's arrival. On learning this development the *lugarteniente* had turned about, and while on the march Díaz's vanguard had caught up with his army and had annihilated it. Márquez himself had succeeded in escaping his pursuers, but he had only a handful of men with him when he had re-entered the capital where he was now in turn besieged.

Escobedo, who was also aware of Márquez's defeat, sent an emissary to Maximilian on the same day with a flag of truce declaring that if the city capitulated immediately the Emperor would be free to depart unharmed. Maximilian, however, refused to enter into any negotiations which provided only for his personal safety, and so the struggle continued. A few days later a concerted effort was made by the whole besieged army to break through the enemy lines in daylight, and although the operation met with an initial success when over 500 enemy prisoners and twenty guns were taken, it was completely spoiled by Miramón who declined to push forward and take advantage of his gains.

On April 24 Maximilian had a narrow escape himself. A twelve-pounder ball from one of the enemy gun emplacements entered the convent through a window and, after striking the opposite wall, fell at the Emperor's feet, covering him and everyone present with fragments of plaster and masonry. Luckily no one was injured. Maximilian referred to this incident, which nearly cost him his life, writing immediately afterwards to the Comptroller of the Household at Miramar and describing his existence at this time :

My old comrades in the navy would be surprised if they knew me as the head of a veritable army. The admiral has gone into retirement, and I am an active Commander-in-Chief, booted and spurred and wearing an enormous sombrero. The only one of the admiral's habits which I have retained is the use of the telescope which never leaves me for a moment. I am discharging my new duties vigorously and it gives me great pleasure to direct military operations, particularly with young and enthusiastic troops. Just as at other times I used to make tours of inspection both by night and day and used to like to take ships and barracks by surprise, so I now make a point of visiting the advance posts and of surprising the men in the trenches at all hours of the night. At such moments as these the enemy has not enough bullets or mortars or shells for me and my staff : we have become in effect a human target. During the action on the 24th a cannon ball, which wounded nobody, fell three paces away from me ; I will send you a piece as a souvenir for our museum at Miramar.

I would have you know that throughout this campaign I have been entirely surrounded by Mexicans : the only Europeans I have with me are Dr. Basch and Grill, my servant. There are no foreigners among the troops [1] although my opponent Juárez is richly supported by North Americans. We have taken prisoners several who are officers.

As April passed into May and the garrison entered into the third month of the siege, spirits began to droop, and although Maximilian had all the bells rung which had not been converted into ammunitionon—the false pretext that Márquez was on his way with reinforcements—the feeling was now widespread in the town that no relief was in sight. Gradually the Emperor came round to the view that his best plan was to try to cut his way out at night with what remained of the army. Whilst this operation was taking place the town was to be held by 3,000 Indian inhabitants of the city who were to be organized by Mejía and armed for the purpose ; they were to fire off a few rounds from time to time to deceive the enemy, and when the latter finally succeeded in breaching the fortifications they were to throw their arms away and retire to their houses.

The sortie was set to take place on the night of May 14, but at the last moment Mejía asked for a postponement of twenty-four hours since he stated he had been able to collect arms for only 1,200 Indians. Although Salm protested that " twelve hundred muskets and four guns were perfectly sufficient for masking our attack by noise ", the Emperor agreed to the change of plans, particularly as Miramón was of the opinion that " it was still time enough and a longer delay would have the good effect of making the enemy more secure and careless ".

The Emperor had already divided the contents of the imperial war chest among his confidants in the secret who, in addition to Miramón and Mejía, included Méndez, Salm, Basch, Blasio and Colonel Miguel López, in order to minimize the chances of the whole sum falling into enemy hands during the sortie. When it came to López's turn to receive his share it so

[1] Maximilian had forgotten Prince Salm. There were also about 500 Frenchmen, chiefly deserters from Bazaine's army, in the Imperialist ranks.

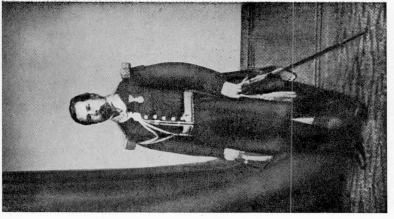

GENERAL RAMÓN MÉNDEZ

GENERAL TOMÁS MEJÍA

From contemporary photographs

GENERAL MIGUEL MIRAMÓN

PRINCESS AGNES SALM

PRINCE FELIX SALM

GENERAL LEONARDO MÁRQUEZ

From contemporary photographs

happened that all the gold had been used up among the others and the colonel was given silver. He was greatly incensed at this arrangement which he took as a mark of mistrust of himself personally. As a matter of fact his receiving nothing but silver was an accident, as nobody distrusted him in the least. It may have been his conscience, however, which reminded López of another and more notorious character in history who had brought off a vital stroke of business with thirty pieces of the same metal.

Indeed nobody in the garrison suspected that, although he had just been decorated by the Emperor and was deep in his confidence, the treacherous colonel had visited the Liberal camp during the previous night and made arrangements for leading the enemy secretly into the city.

7

That night the Emperor could not sleep. He tossed and turned in his narrow bed, and about two hours after he had retired he was seized with a violent attack of colic. Bad food coupled with the effect of the rainy season had made many of the garrison ill with dysentery and now it was Maximilian's turn. He sent for Dr. Basch who stayed an hour with him and administered a sedative. Soon after three o'clock he fell into deep slumber. About an hour later Blasio, who occupied an adjacent cell, was awakened by the sound of rapid footsteps in the corridor outside. Suddenly the door was flung open noisily and someone whom the secretary could not recognize in the darkness burst in. " Hurry and wake the Emperor ! " said the visitor. " La Cruz is in the hands of the enemy. The convent is surrounded by Liberals ! "

Blasio immediately jumped out of bed and lit a candle which he held towards the face of the intruder. He recognized Lieutenant-Colonel Jablonski, whom he knew to be Colonel López's subordinate officer. He then ran out into the corridor, which he soon noticed to his horror was filled with soldiers who wore the uniform of the *Supremos Poderes*, the crack Liberal regiment whose members formed Juárez's bodyguard. When he opened the door of the Emperor's cell, Maximilian was sleeping peacefully, so he shouted to the Mexican servant on duty to awaken the Emperor and he then dashed off to rouse the other members of the staff. Meanwhile the Emperor got up looking deadly pale from his illness and began to dress slowly, for he only half believed the truth of what he had heard. " It is nothing," he said to Basch. " The enemy has got into the gardens. Get your pistol and follow me." A few minutes later Jablonski came in and implored him to hurry. He was followed by Salm, who arrived just as Maximilian was finishing his hasty toilet. The Emperor appeared quite calm. " Salm, we are betrayed ! " he said. " Go down and let the hussars and bodyguard march out. We will go to the Hill of Bells and see what can best be done there. I shall follow you directly."

The Emperor waited some minutes for Basch, and as he did not come back — he had in fact been arrested when looking for his small arms — Maximilian decided to go on without him. Accompanied by his Chief of Staff General Castillo and the secretary Blasio, he was descending the staircase of the convent when Salm, who had been unable to find either the hussars or the guard, reappeared at the bottom. " Your Majesty," exclaimed the Prince pointing to the plaza outside, " this is the end. The enemy is there."

The Emperor was carrying a revolver in each hand, and Salm immediately ran up the stairs to relieve him of their burden, thus constituting himself Maximilian's bodyguard. The party then left the building together. As they stepped into the plaza, an armed sentry stopped them. Involuntarily Salm raised one of the Emperor's revolvers, but Maximilian made a gesture of helplessness with his hand and Salm dropped it. At this moment several Liberal troops came up led by Colonel José Rincón Gallardo. At his side was the traitor López. The Liberal colonel recognized the Emperor in the half light, but he turned nevertheless to the sentry and said, " *Déjalos pasar. Son paisanos.*" [1] Maximilian was wearing a great-coat over his uniform since the morning was cold and he felt far from well, but there seems no doubt that Colonel Rincón Gallardo recognized him as well as his companions and deliberately allowed them to

[1] " Let them pass. They are civilians."

escape. The Emperor attributed this kindness to the fact that Carlota had been friendly with the colonel's sister and had helped her in various ways.

As dawn was breaking, the group succeeded in reaching the main square of the town where they were joined by some further adherents. On their way the villainous López, who was mounted, caught up with them and offered to hide Maximilian in " a perfectly safe place ". The Emperor refused indignantly. Somebody now brought the imperial charger, but as there were no mounts for the rest of the party Maximilian insisted on continuing on foot. " If you gentlemen walk,' he said to his companions, " I will walk also." In this way they reached the Hill of Bells where they were shortly joined by Mejía and a handful of troops who had not been arrested and disarmed. As soon as they appeared they became the target for Liberal gun-fire from the surrounding hills. The Emperor asked Mejía whether they could cut their way out, but the brave little Indian shook his head sadly. Then Maximilian turned to Salm despairingly and said, " Now for a lucky bullet."

Although shells were falling on all sides, the bullet did not come. Maximilian again appealed to Mejía, but the staff were of but one opinion : " There is nothing to do but surrender." Accordingly when he had given Blasio some confidential papers to destroy, the Emperor sent an officer to Escobedo's head-quarters bearing a white flag. The enemy artillery ceased firing, and in a short time the Liberal General Echegaray appeared and, approaching Maximilian, informed him politely that he was his prisoner. Maximilian merely nodded and asked to be taken to Escobedo. Echegaray agreed, but before they reached Escobedo's headquarters they met the Liberal commander himself at the foot of the hill. Maximilian unbuckled his sword and handed it over to his captor. They then proceeded to have an interview in a tent which was hastily erected on the Hill of Bells for the purpose.

The two men faced each other in silence for some moments — the Liberal General whose forces had taken the town after a siege of seventy-one days, and the Emperor of Mexico whose brief reign of three years was thus about to terminate. As

Escobedo did not seem to wish to open the conversation Maximilian did so in a low voice, asking that no more blood might be shed ; if not, then let them be content with his life only. Maximilian also requested that the members of his household who had served him faithfully might be fairly treated. Escobedo replied shortly that he would refer the Emperor's requests to his government and until he had received instructions he would treat Maximilian and his adherents as prisoners of war. He thereupon left, directing Riva Palacio to escort Maximilian to his old quarters in the convent, which the Liberal managed to do tactfully by a roundabout route so as to save the prisoner from the gloating gaze and possible insults of the victorious troops in the principal streets of the town.

It was about ten o'clock in the morning when the dejected party returned to the convent, which included Mejía, Salm and the other members of the imperial staff who surrendered at the same time on the Hill of Bells. Miramón was captured in another part of the town. " I am satisfied that everything has passed off without bloodshed," said the Emperor. " It is better that way." On reaching his cell Maximilian discovered to his surprise and annoyance that it had been stripped almost bare of its contents. Only a table, a chair and the camp bed remained ; even the mattress had been ripped up in the thief's search for money. Amongst the articles stolen was a silver toilet set which the Emperor valued greatly and which was subsequently found, together with a quantity of the Emperor's private papers and other personal belongings, in the quarters of Colonel López.

Maximilian, who felt extremely tired and ill, immediately went to bed ; but he got little rest. Streams of Liberal officers visited his cell anxious to converse with him and satisfy their curiosity. From them he learned the extent of López's treachery, and he reckoned that the colonel had sold him and his troops for about eleven reals a head. On his return from Escobedo's headquarters, which he again visited on the night of May 14, López made himself known to the sentries, who lowered their arms while the Liberal soldiers who accompanied him promptly arrested them. The enemy thus penetrated to the centre of the town without firing a shot. It was indeed a shameful business, as the Liberals themselves admitted. " People like him are made use of," said one of them to Maximilian when speaking of López, " but afterwards you kick them out." Nevertheless the Emperor did not blame the betrayer of the garrison as he did the *lugarteniente* whom he had trusted to return to Querétaro as he had promised. If he had to choose between setting at liberty either López or Márquez, Maximilian stated that he would un-hesitatingly let López go, who had been " a traitor through cowardice ", rather than Márquez who was a traitor " deliber-ately and in cold blood ".

During the next twenty-four hours Maximilian's illness increased to such an alarming extent that Basch, who since his own arrest had been allowed to attend his old master pro-fessionally, requested and obtained permission to move him to healthier as well as more comfortable quarters. The Emperor and the others were accordingly transferred to the Convent of Santa Teresita, from which the nuns who occupied it had apparently already been evicted. The rooms allotted to Maxi-milian were spacious and airy but he was only able to enjoy them for a few days, as, consequent upon a change of jailers and the receipt by Escobedo of orders from Juárez that he and his companions were to be tried by court-martial, he was again moved on May 22, this time to the Convent of the Capuchins. For the first night, to his intense discomfort as well as dread (for he was inclined to be superstitious), the Emperor was obliged to sleep amongst the tombs in the damp crypt, while Basch occupied the table on which it was customary to lay out the dead. Next day they were accommodated in two of the cells in the upper part of the convent whose windows opened on to a patio where there were some trees. The Emperor's cell measured six paces by four, and its sole furniture consisted of his bed, a chair, a washstand and two tables on one of which stood four silver candlesticks. A crucifix hung on the wall. This was a bad omen, for in Mexico it was customary to place crucifixes and candles in the cells of condemned prisoners.

Of the Emperor's principal staff officers, Salm, Castillo, Mejía and Miramón were confined in the same building. The ex-President had been severely wounded in the face while engaging a body of Liberals in one of the streets on the morning of the fateful May 15 and shortly afterwards had been surrendered to Escobedo by the doctor into whose house he had been carried. On the following day the Liberal Commander-in-Chief had issued a proclamation stating that any Imperialist officers who did not present themselves at his headquarters within the next twenty-four hours and were subsequently apprehended would be shot forthwith. This edict had the effect of drawing into the Liberal net every ranking officer of consequence with the exception of Méndez and Arellano who remained in hiding. However, while the artillery commander managed to escape from the city by bribing his captor and successfully made his way to Mexico City, his Indian colleague who had commanded the reserves was betrayed and captured.

During the last days of the siege Méndez had had an altercation with a hunchback tailor who the Indian General considered had insulted him. At all events Méndez struck the tailor across the face with his whip. The tailor was determined to get even with him and, on the day of the capitulation, dogged his steps to his hiding-place and then denounced him to the Juáristas. Méndez, however, had contrived to conceal himself so cleverly that their officers were about to abandon the search when some ground suddenly gave way beneath their weight, and Méndez emerged covered with dust and grime. He knew that he could expect no mercy from the Liberals, for it was he who had ordered the execution of the Juárist Generals Arteaga and Salazar after the passing of the " Black Decree ".[1] He had only one request to make before facing the firing squad, and that was to see Maximilian. His request was granted, and a touching farewell took place between them. " You go in the vanguard, General," said the Emperor as he embraced him for the last time. " We shall soon follow you on the same road."

A few hours later Méndez was led out to execution. He passed along the corridor opposite the Emperor's cell, walking fast as was his custom and smoking a cigar. He grinned and waved goodbye to Maximilian, Salm and the others. When he

[1] See above, p. 182.

reached the bull-ring near the Alameda gardens where the firing squad was drawn up he was compelled to kneel down with his back to the guns, in which posture the Juárists were accustomed to shoot those whom they considered traitors to their country. As the men were about to fire he turned round on one knee, and waving his hat shouted, " *Viva México !* " With the volley he fell forward on his face, but he was not dead, for he pointed with his forefinger behind his ear where a corporal, who stepped forward, obligingly put another bullet.

8

During the afternoon of the day on which Méndez was executed a carriage arrived at the convent to fetch the Emperor to go to the Commander-in-Chief's headquarters. The other prisoners at first thought that Maximilian was about to face the firing squad as well, but Escobedo merely wished to see him, and as it was inconvenient for the Commander-in-Chief to come to the prison he had the Emperor brought out to the hacienda where he was staying. Escobedo happened to be entertaining his sisters on this occasion and there were two military bands playing in the gardens, which provided a somewhat incongruous and embarrassing background to a political conference, for the Republican General felt it might compromise his dignity if he sent them away.

Maximilian, who was accompanied by Prince and Princess Salm, discussed his abdication. He undertook never to interfere in Mexican politics again if he were allowed to renounce the Empire and leave the country with the European officers and troops. At the Emperor's request these proposals were embodied in a note which Salm handed to Escobedo. The Commander-in-Chief undertook to forward them to President Juárez, whereupon the interview came to an end and Maximilian returned to the convent.

Next day Escobedo received an order from Juárez who was at San Luis Potosí directing them to arraign the " so-called " Emperor of Mexico and the " so-called Generals " Miramón and Mejía before a court-martial on charges of traitorously taking up arms against the Republic.

The Emperor's prison life was sombre. Until the Government lawyers came to interrogate him prior to his trial he was allowed to receive visitors freely and also to see his fellow prisoners who were in adjoining cells. A wealthy banker named Carlos Rubio, who owned a cotton factory in the neighbourhood, arranged to have meals sent him regularly. The other prisoners had likewise to depend on the good offices of charitably disposed individuals outside, for, to quote Blasio's words, " our jailers did not concern themselves with whether we had anything to eat or not ". They did not even have beds but were obliged to sleep on the floor on coco-nut matting. For Maximilian the days passed slowly. He played dominoes with his companions, and when not talking to them or his visitors he would read his old friend Cesare Cantù's *Universal History* or else the appropriate if not exactly cheering *History of King Charles I of England*. Sometimes he was certain he would be shot and at other times he believed that Juárez would allow him to return to Europe. Under this last impression he would walk beneath the orange trees in the convent patio with young Blasio and there make dreamy plans for the future. " You shall go with me first to London," he told the secretary. " We'll stay there a year, have my papers brought from Miramar and write the history of my reign. Then we shall go to Naples and rent a house in one of the beautiful suburbs which surround the city with a view of the landscape and the sea. We'll make little voyages on my yacht with Basch, old Billimek and four servants to the Greek Archipelago, Athens and the Turkish coast. Later I shall spend the rest of my life on my island Lacroma in the midst of the Adriatic." Miramón and Mejía, his two faithful comrades-in-arms, were, of course, to share this gilded exile. The Indian, who was greatly touched by the offer of such hospitality, declared that his wants were few and that all he wished to do on regaining his freedom was to fish !

It was natural that the idea of escape should have passed through the Emperor's mind. As it happened the idea found a warm advocate and coadjutor in the person of a newcomer to the scene who was none other than Salm's twenty-three-year-old wife. This remarkable individual was an American whose maiden name was Joy.[1] Beautiful, intelligent and energetic, Agnes Salm had, in spite of her youth, already led an adventurous life which included earning her living as a circus rider before she met her dashing husband during the early months of the Civil War in Washington, where, doubtless because she was a minor at the time, she had married him under an assumed name. On learning that Salm was a prisoner with the Emperor she had hastened first to San Luis Potosí, where she had pleaded with Juárez and then to Querétaro. On her arrival she found all the prisoners in the lowest spirits, for Méndez had been shot that same morning, and they thought that their own fate likewise was a matter of days or even hours.

The Princess's cheerfulness and bustling energy acted as a much-needed tonic. Both she and her husband talked at length about escape and finally convinced the Emperor that an attempt should be made, to which he agreed provided that Miramón and Mejía were included. This condition presented further difficulties, but the Salms hoped to overcome them. Delay was now imperative, as the court-martial was expected to start within three days. The Princess therefore hurried back to San Luis Potosí where she again saw Juárez, and after some argument persuaded him to telegraph Escobedo suspending the legal proceedings for a fortnight in order to enable Maximilian and the others to prepare their defence. Meanwhile Salm was busy bribing the guards and various officers.

The difficulty was to get out of the convent and elude the sentries. "Can't we get out with ropes," asked Maximilian, "putting one hand over the other like sailors in climbing? You know I am good at that — I have been in the navy!" Unfortunately this suggestion was not feasible as Maximilian's window did not open on the outside of the convent, and to reach any window which did meant passing too many guards on duty in the corridors. Once safely out of the building and the town the plan was to make a dash for the Sierra Gorda where

---

[1] She was descended from Thomas Joy, an English architect and builder who played a prominent part in the early development of Boston, Massachusetts.

Mejía, whose influence in that wild hill country was tremendous, would be able to find shelter until they felt able to push on to Vera Cruz. There were few soldiers in the town and no patrols in the streets after eleven o'clock at night, so that once in the streets the chances of escaping to the hills were excellent. Some disguise was necessary, particularly for the Emperor whose tall bearded figure was known to everyone in the country. Maximilian agreed to wear spectacles but he refused to cut off his beard, as he said that should he be recaptured he would look too ridiculous, quoting the example of the Imperialist General Casanova who had removed his moustache with the result that when he was caught a number of his most intimate friends failed to recognize him.

Salm collected all the money which the Emperor had distributed amongst his staff before the surrender which had not fallen into Liberal hands, and with this he bought horses and pistols, taking into his confidence an Italian officer in the Liberal army named Borgo for the purpose. The escape was planned for the night of June 2. Two officers of the guard who were in the secret agreed to help for a cash consideration. The only danger was the Assistant Provost Marshal Colonel Palacios, an Indian whose ferocious appearance was made terrifying by a horrible squint : his duty was to supervise the guard, but as he had his quarters in another part of the convent, it was hoped that he would be in them when the attempt was made.

Everything was ready when suddenly in the late afternoon of June 2 the Emperor told Salm that he would not make the attempt that night. He had forgotten that he had written to the Austrian and Prussian Ministers and other members of the diplomatic corps asking them to come to Querétaro, and now he had just received a telegram saying that they were arriving on the following day together with Mariano Riva Palacio and Martínez de la Torre, two of the foremost lawyers of the day, who had consented to undertake his defence.

" What would the ministers whom I invited here say," he said, " if they arrived and did not find me ? "

" They would be heartily glad to see you anywhere else," replied Salm, to whom the news came as a thunderbolt.

It was in vain for Salm to point out the manifest dangers which any postponement of plans at this late hour would involve. Maximilian refused to be moved. He felt now that the authorities would not be in such a hurry to dispose of his case, "and a few days more or less will be of no account ". Salm, who was convinced this delay boded no good, shook his head sadly, for he remembered too that it was almost the same answer which he received from the Emperor on the fateful night before the betrayal and surrender of the town.

Salm's forebodings were speedily realized. It may have been that the guards in the secret could not withstand the temptation of displaying the gold they had received to their friends. It was also thought that Miramón's wife, who had paid him a visit on the day planned for the escape, may have talked as well. However that may be, Escobedo's suspicions became aroused and two days later he ordered the guard to be doubled and all the prisoners except the Emperor and the two Generals Miramón and Mejía to be removed to another building. At the same time all foreigners were ordered to leave the town ; as for Salm he was bluntly told that he was believed to be the moving spirit in the affair and that if he repeated the attempt he would be shot immediately. To crown all, Borgo, feeling things were becoming too hot, absconded with the horses and balance of the money which had been entrusted to him.

Salm had not played his last card. He could do nothing more himself — indeed he and his companions were now treated so rigorously that they were not even allowed to have knives and forks for the scanty meals which their friends contrived to bring them from outside. But there was the Princess, his wife. This resourceful young woman went to work on Colonel Villaneuva, the officer in charge of all the guards in the city, and succeeded in winning his confidence. Whether Villaneuva appeared ostensibly willing to help while really intending to denounce the affair to his superiors it is impossible to determine for certain. There is a strong likelihood that he was genuine in his offer of assistance, although he doubtless meant to safeguard himself at the same time. He told Princess Salm that nothing could be done without Palacios who controlled the guards in the prison, and if Palacios could be won over then he, Villaneuva, intimated that he would play his part. For his trouble he would require 100,000 dollars for himself and he imagined his colleague would need a similar sum.

The court-martial, which had been appointed to try the Emperor and the two Generals, had already had several preliminary meetings in private, and it had now been announced that the public session was to open on the following day, June 13, in the local theatre which had been selected by Escobedo as the most spacious building in the town to accommodate all concerned as well as those citizens who wished to witness the spectacle. Prisoners and counsel were to occupy the stage, while there was room for 1,500 onlookers in the auditorium. That the final act in the imperial drama should literally be played out in the theatre was humiliating in the extreme for the unfortunate Emperor. He declared that he would only appear under compulsion at this exhibition. Basch wrote out a medical certificate that he was too ill to leave his bed, and this excuse was accepted by the court. Miramón and Mejía, on the other hand, were bound to obey orders. Princess Salm arrived at the convent to see the Emperor on the morning of the trial's opening just as the two Generals were being led out. The former President, she thought, " looked as bright as if he were going to a ball ", but the poor Indian seemed extremely dejected.

As soon as the Princess saw Maximilian she unfolded her plan, explaining that Colonel Villaneuva had undertaken to convey him outside the prison where a guard would be waiting to escort him to the Sierra Gorda and thence to the coast. It only remained for Palacios to be won over. Of course nothing could be done without money, and the Emperor had none. However, he undertook to let her have two bills for 100,000 dollars drawn on the Imperial Family Treasury in Vienna. She agreed to return towards evening for these when she would beard Palacios at the same time.

The Princess returned at the appointed hour and Maximilian handed her the bills. They bore only the Emperor's signature. At first Baron Lago, the timorous Austrian Minister, had been persuaded to sign them as well, but he had later changed his mind and cut off his signature from each with a pair of scissors. Basch told the Emperor that Lago had admitted to him that he had done this as he felt he had compromised himself and if the bill were to fall into Liberal hands he might be executed himself. " It would be a small loss if he were," commented Maximilian dryly.

The Princess now tackled Palacios and after some desultory conversation persuaded him to escort her to her lodging. He accompanied her to her bedroom where with a beating heart she began to talk about the Emperor in general terms in order to test the Colonel's feelings. Palacios admitted that he had formerly disliked Maximilian but that recently, having seen him in captivity, he had come to entertain the greatest sympathy if not admiration for the prisoner. The Princess then decided to come to the point, but before doing so she informed Palacios that she had a matter of the utmost importance to them both to communicate to him and that she must have his word of honour that he would not divulge to anyone what she was about to say, even if he were to reject her proposition. Colonel Palacios then solemnly assented.

In a few words the Princess told him that arrangements for carrying out the Emperor's escape had been made, if only he would turn his back for ten minutes. She knew he was a poor man with a wife and child to support, and for this reason she offered him a comfortable competence which the bill for 100,000 dollars which she now handed him would provide. Palacios took the bill and examined it gingerly. He was an Indian of little or no education and he seemed incapable of understanding that this small piece of paper could provide a life of plenty for himself and his family. He handed the bill back, saying that he really believed it best for Mexico to let Maximilian escape but that as the business was of such consequence he must have the night to reflect on it.

As he seemed to hesitate, the Princess said bluntly : " Isn't the sum enough ? "

Palacios began to talk confusedly about his honour and family.

" Well," went on the Princess in a last desperate effort to secure his compliance, " well, Colonel, here am I ! "

With these words the beautiful young Princess began to undress. The fact that she was offering herself to him as an additional inducement gradually dawned on the Colonel, but it only threw him into a greater state of consternation. Tradition has it that he hurried to the door and, finding it shut, declared that his honour was doubly at stake, and that if she did not let him go he would jump out of the window into the street. The Princess then unlocked the door, reminding Palacios as he went out of the promise he had given her.

The Colonel said nothing, but towards midnight he went to Escobedo and told him everything. Early next morning Princess Salm was placed under house arrest and later in the day escorted out of Querétaro, to which she was forbidden to return.

Thus failed the last attempt to save the Emperor. The same night the court-martial found Maximilian guilty and sentenced him to death by shooting. But the Emperor was past caring what happened to him now, for earlier the same day a report, which at first he believed to be reliable, had reached him that Carlota was dead. "I have just heard that my poor wife is released from her sufferings," he told Baron Lago. "This news, however much it may shatter my heart, is on the other hand an unspeakable consolation to me at the present moment. I have now only one wish on earth, that my body may be laid beside my poor wife, with which mission, my dear Baron, I charge you as representative of Austria."

X. *Homecoming*

ON May 24 Escobedo had received instructions from Juárez to bring Maximilian and the two Generals, Miramón and Mejía, before a military court on charges of promoting invasion and usurping the supreme power contrary to the Presidential law of January 25, 1862. The Public Prosecutor or Fiscal, as he was called, a young lieutenant-colonel named Manuel Aspiroz, visited Maximilian and his companions the same day in order to begin the preliminary examination of the accused in accordance with Mexican legal procedure. During this and the two succeeding days a considerable number of questions, in the form of interrogatories on which his indictment was subsequently based, were put to the Emperor, but apart from identifying himself and stating that he originally came to Mexico " at the solicitation of a large number of Mexican citizens ", he refused to answer any of the interrogatories on the ground that they were of a political nature and he was unable to recognize the competency of a military court to try him. When he was warned by the Fiscal that, if he persisted in his refusal, the charges preferred against him would be taken as admitted, Maximilian had nothing to say.

The Emperor chose as counsel to defend him four of the leading lawyers in the country, Mariano Riva Palacio, Martínez de la Torre, Eulalio María Ortega and Jesus María Vásquez. All of them declined to accept any fees for their services. The first named was the father of the Liberal General and Maximilian's partisans had hopes that his influence with the Government might be productive of clemency on the part of the executive. These four counsel had the assistance of an American lawyer named Frederic Hall who happened to be in Mexico at the time and who seems to have done most of the spade-work for his professional colleagues. Being a foreigner, Hall could not, of course, take any part in the conduct of the case in court, and in any event he was caught by Escobedo's order requiring all foreigners to leave the city following on the discovery of the first attempt to enable the prisoners to escape. It was at his suggestion that the other lawyers had on June 6 submitted a plea to the jurisdiction which was overruled by the Commander-in-Chief, who directed that the case should go to trial a week later.

The public trial began in the Iturbide Theatre at eight o'clock in the morning of June 13. The composition of the court could hardly be described as distinguished. The President was a lieutenant-colonel called Platón Sánchez and the six other members each held the rank of captain. According to Salm, some of them could not read ; they were all young and Hall considered them without exception quite unfit to decide the fine points of law presented for their consideration. Aspiroz, the Fiscal who was in charge of the prosecution, had previously been a practising lawyer, but Escoto, the Assessor or Judge Advocate whose duty it was to review the case at its close and advise the court on the law, was an inexperienced youth of twenty with a ferocious appearance who was a submissive tool of Escobedo's. Indeed the conclusion is inescapable that the Commander-in-Chief deliberately selected the officers of the court-martial with the intention of securing a conviction, and that in his choice of the local theatre, which was decked out with flags and streamers as if for a festival, he wished to stage a popular show rather than a solemn legal proceeding. " God forgive me ! " exclaimed Maximilian when he first heard of these arrangements. " I really believe they have picked out as members of the court those officers who have the finest uniforms ! "

As soon as Miramón and Mejía had arrived and taken their seats next to their counsel on the stage of the theatre, the President declared the court in open session and the Fiscal began to read the indictment. This document consisted of thirteen charges which may be summarized briefly : that Maximilian had offered himself as an instrument of the French intervention with the object of overthrowing the constitutional government of the country ; that he had voluntarily accepted the liabilities of a usurper, including the penalties attached to Juárez's decree of January, 1862 ; that he had disposed of the lives and interests of the inhabitants of Mexico with armed forces and with the aid of foreign troops conducted a " filibustering " war in the course of which he authorized " molestations and atrocities of all kinds " in order to oppress the Mexican people ; and, finally, that he claimed to be entitled to the consideration due to a sovereign in the face of the illegality of the title of Emperor which he had assumed. The Fiscal further submitted at the end of the indictment that Maximilian's refusal to recognize the jurisdiction of the court should be regarded as an admission of the truth of these charges.

Aspiroz then proceeded with his evidence. He read some accounts of the shooting of the Liberals General Arteaga and Salazar, who, it will be remembered, were executed by Méndez's order shortly after the passing of the " Black Decree " in October 1865. Some printed enactments and other documents purporting to be signed by the Emperor were also introduced without any proof of their genuineness. The Prosecutor contended that this evidence was substantiated by the law which permits occurrences of public notoriety to be adduced in proof of a defendant's acts. He did not consider it necessary to call any oral witnesses to establish his case.

When the charges in the indictment were first read over to Maximilian in prison, he had to put his hand over his mouth to keep from laughing because, so he said, " they were so silly ". Maximilian's counsel now sought to develop this view in their defence. They represented that, as the struggle between the Republic and the Empire was a civil war and not a rebellion on the part of the latter which ultimately controlled the greater part of the country and was recognized by nearly every foreign power, the law of January 25, 1862, which was aimed at rebels caught in arms against the Government, was inapplicable to Maximilian. Moreover, this particular law was unconstitutional for it had been enacted by President Juárez, and under the terms of the Mexican constitution at that date the President had no authority to legislate. Also, according to the constitution the death penalty did not exist for such offences as Maximilian was charged with ; it did apply for treason, but Maximilian as a foreigner could not be convicted of this crime. Furthermore, defending counsel submitted that evidence of public notoriety was inadmissible unless proved reliable, which had not been done in this case. Another important point affected the jurisdiction of the court : since Federal as distinct from State interests were involved, the Mexican constitution required Congress or a civil tribunal to adjudicate upon it — hence the court-martial was really incompetent to try the case of one who claimed to be a prisoner of war. Nor did international law sanction taking away an enemy's life save in cases of actual armed resistance. Finally, a touching allusion was made to the much more censurable figure of Jefferson Davis, sometime President of the Confederate States of America, whom other nations had declined to recognize but who was not brought before an incompetent tribunal for trial.

In his closing remarks Aspiroz did not attempt to rebut these points in detail. He contented himself with simply denying the validity of the arguments against unconstitutionality and incompetency and stated that in the Government view the withdrawal of the French had deprived Maximilian and his adherents of all claims to be treated as belligerents instead of rebels. The Fiscal added that he did not attach any importance to objections in point of form, since the constitution was in abeyance and the authorities might have shot all the defendants out of hand on capture had they so wished.

The Government concluded its case at one o'clock in the afternoon of the second day of the trial. The court thereupon retired to consider their verdict. The individual defects of the members did not, however, make for unanimity. They agreed that Maximilian was guilty, but they could not agree on his punishment. Eventually, after nearly nine hours' discussion, the President put the question to the vote. Three members voted in favour of death and three in favour of banishment for life. It therefore fell to young Colonel Platón Sánchez to give the casting vote.[1] He voted for the extreme penalty. It was just ten o'clock at night when the court notary slowly recorded the

[1] The authority for this statement is Prince Salm, to whom it was repeated by a fellow prisoner as common knowledge : *Diary of Prince Salm*, i, 291. It is not mentioned in the official record of the trial.

verdict and sentence, which was the same in the case of all three defendants.

Vásquez and Ortega, who had defended Maximilian in court, appealed on the following day to Escobedo for a stay of execution, and at the same time their two colleagues, Riva Palacio and de la Torre, who were at San Luis Potosí, petitioned Juárez for a pardon. But the Assessor lost no time in approving the legality of the proceedings, whereupon the Commander-in-Chief dismissed the appeal and confirmed the sentence. On the morning of June 16 Escobedo telegraphed this news to Juárez, adding that the three prisoners would be shot the same afternoon at three o'clock.

About eleven o'clock that morning the Fiscal Aspiroz, accompanied by Colonel Palacios and a detachment of troops, visited the condemned men in their cells and read the death warrants to them. Maximilian appeared quite calm. " I am ready," he said simply, and then, looking at his watch and turning to Basch, who was with him, he added : " We have still more than three hours and can easily finish up everything ".

2

Meanwhile frantic efforts were being made by various interests at Juárez's headquarters in San Luis Potosí to obtain a reprieve for the unfortunate Maximilian and the two Generals. Baron Magnus, the Prussian Minister, tried hard without success, as also did the two lawyers, but not even Riva Palacio's friendship with Juárez and great influence with the Liberal partisans could make any impression on the Indian's stony heart. A delegation of two hundred women of the town, who waited on the President, fared no better. Miramón's wife, whom Juárez could not refuse to receive, came in leading her two little children by the hand to plead for their father's life, and she was carried out of the room fainting. Finally, the indefatigable Princess Salm, who had turned up again following on her expulsion from Querétaro, fell on her knees sobbing and offered her own life in place of Maximilian's. In her hysteria she threw her arms round Juárez and swore she would not leave him until he had granted the reprieve. For a moment he seemed moved, but he quickly resumed his cold and implacable manner as he raised the suppliant Princess to her feet. " I am grieved, madam, to see you thus on your knees before me," he said to her sadly ; " but if all the kings and queens of Europe were in your place, I could not spare that life. It is not I who take it, it is the people and the law ; and if I should not do its will, the people would take it and mine also."

Escobedo's telegram announcing the time of the execution arrived in San Luis Potosí shortly after one o'clock in the afternoon of June 16. When Juárez had read it he decided that the three prisoners would not be able to settle their worldly affairs in the few hours remaining to them, and he therefore had Escobedo immediately instructed to postpone the execution for three days, until the morning of June 19.

While this grim exchange of telegrams was taking place, Maximilian and his two companions in misfortune were making their last earthly preparations. The Emperor asked Carlos Rubio the banker, who had sent his meals in to the prison, to advance Basch a sufficient sum, which would be refunded by his family, to enable his body to be embalmed and transported to Europe. At the same time he sent a message to Escobedo on the subject of his execution : he hoped that good marksmen might be selected who would fire at his heart, " for it is not seemly for an Emperor to writhe on the ground in his death agony ", and that he should be shot at one and the same time as Generals Miramón and Mejía. He also wrote letters to most of his relatives and friends, and he made his will in which he remembered them all as legatees. To the Empress of Brazil he bequeathed his little medal with the Madonna which the Empress Eugénie had once given him with the wish that it might bring him luck.[1] He gave Basch his wedding ring and charged him with the task of describing the siege and his last hours to the Archduchess Sophie in Vienna, " And tell my mother ", he added, " that I have done my duty as a soldier and die a good Christian." He then made his confession and received communion at the hands of Father Soria, a priest whom

[1] See above, p. 128.

Vásquez had recommended. When Basch, to whom he dictated most of his farewell letters, brought them to him for his signature at two o'clock he said : " I can assure you that dying is a much easier thing than I imagined. I am quite prepared."

Shortly after this the officer in charge of the firing party came in and asked Maximilian's forgiveness, breaking into tears as he did so. " You are a soldier," replied the condemned man, who in this instance displayed much greater fortitude than his executioner. " You must do your duty."

Besides the physician and confessor, the lawyers Vásquez and Ortega were with the Emperor as the dread hour approached. At the same time Miramón and Mejía were deep in their devotions attended by their spiritual comforters. Maximilian chatted away apparently quite unconcerned, but the short quick movements with which he fingered his beard betrayed the tension of his nerves. Three o'clock struck from the convent clock tower, but no one came to fetch the doomed men. The minutes went by in a terrible agony of suspense. Still no one came, although words of command and movements of the guard could plainly be heard in the patio outside. An hour passed and it was just striking four when Colonel Palacios suddenly appeared with a telegram in his hand. Maximilian's pale features lit up for a moment. Could this be reprieve ? It was merely an order postponing the execution for three days. " It is a pity," exclaimed the Emperor when he heard it, " for I had already finished with life. Whatever happens now, I no longer belong to this world."

During the succeeding forty-eight hours Maximilian wrote a number of further letters and gave additional instructions. He had already expressed the wish to be buried beside the remains of " my poor wife ". He seems now to have been in doubt as to whether she really was dead as he had heard two days previously, for he again wrote to Baron Lago saying that, if the report were without foundation, then his body " should be deposited in some convenient place until the Empress may meet me through death ". He also wrote notes of thanks to the lawyers who had defended him, and to all the officers who had served under his command and who were likewise held prisoner. He finally sent two communications to Juárez. The first was a telegram in which he begged that he might be the only victim and that the lives of Miramón and Mejía, who had on June 16 " suffered all the tortures and bitterness of death ", should be spared. The other was a dignified letter in which he asked for an end to the current bloodshed.

Querétaro, June 18, 1867

Sr. Benito Juárez :

On the point of suffering death in consequence of having wished to prove whether new political institutions could succeed in putting an end to the bloody civil war which has devastated this unfortunate country for so many years, I will gladly yield up my life if its sacrifice can contribute to the peace and prosperity of my adopted country.

Fully persuaded that nothing solid can be founded on a soil drenched in blood and agitated by violent commotions, I implore you in the most solemn manner and with the true sincerity of the moments in which I find myself that my blood may be the last to be spilt, that the same perseverance which I was pleased to recognize and esteem in the midst of prosperity — that with which you have defended the cause which has just triumphed — may consecrate that blood to the most noble task of reconciling the minds of the people, and in founding in a stable and durable manner the peace and tranquillity of this unfortunate country.

Maximilian.

During the afternoon of June 18 a telegram arrived from San Luis Potosí announcing that the President had refused to grant Maximilian's request on behalf of his two companions, and a little later Baron Magnus, who had made a last desperate appeal to Juárez that the three men who had already " died morally " should not be " made to die a second time ", was similarly rebuffed. With these communications the last hope of life for the condemned flickered out.

The Emperor went to bed about eight o'clock in the evening, and after reading some passages from *The Imitation of Christ*, which he had borrowed from Father Soria, he put out the light in his cell and was soon sleeping peacefully. Towards midnight he was awakened by a messenger from Liberal Headquarters who informed him that Escobedo wished to see him. A few minutes later the Commander-in-Chief entered, but he did not stay long. "Escobedo came to say goodbye," Maximilian said to Basch when he had gone. "It is a pity, as I was sleeping so well." However, he snuffed out the candles a second time, and after about an hour, which seemed an eternity to Basch, who had remained in the cell, his regular breathing reassured the physician that the Emperor was again deep in slumber.

He awoke at half-past three, and getting up dressed carefully. For his last journey he decided to wear a black frock-coat and trousers and a broad-brimmed hat. Father Soria then appeared and at five o'clock said Mass for the Emperor and the two Generals : he celebrated on an altar which had been improvised in a niche in the cell. The few witnesses of this service are stated to have sobbed aloud as the three doomed men genuflected at the moment of the elevation of the Host. Shortly afterwards Maximilian partook of a substantial breakfast consisting of coffee, bread, chicken and half a bottle of red wine. When he had finished he took off his wedding ring, which Basch had returned to him three days previously, and again handed it to the physician, repeating the commissions which he had instructed to him. He then removed a scapulary, which he habitually wore, and said as he put it into Basch's waistcoat pocket : "You will give that to my mother". It was his last request, for a few moments later the convent clock struck half-past six and Colonel Palacios appeared with the firing party.

Maximilian stepped firmly out of his cell. The two or three servants who had managed to remain near him now crowded round weeping and kissing his hand. "Keep calm," he told them. "You see that's how I am. It is God's will I should die and we cannot do anything about that." He then approached the cells of the two Generals and said : "Are you ready, gentlemen ? I am ready." Miramón and Mejía immediately came out and the Emperor embraced them both. "We shall soon meet in another world," he said. The "young General" appeared jaunty and cheerful as ever, but the Indian seemed wasted by sickness and could hardly stand upright. They walked down the convent staircase together into the street, where the carriages and escort were waiting for them. Maximilian took a few breaths of the clear morning air, and looking up at the sky, which was beginning to be illumined by the first rays of the rising sun, he exclaimed : " Ah, what a beautiful day ! I always wanted to die on a day like this."

General Escobedo had given orders that the prisoners should meet their end on the Hill of Bells where the Emperor and most of his staff had surrendered. Three ordinary hackney carriages stood ready, which the Republic considered worthy enough vehicles in which to convey the condemned men to the place of execution. Maximilian stepped into the first carriage with Father Soria, Miramón took the second, while the debilitated Mejía brought up the rear of this mournful procession which now set off. The carriages were surrounded by Liberal cavalrymen, while some other troops, including the firing party, came on behind. In order to prevent any attempt at a popular demonstration in sympathy with the prisoners as they passed through the streets, the authorities had advanced the time of the execution by an hour, but notwithstanding this change many of the inhabitants of the town appeared in mourning on the balconies and in the doorways of their houses. Men and women wept openly, and from the roofs abusive epithets and even missiles were hurled at the soldiers. Perhaps the most touching sight of all was provided by Mejía's wife, who had a baby at her breast and made a desperate but unavailing attempt to cling to the carriage which was bearing her brave husband to his doom.

Arrived at the foot of the Hill of Bells, the carriages halted. The door of the Emperor's vehicles stuck and several attempts to open it were unsuccessful, whereupon Maximilian jumped out on the ground, leaving his confessor inside to follow suit. Father Soria was in truth in a bad way. He appeared as if he were about to faint, so that the Emperor with a compassionate look produced from his pocket a bottle of smelling salts which Princess Salm had given him and held it under the priest's nose. Maximilian then looked round and espied Tudos, his Hungarian cook. " Is there no one else here ? " he asked, seemingly disappointed that none of those who had courted favour with him in his prosperous days should be present on this less happy occasion. With the exception of his valet, Grill, none of his other intimates were visible. Basch's courage had failed him at the last moment, while Salm, Blasio and his other friends were either in jail or outside the country. Baron Lago, his brother's minister, had fled in terror, thinking that he had been compromised by Princess Salm's activities. The only member of the diplomatic corps present was the Prussian Minister Baron Magnus, who had exerted himself on the fallen Emperor's behalf very much more actively than had his Austrian colleague.

At the top of the hill about 4,000 troops were drawn up in serried ranks forming three sides of a square and facing a low adobe wall before which the three condemned men were now led. At this moment an order was read out by an officer to the effect that anyone who tried to help any of the prisoners would be shot on the spot. Maximilian's position was pointed out to him in the middle between the two Generals, but he immediately turned to Miramón and said : " General, a brave soldier must be honoured by his monarch even in his last hour. Therefore, allow me to give you the place of honour." With this he insisted that Miramón should take the middle place. He then turned to the unfortunate Mejía, who was in a pathetically weak condition and had had to be practically carried to the fatal spot, and spoke a few comforting words. " General," he said, " what is not rewarded on earth will surely be so in heaven."

The firing party then stepped forward with their rifles. There were fifteen men in all — four for each prisoner and three in reserve. Maximilian approached those in front of himself : he gave each one a gold piece and shook hands with each, pointing to his heart and saying : " *Muchachos*, aim well, aim right here." He then stepped back to his place, took off his hat and wiped his forehead with his handkerchief. He immediately handed both these articles to Tudos and asked him to take them to his mother. He then looked round at the assembled troops and spectators and said in a clear voice in Spanish : " I forgive everybody. I pray that everybody may also forgive me, and I wish that my blood, which is now to be shed, may be for the good of the country. Long live Mexico ! Long live Independence ! " [1]

When the Emperor had finished speaking, Miramón took a piece of paper from his pocket from which he read a few lines disclaiming all charges of treachery and asserting that his children would never have cause to be ashamed of their father. " *Viva México ! Viva el Emperador !* " he concluded. His words were echoed in a faint voice by Mejía.

For a moment the three men faced their executioners, as Querétaro lay in the valley beneath them blissful in the morning sunshine. None of them was blindfolded. Maximilian smiled, parted his beard in the middle, and folded his arms quietly. Miramón pointed to his heart and murmured, " *Aquí.*" [2] Mejía said nothing but grasped a crucifix tightly in one hand as he gazed at the men in front of him. A moment later came some rapidly uttered words of command, the sound of rifles being raised to a dozen shoulders — and then a deafening detonation.

As the smoke cleared away the three men could be seen sprawled on the ground in their death agony. Maximilian, who lay on his face, was heard to murmur the word " *Hombre,*" [3] and the officer who had given the order to fire ran up and, turning over the Emperor's body with his sabre, pointed to his heart in silence. A soldier then fired a shot at such close range that it scorched his clothes. Miramón was already dead, but two more bullets were necessary to despatch Mejía. The hour was just past seven o'clock.

There were a few moments' silence before the troops began to march slowly back to their quarters. Then suddenly by a prearranged signal all the church bells in the town rang out. The Empire was over.

3

As the Mexican Empire was bravely meeting its end in Querétaro, its Napoleonic godparent was having one last gay

---

[1] This version of Maximilian's dying speech is vouched for by a number of eye-witnesses, including Tudos and Father Soria: Basch, *Erinnerungen aus Mexiko*, ii, 220. The longer version printed by Salm in his *Diary* (i, 307) seems to be an embroidery on the original by himself and others who were not present at the time.
   [2] " Here."   [3] " Man."

whirl of life in France. It was the summer of another international gathering in Paris, not of diplomats round the conference table, but of sovereigns and statesmen with their ladies
and thousands of less exalted visitors who had come to witness
the marvels of modern art and science and industry in the
Champ de Mars — the dynamic centre of the Great Exhibition
of 1867. There were the latest furnishings, silks, locomotives,
fifty-ton guns from the Krupp works in Germany, an American
rocking-chair, a remarkable new light metal called aluminium
and an equally wonderful new fuel oil which was destined to
motivate the internal combustion engine. The Russian Tsar
Alexander II and King William I of Prussia were resplendent
among the crowned heads whose eyes were dazzled by the
architectural transformation which the united efforts of the
Emperor Napoleon and Baron Haussmann had wrought in
the French capital. But in spite of the gaiety and gaslight and
Monsieur Offenbach's diverting music, Napoleon and Eugénie
had a premonition of evil. The news of Maximilian's surrender
and imprisonment was not exactly cheering, but Mexico seemed
far away from the bunting and crowds in the Champ de Mars,
and anyhow nobody thought that his life was in danger. More
immediately disquieting was the attempted assassination of the
Tsar by a Polish patriot as he drove along the Bois de Boulogne
with the worried-looking French Emperor — one of a series
which was eventually to succeed in the blood-stained snow of a
St. Petersburg street fourteen years later. Napoleon had hoped
for a military pact with the Tsar, but now Alexander cut short
his visit, determined not to ally himself with a monarch who
was unable to guarantee his personal security.

Worse news followed a week or two later. On June 30 the
Emperor and Empress were to present the prizes to the exhibitors.
As Eugénie was dressing in the Tuileries for this event a telegram
arrived announcing Maximilian's fate in Querétaro. She turned
white as a sheet and tottered almost fainting into her husband's
study. They had a brief discussion as to whether the prize-
giving should be postponed and eventually decided to carry on
with the ceremony on the unlikely chance that the report might
be false. It required an immense effort of will on the part of

Eugénie to go through with it, for all the time she handed out
the gold and silver medals to the successful exhibitors the tall
bearded figure of Maximilian floated before her anguished eyes.
Afterwards she unburdened herself to a friend who had opposed
the Mexican venture. " Why was your advice not heeded ? "
she asked remorsefully. " Had your counsels prevailed, Maximilian would today be leading a happy life in the shades of
Miramar with Carlota by his side — instead of which he is
but a corpse and his poor consort a raving lunatic. What a
ghastly ending to it all ! "

The news could not be kept secret for long. Indeed it
leaked out during the prize-giving itself. It was noticed that
the seats reserved for the Count and Countess of Flanders were
vacant, while the Austrian Ambassador was seen to rise hurriedly
on receiving a message and leave the concourse. All further
festivities in connection with the Exhibition were cancelled, and
the Court of the Tuileries went into mourning. The public
reaction was naturally unfavourable, for large sums of money
had been invested in the Mexican loans, which were now beyond
redemption. Angry voices were raised against the imperial
couple in the Tuileries, particularly the " Spanish woman " who
was now generally blamed — more so than her spouse — for
what had happened. But Napoleon did not escape criticism or
even vituperation. The Liberal Monsieur Thiers declared that
the Emperor would " never recover from this curse ", while
the talk in the London clubs was that the Archduke Maximilian
had been Napoleon's " archdupe ". Queen Victoria could
scarcely believe the news until she saw it in black and white in
the newspapers. " Too horrid ! " was Her Majesty's comment
on the catastrophe. " Poor dear unhappy Charlotte bereft of
her reason and her husband killed. What a shocking end to
their luckless undertaking which I did all I could to prevent
and which dearest Albert was so much against."

In composing the telegram of condolence which he sent to
Franz Joseph in Vienna, when the bad news had been confirmed, Napoleon experienced considerable uneasiness. The
two sovereigns had not met since the day eight years before
when the French Emperor in the victor's role had dictated

armistice terms at Villafranca.[1] Now their mutual positions had greatly altered. They were no longer enemies but friends ; indeed they hoped to become allies drawn together in defence of their common interests against the increasing power of Prussia, who had in the previous year arrested Hapsburg hegemony in Germany and might well do likewise with the third Bonaparte's sovereignty in Europe. For some time the French and Austrian Foreign Ministers had been working hard to reach an accord, and Napoleon had been greatly hoping to cement it through a visit from the Austrian imperial couple, ostensibly to see the wonders of the Exhibition. This little plan now seemed to be spoiled, and Napoleon dreaded the Austrian monarch's reaction to any message, however appropriate, which he might receive from him who after all had been responsible more than anyone else for his brother's untimely death. " I at once deplore and admire the energy displayed by the Emperor [Maximilian] in insisting upon fighting single-handed against a party which has only triumphed by treachery," so telegraphed Napoleon, " and I am inconsolable at having with the best intentions contributed towards such a lamentable result." Franz Joseph's reply was unexpectedly cordial and it came as a great relief both to the inhabitants of the Tuileries and the Quai d'Orsay. Of course there could be no question of an imperial visit to Paris, at any rate in the immediate future, but Franz Joseph's official feeling was one of unanimity with Napoleon in the political relations of their two countries as well as in regret at the loss occasioned by the barbarity and inhumanity of the Mexican Republicans. " Today I joyfully repeat to Your Majesty there is nothing to divide us ", wrote the Austrian Emperor, " and everything must draw us nearer to each other."

With a returning measure of courage and self-confidence Napoleon proposed a meeting on Austrian soil, and the two Foreign Ministers took up the idea warmly, for it suited their book to perfection. Vienna was considered but ruled out on the ground that the French Emperor might be exposed to hostile demonstrations on the part of the masses, for the Viennese had not forgotten Villafranca, and Querétaro was unpleasantly

[1] See above, p. 88.

fresh in their minds. Salzburg was eventually chosen as the meeting-place. Baron von Beust, a scheming Saxon whom Franz Joseph had appointed his Foreign Minister after the disaster at Königgrätz and who fondly fancied himself to be a second Metternich, was anxious that the two Empresses should accompany their respective spouses to the interview. But the two imperial beauties, neither of whom had ever met the other, did not respond at all enthusiastically to this proposal. Elizabeth pleaded illness ; she had in fact just become pregnant. " Perhaps I am with child," she told her husband, with whom she had lately effected a measure of reconciliation. " While this uncertainty lasts the thought of the Salzburg visit is very depressing. I am so utterably miserable I could cry all day. . . . I take no pleasure in anything. I do not want to go for walks or rides either. Everything in the world is insipid." As for Eugénie, she said quite frankly that it would be the most painful thing in the world for her to find herself face to face with a family to whose grief she had contributed by her insistence on the Mexican expedition. Had she known them before, it would have been different. As it was, she was afraid of appearing either too cold or too tragic.

These scruples were eventually overcome when it was represented to the two Empresses by their husbands and their husbands' Foreign Ministers that urgent reasons of state required their attendance. One bright morning in August Their Imperial Majesties solemnly embraced each other on the Salzburg railway station platform and later walked and talked in the shadow of the Kapuzinerberg. It was two months almost to a day since Maximilian had faced his executioners on the Hill of Bells, and at first conversation naturally turned upon the dead man, who was uppermost in the thoughts of all of them. This produced a certain feeling of constraint, but it quickly wore off when other topics were introduced and the party was soon discussing Prussia and the Eastern Question and much else besides. Although one of the latest Parisian models which Eugénie wore, with the skirt mischievously looped up on one side to show her neat little foot, was not quite in keeping with Austrian Court views on such matters, the French Empress behaved tactfully and decorously, and generally speaking her toilettes were described as " very unostentatious ". The Austrian Foreign Minister noted with approval that she took care to " efface herself " before Elizabeth's fascinating beauty. Painful memories were soon forgotten in this picturesque setting, and Franz Joseph even promised to come to see the Exhibition after all.

Nor did the Austrian Emperor allow the Mexican tragedy to interfere with his private pleasure. Shortly after leaving Salzburg he wrote to his crony Prince Albert of Saxony inviting him to come to the usual autumn shoot at Ischl, where in past years Maximilian had been included among the guns although he was but an indifferent shot. Franz Joseph admitted that every stone about the lovely hills in the neighbourhood reminded him of " that unforgettable friend " and at times it almost seemed as though his late brother must turn up in his old familiar haunts. All the same, added the Emperor, " though our party has now lost one of its best members, we may still look forward to good sport ".

4

Immediately the firing party had done their work on the Hill of Bells and the Republican army doctors in attendance had pronounced the prisoners dead, the bodies of Maximilian and the two Generals were wrapped in coarse sheets and placed in common deal coffins. The Emperor's coffin was much too short and his feet protruded from one end.[1] The remains of Miramón and Mejía were handed over to their families by Juárez's instructions, but Maximilian's body was brought back to the convent under the charge of Colonel Palacios and a detachment of infantry. As this sad cortège made its way through the streets of Querétaro, an officer observed a woman weeping and went up to her brandishing a revolver. " Why are you crying ? " he asked her roughly. " I am weeping for my Emperor," she replied. Upon this the officer caught hold of her by the arm to arrest her, but she immediately produced a knife and stabbed him. She succeeded in escaping in the crowd

---

[1] This coffin, which bears distinct traces of blood, is preserved together with other Maximilian relics in the municipal museum in Querétaro.

during the resultant commotion. Other mourners who expressed their grief too ostensibly in the opinion of the authorities were taken into custody.

On arrival at the convent Maximilian's lifeless form was removed from the coffin and placed on a table in the chapel. Palacios thereupon sent for Basch and the late Emperor's other retainers as well as a number of Imperialist officers who were likewise imprisoned in the convent, and, pointing to the corpse, said, " Behold, that is the work of France ! " Palacios informed Basch that he could witness the embalming of his late master, but that, apart from making suggestions, he could not participate in the operation, which would be performed by two Republican doctors. Nor was Basch allowed to take possession of the body to convey it to Europe in accordance with Maximilian's last wishes. Baron Lago, who made the request officially on behalf of the Austrian Government, received a blunt telegram of refusal from Juárez's headquarters.

Rivadeneyra, the chief doctor in the Liberal army, and Licea, the physician who had surrendered Miramón when the latter was lying wounded in his house, arrived to undertake the embalming later the same day. On the authority of an eye-witness, they went to work noisily, smoking and laughing. As Licea plunged a knife into the cadaver, he said brutally : " What a delight it is for me to wash my hands in the blood of an Emperor ! " Palacios, who was present at part of the proceedings, displayed even worse taste when he pointed to two receptacles containing the dead man's intestines and exclaimed : " Those ought to be given to the dogs." He then picked up the receptacles and emptied their contents over the corpse's face, saying as he did so : " You would place crowns on your head ! This should satisfy you for your crown now ! "

Since there was no naphtha available for use in the embalming, the doctors injected chloride of zinc into the arteries and veins, having first removed the heart, lungs, liver and intestines. The frame was then varnished twice and hung up to dry. The portions of the body which had been removed were mixed with powder of tannin and galls, and throughout the whole of one day the heart was seen lying on one of the

VIEW OF QUERÉTARO IN 1867
From a contemporary photograph
The Hill of Bells lies beyond the two churches on the left

THE CONVENT OF LA CRUZ IN QUERÉTARO
From a photograph
Maximilian was first imprisoned in the building on the right

THE EXECUTION OF MAXIMILIAN AND GENERALS MIRAMÓN AND MEJÍA

From the painting by Édouard Manet in the Municipal Picture Gallery in Mannheim

This picture by the leading artist of the French Impressionist school was painted immediately after the event which it so vividly portrays. Its public exhibition in France was forbidden by order of the Emperor Napoleon III

benches in the chapel. The head was free from wounds, and of the six bullets which had pierced the body three had struck the abdomen and three the chest, the latter shots being mortal. According to Basch, all the bullets had been fired at such close range and had so perforated the body that not a single one was subsequently found. The Mexican doctors, however, asserted that one bullet had lodged near the base of the spine, probably that which was discharged when the Emperor was lying on the ground and which scorched his clothes. From the nature of the wounds Basch considered that the death struggle must have been very brief.

The process of embalming occupied a week, after which the corpse was dressed in black trousers, army boots, the blue campaign coat which Maximilian habitually wore with plain gilt buttons buttoned up to the neck, black cravat and black kid gloves. Black glass eyes were inserted in the eye-sockets, as those of the same colour as his own eyes could not be obtained. This figure, whose appearance had been rendered still more bizarre by the loss of part of the hair and whiskers which went to divers Liberal souvenir-hunters, was subsequently placed with the other parts of the body in a somewhat better coffin than was at first selected, made of cedar-wood with a glass aperture and lined with zinc. Maximilian's head could be seen through the glass resting on a black velvet pillow trimmed with gold, while the outside of the coffin was covered with black velvet and gold lace bands.

The coffin with its contents was deposited in one of the churches of Querétaro where it was viewed by numerous Liberal adherents. Some time later it was transferred to the quarters of the Governor of Querétaro, who was made responsible for its security. For the first two or three weeks after the embalming the body looked tolerably well, but after a month it began to darken and it soon became apparent that the work of attempted preservation had been badly carried out. Nor was the coffin particularly well cared for by the Governor. The velvet covering got dirty and spotted with candle-grease, the glass became cracked, and the whole gave the impression of being stowed away as a piece of old junk.

Meanwhile Basch continued his efforts to obtain possession of his master's remains and he was joined by the Prussian Minister Baron Magnus, but all their requests invariably met with a blank refusal. However, towards the end of August Admiral Tegetthoff arrived in Vera Cruz in an Austrian man-of-war and submitted a similar demand on behalf of the imperial family in Vienna. Juárez now began to realize that he could not in common decency persist in his attitude without incurring the censure of the civilized world. He therefore gave as his excuse for refusing Basch and the two German Ministers that none of them supported their requests with any official document either from the Austrian Government or from Maximilian's relatives. Tegetthoff did not have any written authorization either, but he was informed that as soon as he presented it the Government of the Republic would comply with his wishes.

While Tegetthoff was waiting for the necessary papers from Vienna, Juárez gave orders that Maximilian's remains should be transported to Mexico City preparatory to being handed over to the Austrian admiral. The coffin was deposited in the chapel of the hospital of San Andrés in the capital, where it was immediately evident that the contents were exhibiting unmistakable signs of decomposition. Instructions were therefore given by the Government that the embalming should be done over again by three other physicians. When the bandages were removed for this purpose those present were nauseated by the odour of putrefaction, particularly where the flesh had been opened by the gun-shot wounds. The face was observed to be much sunken, and it seemed that the whole features were gradually changing. The new embalmers accordingly adopted a method of desiccation similar to that employed by the ancient Egyptians. The corpse was first bathed in a solution of arsenic ; the fluids which it contained were then drained off until it was dry enough to enable it once more to be wrapped in bandages and varnished. The drying process occupied several days, during which time the body was suspended by ropes from the ceiling of the chapel. During this period no one was allowed to see the corpse, and even those who appeared at the San Andrés Hospital with an official permit were invariably denied admission.

Hence the opinion became widespread that the Government was ashamed to let the true condition of the remains be generally known.

The second attempt at preservation was completed early in November and the body was placed in a new coffin of polished granadilla wood ornamented by carvings.[1] By this time a despatch had arrived from Baron Beust in which the Austrian Foreign Minister tactfully alluded to the " premature death " which had torn the Archduke Ferdinand Maximilian from his relatives, who were naturally anxious that his remains might " find their last repose beneath the vault that covers the ashes of the princes belonging to the house of Austria ". This being deemed sufficient authorization, the President directed that the coffin should be delivered to the Austrian representative without further delay. However, before this was done Juárez himself decided to visit the San Andrés Hospital and see with his own eyes how the work of re-embalming had been carried out. He is stated to have arrived at dead of night accompanied by his personal physician Dr. Ignacio Alvarado, who held the lantern while the little Indian gazed impassively at the blackened features of his late rival. After remarking that Maximilian's legs were too long for his torso, and that his broad forehead, which was accentuated by his baldness, gave a false impression of superior intellect, Juárez, according to the physician, nodded in the direction of the coffin and said, " The smell isn't so bad after all." [2]

As soon as Admiral Tegetthoff had received the coffin he set out for Vera Cruz, whence he weighed anchor on December 4. The vessel chosen to convey the sad burden to Austria was Maximilian's old flagship the *Novara* in which the late Emperor had made so many happy voyages and which had later brought him and his consort to their fateful Empire less than four years before.

As the *Novara* approached Austrian shores a great part of the fleet which lay in Pola sailed out and escorted the funeral

[1] The physicians' accounts for the embalming and other incidental expenses are preserved in the Archives of the Ministry of Foreign Affairs in Mexico City. The coffin cost $65.

[2] There is no doubt of Juárez's visit to the San Andrés Hospital. See below, p. 340.

vessel on the last stage of the sad voyage to Trieste. Here Maximilian's two younger brothers, the Archdukes Karl Ludwig and Ludwig Viktor, were waiting as the coffin, draped in the flags of Austria and Mexico, was slowly rowed ashore. The same day — it was January 16, 1868 — the coffin was placed on a special train bound for Vienna. Heavy snow delayed the train for some hours in the Semmering Pass so that it was not until late the following night that it arrived in the Austrian capital. The pleasure-loving Viennese had willingly interrupted their Carnival frolics to honour the memory of one who had been very dear to their gay hearts. Large crowds waited patiently and in silence at the Südbahnhof and followed the hearse through the narrow streets from the railway terminus to the Hofburg. The funeral carriage was drawn by six black horses and escorted by a company of Hussars of the Imperial Guard who carried flickering torches that threw a weird light on their glittering arms and nodding plumes. Snow had been falling since early afternoon so that the coffin bore a thick coating of white as it was carried through the gates of the Hofburg where the Emperor Franz Joseph and the rest of the imperial family were waiting to receive it.

When the grey-haired old Archduchess Sophie first saw the dark waxen features of her favourite son, which were visible through the glass, she threw herself on the coffin and sobbed aloud for several minutes. Arrangements had been made for the body to lie in state in the Imperial Chapel in the palace, and it was about midnight when the coffin was placed on a catafalque near the altar. Just as she had sat throughout the night by the bedside of the dying " eaglet " a quarter of a century before, so the Archduchess Sophie now insisted on keeping vigil with the guard of honour in front of the bier, where a couch had been prepared for her. Here she remained until dawn. Throughout the morning which followed the chapel was thronged with people of all classes who came to pay their last tribute to the dead. At three o'clock in the afternoon the funeral proper began with the conveying of the coffin to the Kapuzinerkirche for a solemn Requiem Mass which preceded the interment in the imperial family vaults. It was perhaps in the nature of a coincidence that Maximilian should have spent the last days of his life in a Capuchin convent, for now in accordance with Hapsburg family tradition his earthly remains were to lie beside those of his ancestors within the walls of a church of the same religious order.

As it was a State funeral, all the foreign powers sent special representatives — that is, except the United States, which even in death declined to recognize Maximilian and his Mexican Empire. Queen Victoria of England sent Lord Raglan, a veteran General of the Crimean War ; the Duc de Grammont attended on behalf of Napoleon III ; while the Prussian King William I was represented by Baron Magnus, the only member of the diplomatic corps who had witnessed the execution on the Hill of Bells. Among those who had belonged to the Emperor's intimate circle in Mexico there were only a few present — Bombelles, Eloin, Basch and Blasio. The latter had managed to secure a pardon and permission to leave the country. The only other Mexicans there were Maximilian's former Minister in Vienna, Barandiarán, and his secretary.

At the conclusion of the service the coffin was carried down into the crypt, where it was deposited in a marble sarcophagus which one of the Court functionaries duly locked with a golden key. Maximilian's last wish, which he had enjoined upon Baron Lago in Querétaro, that he should be laid to rest beside the remains of his wife could not be carried out since Carlota was still alive, even though she was immured in a living tomb. But Fate willed that the neighbouring sarcophagus should belong to another relative — who knows for certain how close ? — a figure in its own way as pathetic and tragic as Maximilian's — Napoleon Francis Duke of Reichstadt.[1]

5

During the earlier months of 1867 Carlota's condition had shown some signs of improvement. She no longer indulged in

---

[1] This tomb was not destined to remain undisturbed. In 1940, exactly a hundred years after Napoleon I's remains had been transferred from St. Helena to their present resting-place in France, the remains of the Duke of Reichstadt were removed from Vienna to Paris, by order of the German Chancellor Hitler, to lie beside those of his father in the Invalides. *The Times* (London), December 17, 1940. See also below, p. 341 note.

wild illusions about her husband ; in fact, she ceased to speak of him at all. Most of the time she spent quietly reading or writing or at her needlework. Interest in contemporary political history impelled her to steep herself in books about the ancient world. She took up biblical criticism with avidity and read all she could of the history of classical Greece. At the same time she was encouraged to occupy herself with her fingers and in due course she produced a chasuble worked in tapestry which was used during the Whitsuntide celebrations in the chapel at Miramar. News from the outside world left her untouched. She learned of the Paris Exhibition where, as she put it, " all the great of the world seem to be gathered ", and she knew that her brother the King of the Belgians would probably be among them. Personally she was quite satisfied to be where she was. " For myself ", she wrote, " I am out of touch with all that kind of thing. Miramar in its complete peacefulness has the advantage of being very beautiful : to listen to the singing of the birds is also quite lovely."

However contented poor Carlota might appear, her brother and the rest of her family in Belgium resented the strict isolation in which she was kept at Miramar — for instance she was allowed to have no female companion with her — and Leopold determined to put an end to it. The grim news from Querétaro enabled him to do this, since it naturally raised the question of Carlota's marriage contract and Maximilian's will. The Belgian King sent his aide-de-camp, Baron Goffinet, to discuss the arrangements with Franz Joseph and his advisers in Vienna. After a number of stormy scenes it was agreed that Leopold should be given custody of his sister and be responsible for her maintenance. In return he renounced on Carlota's behalf all rights specified in the marriage contract, including any sums payable out of her jointure, and he also agreed to hand over the island of Lacroma, which Carlota had bought shortly after her marriage, to the Intendant of the Imperial Austrian Civil List.

This agreement was immediately put into effect. Towards the end of July the Queen of the Belgians arrived in Trieste to take her sister-in-law back with her to Brussels. This mission was fortunately accomplished without accident, thanks to the

employment of infinite precautions and a number of subter-
fuges, although Bombelles and the other members of the household at Miramar are stated to have made every effort to retain
their charge. A suite of rooms had been prepared for the
ex-Empress in the royal castle of Tervueren and she settled
in there quite happily. To those who saw her on her arrival
she seemed pleased at having left Miramar, and it soon became
apparent that she was dominated by a certain fear which was
occasioned by the fact that she had been brought there by
force from Italy. Queen Marie treated her with the utmost
tenderness and declared that she would never leave her until
she was cured. At the same time the Queen was furious at
what had happened at Miramar. "You would never believe
the barbaric and heathen surroundings from which we had to
tear poor Charlotte away," she said. "I don't imagine there
has ever been in history a case of a young woman who has been
so deserted as this unfortunate Empress."

Neither were King Leopold and Queen Marie prepossessed
with Carlota's physical appearance — "nothing but skin and
bones ". However, she quickly responded to the new treatment,
her appetite improved and she put on weight. She would go
out with the Queen twice a day either on foot or in a pony
chaise ; after a while she was able to receive visitors and was
moved to Laeken, where the royal family was living. However,
her continued silence on the subject of Maximilian and Mexico
gave rise to some uneasiness in the family circle, particularly
when the conclusion of Admiral Tegetthoff's mission became
known. It was obvious that the approaching funeral ceremonies,
which had aroused general interest throughout Europe, would
be described at length in the Belgian press. To anticipate any
visitor or servant from making any accidental allusion to this
event and to forestall the possibility of Carlota herself laying
hands on a newspaper at the time, the King and Queen decided
that the news should be broken to her gently. The Archbishop
of Malines, who had been Carlota's spiritual adviser before her
marriage, was requested to undertake this delicate duty.

The invalid's reaction was much better than the Belgian
royal family expected. For some minutes she lay sobbing in

the Queen's arms and then she said she would like to make her confession. When she had received absolution and had communicated, she put on a mourning dress, but otherwise appeared quite calm and went about her daily round as usual. The blow was apparently softened by the fact, of which she was quite conscious, that her husband had met his end bravely. A few days later she went to her writing-table and wrote a perfectly lucid letter on the subject to her old friend and former governess Countess Hulst :

Laeken, January 28, 1868

My dear good Countess :
    In the midst of my deep grief your words of motherly affection have been sweet. As you say, only God gives consolation for those losses which in a single day take all the goodness out of life. Pray for me, pray for him who for ten years made me happy, and pray that I may always accomplish his sacred will.
    When I remember the night before my marriage which I spent with you, little did I foresee how short all our joys would be in this union so lately broken ! God's will be done. There is no doubt it appeared to Him that my beloved Emperor had already merited eternity and that He did not wish to keep him waiting. Indeed it is impossible to imagine a finer and more Christian end than his which, if I may make the comparison, bears a considerable resemblance to the sacrifice offered on Calvary.
    If mankind thus treated the Son of Man, is it to be wondered that they should not have spared the son of kings whose only crime had been to do good and devote himself to the welfare of others ?
    Pray for me always, my dear Countess, and believe me ever as in the past
                    Your sincerely affectionate
                                    Charlotte

She wrote similar letters to Hidalgo and Mme. Bazaine, enclosing souvenirs of herself and the late Emperor. Unfortunately the improvement in the invalid's condition was not destined to last long. With the approach of the first anniversary of Maximilian's death her vagaries became more pronounced ; with the succeeding months all hopes of effecting a cure were gradually abandoned and she reverted to her earlier demented condition at Miramar. At times the unfortunate woman had outbursts of violence which became so acute in the month of June that a fatal crisis was feared daily. She refused to have meals with any of the members of the royal houshold, and when her brothers appeared she would run off like a naughty child and hide herself in the park. Her lucid intervals became less and less frequent and so she was moved back to Tervueren and complete seclusion. A striking feature about her which was noticed at this time was that her physical state of health remained unimpaired. On the contrary, she looked better and more beautiful than she did before her illness. Of the state of her mind there was, however, no question. "It is a desperate case", wrote Vicomte Conway, one of the Belgian Court officials. "The unfortunate Princess is now totally deprived of her reason."

For the next ten years Carlota stayed shut up in the Tervueren demesne and the outside world heard little and saw nothing of her.[1] If the evidence of one of the servants can be believed, she frequently used to pass her nights beside a window staring out into the darkness, talking and laughing and weeping over things that only her still beautiful eyes could see. During the day-time she liked to stay in her room amongst whose shadows the oddest assortment of articles could be discerned by the visitor. There was a bridal dress hung on the wall beneath a feathered Mexican idol, a bunch of faded flowers and various old weapons. In a corner was a life-size doll which she had dressed in imperial robes and given a flowing blond beard to represent Maximilian. She would spend hours talking away dreamily to this macabre figure.

Indeed she might have remained happy in this world of childish make-believe for many more years had it not been for a strange accident. Early one morning in March, 1879, flames were seen coming out of the wing of the castle which was known to be occupied by the Empress and her attendants. Her doctor, who was awakened, dashed into her room to find it

---

[1] A long rambling letter purporting to have been written by Carlota in a lucid interval to the Duchess of Aosta about 1870 first appeared in the *Revista Germánica* and was republished in translation by John Bigelow in his *Retrospections of an Active Life* (New York, 1909), iii, 511-22. In this letter the writer endeavours to dissuade the Duchess, whose husband had recently been offered the throne of Spain, from accepting a foreign crown. The style of composition make it difficult to believe in its genuineness.

filled with smoke. At first she refused to get up, but the doctor forced her to put some clothes on and then led her down the staircase into the park outside. Looking back at the fire, which had now taken a firm hold of the building, she rubbed her hands and exclaimed gleefully : " How lovely ! " It was subsequently established that the fire had been started by a defective hot pipe in a linen cupboard in one of her attendants' rooms, but this fact did not prevent gossip spreading to the effect that the conflagration had been deliberately caused by Carlota herself.[1]

She returned to Laeken for a few weeks while another residence was being found for her ; but, though she walked and read and played the piano and even had meals at the same table as those she had refused to sit down with a decade before, her state of mind was unchanged. Meanwhile Leopold purchased for her use the castle of Bouchout, a medieval retreat a few miles from Brussels, where on April 5, 1879, she was installed with an establishment befitting an ex-Empress of the Belgian royal house. She was not to know that nearly fifty more years of darkness lay ahead before her troubled spirit could at last find rest.

6

It was Carlota's peculiar destiny that in the remote fastness of a medieval castle in Belgium she should outlive every individual without a single exception who had participated in the imperial drama. Fate dealt differently with each of them whom she thus survived, whether friend or enemy ; and if she knew little or nothing of their subsequent fortunes, it was part of her own tragedy, for their characters were inseparably linked with the Mexican Empire and its aftermath.

First there were the members of Maximilian's intimate circle in Querétaro. Of the Generals, fourteen, including Castillo and Salm, went through the farce of a court-martial and were sentenced to death. After repeated postponements and an agonizing period of suspense, all the sentences were commuted to varying

[1] The story was repeated among others by Count Roger Rességuier, nephew of Maximilian's friend Count Ollivier Rességuier (see above p. 157), in his memoirs ; see the English edition by Herbert Vivian, *Francis Joseph and his Court* (London and New York, 1917), p. 154.

terms of imprisonments. Owing to the combined efforts of his wife and Admiral Tegetthoff, the brave Salm eventually received a pardon from Juárez and was allowed to leave the country. Maximilian had nominated him in his will one of the two persons whom he designated to write the official history of his reign, but after a fruitless endeavour to obtain the necessary material from the Imperial Family Archives in Vienna, he abandoned the task and contented himself with publishing his diary of the Querétaro campaign.[1] A year or two later he found himself again on active service, this time in the Franco-German War, which abruptly ended his adventurous life, for he was killed by a French bullet during the battle of Gravelotte. Agnes Salm, who served in the same campaign as a Red Cross nurse and received the Prussian Medal of Honour for her services, subsequently thought of entering a convent, but on being told by Pope Pius IX that she had no vocation to be a nun, she resigned herself to the routine of German social life and got married again. Her second husband, Charles Heneage, was a member of the British diplomatic service whom she met in Berlin, but he apparently lacked Salm's virtues in her eyes, for they did not get on together and later separated : it is said that he used to beat her. The one-time circus rider made a brief public reappearance in 1899 when she returned to America with the flags of her first husband's regiments and endeavoured to raise money for an ambulance corps for the Boers. Her impetuous spirit at length found rest in Karlsruhe, where she died shortly before the outbreak of the First World War.

Basch, Eloin and the iniquitous Father Fischer returned to Europe and obscurity.[2] They were followed by the youthful Blasio, who made the journey to Vienna in order to attend his late master's funeral, and also to describe his impressions of the

[1] Prince Felix zu Salm-Salm, *Querétaro. Blätter aus meinem Tagebuch in Mexico,* Stuttgart, 1868 (English translation : *My Diary in Mexico,* 2 vols., London, 1868). The other individual nominated by Maximilian as a prospective historian was the ex-minister José Fernando Ramírez, who was already in exile (see above, p. 247). He died in Germany in 1871 without apparently having had any better success than Salm.

[2] Felix Eloin (1819–1888) married, in 1873, Carlota's former lady-in-waiting, Countess Paula Kollonitz. They subsequently separated. Father Augustín Fischer (1825–1887) is believed to have written his version of Maximilian's reign entitled *Memorias*

siege to the Archduchess Sophie and the other members of the family. He subsequently visited Brussels, where he sought in vain for an interview with Carlota. The doctors considered it might produce a fatal crisis in the patient. The faithful young Mexican did, however, succeed in catching a glimpse of the former Empress as he stood outside the gates of Laeken and watched her strolling in the park with two of her ladies. She was dressed in her usual elegant style. " Her gentle and kind face was profoundly sad ", noted Blasio. " Her large eyes, so black and beautiful, appeared even larger and more beautiful under their purple lids. But they stared vacantly, as though questioning her destiny."

A legacy realized from the sale of Maximilian's yacht, of which he received a part share, enabled Blasio to spend the next two years in Europe. He then went back to Mexico, where he secured employment as a book-keeper with the Mexican Railway, which by a spectacular feat of British engineering a few years later extended its line from Vera Cruz to the capital. In due course the Emperor's former secretary rose to be chief cashier of the company. About the turn of the century increasing attacks of the gout obliged him to retire, and the company kindly gave him a pension, for he had then completed more than thirty years' service with the railway. But his life was not over yet. He settled down in a suburb of the capital to write his memoirs of Maximilian and the Empire ; although it attracted but little attention either in Europe or in America when it first appeared in 1905, Blasio's book was eventually to rank as perhaps the most entertaining and instructive of all the recollections of the period.[1] Forgotten like his work, and some say destitute, the gouty and decrepit José Luis Blasio survived other revolutionary storms that broke over his native land. Indeed he lived through the stirring days of Huerta and Pancho Villa and

---

sobre la Historia del Gobierno de Maximiliano, copies of which were deposited in London and in New York with injunctions that the work was not to be published until at least ten years after his death. No such work has ever appeared. Fischer eventually came back to Mexico, where he died in charge of a parish. His dissolute habits did not prevent him from becoming an enthusiastic and well-known collector of old books and coins.

[1] J. L. Blasio, *Maximiliano Intimo. El Emperador Maximiliano y su Corte*, Paris and Mexico, 1905 (English translation : *Maximilian, Emperor of Mexico*, edited by R. H. Murray, New Haven, Conn., 1934). See below, p. 332.

Carranza and did not die until 1923. He was then close on eighty years old.[1]

For Márquez and the other leading Imperialists who had been shut up by the Liberal General Porfirio Díaz in Mexico City, the future held varying fates in store. Some went to the firing squad, some to prison and others to exile. The infamous *lugarteniente*, who had previously perpetrated the most shameful extortions in the Emperor's name amongst the inhabitants of the capital, made an unsuccessful attempt to cut his way out of the city with a few thousand men on the eve of Maximilian's execution. He then went into hiding and his example was followed by Arellano, Vidaurri and a few other partisans such as O'Horan, the prefect of the town, and the former Minister-President Lacunza, who realized that the game was up and knew what their fate would be if they fell into Liberal hands. Two days later the city capitulated, and Díaz marched in at the head of his army. The customary proclamation was published calling upon the remaining Imperialists of prominence to surrender themselves, and in a few days the three prisons which had been prepared for their accommodation were full up. During the inquisition which followed Vidaurri and O'Horan were dragged from their hiding-places by the authorities and promptly shot. Vidaurri, whose whereabouts was betrayed by a woman, was not even given the hollow consolation of a trial ; he was forced to kneel in ordure with his back to the firing party and his execution was carried out with the most horrible brutality. On the other hand, Marquez, Arellano and Lccunza as well as Lares succeeded in escaping and making their way abroad.[2]

The Liberals had set a price of 10,000 dollars on the head of the *lugarteniente*. An American who was serving with the Juárist forces told Prince Salm at this time that he knew very well where Márquez was concealed, but that he would not expose him ; in any event he was sure the Government would not pay if he did so, since the traitorous López had not received his blood money yet. Márquez's hiding-place was indeed as

[1] He died in Mexico City on September 6, 1923, the year in which the Mexican Railway celebrated the fiftieth anniversary of the completion of the line.

[2] Arellano subsequently published his version of events under the title of *Ultimas Horas del Imperio* in which he bitterly denounced Márquez's treachery.

daring as his subsequent escape. For some days he lay in a freshly-dug grave in one of the city cemeteries ; he then put on the ragged clothes of an Indian charcoal vendor and in this disguise made his way, mostly on foot, to Vera Cruz. Here he had to wait for several days, still in danger of detection, before he managed to secure a passage on a ship bound for New Orleans. On this occasion he is said to have posed as an English naval officer with a monocle, having cut off his beard for the purpose. From New Orleans he got another ship to Havana, where he spent the next twenty-seven years incognito eking out a precarious livelihood as a pawnbroker. At the same time it was whispered that he received a pension from the Díaz Government for services rendered. In 1895 he judged it safe to return to Mexico — he was now a bent, white-haired old man of seventy-five, — but only to find that no one took any notice of him, the once all-powerful *lugarteniente* and tiger of Tacubaya. He lived for more than ten years in a second-class hotel in Mexico City, and it was said turned quite religious in his old age. He certainly had plenty for which to ask forgiveness. He also wrote numerous tracts in attempted self-justification which he published but which failed to convince many of his readers. His record was altogether too black for redemption in this world.[1]

The manner in which madness and sudden death alternated as the lot of many who were connected in one way or another with Maximilian's Empire is strangely reminiscent of the ancient Greek drama where these catastrophes were regarded as the favourite examples of divine displeasure. Soon after the executions on the Hill of Bells, Señora Miramón went out of her mind and had to be kept under restraint. About the same time Colonel Platón Sánchez, who had presided at the court-martial in the theatre at Querétaro, was killed by his own men. Nor did Colonel López live long to enjoy his blood money. His wife refused to have anything further to do with him for having betrayed their *compadre* — Maximilian had stood godfather to their child — and the Liberals also shunned and despised him.

General Leonardo Márquez, *Manifiestos (el Imperio y los Imperiales)*. Edited with *rectificaciones* by Angel Pola, Mexico City, 1904. He died on July 4, 1913, whilst on a visit to Havana, aged ninety-three.

Some years later he was bitten by a mad dog and died by hydrophobia. The fact that he should ever have received Maximilian's confidence was regarded as extraordinary, since it was clear that the Emperor had been familiar with his black doings in the past. Amongst the records which Maximilian had omitted to take with him or to destroy on leaving Mexico City for Querétaro, and which the Liberals subsequently discovered in his secretariat on entering the National Palace, was a note-book in Eloin's handwriting prepared at the beginning of his reign containing character sketches of the leading Mexicans who might be considered favourable to the imperial cause. From this it appeared that López had been cashiered from the Mexican army for treasonable conduct during the war with the United States in 1847.[1]

A most remarkable coincidence of dramatic irony lay in the story of Maximilian's natural son by Concepción Sedano y Leguizano, the gardener's wife at Cuernavaca.[2] Sedano was barely a year old at the time of his father's execution and he lost his mother very soon afterwards, as she died of grief a year later. However, some provision seems to have been made for the child's upbringing, for he was sent to France, where he

[1] This interesting MS. was immediately published by Juárez's directions under the title of *Los Traidores Pintados Por Sí Mismos : Libro Secreto de Maximiliano*. It was republished in Mexico City in 1900 with annotations by Angel Pola. López attempted to justify his conduct at Querétaro in a pamphlet entitled *La Toma de Querétaro* which appeared shortly after the fall of the city and which was later republished by Salm as an appendix to his diary. In this pamphlet the author states that owing to the demoralization of the Imperialist forces in Querétaro Maximilian himself requested him to visit the enemy camp and enter into negotiations with Escobedo, with a view to arranging his secret departure from the city along with that of a few chosen followers. On returning to his own lines López alleged that he was arrested by the Liberals who had followed him, and that he then sent his assistant Jablonski to warn the Emperor of the imminent danger so that he might be able to effect his escape.

This version of events has been convincingly refuted by Salm and other contemporaries on the spot. One apparent piece of evidence in López's favour in the shape of a note from Maximilian to López dated May 18, 1867, in which the Emperor supposedly refers to the existence of a " profound secret " between them and Escobedo, has been shown by Blasio to be a forgery : see appendix to the original Spanish edition of Blasio's memoirs. Perhaps the clearest proof of López's treachery lies in his later treatment at the hands of the Liberals, since he was the only senior Imperialist officer in Querétaro at the time against whom no proceedings were subsequently taken. A recent work in which López's behaviour has been critically examined in the light of all the available authorities is Alfonso Junco, *La Traición de Querétaro. Maximiliano ō Lópe₂ ?* (Mexico City, 1930).

[2] See above, p. 187.

was befriended by a wealthy Mexican in Paris named Bringas. Unfortunately he grew up to be a reckless and extravagant adventurer, being constantly in debt and on occasion not above stooping to sharp practice in money matters. He affected the airs of a *grand seigneur*, wore a beard in the same style as his father, and took a particular pride in being known as " the imperial bastard ". For a time he was employed by a business house as a commercial traveller and in this capacity he hovered round the pavilions of the International Exhibition which was held in the French capital in 1910. The outbreak of the First World War four years later found him in Spain practically penniless. While in this plight he somehow got into touch with the German secret service organization in Barcelona, which promptly recruited him for espionage work in France. He returned to Paris in 1915, where he was able without difficulty to carry on his new activities under cover of his former business associations.

For a while all went well. Sedano used to despatch the military information which he collected in the form of letters written in invisible ink, which he posted to an intermediary address in Switzerland and which were there reforwarded to his principals in Germany. However, instead of writing his messages between the lines of an innocuous letter already prepared in ordinary ink, he simply committed them to what appeared to be blank sheets of paper, when one was at last intercepted by the French censorship. It took the French authorities some time to discover the reagent to develop the secret ink but they eventually did so, with the result that a police watch was set on Sedano's movements. Shortly afterwards the unfortunate man was arrested as he was in the act of dropping a letter into one of the postboxes in the Boulevard des Italiens. At his trial by court martial twenty-nine of his letters were produced containing secret writing, and the prosecutor stated that they all contained information of value to the enemy. Although he defended himself cleverly, alleging that he was the victim of friends who had given him letters to post of whose contents he was unaware, he was nevertheless duly convicted and sentenced to death.

On a grey autumn morning, almost exactly half a century

THREE MEXICANS IN OLD AGE

LEONARDO MÁRQUEZ
In 1904

PORFIRIO DÍAZ
In 1904
From contemporary photographs

JOSÉ LUIS BLASIO
About 1905

THREE EUROPEANS IN OLD AGE

CARLOTA
In 1926

FRANZ JOSEPH
About 1910

From contemporary photographs

Rischgitz

EUGÉNIE
About 1890

after his father had met a similar end — it was October 10, 1917 — Sedano was taken from the Santé Prison in Paris to face a firing party at Vincennes. The officer in charge read out the sentence of the court as the doomed man faced his executioners : " Sedano y Leguizano, son of the Emperor Maximilian of Mexico, you will be shot as a traitor ". Sedano said nothing ; like his father, he was determined to keep up appearances to the last. He walked coolly to the wooden post, to which he was bound in accordance with procedure at French military executions, and he refused to be blindfolded or to accept any other assistance. He stared haughtily at the men in front of him until the final volley crashed out.[1]

7

" Maximilian of Hapsburg knew our country only by geography ", wrote President Juárez in an attempt to justify the proceedings at Querétaro. " To this foreigner we owe neither blessings nor evils." The Mexican authorities had naturally no desire to perpetuate the Emperor's memory, although they took care to publish anything discreditable about the Empire they could find in the way of official documents. Neither did they wish to encourage any popular trend towards the building up of a Maximilian legend. When the chapel of San Andrés Hospital, where the Emperor's body had lain during the second embalming, showed signs of becoming a meeting-place of imperial adherents and an inflammatory sermon was preached there on the first anniversary of the execution, Juárez had the building pulled down and a road constructed through the place. Anonymous hands placed wooden crosses on the Hill of Bells, but it was not until thirty-four years had passed by, when

[1] The authority for this curious story is Major Émile Massard who sat on most of the courts martial which sentenced the well-known German agents in Paris during the First World War. In this case Massard had access to the official records of the court, which he later used in publication of his account of Sedano : see his interesting book *Les Espions à Paris* (Paris, 1923), p. 204 *et seq.* The fact of Sedano's paternity has been confirmed by the researches of Mrs. Davila into local history. " After speaking with two old people in Acapacingo who could remember the Royal couple ", writes Mrs. Davila, " and many middle-aged people whose parents had told them parts of the story, and also digging into old records, the writer was able to verify the story of the birth of Maximilian's son in Cuernavaca." See Esta O. de Davila, *Paradise in Mexico. Morelos and its Capital Cuernavaca* (Mexico City, 1937), p. 57 *et seq.*

Juárez was dead and the long dictatorship of President Díaz was well under way, that the Government tolerated the erection by public subscription of a memorial chapel on the spot. Some relics of the dead Emperor were also collected and placed in a museum in Querétaro, but most of his belongings had already been scattered.[1] It is said that Father Fischer had even tried to sell some of his private papers which had been entrusted to him, while the notorious Dr. Licea had retained a considerable amount of clothing, hair and other effects in the hopes of finding a profitable purchaser, until he became involved in litigation with the Austrian imperial family and was compelled to surrender them by order of the court. A great deal of jewellery, furniture and other effects which had belonged both to Maximilian and Carlota found its way into private hands.[2]

For the Mexican authorities another unpleasant reminder of Maximilian's Empire was the reappearance in the 'eighties of young Augustín Iturbide. When Maximilian was contemplating abdication at Orizaba in the autumn of 1866, the child had been restored to his mother, who took him to Cuba ; on the fall of the Empire he had been sent to the United States and later to Europe to be educated. The irrepressible Doña Alicia had

---

[1] During a visit to Mexico in 1943 the author discovered a table and set of dining-room chairs bearing the imperial monogram in a hotel in Querétaro. These pieces of furniture probably came from Chapultepec and were brought by Maximilian to Querétaro for use in the Convent of La Cruz.

[2] Many of their rare printed books and pamphlets on Mexico were acquired by the American historian Hubert Howe Bancroft and now form part of the Bancroft Library in the University of California. The Andrade collection, which Maximilian had purchased in 1865 as the intended nucleus of a national Imperial Library (see above, p. 168) but had not paid for, was hastily packed up by the owner during the last days of the Empire and transported on mule-back to Vera Cruz, whence it was shipped to Europe. It was sold by public auction in Leipzig in 1869 and fetched over $16,500. The greater part of the collection went to Bancroft, who similarly acquired the cream of the libraries which had been formed in Mexico by two of Maximilian's close advisers, José Fernando Ramírez and Father Fischer. For further details see H. H. Bancroft, *Literary Industries* (San Francisco, 1890), p. 187 *et seq.* ; Felipe Teixidor, *Ex Libris y Bibliotecas de México* (Mexico City, 1931), p. 345 *et seq.* ; and the catalogue of the Bancroft Library published by the University of California as vol. ii of *Spain and Spanish America in the University of California Libraries* (Berkeley, California, 1930). The papers entrusted to Father Fischer were subsequently recovered by the Austrian Government (see below, p. 327) as well as some of the books. A list of the latter, which are now preserved in the National Library in Vienna, has been printed by Count E. C. Corti in his *Maximilian und Charlotte von Mexiko*, vol. ii (Vienna, 1924). The list includes a number of works which Maximilian collected before he accepted the Mexican crown and which show how completely he was misled as to the true state of affairs in the country.

always spoken of bringing up the boy to be a good Mexican and with this end in view she managed to secure him a commission in the national army. Unfortunately he was foolish enough to write a letter to a Mexican newspaper in which he criticized the benevolent but despotic administration of President Díaz. For this indiscretion he was brought before a court martial which, having doubtless received a hint from high quarters in advance, sentenced him to banishment and loss of property. He then returned to the United States, where he succeeded in obtaining the post of Professor of French and Spanish in Georgetown University in Washington where he had formerly been a student. His death in 1924, after thirty-four years of academic life, passed quite unnoticed by the general public of both countries.

Fate, too, dealt heavy blows to the chief instruments of foreign intervention. Bazaine, who by Napoleon's order returned to France without the honours due to a marshal and became for a time a popular scapegoat for the failure of the Mexican venture, was ultimately given the supreme command in his country's darkest hour in 1870, only to capitulate before superior Prussian strategy and the needle-gun. Sentence of death passed on him by a military court was subsequently commuted to twenty years' imprisonment, but with the aid of the energetic Pepita he managed to escape from his island fortress in the Mediterranean and end his days as a poor exile in Spain. As for Pepita, whom the Spanish climate did not suit, she returned to Mexico only to die forgotten and neglected in an institution. Meanwhile Napoleon had passed away as the result of a peculiarly painful operation in England, where he had been living since the catastrophe at Sedan, and six years later his son the Prince Imperial had been speared to death by Zulu assegais in wildest Africa. Only Eugénie lived on in exile to survive the second German invasion of her country in half a century, but when she too passed away in her ninety-fifth year the other ex-Empress still existed in her fantastic dream-world at Bouchout.

But the direst Nemesis of all was reserved for the Hapsburgs. The Archduchess Sophie had seen the shadows of coming events while at prayer in the Burgkapelle — it was the morning of the fateful June 19, 1867 ; — she was observed staring wildly from her seat in the chapel at the pattern of a cross let into one of the walls as if at some terrifying vision and was suddenly heard to cry out : " Oh, my poor Maximilian ! My poor murdered son ! " The shock when the truth of this remarkable premonition was confirmed some days later undoubtedly hastened her own end. Not long before her death she attempted to make some slight amends for her harsh treatment of a young girl twenty years before. On learning that Paula von Linden, who had by then got married and become Countess von Bülow, was in Vienna, she sent for her and explained the secret of Maximilian's strange behaviour at the Prussian Court Ball in 1852 when he had avoided the eager girl's questioning gaze without a word. They were standing before a picture of her dead son and favourite. " Ah," said the broken-hearted and white-haired old Archduchess, " my Max was *so* fond of you." As she spoke she emphasized the word " so ". For the first time Paula learned that Maximilian had loved her passionately and on being found out had been forbidden to speak to her.[1]

In one of her last letters to Maximilian his mother had described the Christmas festivities at the Hofburg in 1866. " On December 26 Papa and I for the first time asked our four grandchildren with their parents to a Christmas tree ", she wrote. " The Emperor, who can be so charming with little children, rocked fat Otto in a sledge which they can pull along and in which Rudolf eagerly gave the little ones a ride. Franzi chose the better part ; he sat down on one of the sofas beside Sisi and chattered and played with her. Beauty is a magnet for little boys as much as for grown men, while little girls do not as a rule pay attention to it. On the following Sunday when all the children and grandchildren, including Otto, were gathered round us during and after luncheon, the big clock struck — the one with your works from Olmütz — and it seemed to me like a greeting from you chiming in the family circle from afar. Tears came to my eyes. The Emperor noticed them, I think, and guessed the cause, for he turned away hastily."

This scene of domestic bliss was to be rudely shattered, but

[1] See above, p. 37.

fortunately for the Archduchess Sophie she was spared the pain of witnessing the fates which overtook one of her remaining sons, her imperial daughter-in-law and three of the grandchildren.

First there was the Crown Prince Rudolf, only son of the unhappy union of Franz Joseph and Elizabeth. Carlota remembered him, for though he was only six years old when she had left with Maximilian for Mexico, they had all had their photographs taken together in a family group in Vienna. In the year after she entered the shadows of Bouchout they told Carlota that Rudolf was marrying her brother Leopold's daughter Stephanie. But the marriage was not a success. Rudolf, who in many ways resembled his unfortunate uncle Maximilian, quickly got bored with his wife and, while by a curious coincidence she went to live at Miramar, he turned to Liberal politics and other women for diversion. " We are living in evil times ", he wrote in 1882. " Graft, theft, rabble in high places, the crudest despotism, hand-to-mouth makeshifts. The State is gliding towards ruin." Maximilian had written something very much like this twenty odd years before.[1] For Rudolf history also repeated itself in sudden death, which came to him one dreadful winter's morning seven years later at Mayerling.

About this time Sophie's youngest son, Ludwig Viktor, became involved in some extremely unpleasant scandals. This frivolous Archduke, whom Maximilian had once thought of marrying off to one of the Brazilian Emperor's daughters and making his heir, became addicted to the society of certain members of his own sex in a manner which would not perhaps have provoked comment in ancient Greece but which resulted in his banishment from the Imperial Court of Austria. Then there was the Empress Elizabeth, whose life was a standing reproach to Franz Joseph. This restless and unhappy woman flitted about, spending one winter swimming at Corfu and the next hunting in England, until one day towards the end of the century an Italian anarchist plunged a piece of steel into her heart, as she was about to board a pleasure steamer on the Lake of Geneva, and put an end for ever to her earthly peregrinations.

[1] See above, p. 88.

Neither could the ultimate destinies of Otto and Franzi [1] be regarded as enviable. The Archduke Otto, who indulged in obscene and sadistic orgies which would have put the Roman Emperor Nero to shame — when drunk he once appeared stark naked in a fashionable Viennese restaurant, and on another occasion he stripped and roasted one of his attendants over a burning stove — died as the result of his excesses and a loathsome disease which he contracted in the course of his debaucheries. His conservatively-minded brother Franz Ferdinand, the Franzi of the Hofburg Christmas party, who became heir to the Austrian throne on his cousin Rudolf's death at Mayerling, was, like the Empress Elizabeth, the victim of premeditated assassination. His death, along with that of his morganatic wife as they were driving through the streets of Serajevo on a sunny day towards the end of June 1914, was the signal for the outbreak of the first great world conflict a few weeks later.

As the Austrian army once again mobilized and marched off to war the crazy inmate of Bouchout stood in front of Franz Joseph's photograph and said : " *Du sollst bleiben ! Du musst bleiben !* " [2] Meanwhile the aged and ailing Emperor sat on over his papers at Schönbrunn, minuting, noting and directing in the same neat meticulous hand that he had used for well over half a century. He was still at his desk two years later when the servants found him late one winter afternoon practically unconscious and scarcely able to grasp the meaning of what he was trying to read. As they carried him dying to bed, he protested feebly, saying : "I still have much to do. I must get on with my work."

8

For close on fifty years the pathetic creature that had once been Empress of Mexico lingered in the darkness of Bouchout. Throughout this period her medical attendants carefully noted down the various phases of her illness, and their reports must form instructive reading, at any rate for the student of mental disease. Although she never in any sense recovered her reason,

---

[1] Children of the Archduchess Sophie's third son, Karl Ludwig.
[2] "You should remain. You must remain."

and her lucid intervals, which had once been fairly frequent, gradually disappeared altogether, she did enjoy spells of physical calm when she regained a taste for her usual domestic occupations. At other times she indulged in wild fits of destructive monomania. During these attacks it was noticed that she would break everything that came to hand, tearing up books and slashing pictures and hangings on the walls, but she was always careful to spare any photographs or other objects which reminded her of Maximilian. On one occasion towards the end of her days she is supposed to have caught sight of her image reflected in a mirror and to have realized in consequence that she was no longer young and lovely but a faded and forgotten old woman. Her immediate reaction is said to have been to give orders that all the mirrors and windows in the château should be broken.

In spite of her madness Carlota retained some consciousness of her former position, and she would almost invariably refer to herself when speaking as "*one*". On one occasion she was annoyed by the absence of an attendant. "When I reigned," she said, "I simply lifted a finger to summon my lady-in-waiting." At other times when she had an attack of violence, her doctor was known to reduce her to a state of complete calm by saying, "Madame, of all the Empresses I have known you are the only one to behave like this!" She seemed to be conscious of the nature of her illness. "Pay no attention, Monsieur, if one talks nonsense," she was once overheard saying to herself. "Yes, Monsieur, one is old, one is stupid, one is mad. . . . The mad woman is still living. . . . Monsieur, you are in the presence of a mad woman!" She was also appreciative of what was being done for her by others. When Baron Goffinet, who managed her establishment and administered her property as curator, used to come to lunch she would always dismiss him at the conclusion of the meal with some such phrases as "So very kind. Thank you. You must come again."

To the last she was fastidious about her personal appearance. She would change her comforters which she wore in the morning for an afternoon dress ; she would attend to her hair, which was cut short, slipping on a bonnet with gay ribbons of various colours, and she would also lace up her slippers. In her extreme old age she suffered from a cataract which made fine sewing or embroidery impossible, but she would still play an occasional game of cards and even sit down to a duet at the piano. On the first day of each month she would regularly go and step into a boat which was moored to a bridge which crossed the castle moat. This was some mysterious rite whose meaning was never solved. In her later days, too, she kept up her carriage drives in the park, but most of the time the poor invalid was absorbed either in long reveries or else in passionate conversations with imaginary interlocutors.

" No, Monsieur, not even if you were to offer me the kingdom of Saxony. . . . All the Orleans are the same. . . . Yes, they say the dividing line will extend from Denmark right down to the Tyrol ! "

Her niece Stephanie, widow of the ill-fated Rudolf, has described how she visited her for the last time at Bouchout in 1899. When Stephanie ran forward to kiss her hand, Carlota embraced her rapturously and was obviously delighted to see her. For a while she chattered away incoherently, then she suddenly turned her large sorrowful eyes towards the younger woman. " *Tu viens d'Autriche, chère enfant ?* " she asked. " *Comment se porte ton beau-père l'Empereur ?* " Before Stephanie had time to answer she rose to her feet, took the visitor by the hand, and leading her up to a life-size portrait of Maximilian which hung in the room, curtsied humbly before it and said, " *Et l'autre, ils l'ont tué !* ".

Of Mexico and Maximilian she hardly ever spoke directly to anyone. But her soliloquies suggested that her disordered thoughts from time to time recurred to unhappy memories of far-off days. On November 4, 1912, which was her saint's day, she exclaimed on receiving a visit from the Countess of Flanders, " And Maximilian is not here ! " On another occasion she suddenly sat down at the piano and played the Mexican national hymn.

Then again : " They tell one that one had a husband, a husband, Monsieur, who was an Emperor or a King ! . . . A great marriage, Monsieur, and then madness ! . . . Madness is the result of events ! . . . Monsieur, you are the cause of the murder ! . . . Archduke Maximilian of the House of Hapsburg. *Canaille, misérable !* . . . Napoleon, a prime instigator of the Empire. . . . If he had only been supported by Napoleon. . . . Blücher arrived in time to save the situation, but for Mexico there is nothing, nothing at all ! "

The ex-Empress had a certain conception of dates — not of years, but of days of the month and anniversaries such as her saint's day, her birthday and the date of her first communion. Of passing events she had only the vaguest ideas. She seems to have been quite unaware, for instance, of her brother Leopold's much-criticized misdoings in the Belgian Congo, as also of his morganatic alliance with Baroness Vaughan and the scandalous quarrels which occurred between him and his children. Care was taken to keep deaths in the family from her knowledge, but she certainly learned of some of them. When Leopold II died in 1909 and was succeeded as King of the Belgians by his nephew Albert Count of Flanders, she talked volubly of all the princes in her family, ending up by saying, "And to think I have a nephew who is still very young and already occupies a throne and is called King ! " But her memory failed with the passing of the years, for when King Albert and Queen Elizabeth paid her a congratulatory visit on November 4, 1923, she kept on repeating after they had left her, " One has had a visit from the Flanders ! "

It was hardly necessary for her circle of attendants to attempt to conceal from her the German invasion of the country in 1914 and the horrible events which followed. The First World War passed her by almost completely. The commanding officer in charge of the force which occupied the neighbourhood attached a notice to the gates of Bouchout which informed all members of the German army who might read it that the castle was occupied by the sister-in-law of " our revered ally the Emperor of Austria " and called upon all German soldiers " to pass by without singing and to leave this place untouched ". Yet Carlota probably had some inkling of what was going on when the Germans crossed the frontier and invested Brussels, executing numbers of civilian inhabitants in the process. One day in August

1914 she was heard mumbling to herself. "Monsieur, one sees red. . . . One thinks something is happening for one is not gay . . . the frontier is dark, very dark . . . the prisoners should not be surrendered !" The sound of the guns could be distinctly heard from the castle. On one occasion the members of a German patrol forced their way into the dining-room when the ex-Empress was at the table, and just before the Armistice a German company commander vainly endeavoured to billet his men in the building.

Of her imperial brother-in-law's death at Schönbrunn in 1916 and of his grandnephew Charles's brief shadowy reign which terminated in the collapse of the Hapsburg dynasty and the proclamation of the republics of Austria, Hungary, and Czechoslovakia and the kingdom of Yugoslavia, she seems to have been completely ignorant. The disappearance of the Hohenzollern and Romanov dynasties from their thrones and the council chambers of Europe likewise left her undisturbed, as had the fate of the houses of Bonaparte and Braganza in years gone by. It was a far different world which she was leaving from that in which she had spent her youthful and unclouded years. Even before she died the inhabitants of Europe and America were conversing with each other by means of radio-telephony and a young airman named Charles Lindbergh was preparing to fly from New York to Paris.

Nor does Carlota seem to have been aware of the appearance of a surprising and almost comical figure in England who put forward the most ludicrous pretensions to her person and fortune. William Brightwell, a fishmonger of the city of London, claimed that his proper names were Rudolph Franz Maximilian Hapsburg and that he was really Carlota's child. According to his fantastic story, this adopted son of a Cockney greengrocer, who was in the habit of supplying the public-houses along the Thames with excellent kippers, was actually born during the ex-Empress's hectic stay in the Vatican. Mr. Brightwell claimed a share in Carlota's fortune at her death and also a contingent interest in a number of Maximilian's jewels and artistic treasures which are believed to have gone down in a shipwreck after the Madero revolution in Mexico in 1911. Needless to say, none of his claims were ever substantiated, for Carlota was never unaccompanied for a single moment during her sojourn in the Eternal City, and indeed there is no period throughout the whole of her life which cannot be satisfactorily accounted for by the testimony of reliable witnesses.

As she grew older there is evidence that she occasionally considered death and even sensed that it was a long time coming. "It would be a catastrophe, Monsieur, which would not come suddenly but little by little." On one occasion, when she learned of the passing of some member of her family in spite of the attempts of her attendants to keep her in ignorance of the event, she was heard to exclaim: "I too shall die! *Miserere mei, Deus!*" Not long before the end she spoke to Baron Goffinet. "I want to go to Laeken," she said. "One goes up and up and up and then finally disappears behind the towers." This was a reference to the crypt in the Church of Notre Dame at Laeken which was the burial-place of the Belgian royal family. As a girl she had knelt and wept there beside her mother's tomb.

On Christmas Day, 1926, she looked remarkably well for an old lady of eighty-six. The change came shortly after New Year. She suffered an attack of bronchial influenza which turned into pneumonia. The doctors could do nothing, and she passed away peacefully in the early morning of January 19, 1927. With her going there snapped a last link with the past of imperial Austria and imperial France and imperial Mexico.

It was snowing in the castle grounds outside just as it had been snowing exactly fifty-nine years before when they carried the mortal remains of Maximilian into the Kapuzinerkirche in Vienna. It was still snowing when a handful of Belgian legionaires, all that were left of the brave volunteer regiment which landed at Vera Cruz with the Emperor in 1864, carried Carlota's body through the forest of Laeken to its last resting-place in the royal crypt. Before it reached the sarcophagus the coffin was encased in lead, so that it was clear that this interment was intended to be permanent and that there was no intention of ever transferring her remains to lie beside those of Maximilian, as had been his wish.

But if their earthly remains were separated, as had been their bodies during much of their lives, their spirits were united. Indeed long before her death Carlota had been conscious that she was at one with the " Lord of the Earth " and the " Sovereign of the Universe ", as she liked to think of Maximilian. What she had once written to him during the period of her mental suffering had at last been realized : " I was to blame, my beloved darling, for everything. But now I am happy. You have triumphed ! You are part of God's victory over Evil. . . . Your eyes look down at me from every place and I hear your voice everywhere."

BIBLIOGRAPHY

A. MANUSCRIPT SOURCES

The most important MS. source for the lives of Maximilian and Carlota is the *Archiv des Kaisers Maximilians von Mexiko* or *Maximilianarchiv* which is at present preserved in the *Haus- Hof- und Staatsarchiv* in Vienna. The collection is divided into two parts : (*a*) the *Mexikanische Archiv*, consisting of 34 cartons which concern the Mexican Empire and the diplomatic negotiations which preceded its establishment ; and (*b*) the *Miramar Archiv*, consisting of 39 cartons which contain Maximilian's scrapbooks and diaries of his early life as well as the official and private papers relating to his governorship of the Italian provinces and which were originally preserved at Miramar, Maximilian's castle near Trieste. The whole collection comprises over 10,000 items and includes almost every piece of paper which Maximilian considered worth keeping, such as school exercise-books, engagement calendars, descriptions of travels, poems, visiting-cards, the log of his flagship the *Novara*, etc. A 387-page catalogue of the collection giving full details of its contents exists in the Vienna *Staatsarchiv* (ref. *Archivbehelf*, 302). A photostatic copy of this catalogue is in the Manuscript Division of the United States Library of Congress in Washington, D.C.

When Maximilian was contemplating abdication in the autumn of 1866, he caused to be sent on board an Austrian vessel in Vera Cruz and shipped to Miramar all the official and private papers concerning the Mexican venture which he considered of any importance. These form the *Mexikanische Archiv* mentioned above and comprise all Maximilian's correspondence with Carlota, the Emperors Franz Joseph and Napoleon, King Leopold I, Pope Pius IX, Count Rechberg, General Almonte and many others. They also include Carlota's correspondence with her father and the Empress Eugénie. As a rule Maximilian wrote private letters in German and officially in French, except when corresponding with the Pope, whom he invariably addressed in Italian.

After Maximilian's death the Emperor Franz Joseph took possession of the collection and refused to release any portion of it to the two literary executors whom Maximilian had appointed in his will to write the history of his reign. The archives were transferred from Miramar to Vienna, where they were supplemented from time to time by further

accessions from Mexico.[1]   Here they remained carefully guarded and
inaccessible to historians until after the downfall of the Hapsburg
monarchy.   In 1929 a generous bequest from Mr. John D. Rockefeller,
Jr., enabled the U.S. Library of Congress to secure photostatic copies
of practically all the *Mexikanische Archiv,* and these are now available
to students for research and reproduction in the Library's Manuscript
Division.   Several years later a detailed account of the whole collection
was written by the official archivist Dr. Fritz Reinöhl and published by
the Austrian Government under the editorship of Dr. Ludwig Bittner
in *Inventare des Haus- Hof- und Staatsarchiv,* vol. 5, Vienna, 1937.

The following are the principal additional MS. sources :

Archivo del Imperio.   Official correspondence of the Imperial Government of Maximilian, including the archives of the civil and military cabinets.
About 60 cartons.   In the *Archivo General de la Nación,* Mexico City.

Correspondence of the Juárez Government on the subject of the Emperor
Maximilian : (i) relating to his defeat in Querétaro, trial, execution and
delivery of his body to Admiral Tegetthoff ; (ii) with the U.S. Government
on his imprisonment and execution, 1867.   In the Archives of the Ministry
of Foreign Affairs, Mexico City (Expediente H/504, 2, " 867 "/1-2).

Diplomatic correspondence between the Austrian Ministry of Foreign
Affairs and the Austrian diplomatic representatives in Rome, Madrid,
Brussels, Washington and Mexico City relative to the Mexican Empire,
1861–67.   In the *Haus- Hof- und Staatsarchiv,* Vienna.[2]

Diplomatic correspondence between the British Foreign Office and the
British Ministers in Mexico City, 1859–67.   In the Public Record Office,
London (F.O. Series 50 and 204).

Diplomatic correspondence between the French Ministry of Foreign
Affairs and the French diplomatic representatives in Mexico City and
Washington, 1861–67.   In the Archives of the Ministry of Foreign Affairs,
Paris.

Diplomatic correspondence between the United States Department of
State and (i) the U.S. diplomatic representatives in Austria, France and
Mexico ; (ii) the Mexican Minister in Washington.   In the United States
National Archives, Washington, D.C.

The Bazaine, Lares, Riva Palacio and Uraga papers in the Library of
the University of Texas.   Austin, Texas.   (These MSS. form part of the
Genaro García collection and the Texas University Archives.)

---

[1] Most of the important private and state papers covering the last months of Maximilian's reign were recovered in this way.   They included the papers entrusted by the
Emperor to his notorious adviser Father Fischer: see above, p. 316.   On the other
hand, many of Maximilian's books and other possessions, which he did not take with
him to Mexico, are still (1945) preserved at Miramar.

[2] Photostatic copies exist in the U.S. Library of Congress.

Bibliography

(i) Achille Bazaine. Correspondence and miscellanea, 1863–67. Copies in Spanish with occasional French texts of about 5,500 documents written while Marshal Bazaine was in command of the French Expeditionary force in Mexico.[1]

(ii) Teodosio Lares. Correspondence and other documents, 1833–67. Over 1,000 items.

Lares was Chief Justice, President of the Assembly of Notables and President of the Ministerial Council during the Empire. An extreme Conservative and reactionary who managed to escape to Cuba after Maximilian's execution.

(iii) Vicente Riva Palacio. Correspondence and other documents for the history of Mexico, 1814–96, including his personal papers.

General Riva Palacio was one of the leading Republican Generals who fought against Maximilian at Querétaro and was also perhaps the most distinguished contemporary Mexican historian.

(iv) José López Uraga. Diary, 1853–71.

General Uraga was one of the few Republican Generals who was won over to the Imperialist cause after the establishment of the Empire. He served for a time as Chief of Staff to Maximilian and escorted Carlota on her visit to Yucatan in 1865.

B. PUBLISHED SOURCES

Maximilian intended that his personal archives should be utilized for the posthumous publication of accounts of his reign in Mexico, his governorship of the Italian provinces and his travels in Europe and South America, together with selections from his other early writings. Only the last of these objects was realized in accordance with the Emperor's intentions. Immediately after his death selected portions of his scrap-books and travel diaries for the years 1851–53 and 1859–60, which had already been circulated privately among his friends, appeared in seven volumes as *Aus meinem Leben*. This was followed a year later by the publication of his travel diary for 1850 entitled *Mein erster Ausflug*.

On his return to Austria from Brazil in 1860 Maximilian entrusted the papers which he had collected for a history of his rule in Lombardy and Venetia to Professor Tobias Wildauer of the University of Innsbruck. The latter eventually produced a survey which he called *Storia del Governatore del Lombardo-Veneto*. Maximilian himself revised the text in part but he had not finished his corrections before he left for Mexico. The MS., which remained among Maximilian's private papers at Miramar, was apparently overlooked by

[1] Partly published to November 1865 by Genaro García in his *Documentos inéditos ó muy raros para la Historia de México*, vols. xiv, xvi, xviii, xx, xxii, xxiv, xxvii, xxx and xxxiii, Mexico City, 1907–10.

Count Corti in his researches when the *Maximilianarchiv* were thrown open to students with the rest of the national archives for the period of Franz Joseph's reign. In 1935 substantial portions of this interesting MS. were published by Luis Gasparini in the *Nuova Antologia*.

In his will Maximilian had charged his aide-de-camp Prince Felix zu Salm-Salm and his former Foreign Minister José Fernando Ramírez with the task of writing the history of his reign in Mexico. This work was to be based mainly upon the papers which he had had shipped to Europe at the time of his contemplated abdication in 1866. Unfortunately both these literary executors died shortly afterwards without being able to obtain possession of the documents from the Austrian imperial family, Salm being killed in the Franco-German War and Ramírez following him to the grave a year later.[1] Ernst Schmit von Tavera, an attaché in the Austrian Legation in Mexico who had visited Maximilian in prison and apparently promised to assist in the work, subsequently wrote a history of the Imperial Government based upon such materials as he could collect from the legation chancery and elsewhere in the country. This work was completed about 1875, but owing to the Emperor Franz Joseph's objections it was not published until nearly thirty years later, and even then did not include any of Maximilian's private papers.

Meanwhile a voluminous and uneven literature on Maximilian and the Mexican Empire had been appearing since its fall. It began with a brilliant obituary notice by Lord Acton originally written in the form of a lecture which he delivered in England.[2] For the rest, the authors who were able to include many important and hitherto unpublished documents in their works were mostly either, like Domenech, Détroyat, Salm, Montlong, Basch and Blasio, on Maximilian's staff and therefore much biased in his favour ; or like Kératry, Blanchot, Niox and Gaulot, connected with the intervention and therefore very pro-French ; or else like Lefévre, who was a friend of the Juárez Government and consequently allowed access to the archives left behind in Mexico by Maximilian, extremely opposed to the Emperor and his cause. A number of writers made use of this ill-assorted material and produced biographies, of which perhaps the best is by Percy F. Martin, published in 1914.[3] It was not until after the First World War that Count E. C. Corti was able to begin his researches in the Vienna *Staatsarchiv* which resulted in the appear-

[1] See above, p. 309 and note.
[2] *The Rise and Fall of the Mexican Empire*, a lecture given by Lord Acton in 1868 and republished in his *Historical Essays and Studies*, London, 1907.
[3] *Maximilian in Mexico. The Story of the French Intervention.* London, 1914.

Bibliography

ance in 1924 of his two-volume *Maximilian und Charlotte von Mexiko*. In spite of certain gaps and imperfections, this scholarly work remains the leading printed authority on the subject.

The production of Corti's work encouraged the publication of two well-documented biographies of the Empress Carlota in the French language. The first of these, *La Tragédie mexicaine* by Baron Camille Buffin, included some material in the Vienna archives which had been omitted by Corti ; while the second, *Charlotte de Belgique Impératrice du Mexique* by Countess H. de Reinach Foussemagne, incorporated a great mass of Carlota's private correspondence which had been obtained from the archives of the Belgian royal family and other sources. More recently published biographies of the popular type are *Phantom Crown*, London and New York, 1934, by Bertita Harding ; *Charlotte l'Impératrice fantôme*, Paris, 1937, by Robert Goffin ; *Charlotte et Maximilien*, Paris, 1937, by Lucile Decaux ; and *Passengers to Mexico*, New York, 1943, by Blair Niles.

The history of Maximilian's Mexican Empire has been alternately written by French and Mexican historians as part of the history of their respective countries. Most important on the French side are the scholarly writings of Émile Ollivier, *L'Empire libéral*, 18 vols., Paris, 1895–1915 ; and Pierre de la Gorce, *Histoire du Second Empire*, 7 vols., Paris, 1894–1905 ; and on the Mexican the great works of Vicente Riva Palacio, *México á través de los siglos*, 5 vols., Barcelona and Mexico City, 1887–89 ; and Niceto de Zamacois, *Historia de Méjico*, 18 vols., Barcelona and Mexico City, 1877–82. A useful but little-known work of reference for the Mexican background, particularly for biographical details, is Alberto Le Duc and Dr. Luis Lara y Pardo, *Diccionario de Geografía, Historia y Biografía Mexicanas*, Paris and Mexico City, 1910.

The fullest list of printed materials is contained in Jesus Guzmán y Raz Guzmán, *Bibliografía de la Reforma, la Intervención y el Imperio*, 2 vols., Mexico City, 1930 (*Monografías Bibliografías Mexicanas*, Nos. 17 and 19). The U.S. Library of Congress's *Guide to the Diplomatic History of the United States*, by S. F. Bemis and G. G. Griffin (Washington, 1935), is also helpful.

Either on account of the documents they contain, or because their authors possessed first-hand knowledge of the events described in them, the following printed works must be considered indispensable:

Y

Arellano, Manuel Ramírez de.   *Últimas Horas del Imperio*.   Mexico, 1869.
The author served as a general of brigade under Maximilian and commanded the artillery during the siege of Querétaro, whence he managed to escape after the fall of the city.   A useful eye-witness account violently prejudiced by the writer's hatred of General Márquez.

Arrangoiz, Francisco de Paula.   *Apuntos para la Historia del segundo Imperio Mexicano*.   Madrid, 1870.   *Historia de Méjico desde 1808 hasta 1867*.   4 vols., Madrid, 1871.
Strongly coloured by the author's reactionary and clerical feelings.   He acted for a time as Maximilian's agent in London and resigned on account of his ecclesiastical policy.

Bancroft, Hubert Howe.   *History of Mexico*.   6 vols., San Francisco, 1886–88.
Volume VI contains a scholarly account of the French intervention and the Empire by an eminent American historian based on the most extensive knowledge of the earlier published sources, particularly Mexican. Is very fair to Maximilian.

Basch, Samuel.   *Erinnerungen aus Mexiko.   Geschichte der letzten zehn Monate des Kaiserreichs*.   Leipzig, 1868.
Dr. Basch was Maximilian's German physician and lived with him from September 1866 until the Emperor's death ten months later.   Contains a valuable description of the siege of Querétaro and an interesting diary of the Emperor's life in prison ;   also reproduces a number of documents entrusted to him by Maximilian.   Tends to be unduly laudatory of the Emperor and critical of the Mexicans.   A Spanish translation entitled *Recuerdos de Mexico*, published in 1870, has a useful essay by Hilarión Frías y Soto pointing out Basch's errors and inaccuracies.   Basch's work has unfortunately not been translated into English.

Bigelow, John.   *Retrospections of an Active Life*.   5 vols., New York, 1909–13.
Bigelow was U.S. Minister to France from April 1865 until September 1866, having previously filled the post of Consul-General in Paris.   Vols. II and III contain his correspondence with the Department of State during this period.

Blanchot, Charles.   *L'Intervention française au Mexique*.   3 vols., Paris, 1911.
Colonel Blanchot was a member of the French expeditionary force with ample opportunities for recording his observations in the form of notes and diaries, which he used as the basis for this work.

Bibliography

Blasio, José Luis. *Maximiliano intimo. El Emperador Maximiliano y su Corte*. Paris and Mexico, 1905.

Blasio was a young Mexican who became Maximilian's private secretary early in his reign and remained with him to the end, except for a few months in 1866, when he accompanied Carlota to Europe and witnessed the beginnings of her madness in Rome. His naïve and entertaining memoirs, which reveal much more about the lives of the two sovereigns and their Court than the author intended, are invaluable to the biographer. An English edition by Robert Hammond Murray entitled *Maximilian, Emperor of Mexico* was published by the Yale University Press in 1934. The notes to this edition are useful but they should be read in conjunction with the critical essay written in the light of Mexican sources by Luis Pérez Verdia, *Impresiones de un Libro* (Guadalajara, 1905), which was apparently overlooked by the American editor of the English translation.

Buffin, Baron Camille. *La Tragédie mexicaine. Les Impératrices Charlotte et Eugénie*. Brussels, 1925.

A good biography of Carlota based largely on unpublished Austrian and Belgian sources.

Cantù, Cesare. *L'Arciduca Massimiliano*. An appendix to the author's *Della Indipendenza Italiana Cronistoria*. Vol. iii. Turin, 1877.

Cantù was a well-known Italian nationalist writer who, unlike the majority of his fellow sympathizers, supported Maximilian's rule in Lombardy and Venetia. He was put in charge of public education. His biography includes a detailed account of Maximilian's governorship of the Italian provinces which is particularly valuable, coming as it does from an eye-witness and a member of the administration.

Corti, Count Egon Cesar. *Maximilian und Charlotte von Mexiko*. 2 vols., Vienna, Zürich and Leipzig, 1924.

The most complete and fully documented account yet published, based on the author's extensive researches in the *Maximilianarchiv* in Vienna. Appendices contain complete texts of correspondence between Maximilian and Napoleon III and between Carlota and Eugénie. The author treats the Mexican venture from the European rather than the American viewpoint. There is a good English translation by Mrs. Catherine Alison Phillips, *Maximilian and Charlotte of Mexico*, London and New York, 1928. A revised and abridged version of this work entitled *Die Tragödie eines Kaisers* was published in Leipzig in 1933, but has not yet been translated into English.

Dawson, Daniel. *The Mexican Adventure*. London, 1935.

A careful and well-documented study of the diplomatic negotiations leading to the establishment of Maximilian's Empire based principally on the public archives in Vienna and London.

Détroyat, Léonce. *L'Intervention française au Mexique*. Paris, 1868.

The author was a French officer who was devoted to Maximilian and served in his government as Under-Secretary of the Navy. His book contains important documents, but since it appeared during Napoleon's reign, its references to the French Emperor are very guarded.

Domenech, Emmanuel M. A. *Histoire du Mexique. Juárez et Maximilien.* Paris, 1868.

The Abbé Domenech was chaplain to the French army in Mexico and also worked as Maximilian's press secretary. His political views are reactionary but, while of little value as a history, his book is extremely important for the documents it includes.

Franz Joseph, Emperor. *Franz Joseph I in seinen Briefen.* Edited by Dr. Otto Ernst. Vienna, 1924. (English translation : *Franz Joseph as revealed by his Letters.* London, 1927.)

Briefe Kaisers Franz Josephs I an seine Mutter. Edited by Dr. Franz Schnürer. Munich, 1930. (No English translation.)

These two collections of Franz Joseph's private and official correspondence from the Austrian State archives contain many references to Maximilian as well as a number of important letters to him.

García, Genaro, and Pereyra, Carlos. *Documentos inéditos ó muy raros para la historia de México. Correspondencia secreta de los principales intervencionistas Mexicanos.* 36 vols., Mexico City, 1907–10.

Contains copies of correspondence of Marshal Bazaine and other leading figures in the French intervention in Mexico and the Empire.

Gasparini, Luis. *Massimiliano d' Austria Ultimo Governatore del Lombardo-Veneto nei suoi ricordi.* A series of four articles in the *Nuova Antologia,* Rome, January–March 1935.

Massimiliano nel Messico. Two articles by the same author in the *Nuova Antologia,* September 1938.

These articles contain some interesting and important extracts from previously unpublished material not used by Corti including Maximilian's diary for 1863, an account of his governorship of the Italian provinces prepared by Professor T. Wildauer of the University of Innsbruck under his direction, General Miramón's prison diary in Querétaro, and the correspondence of Curtopossi, Italian Minister to Mexico.

Gaulot, Paul. *L'Expédition du Mexique, 1861–67.* 2 vols., Paris, 1906.

Based on papers of Ernest Louet, paymaster-general of the French army in Mexico. Contains important documents, particularly the secret correspondence between Napoleon III and Bazaine, but the author's laudatory treatment of the latter should be accepted with caution.

Hall, Frederic. *Mexico Under Maximilian. Invasion of Mexico by the French.* New York, 1868.

Hall was an American lawyer who assisted in the preparation of Maximilian's defence before the court martial at Querétaro. Valuable on the

Bibliography

legal side and also for the author's personal sketches of the Emperor and Empress.

Kératry, Comte Émile de. *L'Empereur Maximilien : son élévation et sa chute.* Leipzig, 1867. (English translation : *The Rise and Fall of the Emperor Maximilian. A Narrative of the Mexican Empire, 1861–67.* London, 1869.)
The first documented account to appear after Maximilian's death. Pro-French.

Kollonitz, Countess Paula. *Eine Reise nach Mexiko, 1864–67.* Vienna, 1867. (English translation : *The Court of Mexico.* London, 1868.)
Countess Kollonitz was one of the Austrian ladies-in-waiting who accompanied Maximilian and Carlota to Mexico. Her experiences are frankly and entertainingly related.

Lefévre, E. *Documentos oficiales recogidos en la secretaria privada de Maximiliano.* 2 vols., Brussels and London, 1869. (French edition : Paris, 1870.)
The author was a French journalist of Republican sympathies who was allowed access to the papers left behind in Mexico by Maximilian. The documents are important, but their selection and mode of presentation are not unnaturally prejudiced against the Empire.

Malortie, Baron Karl von. *Mexikanische Skizzen. Erinnerungen aus Kaiser Maximilian.* Leipzig, 1882. (English translation : *'Twixt Old Times and New.* London, 1892.)
Here, There and Everywhere. London, 1895.
Baron Malortie was aide-de-camp to General Franz Thun, commander of the Austrian volunteer corps in Mexico. These volumes contain some interesting reminiscences of Court life at Chapultepec and Cuernavaca, and also an important but not altogether accurate account of Carlota's tragic visit to Europe in 1866 as related to the author by the Empress's lady-in-waiting Countess Manuela del Barrio.

Márquez, Leonardo. *Manifiestos. El Imperio y los Imperiales.* Edited with " *rectificaciones* " by Angel Pola, Mexico City, 1904.
A collection of pronouncements issued in attempted self-justification by the Conservative General Márquez. The editor's preface contains some interesting information about the figures surrounding Maximilian, particularly Márquez and Blasio.

Maximilian, Emperor. *Aus meinem Leben. Reiseskizzen. Aphorismen. Gedichte.* 7 vols., Leipzig, 1867. (English translation without the aphorisms and poems : *Recollections of My Life.* 3 vols., London, 1868.)
Mein erster Ausflug. Wanderungen in Griechenland. Leipzig, 1868. (English translation : *On the Wing.* London, 1868.)
These selections from Maximilian's scrap-books and travel diaries for

the years 1850–53 and 1859–60 are characteristically revealing. The English translation of *Aus meinem Leben* is indifferent.

Montlong, Wilhelm von. *Authentische Enthüllungen über die letzten Ereignisse in Mexiko.* Stuttgart, 1868.
A useful collection of documents by an Austrian staff officer and strong partisan of Maximilian's.

Niox, G. *Expédition du Mexique, 1861–67.* Paris, 1874.
The author was a French staff officer in Mexico. His book gives a well-documented account of the Intervention from the French and anti-Juárez point of view.

Pola, Angel. *Los Traidores pintados por sí mismos. Libro secreto de Maximiliano.* Mexico City, 1900.
This is an edition of a MS. of character sketches of the leading Mexicans who supported the Empire which was discovered in the National Palace in Mexico City when Juárez's forces entered it after Maximilian's death. The work was compiled at the beginning of Maximilian's reign by his Belgian adviser Felix Eloin. The text was first published by Juárez's orders in 1867. The sketches are revealing and in many cases none too flattering to their subjects.

Reinach Foussemagne, Countess H. de. *Charlotte de Belgique Impératrice du Mexique.* Paris, 1925.
The best biography of Carlota hitherto published. The author has made excellent use of the archives of the Belgian royal house and the Empress's private correspondence from a variety of sources. This work is remarkably outspoken for an " authorized " life.

Salm-Salm, Prince Felix zu. *Querétaro. Blätter aus meinem Tagebuch in Mexiko.* Stuttgart, 1868. (English translation : *My Diary in Mexico in 1867. . . . With Leaves from the Diary of Princess Salm-Salm.* 2 vols., London, 1868.)
An interesting and valuable account of the siege of Querétaro by a Prussian soldier of fortune who fought by the Emperor's side and shared his imprisonment. Is particularly good on the military side although it does not do the Mexicans full justice. The selections from Princess Salm-Salm's diary describe her attempts to secure Maximilian's pardon from Juárez.

Schmit, Dr. Ernest, Ritter von Tavera. *Geschichte der Regierung des Kaisers Maximilian I und die französische Intervention in Mexiko.* 2 vols., Vienna and Leipzig, 1903.
Die mexikanische Kaisertragödie. 1903.
The author worked as assistant to Baron Lago, the Austrian Minister in Mexico, and besides recording his own observations he has used official documents to narrate the history of Maximilian's reign from the Austrian point of view.

Bibliography

Sonolet, Louis. *L'Agonie de l'Empire du Mexique.* Two articles in *La Revue de Paris*, vol. 4, année 34. Paris, August, 1927.

The writer has had access to the Castelnau family papers, of which those concerning Brigadier-General François Castelnau's mission on behalf of Napoleon III to Mexico in the autumn of 1866 form the basis of this interesting monograph. In the notes and letters which he wrote at this period Castelnau is extremely severe on Bazaine, whom he accuses with some truth of the most shameless duplicity and even treachery in negotiating with the Liberals behind Maximilian's back. The strong evidence against Bazaine, here adduced in detail for the first time, should be read particularly in the light of Gaulot's work on the Mexican expedition (*vide supra*), which tends to rehabilitate him. It would appear from these documents that Bazaine must bear a considerable responsibility for Maximilian's death.

State Papers published by the United States and Mexican Governments.
The volumes published by order of the U.S. Congress known as *Diplomatic Correspondence* for the period of the Empire contain a number of interesting and important letters to Maximilian which were intercepted by Juárez's representatives in the United States.

Stevenson, Sara Yorke. *Maximilian in Mexico.* New York, 1897.
Mrs. Stevenson, the American archaeologist, lived as a girl with her parents in Mexico during the Intervention and Empire. Her reminiscences of the period, which she wrote many years later, are interesting as a personal history and are well written from the American viewpoint.

The following printed sources have been used for particular chapters :

CHAPTER I

The relations between the Archduchess Sophie and the Duke of Reichstadt are described in Edward Wertheimer, *The Duke of Reichstadt*, London, 1906 ; Jean de Bourgoing, *Le Fils de Napoléon*, Paris, 1932 ; Octave Aubry, *Napoleon II*, London, 1933 ; Lucile Decaux, *Charlotte et Maximilien*, Paris, 1937 ; and authorities there cited.

Maximilian's childhood can be reconstructed from the editions of Franz Joseph's private correspondence by Ernst and Schnürer quoted above. See also biographies of Franz Joseph by Eugene Bagger (New York, 1927) and Joseph Redlich (London and New York, 1929).

The Austrian political and Court background of Maximilian's youth is described by Viktor Bibl in his *Der Zerfall Oesterreichs*, 2 vols., Vienna, 1922 ; and by Heinrich Friedjung in his *Oesterreich von 1848 bis 1860*, 2 vols., Berlin, 1918. See also Bagger and Redlich, *op. cit.*, and, particularly for naval details, Hans Birch Freiherr von Dahlerup's *In österreichischen Diensten*, 2 vols., Berlin, 1911.

Mexican Empire

Maximilian, *op. cit.*, for descriptions of travels. See also George Finlay, *History of Greece*, vol. vii, Oxford, 1877.

CHAPTER II

Social life in Vienna in the 1850's and Maximilian's first love affair are described by Countess Paula von Bülow in her memoirs, *Aus verklungenen Zeiten*, Leipzig, 1924.

Maximilian, *op. cit.*, for visits to Spain and Portugal. On the Dowager Queen Amelia of Portugal and her daughter Princess Maria Amelia see María Junqueira Schmidt, *A Segunda Imperatriz do Brazil* (*Amelia de Leuchtenberg*), San Paulo, 1927.

On Maximilian's visit to Albania see particularly two articles by Luis Gasparini in *Rassegna Italiana*, vol. xiv, Nos. 231 and 232, Rome, 1937. (*L'Arciduca Massimiliano in Albania.*)

Count E. C. Corti, *Elisabeth " die seltsame Frau "*, Salzburg and Leipzig, 1935 (English translation : *Elizabeth, Empress of Austria*, London, 1936), for relations between Franz Joseph and the Empress.

On the Austrian navy see official *Geschichte der K. K. Kriegsmarine*, 3 vols., Vienna, 1884 ; A. Lengnick and R. von Klimburg, *Unsere Wehrmacht zur See*, Vienna, 1904 ; J. K. Laughton, *Studies in Naval History*, London, 1887 ; A. Beer, *Aus Wilhelm von Tegetthoffs Nachlass*, Vienna, 1882 ; and von Dahlerup, *op. cit.*

On Maximilian's visit to Egypt and Palestine in 1855 see Gaulot, *op. cit.* vol. i.

Maximilian's visits to Paris and Brussels in 1856 are well described in the light of previously unpublished documents by Corti, *Maximilian und Charlotte von Mexiko*, vol. i. See also Count Alexander Hübner, *Neuf Ans de Souvenirs d'un Ambassadeur*, 2 vols., Paris, 1904 ; Blanchard Jerrold, *Life of Napoleon III*, 4 vols., London, 1874 ; Count Fleury, *Memoirs of the Empress Eugénie*, 2 vols., London and New York, 1920.

CHAPTER III

Reinach Foussemagne on Charlotte's early life and marriage. See also Corti, *Leopold I von Belgien*, Vienna, 1922 (English translation : *Leopold I of Belgium*, London and New York, 1923) ; *Letters of Queen Victoria*, 1st series, ed. Benson and Esher, vols. ii and iii, London, 1908 ; Theodore Martin, *Life of the Prince Consort*, vol. iv, London and New York, 1879 ; and *Memoirs of Ernest II, Duke of Saxe-Coburg-Gotha*, vol. iii, London, 1890.

For Maximilian's viceroyalty in Italy see particularly Cesare Cantù, *Della Indipendenza Italiana Cronistoria*, vol. iii, Turin, 1877 ; and Luis Gasparini, *Massimiliano d'Austria Ultimo Governatore del Lombardo-Veneto nei suoi ricordi* in *Nuova Antologia*, January–March,

Bibliography

1935. See also on Italian political background, Bolton King, *History of Italian Unity*, 2 vols., London and New York, 1899 ; R. de Cesare, *The Last Days of Papal Rome*, New York, 1909 ; and on military background Count Carl Lónyay *"Ich will Rechenschaft ablegen."* *Die unbewusste Selbstbiographie des Generals Benedek*, Leipzig and Vienna, 1936.

CHAPTERS IV AND V

Maximilian, *op. cit.*, on his visit to Brazil. See also Mary W. Williams, *Dom Pedro the Magnanimous*, University of North Carolina, 1927.

Maximilian's marital relations are discussed by Blasio, *op. cit.*

On the Mexican political background see generally Charles Lempriere, *Notes on Mexico in 1861 and 1862*, London, 1862 ; H. H. Bancroft, *op. cit.* ; and on diplomatic negotiations concerning Maximilian and Mexican crown, Dawson, *op. cit.* See also Hall *op. cit.*, and for United States political reactions Frederic Bancroft, *Life of William H. Seward*, 2 vols., London and New York, 1900 ; John Lothrop Motley, *Correspondence*, ed. G. W. Curtis, vol. ii, New York, 1889 ; and Bigelow *op. cit.* vol. ii. On the Convention of London see article by W. S. Robertson, " The Tripartite Treaty of London ", in the *Hispanic-American Historical Review*, vol. xx, No. 2, Durham, North Carolina, 1940.

On the French intervention in Mexico and particularly military operations see Niox, Ollivier, Gaulot and García, *op. cit.*

On Juárez see biographies by Justo Sierra (Mexico, 1905–6), Rafael de Zayas Enríquez (Mexico, 1906) and Hector Peréz Martínez (Madrid, 1933).

CHAPTER VI

On Maximilian's and Carlota's visit to Paris and Rome in 1864 see *Memoirs of Ernest II, Duke of Saxe-Coburg-Gotha*, vol. iv ; Ferdinand Gregorovius, *Roman Journals*, London, 1909 ; and Gasparini, *op. cit.* The journey to Mexico is described by Kollonitz, *op. cit.*

Maximilian's ecclesiastical policy in Mexico has been exhaustively treated in an article by Professor N. Andrew Cleven in the *Hispanic-American Historical Review*, vol. ix, No. 3, 1923.

On imperial foreign policy see J. M. Callahan, *American Foreign Policy in Mexican Relations*, New York, 1942 ; Dexter Perkins, *Hands Off. A History of the Monroe Doctrine*, Boston, 1941 ; Frederic Bancroft, *Life of Seward*, vol. ii ; and an excellent article by F. Bancroft on " The French in Mexico and the Monroe Doctrine," in the *Political Science Quarterly*, vol. ix, no. 1, New York, 1896.

Bazaine's largely forgotten career has recently been made the subject of an engaging study by Philip Guedalla in *The Two Marshals*,

London and New York, 1943 ; see also Sonolet, Stevenson and Blasio, *op. cit.*

Chapter VII

Reinach Foussemagne and Blasio, *op. cit.*, for Carlota's activities generally. Her journey to Yucatan is narrated with documents by Buffin, *op. cit.*

On Maximilian and the Iturbide family see article by John Bigelow, " The Heir Presumptive to the Imperial Crown of Mexico ", in *Harper's Magazine*, April 1883.

The life at Cuernavaca is described by Blasio and Malortie, *op. cit* ; see also Esta O. de Davila, *Paradise in Mexico*, Mexico City, 1937.

On Maximilian's colonization schemes see D. F. M. Corbin, *Life of M. F. Maury*, London, 1888 ; Charles L. Lewis, *Mathew Fontaine Maury*, Annapolis, 1927 ; and article by George D. Harmon, " Confederate Migration to Mexico ", in the *Hispanic-American Historical Review*, vol. xvii, No. 4, 1937.

Chapter VIII

On Carlota's voyage to Europe see generally Corti, Reinach Foussemagne, *op. cit.*, and Malortie, *Here, There and Everywhere*. See also Fleury, Gregorovius, *op. cit.*

An interesting letter from Velásquez de Léon to Maximilian describing Carlota's insane symptoms was intercepted by Juárez's Minister in Washington and published in U.S. Government's *Diplomatic Correspondence, 1866*, Part III, Washington, 1867.

On the alleged birth of a child to Carlota at Miramar see Robert Goffin, *Charlotte l'Impératrice fantôme*, Paris, 1937.

Chapters IX and X

On the Querétaro campaign and events leading up to it see Bancroft, *op. cit.*, vol. vi and authorities there cited, particularly Juan de Dios Arias, *Reseña Historica del Ejército del Norte*, Mexico City, 1867 ; also Basch, Blasio, *op. cit.*

Eloin's intercepted letter to Maximilian was published in *Diplomatic Correspondence, loc. cit.*

A complete transcript of the official version of the trial of Maximilian, Miramón and Mejía, with the preliminary interrogatories, which is in the Mexican National Archives, has been published in the *Boletín del Archivo General de la Nación*, vols. i–iii, Mexico City, 1930–32. See also *Causa de Fernando Maximiliano de Hapsburgo*, Mexico City, 1868, and Hall, *op. cit.*

For Maximilian's last days and execution the leading authorities are Basch, Blasio, Salm, Schmit von Tavera and Hall, *op. cit.*

Bibliography

For the Paris Exhibition of 1867 and the Salzburg meeting see Frédéric Lolliée, *The Life of an Empress*, London, 1908 ; Philip Guedalla, *The Second Empire*, London and New York, 1922 ; Count F. F. von Beust, *Aus drei Vierteljahrhunderten : Erinnerungen und Aufzeichnungen*, Stuttgart, 1887 ; and an article by Henry Salomon, " Prince Richard Metternich et sa correspondance pendant son ambassade à Paris, 1859–71 ", in *La Revue de Paris*, February 1924.

Maximilian's embalming is described by Salm, Hall, *op. cit.* The evidence of a number of individuals which leaves no doubt of Juárez's visit to the San Andrés Hospital to view the body has been collected by Augustín Rivera in a pamphlet, *Confirmación de la visita de Juárez al Cadaver de Maximiliano*, published in Mexico in 1912. See also the same author's *Anales de la Reforma y del Segundo Imperio*, Guadalajara, 1897.

Tegetthoff's mission is fully described by himself in A. Beer, *Aus Wilhelm von Tegetthoffs Nachlass*, Vienna, 1882.

Details of Maximilian's burial are given by C. Wolfsgruber in *Die Kaisergruft bei den Kapuzinern in Wien*, Vienna, 1887.[1]

On the fate of Maximilian's contemporaries see generally Bancroft, *op. cit.* vol. vi. On Blasio and Márquez particularly see Angel Pola's edition of Márquez's *Manifiestos*, Mexico City, 1904. On Iturbide see W. Coleman Nevils, *Miniatures of Georgetown*, Washington, 1934.

On Carlota's illness and seclusion at Tervueren and Bouchout see Buffin and Reinach Foussemagne, *op. cit.* ; also Herbert Vivian, *Francis Joseph and His Court*, London and New York, 1917 ; and Princess Stephanie of Belgium (Princess Lónyay), " *Ich sollte Kaiserin werden.*" *Lebenserinnerungen der letzten Kronprinzessin von Österreich-Ungarn.* Leipzig, 1935. (English translation : "*I was to be Empress*", London, 1937). On her death see *New York Times*, January 17–20, 23, 1927, and London *Times*, January 17–20, 22, 24, 1927. A photograph of the funeral appeared in the London *Times*, January 24, 1927.

The downfall of the Mexican Empire forms the theme of Franz Werfel's moving drama *Juarez und Maximilian*, which was first performed at the Burgtheater in Vienna in 1924.

[1] Maximilian's tomb, in common with the other Hapsburg family sarcophagi in the Kapuzinerkirche in Vienna, has withstood recent prolonged bombardment and siege, although many of the buildings in the near-by streets were destroyed. The author had an opportunity of examining it shortly after the entry of the first British troops into the city in 1945 and noted the following contemporary inscription :

FERDINANDVS MAXIMILIANVS ARCHIDVX AVSTRIAE NATVS IN SCHOENBRVNN VI IVLII MDCCCXXXII QVI IMPERATOR MEXICANORVM ANNO MDCCCLXV ELECTVS DIRA ET CRVENTA NECE QVERETARI XIX IVNII MDCCCLXVIII FIDEM AVITAM RELIGIOSISSIME CONFESSVS HEROICA CVM VIRTVTE INTERIIT.

INDEX

Index

Billimek, Professor, Austrian naturalist, 185, 242, 243

" Black Decree ", 181-182, 283

Blanchot, Charles, French colonel, historian of French intervention in Mexico, 187, 330, 332

Blasio, José Luis, Maximilian's Mexican secretary, 166 ; anecdotes about Maximilian by, 170, 171 ; on Maximilian's conjugal life, 174-175 ; at La Borda, 186 ; on Carlota's character, 192 ; his account of Carlota's strange behaviour at Puebla, 203 ; visits Miramar, 222 ; in Italy with Carlota, 223, 233 ; returns to Mexico, 242 ; leaves Orizaba with Maximilian, 245 ; at Querétaro with Maximilian, 257, 258, 261, 266-269 ; imprisoned with Maximilian, 274 ; at Maximilian's funeral, 303, 309 ; sees Carlota in seclusion, 310 ; subsequent career and death of, 310-311 ; his memoirs, 310, 330, 332 ; on supposed letter from Maximilian to López, 313 note

Bolzano, 223

Bombelles, Count Heinrich, Maximilian's tutor, 7

Bombelles, Count Karl, gentleman-in-waiting to Maximilian, 203, 236, 240, 303, 305

Borda, José de la, 185 and note. *See also* La Borda

Borgo, Italian officer, 276, 277

Bouchout, castle of, 308, 320

Bourdillon, English journalist, 119

Bouslavek, Carlota's physician, 203, 228

Brabant, Duke of. *See* Leopold II

Brazil, Maximilian's visit to, 96 *et seq.*

Brightwell, Mr., 324

Brincourt, French general, 144

Bringas, 314

Buenavista, palace of, 163, 247

Bülow, Countess Paula von, *née* Linden, 27 *et seq.*, 37, 318 ; her memoirs, 337

Buol, Count Karl Ferdinand von, Austrian Foreign Minister, 52, 81, 85

Cabarrus, Tallien de, 157

Cable, transatlantic, 238 and note

Campbell, Mr. Lewis D., 244

Cantù, Cesare, Italian Liberal, 80 ; his writings, 274, 333

Cape Rodoni, 40

Carlota (Charlotte, Carlotta), Empress of Mexico, Princess of Belgium, 59 ; birth of, 60 ; education, 61 ; courtships, 63 ; engagement to Archduke Ferdinand

Maximilian, 64 ; her opinion of her fiancé, 67 ; her dowry, 69 ; her wedding, 75 ; honeymoon, 76 ; in Italy, 78 *et seq.* ; insulted in Venice, 83 ; goes to Trieste, 84 ; her anxiety for Maximilian, 87 ; purchases Lacroma, 90 ; her voyage to Madeira, 92 ; life at Miramar, 103, 107 ; discusses Mexican project with her father, 121 ; in Paris, 127 ; and London, 128 ; her visit to Vienna, 131 ; proclaimed Empress, 133 ; departs for Mexico, 136 ; in Gibraltar, 139 ; arrives at Vera Cruz, 142 ; her opinion of Mexican roads, 143 ; and Mexican education, 145 ; on Maximilian's first political measures, 148 ; on her new life, 151 ; and Mme. Bazaine, 162-163

Describes her political interests, 173 ; her character, 172, 192, 196 ; at Chapultepec, 149, 160, 172 ; at Cuernavaca, 186 ; her visit to Yucatan, 188 ; supposed poisoning of, 191 and note ; reproaches Maximilian for weakness, 210 ; her voyage to Europe, 203 *et seq.* ; in Paris, 207 ; at Como, 217 ; at Miramar, 220 ; first signs of madness, 221 ; her visit to Rome, 223 ; goes to Vatican, 226 ; removed to Miramar, 233 ; Maximilian learns of her illness, 240 ; taken to Belgium, 304 ; her later years and death, 320 *et seq.*

Nomenclature, 78, 133 ; her conjugal relations, 106-107, 174-175, 187 ; adopts son, 176 ; alleged birth of son to, 324

Letters from, to Duchess of Aosta, 307 note ; to Queen Eugénie, 145, 154, 162, 163 ; to Countess Hulst, 62, 70, 76, 78, 103, 192, 306 ; to her grandmother, 173, 175 ; to Maximilian, 215, 221, 222, 229 ; to Queen Victoria, 61

Carlota Colony, 194

Carlotta. *See* Carlota

Caroline, Dowager Empress of Austria, 125

Carrera, President of Guatemala, 157

Casanova, Mexican general, 276

Castelnau, François, French general, 241, 246 and note, 247 ; his papers, 336

Castiglione, Countess, 55

Castillo, Martín, Mexican Finance Minister, 164 ; becomes Foreign Minister, 183 ; appearance of, 185 ; accompanies Carlota to Europe, 203 ; in Paris, 207 ; feigns indisposition, 215 ; with Carlota in Italy, 223, 225 ; telegram from, 240

Castillo, Severo, Mexican general, 261, 268, 271, 308

Index

Index

Mexican Empire

Miramón, Miguel, Mexican general, President of Mexico, 110-111 ; foreign mission of, 165 ; visits La Borda, 185 ; returns to Mexico, 243 ; defeat of, 251 ; appointed infantry commander, 253 ; attacked by Márquez, 255 ; his tactics at Querétaro, 257 ; oversleeps, 259 ; successful sortie by, 261 ; his speech to Maximilian, 262 ; his animosity against Méndez, 263 ; captured, 270 ; imprisoned with Maximilian, 271 ; moved to another prison, 277 ; court-martial of, 278, 281 ; his last hours, 287 *et seq.* ; his dying speech, 292 ; his body restored to his family, 297 ; his prison diary, 334 ; conduct of his wife, 277
Monroe Doctrine, 159, 339
Monterey, 237
Montezuma, 108, 168
Motley, John Lothrop, American historian and diplomat, 126, 200

Naples, 22
Napoleon, Prince Imperial, 210, 317
Napoleon, Prince (" Plon-Plon "), 50
Napoleon I, Emperor of France, 36, 52 note
Napoleon II. *See* Reichstadt
Napoleon III, Emperor of France, 32 ; Maximilian's first visit to, 49 *et seq.* ; on Franco-Austrian relations, 84 ; meets Cavour, 85 ; and Hidalgo, 113, 199 ; presses Maximilian to accept Mexican crown, 125, 129 ; entertains Maximilian and Carlotta, 127 ; mining concession granted to, 147 ; orders withdrawal of French forces from Mexico, 184 ; sees Eloin, 199 ; rejects Maximilian's proposals, 200 ; telegraphs to Carlota, 206 ; his interviews with Carlota, 209 *et seq.* ; suggests Maximilian's abdication, 239 ; sends Castelnau to Mexico, 241 ; hears news of Maximilian's death, 293 ; condoles with Franz Joseph, 295 ; meets Franz Joseph at Salzburg, 296 ; exile and death of, 317 ; his duplicity, 128 ; Maximilian's opinion of, 53 ; Maximilian's correspondence with, 164, 172, 239, 327
Navy, Austrian, 18, 45 *et seq.*, 87, 89, 219, 220, 239 ; bibliography of, 338. *See also under* Maximilian ; *Novara* ; Tegetthoff
Navy, British, Maximilian's opinion of, 31
Nicholas I, Russian tsar, 13, 39
Novara, 20 note, 220
Novara, Austrian frigate, 20, 30, 49, 134, 193, 301, 327

O'Donnell, Spanish marshal, 92
O'Horan, Mexican prefect, 311
Orizaba, 144, 194, 241-244 ; described by Carlota, 144
Ortega, Eulalio María, Mexican lawyer, 281, 285, 287
Oscar, Prince of Sweden, 54 and note
Osmont, French general, 236, 238
Otto, Archduke, 318, 319
Otto, King of Greece, 14, 120

Palacio. *See* Riva Palacio
Palacios, Mexican colonel, 276 *et seq.*
Paris, 49, 127, 207, 293, 304, 314
Pedro I, Emperor of Brazil, 35, 96 note
Pedro II, Emperor of Brazil, 97, 102
Peña, Manuel de la, President of Mexico, 162 note
Peña, María Josepha de la. *See under* Bazaine
Petropolis, 102
Philip V, King of Spain, 25 note
Pius IX, Pope, 48, 73 ; character, 74 ; blesses Maximilian and Carlota, 137 ; disappointed at Maximilian's ecclesiastical policy, 152 ; Carlota's opinion of, 155 ; mission from Maximilian to, 199 ; Carlota's last audiences with, 224 *et seq.* ; and Princess Salm, 309 ; Maximilian's correspondence with, 327
Pola, 49, 65
Poliakowitz, 160
Price, Sterling, 193
Prussia, 37, 205
Puebla, 144, 203, 245

Querétaro, 254 *et seq.*, 297

Radetsky, Count Joseph, Austrian marshal, 13, 70
Raglan, Lord, 303
Ramírez, José Fernando, Mexican Foreign Minister, 147, 164 ; Carlota on, 148 ; his policy, 156 ; signs " Black Decree ", 182 ; surrenders portfolio, 183 ; accompanies Carlota to Yucatan, 188 ; leaves Mexico, 247 ; Maximilian's literary executor, 329 ; his death, 309 note ; his library, 316 note
Rechberg, Count Bernard von, Austrian Foreign Minister, 104, 107, 115, 156
Reichstadt, Napoleon Francis, Duke of, 1 *et seq.*, 303 and note
Rességuier, Count Ollivier, 157, 308 note
Rességuier, Count Roger, 308 note
Riedel, Dr., Austrian mental specialist 233, 240

348

Index

THE END

Printed in Great Britain by R. & R. CLARK, LIMITED, *Edinburgh.*

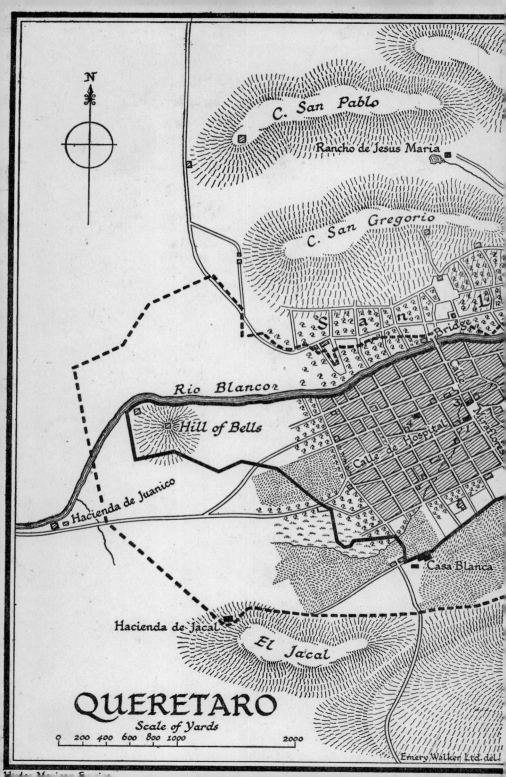

N

C. San Pablo

Rancho de Jesus Maria

C. San Gregorio

S a n

Bridge

Rio Blanco

Hill of Bells

Calle de Hospital

Hacienda de Juanico

Casa Blanca

Hacienda de Jacal

El Jacal

QUERETARO

Scale of Yards

0   200 400 600 800 1000   2000

Emery Walker Ltd. del!